The Ideology
of Racism

The Ideology of Racism

by Samuel Kennedy Yeboah

HANSIB

First published in 1988 by Hansib Publishing Limited.
This Reprinted Edition published in 1997 by Hansib Publications
Third Floor, Tower House, 141-149 Fonthill Road, London N4 3HF.
Printed in Malta by Progress Press Co. Ltd

British Library Cataloguing in Publication Data.
A Catalogue record for this book is available from the British Library
ISBN 1-870518-07-1

AUTHOR'S NOTE
*The ideas expressed in this book are entirely my own and do not
represent the views of the London Borough of Hackney.*

To

The memory of all Black people who died resisting racial oppression and subjugation!

Acknowledgements

I am deeply indebted to my wife, Sally and five children, Melanie, Ruby (the twins), Katherine, Daniel and James for their forbearance during the research for, and writing of, this book. For nearly three years, I spent almost every weekend and public holiday locked away from my family. During this period when I was an 'absentee husband and father', my wife endured a great deal of indignation, but bore it with fortitude and equanimity. But for her patience and understanding, this book would not have been possible.

S.K.Y.
Milton Keynes

Contents

Preface

Even the most casual observer will notice that a common feature of
virtually all multi-racial Western societies (composed of white
people and black people of African descent) is that black people, as a
group, are the most socio-economically disadvantaged. Whatever
socio-economic indices one might choose to measure group differences – level of education/qualification attained, occupation, earnings, household income, private wealth, quality and type of housing
tenure – one would invariably find that black people of African
descent occupy the base of the socio-economic pyramid, and are the
most deprived of the deprived groups.

To compound this phenomenon of socio-economic disadvantage
and deprivation (and no doubt, as partial explanation of this
disadvantage), there is woeful under-representation of black people
in the power structures of these multi-racial societies – with
reference in particular to Britain, Holland, the United States of
America, France, Canada, Brazil, Australia and South Africa.
Whether one is dealing with political institutions such as national
and local governments (as well as the civil servants and local
government officers who implement their decisions, respectively), or
political parties; State law enforcement agencies and coercive
institutions such as the judiciary, police force, prison and penal
authorities, the armed forces; educational institutions such as
education authorities, schools, colleges and universities; or
economic institutions such as manufacturing industries,
commercial and financial organisations, employers' associations,
trade unions, service industries (hotels, restaurants, leisure and
entertainment), black representation will be found to be non-
existent in the power structures and decision making centres, or
where present, will be proportionately much lower (in many cases
just a token) in comparison to the size of the black population.

Since it would be stretching the statistical law of averages beyond
the boundaries of rationality, it should not be accepted that these
uniform social phenomena represent mere accidents. The rational
social thinker must, hence, seek underlying causes: what factors are
responsible for causing such uniform social conditions in so many
different countries? Are these factors biological? Is there something
genetically inherent in black people which, in a competitive
Western society, renders them incapable of competing successfully
against their white counterparts in education, jobs, the political
process, etc.? Conversely, is there something genetically inherent in
white people which makes them superior to all other races in

general, and black people in particular, and which thus endows them with competitive advantage – politically, socially, and economically?

If the causes are not biological, are they socio-cultural? If they are, how do they occur so uniformly in societies with such different histories, cultures, traditions, as well as varied educational, economic and political systems? Could there be an on-going conspiracy between the ruling and dominant classes of these societies to actively suppress the politico-socio-economic development of their black citizens? If so, why? Is the desire to suppress and dominate black people a 'natural' characteristic of white people and, hence, this conspiracy? If it is, how could such a conspiracy be realistically maintained so effectively for centuries? Have black people acquiesced in this effort to keep them down? If not, have they resisted? And if they have, why has their resistance so uniformly failed?

If the causality does not lie in the social conspiracy theory, could it be due to some commonly-shared socio-historical experiences between these countries? Did some historical events occur which brought about a certain social relationship of differential power between black and white peoples? If so, why and how has this power differential been effectively maintained for centuries to the present time?

There is a real danger in social theorising that one could formulate universally applicable theories to explain social phenomena existing in different socio-cultural and historical contexts. Such theories, in many cases offer models of 'reality' which bear little semblance to actual *reality*. I am mindful of this danger! However, in the following Chapters, I shall present overwhelming evidence to demonstrate that there is a universally applicable theoretical model which offers causal explication of the social phenomenon of black disadvantage and deprivation in virtually all multi-racial Western countries. The manifestation and symptoms of this racial discrimination against black people and its consequence may differ from one country to the other due to differences in socio-cultural, historical, political, and economic systems. But I shall demonstrate that the origin and development of this racial problem, and the ideas which sustain and continue to make it operable are either identical, or very similar indeed!

Although I have chosen Britain as the geographical context for the analysis of the ideology of racism, and employment has been selected as an area of focus for the analysis of the effect of the ideology, the resultant theoretical framework will be applicable to the United States of America, France, Holland, Brazil, Australia, etc and the effect of the ideology will equally be applicable to housing, education, political representation, and so on.

Introduction

Britain is now acknowledged to be a multi-racial society, and equal opportunity to all, irrespective of race, colour, nationality or ethnic origin is a declared public policy. Evidence that a multi-racial society in which genuine equality of opportunity exists can be seen when the racial/ethnic composition of the society is reflected in most aspects of national economic life. One would expect to find the racial make-up of the labour market, for example, reflected in industrial, commercial, and financial organisations and organs of state such as the civil service, police, the judiciary and the armed forces. This is not the case in multi-racial Britain. The findings of many empirical research studies have shown Britain's black and ethnic minorities to be victims of systematic and persistent racial discrimination, not only in employment, but also in housing, education and access to many social amenities and services.

Partly from a moral point of view, but even more importantly, from the recognition of the potential threat to social order and stability that an endemic and persistent racial discrimination against a section of the community poses, parliament enacted the Race Relations Acts of 1965, 1968 and 1976. The objective of the legislation was to make racial discrimination unlawful; to seek its eradication; and to bring about equality of opportunity for all citizens, irrespective of race, colour and origin. Regrettably, the end sought has not materialised.

Evidence from current empirical studies reveals that while many acts of overt and 'active' discrimination, such as in advertisements, have disappeared, 'passive' discrimination is still rampant. In practical terms, according to the House of Commons Home Affairs Committee, 'this means that black people tend to obtain the less pleasant jobs and fail to be considered on merit for training and promotion into higher managerial/professional grades.'[a] It has become apparent that mere compliance with the provisions of the 1976 Race Relations Act will not result in equality of opportunities in the employment field.

Central Government has not provided moral or political leadership in the drive to extirpate racial discrimination, apart from the occasional ritual incantations delivered by Cabinet Ministers at meetings with minority leaders. Hugo Young, in an article in *The Guardian* on Monday, November 26, 1984, posed the question "...what action has the government actually taken to redress the institutionalised prejudice and discrimination in housing and employment which has been proved to exist in numerous inquiries by bodies from the House of Commons down?" Predictably his answer was, "little or none".

The Government, as the largest employer in the country, cannot demonstrate that it is an equal opportunities employer. Two examples here serve to illustrate Central Government's effort to deal with racial discrimination in Britain. James Naughtie, Political Correspondent of *The Guardian* reported on Thursday, February 7, 1985 that Alan Clark, *a government minister with responsibility in the Department of Employment for Race Relations*[b] "...was forced into a position of unaccustomed silence yesterday by a ...row over whether he had referred to black Britons as denizens of Bongo Bongo land". On Thursday, May 24, 1984, Malcolm Pithers reported in *The Guardian: A senior race relations adviser*[b] to the Police Federation apologised privately last night to his colleagues for referring to coloured people as nig-nogs during a conference debate... Inspector Johnson *spent 18 months on a Home Office working party into race relations and the police*[b], and is a member of the federation's national executive."

The Inspector was forced to resign from his posts in the Police Federation the next day and returned to the headquarters in Durham. His forced resignation, however, gives a false impression of the attitude of the Police towards racism within the force – empirical investigation has shown that, far from being an exception, Inspector Johnson's Freudian 'slip-of-the-tongue' is the norm. The reader can draw his/her own conclusion as to the degree of government determination to grapple with racism which has been shown to be endemic in social institutions in Britain.

There are no coherent and effective national structures set up to deal with the problem, despite expressions of official abhorrence of discrimination. The Commission for Racial Equality, although staffed by dedicated and committed officers, has been so structured and fettered by the legislation, and circumscribed by judicial interpretation, that it was doomed to be ineffective.

In the meantime, the potential danger of disorder, that many feared persistent racial discrimination would cause, has now become a reality. The inner-city 'riots' of 1981 and 1985 have graphically demonstrated that if a section of the community is continually denied a stake in the society's resources, it will have no vested interest in the preservation of order in that society. That section of the community will, in time, become alienated from the society, reject its values, and regard its institutions with reciprocal hostility.

From 1978, a number of inner-city councils adopted 'equal opportunities policies' in their employment practices with a view to promoting equality of opportunity for black people, women and disabled people. In 1982/83 I undertook a research study, in part-fulfilment of an MA Degree course, to analyse and evaluate the measures that two London boroughs – Lambeth and Camden – had adopted to eliminate racial discrimination and to promote equal opportunities for all. During the course of the study, I undertook an extensive survey of the literature on Race Relations and discovered, to my dismay, that the scope of most studies on racial discrimination in employment was limited to the 'cataloguing' of the incidence and persistence of discrimination with little attempt made to offer causal explication of this social injustice. To many authors and socio-political commentators, the *causes* appeared to be non-problematic.

I found this to be wholly unsatisfactory, for effective strategy in any field of human endeavour must be based on precise knowledge of the goals one wants to achieve; a thorough understanding of the obstacles in the way; the adoption of appropriate measures to overcome those obstacles or 'limiting factors'; and a programme of tactical action to move from the current to the desired position. If an organisation seeks to eliminate racial discrimination and to promote equal opportunity which should lead generally to racial equality, at least in the employment field, then it is imperative that the causes of racial discrimination are identified, and measures taken to eliminate them. However, the dearth of research into, and the general lack of interest in, the underlying causes of racial discrimination has meant that many organisations have adopted policies and programmes of work to achieve equality of opportunity, without an adequate understanding of the obstacles militating against the achievement of that objective. Not surprisingly, their efforts have yielded no perceptible results.

Failure by these organisations to extirpate racial discrimination was inevitable, for, at best, their efforts have been directed at the manifest symptoms rather than the real cause of the problem. A medical doctor might administer drugs to relieve the symptoms of an ailment prior to a systematic and thorough diagnosis into the nature and cause of the ailment. Until the cause has been established and treated, however, no cure can be effected and the symptoms will continue to recur. *Pari passu,* an organisation will not, and indeed cannot, effectively extirpate racial discrimination without understanding the causes and factors which sustain it. Evidence from the following chapters will show that diagnosis and prescription in many organisations are confined to the manifest symptom level; consequently resources are ineffectively utilised while the equality objective still remains a distant dream.

It is my aim in this book to attempt a systematic diagnosis of, and to develop a theoretical framework for, the analysis of racial discrimination. I shall seek to go beneath the surface of this social phenomenon; to investigate its social casualty; to analyse the ideology which explains and justifies this social practice; identify the assumptions which inform the ideology and to subject them to rigorous and critical analyses to ascertain whether they are based on fact or fiction, myth or reality. Finally, I will seek to show the effect of the ideology on contemporary social attitudes.

Definition of terms

There are two terms used extensively throughout the book which need to be defined, since they do not conform to some of the meanings in current usage in the literature on race relations in Britain.

As an analytical category, the term *black* may be used to refer to : (a) black people of African origin (i.e. Africans, Afro-Caribbeans, Afro-Americans, and British-born black people) as well as those of African/European or African/Asian parentage; (b) black people as in (a), but also including people originating from the Indian sub-continent (i.e. Caribbeans of Indian extraction, East African Asians, Indians, Bangladeshis, Pakistanis, Sri Lankans, and other peoples of Third World origins); and (c) all non-white people who suffer or may suffer from racial oppression. The latter is a political rather than a biological usage and lumps together such disparate groups as black people (Negroes), Asians (including people from the Far East such as Chinese and Malaysians), Cypriots, Arabs, and so on.

However, in the context of this text, particularly from Chapter Two onwards, the meaning in (a) above will apply. The reason is that the type of racism which we will be analysing is one based on a continuum of races with white people and black people (of African origin) occupying the polar extremes and ranked top and bottom respectively. All other races are ranked in between by reference to a colour criterion. The investigation in this book, therefore, focuses on the extreme form of racism based on white/black social relationships. From this level, racism of other kinds may be understood according to the position occupied by the victims on the continuum, i.e. the lighter the skin colour (other things being equal), the lesser the degree of racism suffered and, conversely, the darker the skin pigmentation, the greater the degree of racism experienced.

The other analytical category is the term *racism*. The definition adopted in this book is similar to that used by the 'Rampton Committee' (later Swann Committee) and UNESCO's (United Nations Educational, Scientific and Cultural Organisation) committee of experts on race. Whenever employed in this text, *racism* should be defined as "a set of attitudes and behaviour towards people of another race, which is based on the belief that races are distinct and can be regarded as 'superior' or 'inferior'." A racist is, therefore, someone who believes that people of a particular race, colour or national origin are inherently inferior, so that their identity, culture, self-esteem, views and feelings are of less value than his/her own and can be disregarded or treated as less important.

Hence, social and individual differences caused by *cultural* variability are rejected by the racist in favour of *biological* differences caused by hereditary factors. This is the basic difference between racism and ethnocentrism. Ethnocentrism is a tendency to understand the world only from the viewpoint of one's own culture; this tendency usually leads to assumed superiority of one's culture over all others. Because it is based on culture which is socially transmitted, anyone of any race who acquires the culture of that society (which is comprised largely of the language, system of norms, values and beliefs) will be accepted by it. On the other hand, racism assumes racial superiority or inferiority. As race is biologically determined and fixed, a person born to the 'inferior' race will always be assumed inferior.

It is claimed by many analysts in Britain that power is a necessary precondition of racism. In fact, some 'experts' define racism as Prejudice plus Power. A critical analysis of the psycho-social variables involved in racism demonstrates, however, that this need not necessarily be so.

Racism is a social attitude. As an attitude, it has three components: (1) the *cognitive* component – beliefs or knowledge; (2) the *emotional-motivational* component – feelings; and (3) the *performance* component – *tendencies* to act in particular ways on the basis of knowledge and emotion.

But action tendencies do not necessarily lead to action even when buoyed by strong cognition and emotion. I may deeply believe and strongly feel that the possession of nuclear weapons is militarily, politically and ethically wrong, but at the same time, feel powerless to do anything about it and consequently *do nothing*. Likewise, a person may hold racist attitudes on the cognitive/affective level and yet not act on his/her beliefs and action tendencies because of social or legal constraints or lack of power. Therefore, one may be a racist without the power to act on the implications of one's racist beliefs.

Racial discrimination, on the other hand, requires power for it depends on (a) the ability (power) to give or withhold social benefits, facilities, services, opportunities, etc. from someone who should be entitled to them; and (b) denying the above on the basis of race, colour or national origin. Therefore power is a necessary pre-condition of racial discrimination, but the same cannot be said of racism. A proletariat or peasant may be a die-hard racist although lacking the power to racially discriminate.

The use of the masculine pronoun:

I was determined from the beginning that the use of the traditional masculine pronoun to refer to humankind in general or an individual human being who could be of either sex, in particular, would not become a feature of this book. However, it soon became apparent that using the pronouns she or he and her or him in every relevant sentence, made some sentence structures clumsy and the reading quite tedious, while contributing little to anti-sexism. I consequently abandoned the attempt. The use of the masculine pronoun throughout the text, therefore, is purely for the sake of convenient grammatical expression. It is not meant to present a male-centred or male-orientated approach to the analysis of social reality.

CHAPTER ONE

Racial Discrimination in Employment: Fact or Fiction?

To most people involved in race relations and to black people in particular, the existence of pervasive racial discrimination in Britain is axiomatic. The findings of many empirical research studies have produced so much voluminous evidence of systematic discrimination that to begin analysis of the problem by first proving its existence is deemed superfluous. To the initiated or converted, therefore, this Chapter will be a tedious repetition of familiar facts; I recommend such readers to proceed to the next Chapter. To the readers who require clear evidence beyond reasonable doubt, I shall begin with a detailed literature survey of the most comprehensive and authoritative empirical studies on racial discrimination carried out in Britain. These studies were undertaken by the former Political and Economic Planning (PEP), now Policy Studies Institute (PSI) between 1966 and 1982.

The PEP Studies

The first Race Relations Act in Britain was passed in 1965. It followed a dramatic acceleration in black immigration in the 1950s and early 1960s, a factor which, according to many observers, met with hostile reaction from some sections of the host community ranging from verbal and physical assaults to systematic and wide-ranging discrimination which effectively and traumatically deprived the immigrants of many of the rights and opportunities enjoyed as a matter of course by white people.

The Race Relations Act, 1965, declared unlawful any discrimination on grounds of colour, race, or ethnic or national origin in certain places of public resort (hotels, restaurants, public houses, theatres, dance halls, swimming pools, public transport, etc.); it prevented the enforcement on racial grounds of restrictions on the transfer of tenancies, and it penalised incitement to racial hatred. A Race Relations Board (RRB) was set up (February, 1966) to help secure compliance with the provisions of the Act.

It was apparent from the start that given the insidious and wide-ranging nature of racial discrimination, the Act did not go far enough. So in 1966, the RRB and the National Committee for Commonwealth Immigrants (the latter was set up by the Prime Minister in September, 1965, to advise the government on matters relating to the integration of Commonwealth immigrants), with a grant from the Joseph Rowntree Memorial Trust, decided to sponsor a study to assess the extent of discrimination in Britain in fields not covered by the Act. These included employment, housing and commercial services such as insurance, credit facilities and financial services.

The survey was carried out by Political and Economic Planning (PEP) and Research Services Ltd under the direction of John Pinder, Donald Monk, William Daniel and Rod Meadows.

The researchers adopted a three-pronged methodological approach. The first involved a questionnaire survey among a sample of 1,000 immigrants (Westindians, Indians, Pakistanis and Cypriots) in six towns in England known to contain a relatively high density of immigrant population. Respondents were asked in an interview if they had experienced discrimination and if so to document in detail any instances they proffered.

In the second approach, a sample of 500 potential discriminators were interviewed by experienced specialist interviewers. The sample population consisted of employers, trade union officials, staff of employment exchanges and of private employment bureaux in the field of employment, estate agents, accommodation bureaux, local government officers in housing; and bank managers, and officers of insurance companies in commercial services.

The third methodology (situation tests) aimed at providing objective evidence of the findings of the interviews with immigrants and potential discriminators. In the situation tests, a team of three applicants, first a "coloured" immigrant, then a white immigrant of Hungarian origin, and finally a white Englishman were sent to apply for employment, housing and commerical services. In each test, the three applicants had equivalent occupational qualification or housing requirements. The Hungarian was included in the team to test whether discrimination was based on 'foreignness' or on 'colour'.

The Findings were released in a PEP report: *Racial Discrimination in Britain,* in April, 1967 which was rewritten by W.W. Daniel and published by Penguin under the title *Racial Discrimination in England.* Among the major findings of the study were:

1. That there was widespread racial discrimination in England.
2. That discrimination was on a far greater scale than the victims' own

awareness of it would suggest.[1]
3. That, contrary to popular myth, "the experience of discrimination is most widespread among people who, on every criterion of ability, are the most able and best qualified".[2]

The reason offered by the author for this paradox is that the less able and less qualified black worker seeks employment at the bottom end of the scale where employers find it most difficult to recruit white labour for the wage offered, whilst the more able and more qualified seek positions higher up the organisation hierarchy where employers are most reluctant to place black people.

4. That a process of 'stereotyping' had occurred in which a generalised image of the coloured person, based on the characteristics of the less able is developed and projected on to all coloured people, without taking proper account of individual differences among them. Thus a well qualified coloured person is heavily penalised compared to a white person who has similar or inferior characteristics.
5. That there were a minority of employers who had employed blacks above the level to which the majority of employers believed them to be suited. "Certainly the minority of employers who had experience of coloured staff above unskilled manual level reported that they found them effective and successful at all such levels, including senior jobs, and that they had no regrets. There were coloured people doing effective work in all types of jobs, even in those roles that were taboo for the large majority of employers (such as having coloured people with white people under their control). Morever not only had employers found their own prejudices to be contradicted by experience but they had also found that the resistance they had expected from white staff had either died down after a time or not materialised at all."[3]

In the light of this report as well as a recommendation by the RRB, in its first published report, "that the Race Relations Act should be extended to cover housing, employment, financial facilities and places of public resort not covered by the present Act", the Labour Government passed the 1968 Race Relations Act, making unlawful most of the forms of discrimination shown to exist by the PEP report.
    In 1974, PEP undertook another study to ascertain whether employers and trade unionists; (a) had taken effective steps to prevent discrimination within the terms of the 1968 Race Relations Act; (b) had taken positive steps to ensure equality of opportunity for all groups; and (c) had striven to create conditions in which members of minority groups are encouraged to overcome their disadvantages. The focus of the enquiry was not whether discrimination had occurred, but on how far employers and trade unionists had taken active steps to prevent it and to combat the conditions in which it takes root.
    This enquiry by Neil McIntosh and David J. Smith, involved a

survey of 283 employers at plant level using a structured questionnaire, case studies of 14 plants (all plants in employment exchange
areas where immigrants from India, Pakistan and the Westindies
formed at least 1% of the local population), interviews at the
head offices of 27 of the largest groups and nationalised industries,
and of eight trade unions.

The report provided evidence that some firms had formulated
anti-discrimination policies and that the larger the plant, the more
likely it was to have such a policy. 14% claimed they had policies of
this kind, while only 8% had taken concrete steps to implement
these policies and a still smaller proportion (1%) could mention a
specific instance in which action had been taken.[4]

Their findings suggested that out of the 14 plants there were eight
which clearly practised some form of discrimination, and in a
further two cases discrimination seemed likely, though the facts
were less clear cut.

Furthermore, the data revealed that there was a strong concentration of black workers in non-skilled manual jobs (67% compared
with 37% of the total workforce), and a low concentration in non-
manual jobs (14% compared with 42% of the total workforce). Of the
283 plants included in the survey, 95% employed some manual
workers. Of these, 22% claimed that they had at least one black
supervisor although among plants where black people represented
5% of the workforce, this proportion jumped to 39%. "However, there
is still a substantial proportion of plants with high concentrations of
the minorities which do not have supervisors from minority groups
now, and do not intend to have them in the near future."[5] 16% of
plants having non-manual staff had at least one minority supervisor
and there was a strong tendency for minority supervisors on the
staff to be Indians.

In a survey of managers' attitudes to black workers, the study
found that of the 50% who responded, there was evidence of
stereotyped thinking and a strong tendency for the
stereotypes to be unfavourable to the minorities; furthermore, these
views were not significantly related to managers' actual experience
of the various minority groups.

Despite the Trades Union Congress resolution passed in 1955
condemning "all manifestations of racial discrimination or colour
prejudices whether by governments, employers or workers", as well
as several initiatives (from the TUC) urging open discussions
between management and unions of racial issues, evidence from the
survey of employers showed that only 8% of plants had any contact
with trade unions on race relations policy. On the other hand, only
3% of plants said that a union had ever disagreed with their policy
on racial issues, and only 2% thought that unions tended to resist

the introduction of black workers. There was also evidence of cases in which unions had either encouraged discrimination or had allowed discriminatory practices to develop through inadequate representation.

In a second report publicised in September, 1974, Neil McIntosh and David Smith aimed in their research to measure the size and nature of the disadvantages suffered by members of the racial minorities (Asians and Westindians) compared with the white population, and to assess, as far as possible, how far these disadvantages were associated with discrimination on grounds of race, and how far they sprung from other causes.

The methodology of the study was similar to the situational tests adopted by Daniel et al (op.cit.), except that each test involved only two matched applicants – a native *white* English person paired with an Italian, a Westindian, an Indian or a Pakistani. The two applicants always had similar (British) qualifications and experience. In all, 305 correspondence tests were carried out in six towns for white collar jobs: Salesman (male), Accountant (male), Management trainee (male), Clerical (female), and Secretary (female).

In the second test, a team of actors was used to carry out tests in four situations two of which involved: (a) personal application for unskilled or semi-skilled manual jobs; and (b) telephone enquiries about skilled manual jobs advertised in newspapers. These tests were carried out in London and Birmingham, and the pair of actors consisted of a native British white actor and a Westindian, an Indian, a Pakistani, or a Greek actor.

In the correspondence testing, an Asian or Westindian applicant was discriminated against in 30% of cases while the Italian applicant faced discrimination in only 10% of cases. "In the light of the fact that the method only identifies discrimination at the screening stage a level of 30% is very substantial. The very much lower figure for the Italian applicant shows that the discrimination is associated largely with racial rather than simply with foreign origin."[7] In the situations and roles tests, Asians and Westindians applying for unskilled jobs faced discrimination in 46% of cases and for skilled jobs 20%.

"This finding implies that there are tens of thousands of acts of discrimination of this kind in a year.... Although the level of discrimination seems, therefore, to be lower now than it was before the Act, the general conclusion from these findings must be that the number of cases of discrimination that are dealt with by the law (either by means of conciliation or by means of legal sanctions), forms a very small proportion of the number of acts of discrimination that actually occur."[8]

In the last of four reports, two of which have been reviewed above (the fourth covered housing), the PEP published in February, 1976, the findings of a national survey on *The Facts of Racial Disadvantage*. The study aimed to find out the extent to which racial minority groups tend to suffer disadvantages (compared with the white majority), and whether or not these disadvantages were the result of unlawful discrimination against them. In a nationwide survey, a large sample of 3,292 people (Westindians, Indians, Pakistanis, Bangladeshis and African Asians) were selected for interviews. For purposes of comparison, a national sample of 1,239 white British men were interviewed within the same period.

Among the major findings of this research was the wide disparity between the level of qualifications and the level of jobs held by the minorities. For example, 79% of white men with degree standard qualifications were in professional or management positions, compared with only 31% of minority men. Furthermore, 21% of minority men with degree standard qualifications were doing manual jobs (including 3% who were doing unskilled manual jobs), whereas none of the white men with equivalent qualifications were doing manual jobs of any kind. This is in spite of the fact that only Asian further degrees were treated as equivalent to English degrees.[9]

Three possible explanations were put forth to justify the wide disparity between the level of qualification and the level of jobs of white men and minority men. The first was that minorities found it more difficult to get suitable jobs because of racial discrimination; "Certainly there is conclusive and up-to-date evidence of substantial levels of discrimination against the minorities in recruitment to employment."[10]

The second possible causal factor was that the minorities met with special difficulties because they did not enter the British employment market at the best age. For example, an employer looking for managers aged 30, will expect candidates to have had, in addition to the appropriate academic qualification, a certain degree of experience which he would evaluate. Although the author could not say how important this difficulty was, "there (was) some evidence that it (had) some significance".[11]

A third possible explanation, rejected by the author, was that minority men actually had less relevant experience or competence in the professional or managerial field than equivalently qualified whites. For example, he rejected language competence as a possible factor; "The relationship between fluency in English and academic qualifications is so strong that nearly all Asian men with degree-equivalent qualifications speak English fluently. Yet it is among this very group that we find the greatest disparity between the level of qualifications and the level of job."[12]

The enquiry also found that

"among skilled manual workers aged 25-54, median gross weekly earnings for white men at the time of the survey were £39.30, compared with £35.60 for minority men. This further disadvantage is superimposed on the difference that already exists in terms of job levels between the minorities and whites. Further, the differences in earnings exists in spite of the fact that the minorities do more shiftwork than whites. It is also highly significant that educational level is little related to earnings among the minorities, while among whites, the better educated earn substantially more than those with poorer education."[13]

Trade union membership was also found to be higher among the minority groups who were in employment than among whites – 61% compared with 47%.

The study concluded that there was, independently, "some evidence that actual levels of discrimination have decreased since the 1968 Race Relations Act; but the fall in perceived discrimination may reflect most of all the fact that discrimination is now less open, admitted and obvious to all."[14]

In 1982, Policy Studies Institute undertook an investigation into the circumstances of the British black population,[a] a project sponsored by among others, the Home Office, the Department of the Environment, the Department of Health and Social Security, the Department of Employment and the Greater London Council.

The survey methodology involved individual interviews with 5,001 black adults in 3,083 separate households, and comparison interviews with 2,305 white adults, each from a separate household. The response rate of the survey was: Asians 82.3%, Westindians 70%, and Whites 82.5%. It can be noted that, by any sampling standard, this was a massive investigation. Wherever possible, comparisons between the 1974 and 1982 surveys were made in order to highlight changes that had taken place.

The findings published in 1984, showed that in the labour market,

"The survey gives us a depressing picture of the economic lives of people of Asian and Westindian origin in Britain today. They are more likely than white people to be unemployed, and those who are in work tend to have jobs with lower pay and lower status than those of white workers. Examination of the changes in the employment patterns of white, Asian and Westindian people over the eight years between 1974 and 1982 shows that there has been little convergence of the types of jobs done by the majority and minority ethnic groups, while their unemployment rates have sharply diverged."[15]

The factors causing this pattern of poor jobs among black workers, according to Colin Brown of PSI, were; (a) the different educational backgrounds of workers from different ethnic groups; (b) the frequent lack of fluency in English among Asian workers; (c) the different residential locations of the majorities of white and black workers; (d) an ethnic minority labour market which seems to be in some respects quite different from that of white workers; and (e) racial discrimination, both direct and indirect.

Although the large differences in job levels between white people and black people may be partly explained by differences in their formal qualifications, "like-for-like comparisons showed that there is still a large difference between white and black job levels among those with and without qualifications".[16] 57% of the black and 44% of white responents had no formal qualifications, but whilst 22% of the latter have non-manual jobs, only 5% of the former (Westindians) had non-manual jobs. This indicates that among a substantial proportion of the workforce, differences in job levels between whites and blacks cannot be attributed to differences in qualifications.

The survey further revealed that "one of the most important consequences of black workers' inferior position in the labour market is their low level of wages. The median weekly earnings of full-time white employees in the survey are £129, compared with £109 for Westindians and £111 for Asians".

In September 1985, PSI, following a survey of applicants for employment by candidates with equivalent qualifications from a variety of ethnic backgrounds, published its latest report: *Racial Discrimination: 17 Years After the Act*. At least 30% of employers were found to have discriminated against the black applicants. The report concludes that, in this respect, little has changed in ten years.

This consistent pattern of racial discrimination and disadvantage suffered by black people in the British labour market is supported by other empirical studies, including the Tavistock Institute of Human Relations investigation (1976-7) into the recruitment, postings, training, promotion, etc., practices in the civil service; the CRE and Nottingham and District Community Relations Council study into job discrimination against young blacks in Nottingham (1980); and CRE spot checks of 300 London-based firms (1982) who were recruiting employees, found that 50% discriminated against blacks at the point of recruitment.

None of these studies, however, offer any causal explanation of racial discrimination. For example, the PEP study in 1966 reviewed above, found "that a process of 'stereotyping' had occurred in which a generalised image of the coloured person, based on the characteristics of the less able is developed and projected on to all coloured people, without taking proper account of individual differences among them".

Some of the questions the investigators failed to address were: Why and how did the stereotyping occur? When did it occur? What were the factors that brought it about? How and why did it spread throughout the population? Why is it that less able whites are not used as bench marks by which all whites are negatively stereotyped as in the case with blacks? Why is it that the most able and most qualified blacks suffer the greatest degree of discrimination? Why do whites find it unacceptable that blacks should supervise whites? In short, why do black people suffer from racial discrimination? When did this social practice emerge? What were the factors which brought the practice into being? How did it become so pervasive? And, more importantly, why does it still persist?

The problem of racial discrimination, in other words, was only partly defined. But how can one solve a problem which has not been adequately defined? How can employers, managers, personnel managers, trade union officials, etc. who are opposed to racial discrimination, propose solutions to eradicate the practice when they do not know its causes? In the absence of that knowledge, how can one evaluate the efficacy of the many varying prescriptions proffered by the CRE, 'Positive Actionists', equal opportunities 'consultants' and so on?

In the 1982 PSI survey, Colin Brown attempted to address the issue of the causes of the persistence of inequality between blacks and whites. His efforts, however, raised more questions than answers. He states:

"As we systematically compare the jobs, incomes, unemployment rates, private housing, local authority housing, local environments and other aspects of the lives of people with different ethnic origins, a single argument emerges in respect of the way the circumstances of black people came to be and continue to be worse than those of white people. In its most general form, the argument runs as follows: Asian and West Indian immigrants came to Britain not as a result of a spontaneous migratory fervour, but as a result of the availability of jobs that offered rates of pay that were higher than those that could be obtained by the migrants in their countries of origin. There were openings for immigrants because the expanding economy of the 1950s and early 1960s created demands for labour that could not be satisfied from within the indigenous workforce. However, these openings were located at the lower levels of the job market, in jobs left behind by white workers who could in this period more easily become upwardly mobile. The result was that even *highly qualified immigrants found themselves doing manual work*[b] while those without qualifications were given the very worst jobs. The same mechanism operated with regard to housing and residential area. Asians and West Indians settled in the areas that white people were leaving, and in the poor housing stock no longer wanted by whites who could afford to move on or who were housed by the councils. Black people came from the former colonies into this country to a position of ready-made disadvantage; their entry to British society was a replacement for the lost battalions of urban manual workers, not, as it might have been, as a group of newcomers with a varied range of qualifications, skills and abilities who could make contributions at all levels of society...The patterns of disadvantage were therefore set early in

the history of Britain's present black population and became in many
respects self-sustaining. The processes of direct and indirect racial
discrimination in employment operate as if to recognise the legitimacy of
recruitment of black workers to some jobs but their exclusion from others,
while a variety of factors maintain the geographical distribution of black
families in the areas of original immigrant settlement".[17]

Ah! at last it appears we have a causal explanation of racial
discrimination in Great Britain! But do we? A closer analysis
reveals contradictions not only with previous PEP and PSI findings,
but also with Brown's own findings in his survey. Firstly, if, as a
result of economic expansion, whites who previously occupied the
bottom of the socio-economic pyramid because of lack of qualifications, skills, etc. were then upwardly mobile (ie were moving into
more skilled, higher-graded, higher status, higher paying jobs), why
were the "highly qualified immigrants" not able likewise to obtain
jobs commensurate with their qualifications, but found themselves
"doing manual work"? Surely, in an expanding economy in which
white British workers with no qualifications or skills were able to
achieve upward mobility, highly qualified black workers, once they
had arrived in this country, ought to have been able to secure
commensurate jobs, unless there were other factors militating
against them!

Secondly, how does Brown's theory explain the 1974 PEP
situational test (itself a replication of the 1966 PEP survey)
reviewed above, in which white and black applicants, matched for
similar (British) qualifications, were used in correspondence tests
for white collar jobs? The black applicant was discriminated
in 30% of cases. A similar study by CRE and Nottingham District
Community Relations Council in Nottingham found blacks were
discriminated against in 48% of cases.

Thirdly, how does Brown's theory explain the PEP's 1966 findings
"that, contrary to popular 'myth', the experience of discrimination is
most widespread among people who, on every criterion of ability,
are the most able and best qualified"?

Fourthly, there have been several migrations into Britain,
particularly from Eastern Europe. Most of the emigrés found
themselves initially in socio-economic circumstances not very
dissimilar to the black immigrants of the 50s and 60s. Why did their
disadvantage not become self-sustaining like that of the blacks?

Fifthly, why did landlords, in advertising vacant properties for
letting, state: "No Coloureds", thus forcing blacks, notwithstanding
their economic circumstances, into 'slum' properties?

Brown's explanation evidently offers no answer to the cause of the racial discrimination which he so clearly establishes in his survey:

"Our expectation when embarking on this study was that we would find substantial reduction in the levels of inequality and that there would be pointers towards the way these changes might be further encouraged. Instead we find a complex jumble of old and new inequalities, rooted in three linked problems. First, it is clear that racialism and direct racial discrimination continue to have a powerful impact on the lives of black people. Second, the position of the black citizens of Britain largely remains, geographically and economically, that allocated to them as immigrant workers in the 1950s and 1960s. Third, it is still the case that the organisations and institutions of British society have policies and practices that additionally disadvantage black people because they frequently take no account of the cultural difference between groups with different ethnic origins."[18]

It is my firm belief that until one understands *why* white people racially discriminate against black people, one cannot, understand the nature of the obstacles in the way of equal opportunities and racial equality, and, hence, one cannot prescribe effective solutions to the problem. A problem adequately defined, is a problem half-solved.

In the following chapters, therefore, I shall attempt a systematic socio-historical analysis of the origin and development of racism in order to provide a framework for the analysis of racial discrimination. I shall analyse the economic circumstances and social relationships which led to the initial development of the ideology of racism. Evidence will be proffered to show how, once originated, the ideology insidiously pervaded every stratum, institution and social practice of British society. Finally the effect of the ideology of racism on the life chances of black people in Britain will be demonstrated.

Notes

a. This excluded black people who came from Africa, but included African Asians.
b. emphasis mine.

CHAPTER TWO

Ideology of Racism – The Origin of Racial Prejudice

Most of the literature on race relations in general, and racial discrimination in particular, either explicitly or implicitly suggests that problems of racial discrimination originated from the 1950s and early 1960s when there was an accelerated increase in black immigration to Britain due to labour shortage caused by the post war boom in economic activity.[1]

The argument thus developed is that, faced with 'a flood' of immigrants, the British people who have national characteristics of insularity and xenophobia, reacted with justifiable resentment. The strange culture, life style and 'unhygienic manners' of the immigrants were perceived as a threat by the host community. Trade unionists feared that the arrival of such a large pool of labour would lower wage levels and weaken the bargaining power of the unions. The qualifications of the skilled workers among the immigrants were said to be suspect and many craft unions feared a lowering of standards of skills of their trades. Faced with these socio-cultural and economic problems caused by these immigrants, it was only natural that the host community should react with suspicion, anxiety, hostility and racial prejudice. The logical inference to be drawn from this line of argument is that but for the large scale 'coloured' immigration of the fifties and sixties, there would be no racial prejudice. Furthermore, that if some means could be found to reduce their number by repatriation, for example, or if all further black immigration were stopped, race relations would improve.

This argument, however, is a gross obfuscation of reality for a number of reasons:

Firstly, black presence in Britain and white negative attitude towards black people goes back four centuries:

"Black slaves first appeared in Britain at the end of the sixteenth century, as an aftermath of the Spanish wars, (Fiddes, 1934, p.500) and, although in 1596 the Privy Council ordered some of them to be removed from the country in case they deprived Englishmen of employment, they reappeared in

increasing numbers, throughout the seventeenth century, as a by-product of
the booming slave-trading carried out on the African coast by Britain, and
the other major European powers."[2]

James Walvin takes up the same theme when he observes:

"Indeed no less a figure than the Queen herself had already expressed herself
forcibly about the growth of a black minority in the capital. In the last decade
of the century the expanding population of England was troubled by famine.
As hunger swept the land, England was faced with a social problem which
taxed the resources of government to the limits. Immigrants added to the
problems. No group was so immediately noticeable as the Blacks. In a letter
to the lord mayors of the country's major cities, Elizabeth noted 'that there
are of late divers blackamoores brought into this realm, of which kind of
people there are already here too many considering how God hath blessed
this land with great increase of people of our nation as any country in the
world'. The Queen therefore ordered 'that those kind of people should be sent
forth of the land', in particular those Africans recently imported by Sir
Thomas Baskerville. In the July of 1596 the Queen reiterated her objection to
black settlement; 'those kind of people may be well spared in this realm,
being so populous'. An ideal opportunity to reverse the flow of Blacks came
with an offer from Casper van Senden, a Lubeck merchant, to ship Negroes
from England to Spain and Portugal, as a part of a deal to recoup some of his
losses on an earlier mission. Elizabeth agreed to the suggestion, ordering her
subjects to turn over their black servants to van Senden and 'to be served by
their own countrymen (rather) than those kind of people... In January 1601,
Elizabeth issued a a Proclamation repeating her licence to Senden to take
'such Negroes and blackamoores which... are carried into this realm... who
are fostered and powered here, to the great annoyance of her own liege
people.'"[3]

Queen Elizabeth obviously failed to rid Britain of black people, for
Britain's increasing involvement in the African slave trade in which
the Queen became an investor, was bound inevitably to increase the
size of the black population. In fact, London's total population of
676,250 in 1764, was said to have included 20,000 Negroes (see
Nigel File and Chris Power, *Black Settlers in Britain 1555-1958*
(1981), p.1).

Secondly, that argument cannot explain the plight of black people
in Liverpool: "In Liverpool, unemployment among the ethnic
minorities is the most visible symptom of racial disadvantage, and
not least among black Liverpudlians of three or four generations....
Racial disadvantage in Liverpool is in a sense the most disturbing
case of racial disadvantage in the United Kingdom, because there
can be no question of cultural problems of newness of language, and
it offers a grim warning to all of Britain's cities that racial
disadvantage cannot be expected to disappear by natural causes."[4]
The Liverpool experience thus clearly argues against the claim that
cultural differences between black people and the indigenous white
people are the main causes of racial prejudice and intolerance.

Thirdly, Clause 87 of the new Government of India Bill 1833, prohibited racial and religious discrimination in the public service. The East India Company which up till then had ruled indirectly on behalf of the British Government, had excluded Indians from the 'covenanted' civil service posts which were the high grade, high status, high paying jobs. Lester and Bindman (1972) give a graphic account of how for nearly one hundred years, the British Government and the Colonial Government in India, systematically and deliberately colluded to frustrate the implementation of Clause 87 in order to preserve the 'covenanted' jobs for whites only.[5] Such job segregation was widespread throughout the British colonies; and was discrimination against the colonised in their own countries -- immigration was not a factor!

Fourthly, the attribution of racial discrimination to immigration is negated by the American experience. Racial discrimination in the US has absolutely nothing to do with immigration – black people have been there for four centuries. Although the socio-cultural and historical contexts in the US are different from those in Britain, there are many similarities in the nature and manifestation of racial discrimination (at least in employment) between the two countries.

Fifthly, racial discrimination by white people against black people is a feature of virtually all contemporary multi-racial societies composed of black and white peoples and in most of these societies, immigration is certainly not a factor of the racial intolerance and discrimination.

The large-scale immigration of black people into Britain in the fifties and sixties therefore offers no satisfactory causal explication of racial discrimination in Britain. Yet most political and social commentators on race relations in Britain choose not to go beyond the fifties in search of explanation, and the main reason, as we shall demonstrate, is that the history beyond that epoch is too barbaric for them to confront. Indeed Dr Stuart Hall, then Director of the Centre for Cultural Studies, University of Birmingham, now Prof. of Sociology at the O.U. was driven to comment in a public talk arranged by the British Sociological Association: "...the development of an indigenous British racism in the post-war period begins with the profound historical forgetfulness – what I want to call the loss of historical memory, a kind of historical amnesia, a decisive mental repression – which has overtaken the British people about race and empire since the 1950s. Paradoxically, it seems to me, the native, home-grown variety of racism begins with this attempt to wipe out and efface every trace of the colonial and imperial past."[6]

To understand the origin and development of racial prejudice, it is imperative to go back into the history of the first contact and

subsequent relationships between Europe on the one hand, and
Africa, America, Asia and Australasia on the other. However,
because Africa, for reasons that will become apparent, offers greater
explanation for the current analysis, most emphasis will be placed
on the relationship between Europe and Africa. I do not intend to
present here a history of slavery or colonialism; nor do I intend to
deliver an apologia of black pre-colonial civilisation since this task
has already been undertaken by more emminent scholars. It is
nonetheless essential to cite established historical data in order to
develop a theoretical framework for the analysis of the origin and
development of racial prejudice; to trace its effect on social beliefs
and values; and how these in turn, have helped to structure social
attitudes which have affected past and contemporary race relations,
particularly in employment.

The Initial Contact

It all began, according to Professor Basil Davidson,[7] in 1441, half
a century before Columbus crossed the Atlantic, when a little ship
under the command of one Antam Gonçalvez sailed from Portugal.
Gonçalvez had been asked by Prince Henry of Portugal to prove his
worth by shipping a cargo of skins and oil of sea lions which had
been discovered on the Atlantic coast of Africa. Having sailed as far
as Morocco, Gonçalvez conceived the idea of winning a reputation by
capturing and bringing to his royal master some inhabitants. After
capturing two Africans – man and woman – Gonçalvez and his crew
met another Portuguese venturer, Nuno Tristao and together they
attacked two African encampments, killing four and capturing ten.
It was hoped that, in Portugal, information could be extracted from
the captives about the nature and people of their land.

When they arrived with their twelve captives, Prince Henry sent
a special envoy to the Pope, explaining his intention to carry out
further raids and even conquests. The Pope welcomed this new
crusade and granted to all who would participate in such war,
complete forgiveness for all their sins. In 1444, another 235 men,
women and children were kidnapped in Africa, transported to
Portugal and sold as household servants.

But this initial encounter was not an accident – the Portuguese
and Spaniards had been planning such a foray into Africa and Asia
prior to 1441. Following the rapid conquests and colonisation by the
Moslem Arabs in the seventh century AD which eventually created
an Islamic empire stretching from the Indus River in the east, Spain
(and for a while, part of France) in the west, and Constantinople in
the north, the Arabs and Berbers controlled the entire coastline of
North Africa, along the Mediterranean. With this geo-political

control went the control of trade in gold with West Africa and spices from India. The European need to circumvent the Moslem Arab monopoly of these trade routes stimulated the exploration of the fifteenth century.

The Renaissance had aroused Europe from its Dark Age slumber, thanks to the translation into Arabic of knowledge from ancient Egypt and the Mediterranean. Armed with the gun, the manufacture of which had been made possible by gun powder learned from the Chinese firecracker; with their ships equipped with lateen sails, astrolabes and nautical compasses, all invented by the Chinese, the knowledge of which had been acquired via the Arabs; motivated by the desire to plunder the resources of others, the Europeans unleashed a concerted and, in some cases, genocidal (eg the Aborigines and some of the Amerindians) onslaught against the rest of the world.

The European foray, as noted, was initiated by Portugal who was granted, by a papal bull of 1455, authorisation to reduce to servitude all infidel peoples. By 1471 Portuguese ships had reached the Gold Coast; by the early eighties, the mouth of the Congo; by 1488, had rounded the Cape; and by 1498-9 had made, under Vasco da Gama, the voyage to India and back. Such success was not to go unchallenged, for the Spaniards soon sought to compete in the lucrative trade. Portugal claimed monopolistic rights under the papal bull of 1455 and so to circumvent this obstacle (as well as Portuguese armed vigilance), the Spaniards attempted to reach the spice islands of the East by circumnavigating the world via the West. When Columbus reached the Caribbean, he claimed he had reached the spice islands and named the Islands the (West) Indies.

Continuing rivalry led to a series of papal bulls issued in 1493 which established colonial demarcations between the two powers – the East to Portugal and West to Spain. The subsequent Portuguese conquest of Brazil was legitimised not under the papal bull, however, but under the Treaty of Tordesillas between the two countries in 1494.

The Spaniards soon discovered gold and the conquistadores marched on mainland America. In a most murderous and brutal assault, Cortez overwhelmed the Mexican Aztecs and Pizarro subdued the Peruvian Incas. As a foretaste of things to come, two great ancient civilisations were destroyed with the utmost cruelty and barbarity, and their land plundered of gold and silver.

The Spanish settlers put the surviving Indians to work, mining silver and gold; planting spices and sugar; and raising hides. The plantations expanded rapidly, fuelling the need for labour. The colonised Amerindians were unable to provide sufficient labour for the fast multiplying plantations and revealed an incapacity to survive in servitude. They died off in great numbers, partly due to diseases which were introduced by the colonisers and against which the Indians had no immunity. A few European slaves and indentured labourers were transported there from Europe, but were insufficient to meet the growing demand. The solution was obvious to the colonialists: if the plantations could not be set up in Africa because of fierce opposition from powerful African kingdoms and other inhospitable factors (such as mosquitoes), then Africa's plentiful labour supply (who have shown themselves capable of surviving European diseases) must be transported to America.

The first recorded shipment of African slaves to the Americas was in 1505 when the King of Spain sent a ship from Seville to the Americas with 17 black slaves. A Portuguese fleet bound for the Indian Ocean, meanwhile, had been blown off course and landed in Brazil, leading to similar consequences for the Indian population as that which befell those in the Spanish colonies – massacre, brutal servitude and rapid depopulation. The plantation systems (like massive raging fires requiring a large amount of oxygen to continue to burn) needed a large labour force to sustain it, and Africa, to its eternal tragedy, was eventually to become the sole supplier.

From 1510 the Atlantic slave trade began in earnest, for in that year, the first consignment of black slaves for sale carried from Spain or Portugal, was sold in the Westindies. In 1518 the first slaves to be shipped directly from Africa to the Americas (rather than indirectly via Spain or Portugal) set sail. What had started as a trickle soon became a massive flood.

The first English voyage to West Africa, that of William Hawkins in 1530, and the next few subsequent voyages, stayed clear of slaves and instead, concentrated on ivory, pepper and gold. Later, however, though formally debarred from what was becoming a commercially profitable trade for the Portuguese and Spanish, English and French interlopers soon took a hand. "English involvement in the African slave trade was pioneered by John Hawkins. Hawkins had been sponsored by Queen Elizabeth I, amongst others. John Hawkins made a great deal of money from trading in slaves."[8]

"At first the trade was in the hands of the Portuguese who supplied the Spanish colonies as well as their own; but the enormous profits made out of slaving, with the mounting demand for plantation labour produced by the colonial endeavours of other European states, soon provoked ferocious competition. The Dutch ousted the Portuguese from the Gold Cost in 1642 and for a short time enjoyed a virtual monopoly of the transatlantic trade;

but then the English and the French intervened, and by the end of the eighteenth century Britain had outstripped all her rivals, to carry in her own ships more than half the slaves who crossed the Atlantic."[9]

The French Government by a royal order of 1670 threw open the slave trade to any Frenchman who wished to engage in it.

In three centuries – between the sixteenth and eighteenth centuries – a total of 15 million slaves were landed in the Americas. The number who died during the transfer to the ships for embarkation and in the middle passage were estimated at about 5 million. But other estimates suggest that Africa lost between thirty and forty million people through the slave trade (see Colin Brown, 'The Making of Africa', p.37). This was the most massive forced movement of human population of all time!

The institution of slavery had, of course existed from time immemorial – in ancient Egypt, Greece, Rome etc. But this was before the advent of capitalism as an economic system. For example, the Christian raiders in Eastern Europe, according to Basil Davidson,[10] sold non-Christian captives to the Franks, and the Franks employed them at home, and also sold them again to the Muslim princes of North Africa and Spain.

The system operated in the Italian city states and the Pope at one time excommunicated the Genoese, operating from the Black Sea, for selling Christian as well as non-Christian Europeans into slavery in Africa, contrary to the norm which permitted the sale of the latter category only. The sale and purchase of slaves was equally widespread in Africa. As Basil Davidson and many other historians have clearly demonstrated, slavery was of a different kind – although generally not an enviable state to be in, the condition of the slave was often economically better than that of many free people.

Moreover, slavery was confined to only a certain category of people. "Every king or potentate had his quota of 'disposable persons' for local use or sale abroad. Most of these were captives taken in raids on neighbouring peoples, or in wars between states, or else were convicts sentenced by courts of law to the loss of their civil rights."[11]

The Dutch merchant, Bosman confirms this of African pre-transatlantic slavery: "Not a few in our country fondly imagine that parents here sell their children, men their wives, and one brother the other. But those who think so deceive themselves, for this never happens on any other account but that of necessity or some great crime. But most of the slaves that are offered to us are prisoners of war, which are sold by the victors as their booty."[12]

The price of a slave was very high and, therefore, acquisition was the preserve of royalty and rich men. For example, a slave in Fatimid Egypt (c. 970-1100) cost almost 20 gold dinars, or nearly one year's income for a family of modest means.[13] "Andalusian records list the price of a black slave in Cordoba at 160 mitcals, or about 150 dinars; and that, for comparison, was also the price of a small house in the same list."[14]

The status of, and the treatment meted out to, slaves was vastly different from the slavery that was to develop in the sixteenth century. As Davidson has observed, "with rare exception, there was no large-scale use for slaves. Above all, there were no plantations. Slaves were used predominantly as domestic servants, or as concubines if they were women. However, a number of slaves became skilled workers, trusted clerks, officials, eunuchs in harems, or warriors in royal guards."[15]

Goitein has said that medieval slavery "was a personal service in the widest sense of the word, which, when the master served was of high rank and wealthy, carried with it great advantage as well as social prestige. In or out of bondage, the slave was a member of the family". In medieval Egypt, "the acquisition of a male slave was a great affair on which a man was congratulated almost as if a son had been born to him. No wonder, for a slave fulfilled tasks similar to those of a son".[16]

The practice in West Africa was not dissimilar. Slaves were either captives of war, criminals sentenced to be sold into slavery, or people sold to recover debts. "I must own that I was first kidnapped and betrayed by my own complexion, who were the first cause of my exile and slavery. But if there were no buyers there would be no sellers. So far as I can remember, some of the Africans in my country kept slaves, which they take in war, or for debt. But those which they keep are well, and good care taken of them, and treated well..."[17]

Once bought, they were taken into the family as bonded, wageless, servants. They could work themselves free, marry their masters' sisters or daughters, acquire wealth on their own account, and become kings through coup d'etat. Some kings formed special bodyguards composed entirely of slaves. The Mamelukes who were to unleash such murderous onslaught on their former masters, are an example. With the Arab conquest of Egypt in 642 AD and their sweep into Europe, several white slaves were brought into Egypt and other countries occupied by the Moslems. They seized power in Egypt in the thirteenth century and reigned till the sixteenth century. For a further 200 years, they survived as a military caste. Slave kings of African origin also ruled states in medieval India, whilst in West Africa, one of the most successful Mali Emperors was a slave usurper.

To conclude the analysis of the ancient and medieval institution of slavery prior to the advent of the plantation system, it is instructive to quote Davidson: "From a marketing standpoint, slaves were valued for their beauty if they were women, or for their strength if they were men, but they were also valued, men and women alike, according to their skills. Once in safe employment, slaves tended to live better, and sometimes far better, than non-slaves, so that medieval slavery was by no means the worst fate open to working people".[18]

More importantly, the change from previous experience was not only quantitative, but qualitative as well. Slavery as previously practised did not dehumanise its victims; they were still humans and treated as such, with few exceptions. The transistion from mercantile capitalism based on trade with equals to large-scale capitalist plantation system, as noted above, created a massive need for labour. To make it highly profitable, the system could not rely on waged labour, nor could the degree of exploitation required be voluntarily exacted even from slaves of the medieval variety. A new breed of slaves had to be created – a slave dehumanised, depersonalised, deculturised, debased and deprived of every human right. The black people who were solely to compose this new breed of slaves, were stripped of their humanity, made 'commodities', items of trade, personal properties to be used and disposed of as the owner chose. It is crucial to take a closer look at the brutality and savagery of the slave trade and the plantation slavery itself, because an adequate understanding of contemporary racism depends on the appreciation of the nature of the Atlantic slave system.

The European slavers obtained their black slaves initially by kidnapping individuals or small groups of Africans along the coasts, in the coastal waters while they were out fishing, on small farms near the coast, or by attacking small coastal villages and making off hastily with their captives in ships anchored just off-shore.

Other slaves were purchased from African slave traders. But the numbers of slaves who could be procured from these two sources were quite limited and supplies were irregular. The slavers had, therefore, to rely more and more on the convicts and prisoners of wars who could be purchased only from the chiefs, kings or their agents. As demand escalated with the expanding plantation system, the available supply could not meet it. Somehow, greater supply had to be stimulated. With no sign of a large-scale increase in the crime-wave which might have increased the supply of convicts, there was

only one way to stimulate supplies – provoking increasing wars
between the black kingdoms and tribes, since African chiefs would
not sell their own free people into slavery. The needs of some
African kings/chiefs and those of the white slavers became inextricably bound – the former needed the muskets to enable them to build
powerful armies, to protect their territories from neighbouring
'enemies', and to expand their kingdoms through military conquests. The latter needed the captives from the wars waged by the
former for the plantations of the Americas. As a result of such wars,
entire provinces were depopulated and their formerly proud and free
citizens marched off in chains into slavery.

Whichever way they were procured, once bought, the slaves
started a journey of the utmost physical and psychological agony
and brutality. After a humiliating bodily examination (the first of
many to come), the African was paid for and marched towards the
coast, if purchased inland. The journey to the coast was one of
frightful suffering and hardship. The slaves were chained, collared
and joined together with heavy poles and marched for long
distances, in some cases up to two hundred miles or more. Those who
could not make it were shot by the overseers or left to die of thirst
and starvation in the bush. Many committed suicide whenever the
opportunity arose. Noisy babies who could not be silenced were
wrenched from their mothers and bludgeoned to death by the
overseers. Some mothers deliberately smothered their babies to
save them from a nightmarish future with the 'white devils' whose
skins were the colour of 'plucked chicken'. Survivors were forced on,
threatened by the guns and ships of their captors.

On arrival at the coast, they were again meticulously, intimately
and degradingly body-searched for blemishes, diseases, etc. Those
found commercially acceptable were put in cells of the many 'castles'
which served to protect the European slavers as well as providing
accommodation for thousands of slaves awaiting transportation to
the Americas. For example, the Gold Coast (now Ghana) alone had
more than 40 such 'castles'. Prior to their shipment, the slaves were
branded on the breast like sheep or cattle, with the owner's brand.

They would wait for a few weeks or even months in the dungeons
of the 'castle' before the boats came. The dungeons were high,
vaulted rooms, guarded by iron gates; the only source of air and
light came from narrow slit windows. But nothing that had occurred
up till now could have prepared the Africans for the horrors of the
'middle passage' – the transatlantic crossing. They had hitherto
suffered severe psychological trauma, physical pain from the whip
and butt of the gun, exhaustion from an often long and difficult trek,
thirst and hunger, and degradation never before experienced.
However all these would pale into insignificance compared with the

utter hell of the 'middle passage'. The ship's captain, who was often an investor, had to decide how many slaves to carry in his ship. He would try to establish an optimum number, offering more tolerable conditions which would offer the best chance of least loss at sea and hence maximum revenue over cost price. Or he could fill every available space on the ship, risking higher percentage of loss on the assumption that the numbers actually landed alive would more than make up for those lost at sea. Either option was risky, but the odds tended to favour the latter. Moreover, much of the loss at sea could be recompensed to the investors by insurance.

An extract from the evidence of Dr Thomas Trotter, a surgeon in the Royal Navy, is highly instructive:

"Question: Do the slaves appear dejected when they first come on board? Trotter: Most of them at coming on board, show signs of extreme distress, and some of them even looks of despair, this I attribute to a feeling for their situation, and regret at being torn from their friends and connections. The slaves in the night were often heard making a howling melancholy noises, something expressive of extreme anguish. I found that it was occasioned by finding themselves in a slave room, after dreaming that they had been in their own country amongst their friends and relatives.
Question: Were the slaves much crowded in your ship in the Middle Passage?
Trotter: Yes; so much so that it was not possible to walk amongst them without treading on them.
Question: Had they room to turn themselves, or in any sort to lie at ease?
Trotter: By no means; the slaves that are out of irons are locked spoonways, according to the technical phrase, and closely locked to one another.
Question: Did the slaves appear to suffer from want of air?
Trotter: Yes; I have seen their breasts heaving and observed them draw their breath with all those laborious and anxious efforts for life which we observe in expiring animals subjected by experiment to foul air of different kinds. I have also seen them, when the tarpaulins were, through ignorance, or inadvertently thrown over the gratings, attempting to heave them up, and crying out 'Kickeraboo! Kickeraboo! which signifies, 'we are dying!'. On removing the tarpaulins and gratings, I have seen them fly to the hatchways with all the signs of terror and dread of suffocation."[19]

Another British surgeon described his experience of conditions aboard the slave ship:

"Some wet and blowing weather having occasioned the port-holes to be shut, and the grating to be covered, fluxes and fevers among the negroes ensued. While they were in this situation, my profession requiring it, I frequently went down among them, till at length their apartments became so extremely hot as to be only sufferable for a short time. But the excessive heat was not the only thing that rendered their situation intolerable. The deck, that is the floor of their rooms, was so covered with the blood and mucous which had proceeded from them in consequence of the flux (dysentery), that it resembled a slaughter-house. *It is not in the power of the human imagination*

to picture to itself a situation more dreadful or disgusting.[a] Numbers of the
slaves having fainted, they were carried up on deck, where several of them
died and the rest were, with great difficulty, restored. It had nearly proved
fatal to me also."[20]

In addition to the epidemics caused by such frightful overcrowd-
ing and insanitary conditions, there was so much appalling
degradation and filth to endure. Some of these journeys lasted the
length of two menstrual cycles for the women among the 'black
cargo'; it requires very little human imagination to appreciate the
effect that this would have on those women as well as others beside
them. But what about the even more regular human need for
excretion? "In each of the apartments are placed three or four large
buckets of a conical form... to which, when necessary the negroes
have recourse. It often happens that those who are placed at a
distance from the buckets, in endeavouring to get to them, tumble
over their companions in consequence of their being shackled. These
accidents, although unavoidable, are productive of continual quar-
rels in which some of them are always bruised. In this distressed
situation, unable to proceed, and prevented from getting to the tubs,
they desist from the attempts; and, as the necessities of nature are
not to be repelled, ease themselves as they lie."[21]

The account of many British sailors eloquently describes the
incredible horrors of the 'Middle Passage':

"There was misery, unending misery. There was so much death in the
Americas that whole slave populations had to be renewed every few years.
The records are eloquent enough...
    In 1829 an Englishman called Walsh took passage from Brazil in a British
frigate, the North Star. Somewhere in the South Atlantic they chased and
stopped a slaver.[b] Walsh went on board and afterwards described what he
saw – the familiar horrors of the Middle Passage. The slaving ship's cargo
was of five hundred and five men and women – the crew had thrown fifty-five
overboard during their seventeen days at sea – and the slaves 'were all
enclosed under grated hatchways, between decks. The space was so low that
they sat between each other's legs, and stowed so close together, that there
was no possibility of lying down or at all changing their position, by night or
by day. As they belonged to, and were shipped on account of different
individuals, they were all branded like sheep, with the owners' marks of
different forms. These were impressed under their breasts, or on their arms,
and, as the mate informed me with perfect indifference, burnt with a red hot
iron...'
    Many of these branded chattels, Walsh found, had no more than 0.9 square
metres or one square foot of sitting space, with no chance of standing up, and
all suffered from a deadly shortage of water. Walsh was shocked, but his
naval companions, 'who had passed so long a time on the coast of Africa, and
visited so many ships' in the course of their anti-slaving patrols, said that
this slaver was 'one of the best they had seen'. Headroom for slaves was as
much as one metre whereas sometimes, Walsh was told headroom was no
more than forty-five centimetres and slaves were generally chained, as these

were not, by the neck and legs during their crossing of the Atlantic. Such scenes were not rare. They had occurred month after month for nearly three hundred years by the time that Walsh took passage from Brazil. This was the physical degradation of the trade."[22]

"A Spanish frigate ludicriously called the Amistad, the Friendship, loaded 733 captives on the West African coast and disembarked in Havana, fifty-two days later, only 188; all the rest had died during the voyage. A doctor who examined the frigate on its arrival found that its captain must have 'packed' his captives so 'close' as to allow each of them on departure from Africa, just over one-third of a square metre. Such horrors multiplied during the decades of the illegal trade."[23]

"Slave revolts at sea were put down with grim ferocity. John Atkins has left an account of how the master of the Robert of Bristol, one Captain Harding, dealt with an insurrection early in the eighteenth century:
'Why, Captain Harding weighing the Stoutness and Worth (of the ringleaders) did, as in other countries they do by Rogues of Dignity, whip and scarfiy them only; while three other Abettors, but not Actors, nor of Strength for it, he sentenced to cruel deaths; making them first eat the Heart and Liver of one of them killed. The Woman (who had helped in the revolt) he hoisted up by the Thumbs, whipp'd, and slashed her with knives, before the other Slaves, till she died.' "[24]

As painful as such physical agonies were, the psychological trauma was much worse to many of the slaves. The West African, unlike the European, was never an individualist by tradition. He was part of an extended family, a community, a clan. He was part of, and depended on, the community; every social practice had meaning only in the context of the community to which he belonged. His identity or role was defined by the community and all worked to protect and to maintain the integrity of that community or 'extended family'. Unlike the Englishman, he did not compete 'to keep up with the Joneses' or to be better than the neighbours. Upon becoming a slave, the African found himself cruelly wrenched from all such ties and known environment; from a known personality, he became a non-entity, an item of commerce, a personal property. His value and worth was now determined by economic or commercial factors. Such an existence was not worth enduring -- every opportunity was taken to end this nightmare of unspeakable physical and psychological 'hell'.

"Some captives refused or were unable to surrender. For them the realities always remained too real. Some of them through defiance, some of them through panic, would elect death for themselves rather than accept what their minds saw and their spirits felt. At every possible chance they would try to jump overboard and drown themselves in the sea. Some would refuse to eat, starving themselves to death. All slave ships were equipped for such as these. Nets were hung over the sides to catch those who would jump. Devices would be inserted between the teeth of those who refused to eat and screwed until their prongs widened, forcing the mouth to open so that food could be

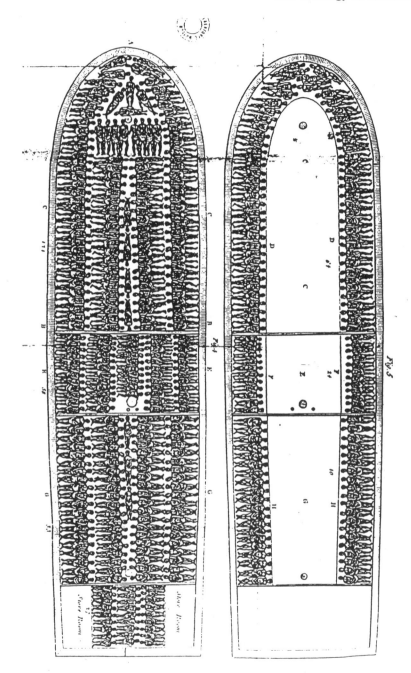

Illustration of *Spoonways* packing. The slaves were unable to change their position

pushed in. Thus, the body could be made to stay alive, overruling the will to die.

The surrender of the spirit and the will to numbness was in its own way a choice of death, a retreat of the consciousness into a tomb of insensibility. Only the automatic physiological reflexes acted as nervous response to keep the biological apparatus functioning. Sometimes the psychic shock was so great, the entombment of spirit so profound, that biological death would soon follow. Many captives simply retreated, thus, into death – from no disease and no apparently conscious act. Europeans were baffled for an explanation. Some claimed these captives had wanted death so badly that they had held their breath, suffocating themselves. But is that possible? Rather it would seem that these captives died of shock. Almost in a void of will, the biology had perhaps ceased functioning, and life extinguished itself – an involuntary suicide.

Whether or not medical science had ever known such a phenomenon, the captains of slave ships sought an answer to it, because not only did they observe such deaths among their human cargo, but they believed it to have an epidemic character unless arrested. The solution was that each day during the voyage, weather permitting, the captives would be made to gather on deck and jump up and down in what the crew called a dance. Drums were used for rhythm; the whip was used as a goad. It made a difference. The forced activity caused the heart to beat faster and the blood to flow, whether or not there was a will. Thus, it seemed, when all the sources that fed the spirit and the mind were attenuated, an external will had to be brought into play to sustain life. Apparently, the rude metamorphosis of men into commodities left little will to live. But they were forced to live. Only then could their captors profit."[25]

Falconbridge also witnessed the effect of captivity on many of the slaves:

"It frequently happens that the negroes, on being purchased by the Europeans, become raving mad, and many of them die in that state. In a former voyage, on board a ship to which I belonged, we were obliged to confine a female negro of about twenty-three years of age on her becoming a lunatic. She was afterwards sold during one of her lucid intervals...."[26]

The Ideology of Racism

Without the slightest doubt, the transatlantic slave trade was one of the most ignominious epochs in the entire history of humankind. It is an eloquent account of man at his most bestial. The evidence is overwhelming – never in the history of human cruelty have so many suffered so much savagery from so few for so long. But how could human beings so deliberately and callously inflict so much suffering on other human beings? Was the European so bestial by nature, so vicious by temperament, so sadistic by character, so bereft of every modicum of morality by culture, that he could inflict such physical and psychological pain without the slightest sign of remorse?

For those who perpetrated such acts of bestiality, a rational justification had to be found, for surely, those laying claims to being humans, could not otherwise inflict such savage and barbarous acts of inhumanity on other innocent human beings! The justification was what later came to be known as 'the doctrine of inherent black inferiority'. The black man, it was claimed, was inherently inferior and could not, therefore, be accorded equality of treatment with the white man. The white slave traders could consequently not be bound by the same ethical and moral codes when dealing with black people.

Writing of the Guinea Coast in the late eighteenth century, a German named Soemmering observed that the people there 'are more insensible than others towards pain and natural evils, as well as towards injurious and unjust treatment. In short, there are none so well adapted to be the slaves of others, and who therefore have been armed with so much passive obedience'.[27]

The Bishop of Rochester, in a statement which echoed previous sentiments of earlier slave traders, said in the House of Lords in 1799:

> "There is a great peculiarity in the negro constitution: that it is particularly conducive to the health of the negro to be close shut up in foul air. This is death to us white men as we know by the experiment of the Black-hole, and other tropical instances; but for your negro, it is the reverse. Keep him hot enough, he will always do well; and the better, the more you try to stifle him..."[28]

Alas! the ideology of racism was born.

> "The first ideology of race grew up with the expansion of Europe, and it is instructive, for it contains all the necessary ingredients to call forth such systems of ideas. In Africa, Asia, and especially in the New World, men of different appearance and different culture were encountered. The Spaniards, with their legalistic and religious notions, could not slay men, take over an area, and subjugate a people without some sort of rationale or ideology to justify these activities. No group of men is able systemtically to subordinate or deprive another group of men without appeal to a body of values which makes the exploitation, and disprivilege, the expropriation, and the degradation of human beings a 'moral' act.... Racial ideologies have the function of defining the subordinate people as 'lesser men', or 'non-men', or 'expendable men'. They thus provide the rationale for the activities or deprivation and heal the breach in the value system."[29]

Ronald Segal develops the same theme when he states that "The doctrine of inherent Negro inferiority was developed to excuse conduct which the teachings of Christianity and the twinges of traditional conscience alike disparaged, and a civilisation which had barely emerged from the sick-bed pronounced itself the only one sound and capable of up-lifting humanity."[30]

The doctrine of inferiority which informed the ideology of racism, served a number of useful purposes:

(a) It provided a moral justification for the acts of bestiality and thereby prevented any possible moral outrage, indignation and opprobrium which might otherwise have come from certain quarters at home.

(b) It soothed any vestige of conscience that the slave traders and colonialists might have possessed, by enabling them to reconcile their cultural values with their brutal activities.

(c) It aimed to prevent an uprising of the enslaved and the colonised. By undermining the self-esteem of the black man, by seeking to convince him of the white man's superiority and (almost divine) right to rule, it was hoped the former would legitimise the rule, domination and exploitation by the latter indefinitely.

Even the Church was not an innocent bystander. Official spokesmen for the Christian conscience of Britian condoned the slave trade; the Society for the Propagation of the Gospel branded its new slaves with the word 'Society' to distinguish their ownership, and the churches of Bristol pealed their rejoicing at Parliament's rejection of abolitionism. The Church of England had, through its leading clergy, stated its position on a number of occasions. The Bishop of London, in dealing with the question of the effect of baptism on ownership in a slave, declared that conversion to Christianity did not make the slightest alteration in the duties arising out of the civil relationships of master and slave except that the converted slave would be under an even stronger obligation to perform his duties. The only freedom which Christianity gave him was the freedom from the bondage of sin and Satan."[31] In other words, under Christianity, the black slave would indeed be more of a slave. Any disobedience, rebellion or attempted escape would be a sin not only against the master, but also against God. With the Bishop of London for a friend, who needs Satan for an enemy?

Eric Williams[32] has also documented the widespread involvement of the Church, and states categorically that the Church supported the slave trade. The story is told of an old elder of the Church in Newport who would invariably, the Sunday following the arrival of a slave-ship from the coast, thank God that "another cargo of benighted beings had been brought to a land where they could have the benefit of a gospel dispensation". Sherlock, later Bishop of London, assured the planters that "Christianity and the embracing of the Gospel does not make the least difference in civil property". To the very end the Bishop of Exeter retained his 655 slaves, for whom he received over £12,700 compensation in 1833 following the abolition of slavery in the British Empire.

Nor was this only a British heresy. The Spanish Jesuits,

Dominicans and Franciscans invested considerable resources in slave-worked plantations, and a slave ship named *The Willing Quaker* plied between Boston and Sierra Leone. The Portuguese clergy was, if anything, worse than his Spanish and British counterparts. As Chancellor Williams observes: "It was a revolting mess, no matter from what angle it is viewed. To begin with, priests were not only among the leading slave traders, but they also owned slave ships to carry the 'black cargoes' to distant lands. Priests also had their harems of black slave girls, some having as many as twenty each. They were called 'house servants' by these 'holy fathers'. The great majority of the whites were the scum of the land from which they came."[33]

Serious argument ensued at the beginning of the African slave trade as to whether the black man was besouled. The polemics ended several decades later when it was decided that he did in fact have a soul. From thence, Missionary expeditions were mounted to convert the 'wild savages' to Christianity and to Western civilisation.

It is difficult, however, to see how the Church was able to reconcile its conscience with regards to its proselyting of black people, its assumptions and beliefs of the nature of the black man, its collusion with the slavers, its participation in the system of slavery and its indoctrination of the slaves to accept their slave status. Montesquieu, the first internationally reputed philosopher to lend his voice to the cause of abolitionists, satirically stated in De l'Esprit des Lois (1748): "Were I to vindicate our right to make slaves of the Negroes, these should be my arguments. The Europeans, having extirpated the Americans, were obliged to make slaves of the Africans for clearing such vast tracts of land. Sugar would be too dear if the plants which produce it were cultivated by other than slaves. These creatures are all over black, and with such a flat nose, that they can scarcely be pitied. It is hardly to be believed that God, who is a wise Being, should place a soul, especially a good soul, in such a black and ugly body." The ideology of race could not be better enunciated! "It is impossible to suppose these creatures to be men", Montesquieu went on, "because allowing them to be men a suspicion would follow that we ourselves are not Christian." In other words, if the African was human, the European could not be Christian for either treating him so bestially, or condoning such treatment. If the African, on the other hand, was not human, then the Church's mission in Africa and the Americas was a fraud, for no creature other than man can be christianised. Somehow, though, the Church managed to reconcile these contradictions, and the missionary activities became one of the decisive factors which paved the way for the transition from slaving to colonisation.

Hitherto, the concept of *ideology* has been used without an attempt to define it. We have looked at some of the historical evidence of the bestiality of the transatlantic slave trade which was so appalling that even animals without a sense of morality could not descend to such depths of barbarity as that perpetrated by the slave traders. We also noted that, to reconcile the claim of humanity and sanity with such barbarous acts, some justification and rationalisation, ie an *ideology* was required. So what on earth is this concept, *ideology*, which was capable of justifying such degree of brutality and which enabled the perpetrators of such acts to live with their consciences?

Colin Sumner defines ideology as "elements of consciousness generated within, and integral to social practice, reflecting the structure of such practice and the appearances of practical context".[34] My preferred working definition is that *ideology* is a set of ideas, beliefs, images, impressions, etc., which explains, rationalises, legitimises, and/or justifies specific social practice(s).

At the psychological level, there are three interrelated assumptions which underlie all human behaviour: (1) behaviour is *caused;* (2) behaviour is *motivated;* and (3) behaviour is *goal directed.* If valid, the above assumptions lead to another assumption viz., that human behaviour cannot be random and spontaneous. There must be a goal – explicit or implicit – towards which behaviour is directed, generated in response to an internal or external stimulus. For example, in the administration of justice, there is an underlying assumption that a murderer has a *motive* and that this must be ascertained in order to determine the appropriate charges and punishment, if found guilty. Law and order becomes impossible if human behaviour is random.

Similarly, at the sociological level, all social practice (ie repeated social behaviour) occur only through ideology: "... there is no [social] practice except by and in an ideology..."[35] Ideology itself originates within social practice, in fact the relationship between social practice and ideology is one of interdependence – social practice, generated in specific social relation, creates a need for a set of ideas, beliefs, assumptions, etc. to explain the purpose of the practice or to justify the practice; and once formed, the ideology becomes necessary – the underlying reason – for the repetition of that social practice. As Sumner puts it, "All ideologies originate within social practices and, once formed, are integral to their operation and development".[36]

Ideologies are important features of social practice since: (1) they define the purpose of the practice; (2) they define the actor's reasons for engaging in the practice and his mode of engagement (and disengagement); (3) they form part of the social context of the

practice; (4) they will effect the shape of the product; (5) they will be
generated within the practice; and (6) they will be embodied (as past
forms) in the material conditions (the raw materials, the tools, the
geography, etc.).[37]
    Social practice may be usefully classified into three main types:
economic, political and cultural. Though closely interrelated in
reality, the three types of social practice may be distinguished by
their products: economic practices result in use values (for personal
use or exchange); political practices result in forms of institutionalised social power, eg. political parties, trade unions, employer
associations, etc.; and cultural practices result in expressions of
forms of signification in fields such as art, music, science, the
dissemination of news, ritual, the dissemination of beliefs, literature, drama, dance, etc. Ideologies will emerge in any one of the
three main types of social practice and, once formed, may pervade
and operate not only in the specific type of social practice in which
they emerged, but also in the other or all three types.
    To appreciate the social imperative of ideologies, let us look
briefly at the 'Necessity theory' of ideologies. "The necessity thesis
is a theory of the logical and historical necessity of the emergence of
a particular ideology out of a particular social relation... The thesis
holds that for a particular social relation to be carried out on a
regular basis, certain ideas are required to be present as a *sine qua
non. Without these ideas the practice is impossible socially and thus
ceases to be a social practice.*[c] Now, since social practices entail the
purposive living out of certain social relations in a specific socio-
geographical context, it must be the case that these ideas are the
reflections of those relations (the assumptions or beliefs which make
them socially operable), and that the ideas adopt their historical
imagery, terminology and elaborated substance from the material
circumstances, existing ideologies and socio-geographical contexts
which constitute the environment in which they are brought to
life."[38]
    From a socio-psychological point of view, therefore, we all
approach phenomena – natural or social – with a whole range of
ideologies. Ideologies are a *sine qua non* of, and integral to, our
perception, definition and reaction to both natural and social
phenomena. This is more especially so in the case of the latter in
which 'reality' is socially constructed and can be made sense of, only
through ideologies. Take, for instance, the social concept, institution
and practice of marriage. It is not a randomly occurring social
behaviour; it is socially constructed and defined; the rituals by
which they may be entered into and disengaged from, are socially
prescribed; the roles and expectations of both partners are socially
determined, etc., etc. All these social practices involved in the

institution of marriage are contained in ideologies which emerged following the original institution of marriage in different primitive societies and as later modified. The perpetuity of the practice depends on the ideology of marriage; and the ideology of marriage continues to exist only to the extent that the social practice of marriage continues to occur. If people in a given society refuse to reproduce or re-enact the social practice of marriage, the ideology of marriage will disappear; if the underlying ideas, beliefs, values, etc. about marriage were to disappear, the social practice of marriage would disappear: "...once an ideology has emerged, its generative social relations can only be practically realized under the guidance of that ideology. Thus, withdrawal of assent to the ideology can result in a standstill in practice, just as much as the cessation of the practice can lead to a shattering of the ideology."[39]

The reality of social stratification in which different groups or classes have different relationships to the means of production, or the technical division of labour within a society, capitalist or non-capitalist, leads to the formation of distinct economic interests, patterns of consumption and lifestyles. These distinctive life-patterns and interests generate different political and cultural practices, leading to the emergence of different and, in some cases, opposing ideologies. There is, in other words, heterogeneity rather than homogeneity of ideologies. However, despite the different subcultures and different class ideologies, there emerge certain ideologies which are dominant and pervade all levels of the social strata. Because of their control over the coercive institutions or apparatuses of state (eg law enforcement agencies such as the judiciary, the police force, prison wardens, the armed forces, etc.); mass communication (as instruments of propaganda and opinion-forming); and institutions of socialisation (eg schools, colleges, universities, etc.); the dominant class is able to impose its ideologies on the subordinate social classes, either through coercion or through socialisation. The latter, of course, is a far more effective way of imposing the dominant ideology than the former, for it leads to internalisation in which the dominated imbibe the ideologies of the dominant and make them part of their own system of ideas, beliefs, values, norms, morality, etc.

It follows, therefore, that particular ideologies, emerging from social practices generated in specific social relations of a particular social class, may pervade the economic, political and cultural practices of the entire social strata within a given society. Of course, certain individuals may refuse to conform to such ideological hegemonic control; but such individuals will be branded 'deviants' and dealt with by the state apparatuses empowered to deal with social deviancy. For the rest of the masses though, the dominant ideology becomes a 'shared common sense'. It is equally true that many ideologies developed from the social practices of subordinate classes will be co-opted into the dominant ideologies as long as they do not threaten the fundamental ideologies of the dominant class. Social consensus is much more readily achieved when the rights, powers and interests of subordinate classes appear to be an integral part of the general ideology.

Finally, it is important to stress that ideologies are not static, but dynamic. Changes in social practices, caused by changing circumstances, will lead to modification of the ideologies underlying those practices. Conversely, changes in the form of the ideology, caused by the influences of new ideas, concepts, or beliefs, will, *pari passu,* lead to modification of the social practice. For example, the introduction of a new religion into a society will lead to changes in the values underlying the institution of marriage as well as changes in the ritual practices of marriage.

It is the basic and fundamental thesis of this treatise that the development of the capitalist plantation system, generated by the need for raw materials to feed the emerging industries, created a massive demand for labour which could not be met by the colonised Amerindians, white slaves from Europe, convicts and indentured European labourers. African slave labour was found most suitable to meet that demand, but the African slave or captured free persons were not going to consent to be transported passively, thousands of miles by some 'white devils' and worked like mules. Maximum coercion, therefore, had to be used and this, coupled with the slavers' greed for maximum profit, led to the most bestial, savage and barbarous treatment of the black man, the scale of which was unequalled in the annals of man's inhumanity to man.

Such bestiality, inhumanity and exploitation had to be rationalised and justified not only to mollify the consciences of the perpetrators and would-be perpetrators, but also to prevent the deserved condemnation and opprobrium of their own societies. The justification was the *Ideology of Racism* whose basic assumption was that the black man was inferior biologically, sub-human, in fact; and hence, in any social relationship involving the white slave trader, plantation owner, mine owner, colonialist on the one hand, and the black slave, labourer, or colonial subject on the other, the normal moral codes and norms of behaviour of civilised (or even primitive) societies did not and indeed, could not apply.

As Basil Davidson observed: "For racism was born out of the need to justify the enslavement of blacks, after the enslavement of whites had long become a crime. From the first, in other words, racism was a weapon of exploitation".[40]

Eric Williams agrees:

"Here, then, is the origin of Negro slavery. The reason was economic, not racial; it had to do not with the color of the laborer, but the cheapness of the labor. As compared with Indian and white labor, Negro slavery was eminently superior. 'In each case,' writes Bassett, discussing North Carolina, 'it was a survival of the fittest. Both Indian slavery and white servitude were to go down before the black man's superior endurance, docility, and labour capacity.' The features of the man, his hair, color and dentrifice, his 'subhuman' characteristics so widely pleaded, were only the later rationalizations to justify a simple economic fact: that the colonies needed labor and resorted to Negro labour because it was cheapest and best."[41] "Negro slavery therefore was only a solution, in certain historical circumstances, of the Caribbean labor problem. Sugar meant labor – at times that labor has been slave, at other times nominally free; at times black, at other times white or brown or yellow. Slavery in no way implied, in any scientific sense, the inferiority of the Negro. Without it the great development of the Caribbean sugar plantations, between 1650 and 1850, would have been impossible."[42]

The falsehood of the basic assumption of the ideology was irrelevant as long as profit flowed to Europe and the consciences of the slavers were mollified.

Race, Ideology and the Economic Dimension

The massive profitability and consequent accumulation of capital from the slave trade and subsequent colonisation, created powerful groups with vested interests who had every reason for wanting to see the doctrine of inferiority propagated and perpetuated. Massive cultivation of tobacco, cotton and, most important of all, sugar was made possible with slave labour. In what became known as the 'golden triangle' trade, the slave ship sailed from its home port with a cargo of cheap manufactured goods – cloth, firearms, beads, spirits, kettles, hats, glass – which it exchanged on the African coast for slaves at a profit; it then crossed the Atlantic and traded the slaves, at further profit, for colonial produce (produced with slave labour); finally, home again, it sold its cargo – sugar, cotton, tobacco, rum, etc. at a massive profit for processing and domestic consumption or for manufacturing into articles of trade.

The British capitalists themselves acknowledged the significance of the system;

"The most approved Judges of the commercial Interests of these Kingdoms have ever been of Opinion that our Westindian and African Trades are the most naturally beneficial of any we carry on. It is also allowed on all Hands, that the Trade of Africa is the Branch which renders our American Colonies and Plantations so advantageous to Great Britain; that Traffic only affording our Plantations a constant Supply of Negroe-Servants for the culture of their Lands in the Produce of Sugars, Tobacco, Rice, Rum, Cotton, Fustick,

Pimento, and all other [of] our Plantation-Produce: So that the extensive
Employment of our Shipping in, to, and from America, the great Brood of
seamen consequent thereupon, and the daily Bread of the most considerable
Part of our British Manufacturers, are owing primarily to the Labour of
Negroes; who, as they were the first happy Instruments of raising our
Plantations; so their Labour only can support and preserve them, and render
them still more and more profitable to their Mother-Country. The Negroe-
Trade therefore, and the natural Consequences resulting from it, may be
justly esteemed an inexhaustible Fund of Wealth and Naval Power to this
Nation."[43]

In 1788 the sugar planters in the Westindies valued their holdings
at £70,000,000 and in 1798 annual income from the Westindian
plantations was £4,000,000 compared with £1,000,000 from the rest
of the world (vast sums indeed in those days).
Liverpool, the greatest of the slaving ports in the late eighteenth
century grew in population from 5,000 in 1700 to 34,000 in 1773,
while customs receipts rocketed from an average £51,000 a year for
1750-57 to £648,000 in 1785. In Bristol (which became the second
city of England for most of the eighteenth century on the success of
the slave and sugar trades) custom duties rose from £10,000 in 1634
to £334,000 in 1785.[44]

"The slave trade... was the basis of British – as well as French and American
– mercantile prosperity and the source of industrial expansion... It was the
huge profits from the slave and sugar trades which produced much of the
capital for Britain's industrial revolution; the ships of Liverpool paid for the
factories of Manchester. The technological achievements which were to give
the West political and economic dominance over so wide an area of the world
were made possible by the miseries of the middle passage.
    The slave trade enriched – and sometimes ennobled – men to the upper
reaches of social acceptability and political influence. The Earl of Westmor-
land told his peers in the early nineteenth century that many of them owed
their place to slaving and that cries for the abolition of the trade were
nothing less than Jacobinism. Some of these English merchants were widely
renowned for their good works in establishing schools for the poor, homes for
the aged, libraries and associations for the learned. Like their moral
kinsmen in the slave states of America, or their twentieth century
descendants, with mining and industrial interests in Southern Africa, they
saw charity as beginning – and ending – at home, within whitewashed
walls."[45]

Discussing the importance of the 'golden triangle' trade to the
industrial revolution, Basil Davidson writes;

"For if the profits of the slave-carrying trade were by no means exceptional in
the commerce of those times, the profits of the whole Circuit trade were
evidently another matter. They were large and they were continuous. So
important were they, indeed, that there appears no reasonable doubt but that
the overall profits of the whole Circuit trade became a major factor in the
accumulation of English and French capital; and, secondly, that this
accumulation was a large, and at certain points probably decisive, contribu-

tion to the whole process of industrialization."[46]

Eric Williams in his *Capitalism and Slavery* has also analysed the enormous economic advantage to Britain of the triangular trade. "The triangular trade thereby", Williams wrote, "gave a triple stimulus to British industry. The Negroes were purchased with British manufactures; transported to the plantations, they produced sugar, cotton, indigo, molasses and other tropical products, the processing of which created new industries in England; while the maintenance of the Negroes and their owners on the plantations provided another market for British industry, New England agriculture and the Newfoundland fisheries." By 1750 there was hardly a trading or a manufacturing town in England which was not in some way connected with the triangular or direct colonial trade. The profits obtained provided one of the main streams of that accumulation of capital in England which financed the Industrial Revolution.

> "The Westindian islands became the hub of the British Empire, of immense importance to the grandeur and prosperity of England. It was the Negroe slaves who made these sugar colonies the most precious colonies ever recorded in the whole annals of imperialism."[47]

The profitability of the triangular trade, the consequent capital accumulation, and the stimulus to industrial production, created hundreds of thousands of jobs which, despite massive exploitation by the new industrial capitalists, led to a rising standard of living for the masses in Britain. Increasing disposable income for the masses, also stimulated demand at home for industrial products, further stimulating industrial production. The development of shipping and shipbuilding and its effect on the build-up of British naval power; the growth of the great British Seaport towns such as Bristol, Liverpool and Glasgow; cotton manufacturing, sugar refining, rum distillation, pacotille production, metallurgy, etc,; all received direct stimulus from the triangular trade and promoted the growth of several ancillary trades and the development of concomitant skills.

Africa, the African slave, and the Westindian plantation system formed the hub of British mercantilism and industrial capitalism with all their implications on tax revenue to the Exchequer, jobs for the masses, massive profits to the plantocracy and industrialists, capital accumulation for further industrial growth, the development of economic and social infrastructure and so on. British economic well-being had become inextricably linked with the triangular trade, creating fertile ground for the germination and growth of the ideology of racism. If the brutal slavery system and the massive plundering of the resources of Africa were essential to British economic well-being, then self-interests dictated that it was necessary to embrace the ideology of racism which rationalised the relationship and justified its maintenance.

Scientific Racism

The initial formulation of the doctrine of inherent black inferiority was largely the work of the slave traders and early European travellers who chose to write down or to publish what they 'saw'. The mythology about the African was, therefore, based on their stories. A necessary prerequisite for the formation of prejudice is ignorance. Europeans at home were wholly ignorant of the African – his history, culture and character. European racial prejudice towards the African was thus entirely based on the account of these travellers, which as time went on, would become inconsistent and, at times contradictory, thereby creating room for doubt.

But pseudo-scientific 'theories' were soon developed to give credence to, and to endow such mythology with, 'scientific' authority and authenticity.

Professor Philip Curtin (1964) suggests that before anthropology became a separate and distinct discipline, the physical structure of man belonged institutionally to anatomical studies, as a branch of medicine. Data about human culture and society outside of Europe was collected by travellers who happened to have the interest to write down what they saw. Analysis of the data was mainly left to a rather vague and still undifferentiated social science, most often under the rubric of 'moral philosophy'. The scientific study of human varieties therefore fell by default to the biologists, as a kind of appendix to their general systems of nature.

The major eighteenth century classifications of nature began with Linnaeus' *Systema Naturae,* first published in 1735, and later revised with additions. This work and its successors formed the basic framework of modern bological classification. One of the major assumptions underpinning biology at the time was the ancient belief that God had so organised the world that all creation was arranged in a 'Great Chain of Being'. All living things could, therefore, be classified and fitted into a hierarchy from man down to the smallest microscopic cell. Since man was placed at the apex of this hierarchical scale the varieties of man had also to be taken into account and the biologists assumed from the beginning that they too could be arranged in a hierarchich order. Linnaeus thus included racial classification – white, red, yellow and black races in that order – in his work.

It is very important to note that these early classifications into superior and inferior races was not based on any scientific investigation or evidence, despite the label. It was merely to accord the ideology of racism the status of a 'science'.

Further efforts by biologists to explain the origin of race were to lead to two schools of thought – *Monogenesis* and *Polygenesis*. Monogenesis was a scientific version of the traditional orthodox Christian belief that God created man, a single pair, at a finite time in the not-very-distant past. The acceptance of the basic monogenetic tenet leads, *ipso facto*, to the need to explain the origin of later variations of Adam's descendants. "The unconscious assumption in all these ideas was that God had created man 'in His image', which was necessarily the image of the biologists. Other varieties must therefore be worse varieties, and thus 'degenerations' from the original stock."[48] The lighter the skin, therefore, the nearer to the ideal; and conversely, the darker the skin, the more degenerate. The monogenetic view, albeit, allowed all races a place in humanity, and people who had 'degenerated' might well 'improve' again.

The theory of polygenesis, although a minority position and openly contradictory to the biblical account of creation, was nevertheless, to have a widespread influence. One of the most widely read polygenists was Isaac La-Peyrere's *Prae Adamitae*, published in 1655, which held that Adam and Eve had been the last of a series of special creations, and some of the living non-Europeans were descended from the earlier pre-Adamites. In other words, in contrast to the monogenetic assumption that Adam and Eve (created in the image of God) were white and that other races are degenerations by colour from white to black, the La-Peyrere polygenetic 'hypothesis' held that there were different prototypes created. Blacks descended from, perhaps, Adam Mark I, the Browns (or was it the Yellows next?) Mark II and so on, until the Whites, when Adam and Eve reached perfection – physically, intellectually and morally.

An anonymous work, *Co-Adamitae*, published in 1732 took a different position, speculating that all races were created simultaneously, but not endowed with the same ability.

Polygenesis was especially attractive to those philosophers who were less influenced by religious orthodoxy. Thus both Voltaire and Rousseau suggested that Negroes were naturally inferior to Europeans in their mental ability. David Hume (1898) argued that "There never was a civilized nation of any other complexion than white, nor even any individual eminent either in action or speculation. No ingenious manufacturers among them, no arts, no sciences... Such a uniform and constant difference could not happen, in so many countries and ages, if nature had not made an original distinction betwixt these breeds of men."[49]

Drawing on Buffon's *Histoire Naturelle* which was a comparative anatomy showing the amazing similarities in physical structure between all animals, especially between men and certain apes, the polygenists speculated in the early eighteenth century that Hottentots and orangoutangs might be side by side in the 'scale of life', separated only by the fact that orangoutangs could not speak (Lovejoy, 1936, p.233, 1904, p.204).

Curtin suggests that the work which was to be immensely more important in giving a pseudo-scientific base to polygenist theories was the *History of Jamaica* by Edward Long. Long, the son of a plantation owner, was born in Cornwall. He studied law, migrated to Jamaica, and, after a while, became a Judge.

In a key section of his book, Long, drawing partly on Buffon, tried to assess the place of the Negro in nature. Africans, in his opinion were 'brutish, ignorant, idle, crafty, treacherous, bloody, thievish, mistrustful, and superstitious people'. Their skins were dark, their features different, and they had a 'covering of wool, like the bestial fleece, instead of hair'. They were inferior in 'faculties of mind', had a 'bestial and fetid smell', and were even parasitised by black lice instead of the lighter-coloured lice of the Europeans. Long in fact suggested that Europeans and Negroes did not belong to the same species.

"In general", Long wrote, "they are void of genius and seem almost incapable of making progress in civility or science... Africans are represented by all authors as the vilest of the human kind, to which they have little more pretensions of resemblance than what arises from their exterior form."[50] Europeans had known millions of Africans, but few had been encountered who "comprehend anything of mechanic arts, or manufacture; and even these, for the most part, are said to perform their work in very bungling and slovenly manner, perhaps not better than an oran-outang might".[51] Long saw a close relationship between the African and orangoutang: "Ludricous as it may seem I do not think that an orang-outang husband would be any dishonour to an Hottentot female. The orangoutang has in form a much nearer resemblance to the Negro race, than the latter bear to white men".[52]

To Long, the African was more of a beast than man: "At their meals they tear the meat with their talons and chuck it by handfuls down their throats with all the voracity of wild beasts." Of the slaves from Guinea: "Their hearing is remarkably quick; their faculties of smell and taste are truly bestial, nor less their commerce with the other sex; in these acts they are libidinous and shameless as monkeys and baboons."[53]

The 'natural hierarchical order' in which humans were ranked from superior (whites) to inferior (blacks) which scientific racism espoused, was further expanded by Long. The theory found its proof in Africa: "As we receded from Negro-land this blackness gradually decreases... We observe the like gradations of the intellectual faculty, from the first rudiments perceived in the monkey kind to the more advanced stages of it in apes, in the orang-outang, that type of man, and the Guinea negro; and ascending from the varieties of this class to the lighter casts, until we mark its utmost limit of perfection in the pure white."[54]

The publication of the 'origin of the Species' in which Charles Darwin set forth the theory of evolution of biological organisms from lower to higher forms of life was quickly cited as further proof of scientific racism. Whites and Blacks may have both evolved from a common ancestral tree – from Dryopithecus, down to Ramapithecus, Australopithecus, Homo Erectus to Homo Sapiens Neanderthalensis (Neanderthal man), but either black people remained at the latter stage of evolution while white people evolved to Homo Sapiens (Modern Man); or the blacks evolved with the whites to Modern Man, but somehow never evolved to the same intellectual level.

But some 'scientists' were not even willing to make that 'concession' and continued to insist that black people and white people were separate species. When it was pointed out to them that miscegenation produced fertile mulattoes unlike, for example, the mule (the offspring of a mare and an ass) which was infertile – surely a proof that all homo sapiens belonged to the same specie – they responded by saying that there was some kind of delayed infertility which would be inherited by, and affect the progeny of, the mulattoes after several generations.

Furthermore, the concept of the survival of the fittest which was extended from the biological to the social order by Herbert Spencer, provided further support to the ideology of racism. Social Darwinism suggested that the most capable and resourceful would rise to the top of the social hierarchy and that this was the natural order of things. It was therefore only natural that whites, as the 'superior race', should be at the top while blacks, the 'inferior race' remained enslaved.

Anthropometry was used by some to provide further 'scientific evidence' of the natural inferiority of the blackman. Measurements were taken of the head, face, ears, nose, trunk, limbs and skeleton, including the bones of the skull; alleged differences between blacks and whites were found, proving the 'natural inferiority' of the former. For example, the Dutch surgeon, obstetrician, artist, sculptor and an authority on medical jurisprudence, Pieter Camper, speculated that a wide facial angle (measured by the extent to which the jaw juts out from the rest of the skull) indicated a higher forehead, a bigger brain, more intelligence and a more beautiful appearance. The angle, he claimed, grew wider as one went from Africans, through Indians, to Europeans. Camper found a striking resemblance between the race of monkeys and black people. Other 'craniologists' such as Johann Friedrich Blumembach, Louis Daubenton, John Hunter and the German anatomist, Thomas Soemmering, propounded similar 'theories'.

It is important to note that the conclusions drawn from 'Darwinism' by the 'scientific racists' were not shared by Darwin who argued that, "Although the existing races of man differ in many respects, as in colour, hair, shape of skull, proportion of the body, etc., yet if their whole structure be taken into consideration they are found to resemble each other closely in a multitude of points. Many of these are of so unimportant or of so singular a nature, that it is extremely improbable that they should have been independently acquired by aboriginally distinct species or races. The same remark holds good with equal or greater force with respect to the numerous points of mental similarity between the most distinct races of man."[55]

"But the most weighty of all the arguments," says Darwin, "against treating the races of man as distinct species, is that they graduate into each other, independently in many cases, as far as we can judge, of their having intercrossed."[56] And finally, Darwin writes, "As it is improbable that the numerous and unimportant points of resemblance between the several races of man in bodily structure and mental faculties (I do not here refer to similar customs) should have been independently acquired, they must have been inherited from progenitors who had these same characteristics."[57]

In other words, according to Darwin, despite the apparent superficial differences between the human races, we all originated from a common ancestor because the similarities in anatomical structure, physiological processes, and most especially, the successful miscegenation, far outweigh the superficial differences. Furthermore, intellectual attainment between different races is 'culturally', not 'biologically' determined.

Darwin's position was, however, among a tiny minority of 'dissidents'. To the overwhelming majority of 'scientists' and scholars, the hierarchical arrangement of the races was an indisputable 'natural order'. Armed with such 'scientific evidence' white Europe could dispossess the non-whites, particularly the blacks, without the slightest twinge of conscience. The near extermination of the Australian Aborigine is an example. On arriving in Australia, the British found the land inhabited by the Aborigines. But as black people were deemed to be non-human or at best, subhuman, their ownership of the land could not be acknowledged. The land was hence declared *empty* and, therefore, open to lawful take-over by the British. The Aborigines, on the other hand, were not going to be passively dispossessed of the land they had inhabited for thousands of years. The scene was set for one of the most barbaric and shameful acts of genocide, even by European standards. In a behaviour that stands out as an eloquent testimony of the level of bestiality to which humanity can degenerate, "nigger-hunt" became a sport in which hundreds of Aborigines were hunted and shot like animals. In a documentary screened on British TV, in 1985 Aborigine children were said to have been buried alive from the shoulders down and their heads kicked until they fell off their bodies. The black Tasmanian race became extinct, thanks to the savagery, bestiality and killing 'efficiency' of the British migrants. The justification, as one high official put it (according to a BBC I programme *Everyman* broadcast on 3rd July, 1983), was that "there is no scientific evidence that the Aborigine is a human being".

The early scientific racists thus offered 'scientific evidence' which had the effect of defining colour, not as an identifying mark of a class of people (eg blondes, brunettes, etc.) but as a *cause* of inherent inferior characteristics. The ideological origin and nature of the doctrine of inherent black inferiority had become most effectively obscured! The doctrine was now enshrined in "science". As the influence of Christian dogma waned and "Thus saith the Lord" no longer conclusively settled all arguments, *science* became the new authoritative voice; and as the status of science increased, so did the belief in 'scientific' theories of which the doctrine of black inferiority was one. An ideology generated within an economic (social) relationship to justify the Europeans' brutality to, and exploitation of, the African had now penetrated the cultural (social) relationship.

These 'theories' were to have a profound influence on the formation of social attitudes and the course of race relations in Africa, America, Britain and elsewhere. For in future the blackman was to be stereotyped and categorised into a pigeon-hole of 'inferiority' not on the basis of the individual's personality, intellectual capability, or inherent talent, but on the basis of membership of a class defined by an immutable natural characteristic: skin colour.

Notes

a. emphasis mine.
b. Parliament had passed an Act in 1807 abolishing the slave trade and the Emancipation of Slaves Act was passed in 1833. The trade, however, continued illegally until the 1880s, following the victory of the abolitionist North in the American Civil War, 1861-65.
c. emphasis mine.

CHAPTER THREE

Creeping Racism – The Spread of an Ideology

The white-black dichotomy of the ideology of racism in which the two races occupied polar extremes and represented opposite values, qualities and characteristics (whose origins go back to the Bible[a]) became even more deeply entrenched in everyday discourse and imagery from Elizabethan times onwards. White represented beauty, righteousness, virginity, innocence, virtue, godliness and purity. God was assumed to be white and His Angels were as white as snow. Conversely, the devil was as black as coal. Almost everything undesirable was representd by black in the English language: black was base, evil, sinful, vile, impure, ungodly and Satanic; hence black-boding, blackbrowed, blackday, black-guard, blackhearted, blackleg, blacklist, blackmail, black-mark, black-Monday and black-sheep.

For example, Dennis Nielsen, a white civil servant in London, had been convicted of murdering at least 15 homosexuals. In a macabre 'tale' of horrors, Nielsen would pick up homosexuals, engage in acts of homosexuality with them and murder the victims at night while they were drunk. To dispose of the bodies, he would dismember the victims, boil them in pots and flush the pieces down the toilet. After the sentence, the contents of Nielsen's kitchen were removed and set up as a replica in Scotland Yard's "Infamous Black Museum". Heinous crimes had been committed by whites against other whites and the museum set up to exhibit the tools and methods of their gruesome deeds is called a *Black* Museum! Such social practice has a history going back several centuries.

The ideology of race with its concomitant assumptions and imagery proliferated in the literature of the eighteenth and nineteenth centuries. A whole set of stereotypes were created and ascribed to the African. He was lazy, sexually licentious, emotionally childish and intellectually stupid. James Walvin (1973) traces the development of racial attitude portrayed in British literature through this period. It is essential to take a closer look at the spread of the ideology of racism through the literature and the arts in order to fully appreciate the development of British social attitude on race. "The purveyors of racialist thought in the eighteenth and early nineteenth centuries" writes Walvin, "drew much of the inspiration from 'factual' material, from travel accounts dating from the sixteenth century. In their turn these accounts, as we have seen, had been profoundly influenced by speculative writing of an even earlier date. The literature caricature of the central period 1770 to 1860 in its turn influenced the emergence of more modern racialist thought, for it employed traditional and, in some cases, ancient ideas about black humanity, and put them in a more coherent form."[1]

The *Gentleman's Magazine,* perhaps the most popular and influential periodical of the day, encapsulated in 1788 the many assumptions and stereotypes of the ideology of racism which were to be mass-produced and mass-circulated right through to the more contemporary period of the 1960s. "The negro", it wrote "is possessed of passions not only strong but ungovernable; a mind dauntless, warlike and unmerciful; a temper extremely irascible; a disposition indolent, selfish and deceitful; fond of joyous sociality, riotous mirth and extravagant show. He has certain portions of kindness for his favourites, and affections for his connections; but they are sparks which emit a glimmering light through the thick gloom that surrounds them, and which, in every ebullition of anger or revenge, instantly disappear. Furious in his love as in his hate; at best, a terrible husband, a harsh father and a precarious friend. A strong and unalterable affection for his countrymen and fellow passengers in particular seems to be the most amiable passion in the Negro breast... As to all the other fine feelings of the soul, the Negro, as far as I have been able to perceive, is nearly deprived of them."[2]

The most constantly recurring stereotype of the African was his indolence or laziness. As Professor Curtin observed: "Laziness was the vice most frequently reported, and the emphasis was repeated from several sides. It was believed to be characteristic of Negro slaves in the West Indies. It was reinforced by mistaken observation in West Africa, where the myth of tropical exuberance encouraged the Europeans to think that Africans had no need to work. In addition, agricultural work in West Africa was often seasonal, on account of alternation of dry and wet periods. The usual dry-season under-employment became a wet-season labour shortage. The dry-season pattern might look like simple laziness."[3]

Whatever gave rise to this stereotype is not highly relevant here, for assumptions underlying a specific ideology need not be factual. The important thing is that it be socially accepted as being a 'reality', and hence, the reason for engaging in the specific social practice which the ideology justifies.

The African, either in Africa or in the Westindies inhabited a land of natural richness, of tropical soil and vegetation, with heavy rainfall and several hours of sunshine per day, leading to luxuriant growth of fruit and vegetation and, consequently, very little effort was required to procure the necessary victuals from the soil, or so the European believed. The combination of favourable geo-physical conditions on the one hand, and his inherent indolence on the other, it was believed, removed any incentive or stimulus for the African to work.

As Dr George Pinckard, a Fellow of the Royal College of Physicians observed of the black slaves in the Westindies in 1806, "Their wants being few, and their food easily procured, their exertions would only be commensurate to their cravings: disdaining labour, they would repose under the soft shade of the plantain, equally regardless of the riches of commerce and the honours of industry. The yam, the plantain, and the pepper-pot, the banjar, the merry dance, and their beloved Wowski would gratify all their wishes and crown their highest ambition".[4]

The alleged indolence of black people was one of the most vociferous arguments used against the emancipation of the slaves, and when emancipation finally came, it was used to explain the collapse of the sugar industry. Thomas Carlyle commented bitterly: "Sitting yonder with their beautiful muzzles up to their ears in pumpkins, imbibing sweet pulps and juices; the grinder and incisor teeth ready for ever new work, and the pumpkins as cheap as grass in those rich climates, while the sugar crops rot around them uncut because labour cannot be hired so cheap as pumpkins."[5]

To Carlyle, the "black gentleman", no longer under coercion, was reverting back to the condition of his African ancestry "with rum-bottle in hand... no breeches on his body, pumpkin at discretion, and the fruitfulest region of the earth going back to jungle around him".[6]

Anthony Trollope, after a Westindian tour for the Post Office in 1858, took up the same theme when he alleged that the Westindian Negro "is idle, unambitious as to worldly position, sensual, and content with little... He lies under the mango-tree, and eats the luscious fruit in the sun; he sends his black urchin up for breakfast and behold the family table is spread. He pierces a coco-nut and lo! there is his beverage. He lies on the grass, surrounded by oranges, bananas, and pine-apples".[7]

The Explorer, Sir Samuel Baker observed confidently: "The natives of tropical countries do not progress, enervated by intense heat, they incline rather to repose and amusement than to labour.

Free from the rigours of winters, and the excitement of changes in the seasons, the native character assumes the monotony of their country's temperature. They have no natural difficulties to contend with – no struggle with adverse storms and icy winds and frost-bound soil; but an everlasting summer, and fertile ground producing with little tillage, excite no enterprise; and the human mind, unexercised by difficulties, sinks into languor and decay".[8]

The question any rational person is bound to pose is why the European, 'the wisest and most intelligent of all humanity' should, for three hundred years, transport over thousands of miles, millions of humanity's laziest race to work the mines and plantations on which their economic well-being and prosperity so much depended?

The black man, it was claimed was endowed with extraordinary sexual prowess. In a popular pamphlet in 1772, it was alleged that "The lower class of women in England, are remarkably fond of the blacks, for reasons too brutal to mention".[9] This fondness was of course not confined to the lower classes, for as James Walvin, op.cit., has demonstrated, there were several sexual encounters and scandals involving black people and the upper classes in England.

The biologists, both monogenists and polygenists, thought that the Negro had a much larger penis than the European; and that Negro women were sexually more desirable for physiological reasons left unexplained. "Mandingo men", wrote Richard Jobson in 1623, "were furnist with such members as are after a sort burthensome unto them".[10]

Bryan Edwards, Jamaican planter and English politician, asserted that "The Negroes in the West Indies, both men and women, would consider it as the great exertion of tyranny, and the most cruel of all hardships, to be compelled to confine themselves to a single connection with the other sex. Their passion is mere animal desire, implanted by the great Author of all things for the preservation of the species. This the Negroes, without doubt, possess in common with the rest of the animal creation, and they indulge it, as inclination prompts, in an almost promiscuous intercourse with the other sex."[11]

The alleged imminent low level of the black man's intelligence is a subject I shall return to in a critique of contemporary scientific racism. Suffice it here to say that it was this assertion that was to have the most devastating consequence on the life chances of black people in Europe and America. "The dull stupidity of the Negro", one early humanitarian wrote, "leaves him without any desire for instruction. Whether the Creator orginally formed these black people a little lower than other men, or that they have lost their intellectual powers through disuse, I will not assume the province of determining; but certain it is that a new Negro (as those lately imported from Africa are called), is a complete definition of indolent stupidity." He concluded: "The stupid obstinance of the Negroes may indeed make it always necessary to subject them to a severe discipline from their masters."[12]

Several Europeans, after the briefest of contact with few Africans, pronounced with the certitude of omniscient experts, unlimited knowledge about *all* Africans. The truth is that the ideology of racism had already operated to inform their perspectives and to construct their reality for them prior to their contact with the African. The nature and characteristics of the African which they theorised about was, therefore, a near parrot-fashion reproduction of the ideology of racism which they all shared.

Pickard, a Belgian visitor, after a brief trip to the Congo in 1896 affirmed with omniscient arrogance: "In spite of all our humanitarian goodwill, we have to acknowledge the irreducible difference of race between us; no Christian dreams, no well-intentioned efforts to project to them our own sentiments, our thoughts, our capacities, can change this,... Like monkeys, the blacks are good imitators – to a surprising degree. One sees here... masons, blacksmiths, mechanics who have become really skillful... It is this undeniable dexterity of theirs which has given birth to an illusion... on the part of those who cannot distinguish between an imitator and a creator. Here, in fact, is the *unbridgeable gulf* [b]. The negro can collaborate with the white man as a subaltern, he can correctly carry out a concrete individual piece of work...

"But will he ever feel stirring in himself the need to be free from social servitude?... Will he ever see invisible realities, the hidden links in society, the way things hold together – necessity for men of our race? Will he not always be a disguised slave, indirectly a serf, in carrying out his partial and localized tasks under the domination of the white man? Perhaps," he concludes, "this is why, instinctively, the white scorns the black, and the black shows a natural submission, a childish humility, a reverential and timid awe before the white man."[13]

To Edward Long, the black man's low intellect was self-evident. "If no rules of civil polity exist among them, does it not betray an egregious want of common sense...? The jurisprudence, the customs and manners of the Negroes, seem perfectly suited to the measure of their narrow intellect. Laws have justly been regarded as the masterpiece of human genius: what are we to think of those societies of men, who either have none, or such only as are irrational and ridiculous?"[14]

By 1905, the terms 'Negro' and 'low-intellect' had become synonymous. "Negroes, Negres (Latin niger: black), man, woman with black skin. This is the name given especially to the inhabitants

of certain countries in Africa... who form a race of black men inferior
in intelligence to the white or Caucasian race."[15]

The *Encyclopaedia Britannica* needs no introduction; its claim to
the use of scientific methodology, objectivity and scholastic authority is unchallenged. Its influence on the educated, directly or
indirectly, through other authors using it as source of information,
cannot be over-emphasised. Its contributors are chosen precisely
because they are among the foremost authorities in their respective
disciplines, and are recognised as such. In 1810, it said of the Negro:
"Vices the most notorious seem to be the portion of this unhappy
race; idleness, treachery, revenge, cruelty, impudence, stealing,
lying, profanity, debauchery, nastiness, and intemperance, are said
to have extinguished the principle of natural law, and to have
silenced the reproofs of conscience. They are strangers to every
sentiment of compassion, and are an awful example of the corrup-
tion of man left to himself."[16]

I doubt very much if the Bible has as many adjectives describing
'Satan'. It appears that, to the *Encyclopaedia Britannica*, with all
its claim to objectivity and scholarly impartiality, the black man
had sunk to a depth of irredeemable notoriety, surpassing 'Satan'
himself.

The 1884 version, in a more moderate tone, asserted: "No full-
blooded Negro has ever been distinguished as a man of science, a
poet, or an artist, and the fundamental equality claimed for him by
ignorant philanthropists is belied by the whole history of the race
throughout the historic period."[17]

As far as knowledge about the black man and his history were
concerned the *Encyclopaedia Britannica's* claim to scholastic authority, objectivity and impartiality was an absolute farce! Evidence
will be brought forth in the following chapters to rebut, and to show
the utter falsehood of its premise. I shall demonstrate that, either
its claim to scholastic authority cannot stand the test of reality, or
the above quotations furnish the clearest proof of the potency of
ideology to create a 'reality' for its adherents which has very little
semblance to 'the real world'.

The African by temperament, it was claimed, was childish, over-
emotional, and dependent. A medical officer of the African Company, James Houston, said of the African in 1725: "their natural
Temper is barbarously cruel, selfish, and deceitful, and their
Government equally barbarous and uncivil; and consequently the
Men of greatest Eminency among them, are those who are most
capable of being the greatest Rogues... As for their Customs they
exactly resemble their Fellow Creatures and Natives, the
Monkeys."[18]

The *Pall Mall Gazette* referred to the 'poor deluded Negroes' as

"the most inflammable and unreasoning population on earth".[19]
"Negroes", the *Times* observed on 10th April, 1860, "were careless,
credulous, and dependent; easily excited, easily duped, easily
frightened".[20]

A continuing evidence of their inferiority was provided by the
widespread caricature of black people in English literature, car-
toons, comic characters, theatrical plays and popular songs in the
eighteenth and nineteenth centuries. During the 1800s, Jack
Gratus states that the blackman "...was shown as the grinning
black servant serving food and drink to the upper-class whites; he
was seen aping the white man by affecting his clothes and manner.
His wife was usually portrayed as fat and ugly, but his children, like
himself, were roly-poly, laughing creatures: childlike, silly and
harmless".[21] Note that the early satirical stereotype had characterised black people as excessively violent, but fearing that this might
lead to a self-fulfilling prophecy threatening white people, black
people underwent a metamorphosis and became 'docile', 'harmless',
'easily frightened'.

Characters such as Sambo, Mungo, Tambo, Rastus, Sam, Pompey
and Mammy, were created and mass-produced in literary works and
folk imagery in comical theatres. Let us look at a few examples of
some of the most influential of these works. In a collection of poems
published in 1789, William Blake wrote in *The Little Black Boy:*

"My mother bore me in the southern wild,
And I am black, but O! my soul is white;
White as an angel is the English child,
But I am black, as if bereav'd of light
My mother ... began to say:
...And we are put on earth a little space
That we may learn to bear the beams of love;
And these black bodies and this sunburnt face
Is but a cloud, and like a shady grove.
For when our souls have learn'd the heat to bear,
The cloud will vanish; we shall hear His voice,
Saying: 'Come out from the grove, My love and care,
And round my golden tent like lambs rejoice'.
And thus I say to little English boy.
When I from black and he from white cloud free,
And around the tent of God like lambs we joy,
I'll shade him from the heat, till he can bear
To lean in joy upon our Father's knee;
And then I'll stand and stroke his silver hair
And be like him, and he will then love me."[22]

A more contemporary version is offered by the English writer Hugh Lofting in Dr Dolittle stories read by millions of European and American children since 1920. Dr Dolittle, an animal doctor had travelled to Africa to cure a plague among monkeys, accompanied by a dog, a duck, a pig, an owl, a monkey and a parrot. Dolittle and his animal entourage become prisoners of a black king; and in the king's garden the parrot and the monkey meet the king's son, Prince Bumpo, who is pictured as an ugly gnome-like black man with a huge nose that covers most of his face. On hearing the ugly prince yearn aloud, "if only I were a white prince", the parrot promises that Dr Dolittle will change his colour if he helps them escape. To Dr Dolittle, the unhappy prince tells his story:

> "Years ago I went in search of the Sleeping Beauty, whom I had read of in a book. And having travelled through the world many days, I at last found her and kissed the lady very gently to wake her – as the book said I should. 'Tis true indeed that she woke up. But when she saw my face she cried out, 'Oh, he's black!' And she ran away and wouldn't marry me – but went to sleep again somewhere else. So I came back, full of sadness, to my father's kingdom. Now I hear that you are a wonderful magician and have many wonderful potions. So I come to you for help. If you will turn me white, so that I may go back to the Sleeping Beauty, I will give you half my kingdom and anything besides you ask."[23]

The prince asks not only to be turned white and blonde, but with 'blue eyes' thrown in for good measure. Of course, for the black prince, such a story could not have a 'happy ending' – his inferiority is predetermined by nature and not subject to redemption, at least not in this world! Dr Dolittle concocts a paste which whitens his face, refuses to give him a mirror, and they make good their escape. Hawthorne, Poe, Melville and several authors mass-produced such tripe imagery of blacks and blackness throughout the period.

William Shakespeare had made his own contribution much earlier. In *Love's Labours Lost,* the king says "Black is the badge of hell, The hue of the dungeons and the suit of night". In the *Tragedy of Othello, the Moor of Venice,* Iago says:

> " 'zounds, sir, you're robb'd; for shame, put on your gown;
> ...Even now, now, very now, an old black ram
> Is tupping your white ewe. Arise, arise;
> Awake the snorting citizens with the bell,
> Or else the devil will make a grandsire of you;
> Arise, I say."

Later, Othello, consumed with jealousy says of Desdemona, his wife:

> "Her name, that was as fresh
> As Dian's visage is now begrimed and black
> As mine own face."

Reluctant to shed her blood, he says of the sleeping Desdemona:

"Nor scar that whiter skin of hers than snow
And smooth as monumental alabaster."

When the deed is done, Emilia, the servant, and wife of Iago, screams at him:

"O, the more angel she,
And you the blacker devil!"

In the theatre, Sambo was portrayed as childish and comical. His outlandish gestures and physical gyrations made him the buffoon par excellence. He was the 'natural' servant and slave, non-violent, dull and humble. A Southern novelist and poet, Robert Penn Warren summed up the personality of Sambo as perceived in American folklore: "He was the grinning, slack-jawed, docile, dependent, slow-witted, humorous, child-loving, childlike, watermelon-stealing, spiritual-singing, blamelessly fornicating, happy-go-lucky, hedonistic, faithful black servitor who sometimes might step out of character long enough to utter folk wisdom or bury the family silver to save it from Yankees."[24]

Thomas D. Rice's character 'Jim Crow' was to become one of the foremost exponents of the minstrel character. It became one of the most popular forms of theatre, reaching into all sections and into the most remote corners of America between 1830 and 1880. By the early twentieth century, almost every community boasted of a minstrel group. Books, pamphlets, and scores provided minstrel compendia from which schools, civic groups, church organisations, and others could choose materials to produce a show. Needless to say, the *Black and White Minstrel Show* achieved long running success in theatres throughout Britain also.

The use of dialect was one of the surest ways to get a laugh when used either in speeches or in songs as the following nineteenth century song illustrates;

Nelly Bly! Nellie Bly! bring de broom along,
We'll sweep de kitchen clean, my dear,
An' hab a little song.
Poke de wood, my lady lub;
An' make de fire burn,
And while I take de banjo down;
Just gib de mush a turn.[25]

The introduction of the silent movie offered yet another opportunity to extend the comic version of the ideology of racism through white culture. Thomas Edison's Company's early film series *Black Maria,* eg 'Negro Lovers', 'Chicken Thieves', and 'Coloured Boy Eating Watermelons'; Edwin S. Porter's *Uncle Tom's Cabin;* pre-World War short films such as *Rastus in Zululand* and *Rastus Got His Turkey;* 'Sambo' title of the all-Negro comedies which included *Coon Town Suffragettes,* and the Charlie Chan's film services; all epitomised the black man as the stupid, childish and cowardly buffoon, good enough to be a faithful, though dull, servant but nothing else.

Of course, whether in science (as noted in Darwin), in literature, in the theatre, or in music, there were a few dissenting voices here and there, projecting a more positive image of the African, but these were voices in the wilderness. Had their voices been heeded and believed, racial discrimination might now not exist in the world let alone be a subject of investigation.

It is vital to grasp the logical relationship between the concepts and characteristics ascribed to the black man and the hierarchical rank order classification of the human races which underlie the ideology of racism: white people, as noted above, were at the apex of God's creation or at the pinnacle of the evolutionary process, and black people occupied the base, with other races ranked in between. The nearer to white people (in terms of colour), the more superior a race was; the further away from white people, the more inferior. All desirable human qualities (as defined 'naturally' by white people) were, therefore, most often found among white people, descending down the hierarchy to black people among whom the most desirable qualities were almost non-existent; conversely, human vices were most pronounced in behaviour among black people, diminishing as one ascended the 'race ladder' until one reached white people at the top where their manifestations in behaviour were lowest. Of course, within each racial group, 'class' played an important part in the distribution of human qualities and vices, with desirable qualities descending from the upper to the lowest classes in diminishing returns and vices ascending in diminishing order from the lowest to the upper classes. But in keeping with the objective of this thesis, the level of analyses will be confined to 'race' which is conceptually distinct from class.

A train is bound by technical constraints to travel in the direction predetermined by the rail lines; it changes course not by choice of the driver, but by the pre-determined direction of the rail tracks. A vehicle may, at the discretion of the driver, leave the road, drive through a field and join another, geophysically unconnected, road going in a different direction. A train which thus diverts, derails! Likewise, basic or fundamental assumptions about a particular phenomenon – natural or social – create 'frames of reference' or conceptual structures which predetermine the logical direction of our thoughts and many of our behaviours in relation to that phenomenon. All statements, arguments, assumptions, and conclusions about that phenomenon, to be valid, *must* proceed from, and not be contradictory to, the basic assumption.

The original and basic assumption of the 'natural inferiority' of black people, set the development of the ideology of racism on a path, the validity of which the social relationship between black people and white people had to demonstrate, or be seen to demonstrate. Black people had not only to be *assumed inferior*, but had to *be seen to be inferior*; there had to be perfect correlation between assumption and perception of reality (and we shall soon see how this was achieved). All theories had to be consistent with this basic assumption. Evidence to the contrary had to be explained away or rationalised within the 'logic of the ideology'. As I shall encompassing principle, "to every rule, there is an exception", was validity of the premise of the ideology were encountered; but the all-encompassing principle: "to every rule, there is an exception", was used to defend the integrity of the ideology when it was impossible to explain away, such evidence.

By the end of the nineteenth century, the ideology of racism had penetrated and pervaded every stratum of British and American (as well as Portuguese, Spanish, French, German and Dutch) social life, consciousness and institutions; it had become deeply embedded in social perception, attitude, and 'psyche'. No section of social practice was untouched by its assumptions and stereotypes. As Peter Fryer points out: "...racism was not confined to a handful of cranks. Virtually every scientist and intellectual in nineteenth-century Britain took it for granted that only people with white skin were capable of thinking and governing".[26]

But what was to give racial ideology its greatest potency and triumph was that by the twentieth century, the assumption had become axiomatic – a self-evident truth. There was a near-perfect correlation and unity between the assertion of biologically-determined black 'inferiority' and the socio-politico-economic status of the black man the world over. Whether in Africa, in the Americas, the Westindies, or in Europe, the black man was 'demonstrably inferior' politically, socially, economically, educationally, technologically and culturally. The belief in the African's innate inferiority no longer required an act of faith – observed 'reality' demonstrated it beyond a shadow of doubt. The need and urgency to preach the doctrine of immanent black inferiority became superfluous in the face of openly available self-evident fact. In the following Chapter, I shall address two questions which arise from the statements made in this paragraph: (a) How did the black man become socio-politico-economically inferior all over the world? and (b) Could not this universal socio-politico-economic inferiority be indicative of the validity of the ideology of racism's basic assumption of 'inherent black inferiority'? To this task, the next Chapter is devoted.

Notes

a. Cheikh Anta Diop suggests that the Biblical origin of ascribing negative concept to blackness has its roots in the departure from slavery in Egypt by the Jews. It was a reflection of the Israelities' hatred for their enslavement by 'Black Egypt' as can be demonstrated in the following text.
b. emphasis mine.

CHAPTER FOUR

The Power Equation –
Rendering a People Inferior

I submitted evidence in Chapter Two of the origin and development of modern racism, and the contribution made by 'science' to authenticate the ideology and to validate its basic assumption. I showed in Chapter Three how this racism insidiously spread through the whole socio-politico-cultural structures of British (as well as Portuguese, Spanish, Dutch, French, German and American) society through the seventeenth-nineteenth centuries. By the twentieth century, I stated, black inferiority had become axiomatic – a self-evident truth – thereby obviating the need for continuous re-affirmation of the ideology's basic premise. But how did black people become socio-politically/economically inferior? Surely, does not the uniformity of the black man's inferior status vis-à-vis the white man the world over, offer incontrovertible proof of the validity of the assumption of the ideology of racism?

The answer, as I shall presently demonstrate, is categorically NO! One variable in the equation of social relationships between black people and white people which I have not hitherto introduced is the concept of *power*. The European, whether as a slave trader, captain or sailor of a slave-ship, plantation owner, slave-driver or master/ mistress of a domestic slave, had the gun and almost absolute power over the African slave – the power of life or death in most cases. Once the African had been assumed or alleged to be inferior as a justification for his enslavement and for the barbarity of his treatment, it was incumbent on the European to demonstrate that the African was, indeed, truly inferior, if the slave-owner-slave relationship was to be effectively maintained.

No effort was spared to achieve that objective. Once purchased, the African was left in no doubt of his 'inferiority'. He had been reduced to an item of commerce, a thing, a personal property (given legal affirmation by English, French, Belgian, Portuguese, American, Dutch, Spanish, etc. laws). He was branded as sheep or cattle are, with a burning hot iron! He was transported in chains in such restricted and atrocious conditions that most, as was noted earlier, excreted and lay in their faeces. He was humiliated, brutalised, viciously assaulted, and in many cases, killed casually and callously. The African woman, in addition to suffering all the above with her menfolk, suffered the indignity of menstruating (in some cases twice on the same voyage) without any facility to mitigate her condition in the appalling and inhuman conditions in which she was transported. She was given the opportunity to clean up and maintain decent personal hygiene only when she was required by her oppressors to satisfy their sexual needs.

For those who survived the dehumanisation of the Middle Passage, the process of deculturisation and depersonalisation began and/or continued on arrival in the Americas. After being purchased, either in the Westindies, Brazil, Cuba or in North America, his owner gave him a new name symbolising, among other things, the effacement of his previous self. The unintended effect of this, as was also the case with Africans who adopted Arabic names through Islamisation, was that if in future their progeny achieved brilliance in any field of human endeavour, they would be assumed to be white or Arabs except to those who would know them personally or those informed of their race.

The African slave was not allowed to speak his language with other slaves of the same linguistic background, because it was feared they might conspire to plot insurrection. They were even banned from playing the 'talking-drums' in America when white people realised that it was a means of transmitting coded messages to each other. And of course, with the loss of language came the loss, over successive generations, of most of his African culture, history, religion, social practices, etc.

Armed with a gun, the white slave-owner could exact absolute obedience at the threat of inflicting maximum physical pain or even death. Everything was done to strip the black man of his humanity. The white man needed the black man's physical structure – his brawn – and only a little of his brain. Having dehumanised him, the 'master' then set about remoulding him into a 'work-horse'.

Any attempt to reassert his humanity, met with swift retribution: such insolence and self-assertion could become infectious! Armed with a gun, the white man could enforce his supposed 'superiority'.

As slaves, with no rights whatsoever, the African was brutalised, violated, punished violently, in some cases murdered, all at the master's whim and caprice. He could marry only with his master's permission and indulgence – a direct challenge to his manhood – and where the couple belonged to different owners, on different plantations, their problems became more complex. But whether they belonged to one owner or different owners, either husband or wife could be sold off at the behest of the master, as a result of insolvency of the plantation (or mine, or whatever business), or at the death of the master. Several slave marriages broke down in this manner with devastating psychological consequences, particularly on those couples who shared deep love and affection for each other, for such affection, where it existed, often offered the only hope in an otherwise unmitigated miserable existence. Children of slaves could be, and were, sold off if and when the master decided, with incalculable emotional/psychological effect on the parents.

The African woman could be, and was, sexually violated and raped, with nauseating regularity, by white people, without the latter facing any judicial retribution. Whether the victim was under age, or married, was irrelevant – the slave who sought by violent means (the only means available in such a circumstance) to defend his daughter or wife from such violation, faced the full rigours of the white man's law! After all, the slave had no right in law. For most black people, the concept of justice was 'mythical' – the only justice they knew was mob justice, a white mob consumed with an extreme and pathological passion of racial hatred!

Any attempt at self-assertion or any display of dignity was construed as insubordination and met with severe punishment. Black people were lashed to insensibility at the slightest demonstration of rebellion. Slave gangs roamed the country to ensure slaves knew their place and were kept there. Escaped slaves were hounded down, returned to their owners and severely punished. Indeed, physical suffering was part of the daily life of the African, mitigated only by the rare fortuitous opportunity of being owned by a kindly, more humane, master.

The African slave was denied access to education. Learning to read and write was a punishable crime. White people who were caught aiding and abetting black people to acquire such skills, were themselves punished. The slave was denied access to any opportunity which might improve him and lead to his personal development. He could acquire skills only when such skills were perceived as economically beneficial to his master. He was denied access to all decision making processes – economic, political, or social.

The end of slavery, when it came, made little difference to the legal and socio-economic status of the 'Negro'. When the Colonial Secretary, Edward Stanley, presented his Emancipation Bill to the British Parliament on May 14, 1833, the plan was in the form of resolutions.[1] In a three-hour-long speech, Stanley said, *inter alia*, "I propose that every slave on the passing of the Act, shall have the power of claiming to be put in a situation... in which they would be entitled to every right and every privilege of freemen subject to this condition, and to this condition alone – that for a certain period they shall contract to labour under their present owners but now their employers." The justification for this extraordinary new contractual relationship labelled 'emancipation' was that "To throw the slave suddenly into freedom will be to destroy all his inclinations to industry; it will be exposing him to the temptation of recurring to his primitive habits of savage life, from which he has but lately been reclaimed."[2] *The ideology of racism could not be better enunciated!*

Stanley's proposal was for £15 million loan to be paid as compensation (within three weeks, this had been increased to £20 million and changed from loan to an outright grant) to the Westindian planters. The repayment of such loan was to be borne by the ex-slave. Of his total time worked as an 'apprentice', he would work three-quarters of the time for his master and one-quarter of the time for himself. During the latter time, the slave would be at liberty to employ himself elsewhere and from his earnings, repay his master.

By this master stroke of ingenuity, the Colonial Secretary could kill two birds with one stone: "I think it likely that the negro will be encouraged to continue his industry and exertions if out of his wages for the fourth of his labour some deduction should be made for the purpose I have adverted to... [It would be] more conducive to create in him habits of industry and of self-denial than if, having all his wants provided for by the planter in consideration of three-fourths of his labour, he should feel that the only object of employing the remaining fourth would be, at his own option, to provide himself superfluities."[3]

To add insult to injury, the Colonial Secretary was telling the African that not only was all the brutality and bestiality suffered at the hands of the British an act of mercy to rescue him from himself in his native Africa; that after three hundred years of living under the blessing of white civilisation, he was still not mentally fit for freedom; that he was being offered the opportunity of 'emancipation' for which he would work three-fourths of his time for his master (now employer) without wages; but that to prevent him sinking back into savagery, he would have to work the remaining one-quarter (his liberated time) in order to repay his master, from the wages thus earned, the privilege of his freedom? What freedom? one might ask!

It took five years of flogging, forced labour, more humiliation, degradation and deprivation for this enforced servitude to be ended by legislative Acts of the Islands themselves rather than by the British Parliament. From 1833 onwards, the black people had the freedom of choice to sell their labour for wages or die of starvation! The black people in Britain (the Mother Country) fared hardly better!

In the United States, many Northern States had opposed the

expansion of slavery and refused to allow its extension in the newly acquired territories of the West. Abraham Lincoln, who had been opposed to slavery (although willing to allow its perpetuation in the Southern States), was elected in 1860 as US President. The Southern States seceded and formed a Confederacy, leading to the American Civil War of 1861 to 1865. Although Lincoln had issued the Emancipation Proclamation on 1st January, 1863, and although the Northern forces (in which 200,000 black people served and 36,000 gave their lives) won the war, freedom in the South soon became nominal.

The end of the Civil War brought some limited, but spectacular gains for some black people in the South. For example, South Carolina's first state legislature following the war consisted of 87 black people and 40 white people. At the national level, 22 black people were elected to Congress from the South. Two black men – Alonzo Ransier in 1870 and Richard H. Graves in 1874 – served as lieutenant governors, in South Carolina while Jonathan J. Wright, a black Judge, became an associate Justice of the state supreme court for seven years.

But the Southern backlash was swift and effective. A period of retrenchment and claw-back followed. The net result was that although 'emancipated', black people found that all socio-politico-economic power was firmly entrenched in the hands of white people who constructed effective social barriers to keep them out of the corridors of power. The Civil Rights Act of 1866 had little meaning when most Negroes had to work for their former masters or starve. Any attempt to claim their rights under the Act led to threatened dismissal and starvation. The Ku Klux Klan emerged to replace the old slave gangs; to terrorise black people; to lynch many of them; and to ensure that the reality of white supremacy endured. Indeed, in many Southern States, the old laws which made it illegal to educate black people continued to be enforced after emancipation.

'Jim Crow' laws were enacted to ensure segregation between black people and white people in all social relations. Black people could not go to white schools, which effectively meant that there was no access to education for most black people as virtually all schools in the South were white schools. Massive racial discrimination excluded black people from virtually all skilled jobs and the professions.

As late as the 1950s there were laws which required black people to give up their seats for white people in buses. It was this law which brought Dr Martin Luther King into prominence and leadership of the American Civil Rights movement of the 50s and 60s. Rosa Parks, a 'negro' seamstress, exhausted from work, refused to give up her seat for a white passenger and was arrested by the police on 1st

December, 1955; Dr King organised a boycott of the buses. Rosa Parks was convicted and fined $10, but the boycott of the buses continued for two years and ended only after the US Supreme Court ruled that the local law requiring segregation on the buses was unconstitutional.

Black people had the utmost difficulty to register to vote in the South. Although the position of black people in the North was much better than those in the South, they still suffered massive discrimination in education, housing, employment, etc. The Civil Rights Act, 1964, the setting up of the Equal Opportunities Commission, the 'riots' of the sixties throughout American cities, all attest to the fact that racial discrimination and racial disadvantage had consigned black people to a socio-politico-economic status of inferiority.

The process by which the assumptions of the ideology of racism acquired the status of an axiom, as stated above, was that firstly, in order to rationalise and justify the barbarity and bestiality of the slave system of the sixteenth century, the white slave traders, slave transporters and slave owners, alleged that the black man was innately inferior – a sub-human, in fact – and hence the moral code to be observed in human social relations, did not and indeed could not apply when dealing with the black man. Secondly a set of negative stereotypes were invented and applied to him as immutable natural characteristics; these were later authenticated by 'scientific racism'. Thirdly, as all effective power was concentrated in the hands of the white man, he had the means to create a self-fulfilling prophecy; this he proceeded to do by systematically denying to the black man all access to opportunities for human progress and self-development. Fourthly, by denying him access to all opportunities for self-development, the black man was, *ipso facto,* rendered socio-economically inferior. Fifthly, the manifest inferiority status to which he had been consigned through blatant racial discrimination was cited as evidence of his innate inferiority, thereby justifying future discrimination, i.e the *effect* of his deliberate deprivation by the whites, was now cited as the *proof* of his inferiority.

By this process, the black man in the Westindies, the US, Brazil and Europe was rendered manifestly inferior, making the claims of the ideology of racism a self-evident fact. The African in Africa has been deliberately left out; let us now see how, through his power position, the white man brutally and systematically rendered him socially, politically and economically inferior.

We have noted above that the capital accumulation made possible by the triangular trade, had stimulated and accelerated the industrial revolution in Britain. But this industrial monopoly was not to remain Britain's prerogative for long; other European countries soon followed Britain and began industrialising. It was not long before overproduction and competition saturated the European market. "By the 1880s," Colin Nicholson states, "the whole of Europe had become – or was becoming – industrialised. Competition for market, raw materials and fields of investment made expansion necessary. Yet it was impossible for any state to expand in Europe itself without provoking a war."[4]

This situation had been foreseen and solutions had been suggested by people with foresight more than ten years earlier. "This is what England must do or perish", John Ruskin had declared in 1870, "she must found colonies as fast and as far as she is able... teaching her colonists that their chief virtue is fidelity to their country, and that their first aim is to advance the power of England by land and sea."[5]

Industrial capitalism had created a new socio-economic order. Feudalism as an economic system had been destroyed or was in the process of being destroyed and, in its place, a new social category – the proletariat or working class – had emerged. Under this new system of production a new social relationship was created in which a worker contracted to sell his labour power to the capitalist for a specified period of time in a given day. At the end of that period most of these workers had to fend for themselves (in contrast to the feudalist socio-economic order), by procuring from their wages the necessities of life, including shelter. The capitalist, unlike the feudal lord, had no responsibility for the personal well-being of his employees. Where shelter, food, clothing, etc. were provided, these were largely supplied with a view to a higher form of exploitation and greater profit.

This system of production, and the new social relationships it developed, lacked the security that the feudal system provided. The worker's job depended on the demand for the products coming out of the factories, mines, etc. When demand fell below supply, production capacity had to contract and workers were thrown out of their jobs. Alternatively, even with rising demand, increasing competition among producers led to bankruptcy amongst the inefficient, leading to loss of jobs. The worker who lost his job under these circumstances, literally lost the means of livelihood. He could find himself destitute – without food, clothing, shelter, etc. A social security 'safety net' for the unemployed and destitute was social science fiction at the time. This insecurity created conditions in which social cohesion, law and order could be threatened as desperate men sought other means of survival or more seriously, attempted to organise a rebellion against the established social order. If a revolution was to be prevented, the large mass of proletariat had to have a more secure employment prospect in an expanding economic system in which the proletariat got larger 'crumbs' from his production.

The solution was to secure larger markets, greater access to cheap raw materials and, at all cost, a more rapid expansion of the economy. "Is it not clear," the French Prime Minister Jules Ferry asked his fellow countrymen in the National Assembly in 1885, "that the great states of modern Europe, the moment their industrial power is founded, are confronted with an immense and difficult problem, which is the basis of industrial life, the very condition of existence – the question of markets?" The solution as he saw it was in economic expansion through colonisation. "European consumption", he continued, "is saturated: it is necessary to raise new masses of consumers in other parts of the globe, else we shall put modern society into bankruptcy and prepare for the dawn of the twentieth century a cataclysmic social liquidation of which one cannot calculate the consequences... Colonization is for France a question of life and death: either France will become a great African power, or in a century or two she will be not more than a secondary European power; she will count for about as much in the world as Greece and Romania in Europe."[6]

Britain, as Joseph Chamberlain observed, faced an identical problem. "Is there any man in his sense," he asked in 1888, "who believes that the crowded population of these islands could exist for a single day if we were to cut adrift from us the great dependencies which now look to us for protection and assistance, and which are the natural markets for our trade?... If tomorrow it were possible, ...to reduce... the British Empire to the dimensions of the United Kingdom, half at least of our population would be starved."[7]

Europe had accumulated tremendous capital from African gold, ivory, spices and above all, African labour (and African blood!) from which the produce of the plantation systems in the Americas had been obtained. This had made possible their transition from mercantile to industrial capitalism. Now the latter was threatened by over-production and economic stagnation, the solution lay, once again, in Africa (as well as Asia, Australia, New Zealand, the Far East, etc.). Africa, in particular, was to be ruthlessly plundered and the African exploited to the maximum (and severely impoverished for centuries to come) for the economic benefit, prosperity, development, advancement, health and well-being of Europe.

It is beyond the scope of this treatise to go into detailed historical analysis of the military conquest of the continent and the subsequent exploitation and restructuring of the economy which was to render the African socio-economically inferior and thereby 'proving true' the ideology of racism's assumption of the innate inferiority of the African. Readers interested in a summary of the historical account will find Chinweizu's book[a] instructive. Our objective here will be to look at the mode of European imperialistic exploitation of the continent, the restructuring of African economies in order to make them satellites of European economic systems, and the consequent improverishment of the African peoples which had a secondary function of providing an apparent 'proof' of the assertion of black inferiority.

To regulate the conduct of the European powers in their scramble for Africa and to prevent wars between themselves over this carving up process, the Berlin Treaty of 1885 was drawn up and ratified by member countries. Of course Europe felt confident enough in 1885 to share out Africa almost as if they were playing a game of 'monopoly' because four hundred years of the slave trade and its consequent depopulation of vast areas of the continent, had had a debilitating effect on Africa. Moreover, the shameful wars fought between the tribes and nations to secure slave labour for the insatiable European plantations in the Americas, had by this time, exhausted the continent's power to resist outside aggressors and had all but disintegrated Africa's powerful political kingdoms. Furthermore, those taken from Africa were the young, strong, healthy, and hence productive, labour force. They were also at the age of child-bearing. It takes little imagintion to visualise the effect that four centuries of such drain in human resources would have had on Africa! The continent was now well anaesthetised for Europe's surgical operation in Africa – the second and most devastating holocaust on the Continent (the first being the transatlantic slave trade) was about to commence.

The missionaries and explorers had also by this time played their indispensable role. Under the guise of preaching Christianity, or as traders, they had gathered and sent home to their governments, intelligence information, including maps, the size and strength of the African forces, the location of mines, etc. The missionaries had been teaching the Africans to seek the Kingdom of God and while they were thus engaged, Europe was contriving to dismantle their earthly kingdoms. Men such as Mungo Park, David Livingstone, Richard Burton, Heinrich Barth, John Clapperton, Rene Caille, Count Belzoni, Count Savorgnan de Brazza, Henry Morton Stanley, John Speke, Major Dixon Denham, William Balfour, Gaspard Mollien and Richard and John Lander, for over a century served as intelligence agents for their respective countries. Like anaesthetists, they prepared the patient – Africa – for the surgeon's scalpel.

Another important factor was that at the time of signing the treaty, Europe already had various toeholds in Africa: Spain occupied the Canary Islands and the island of Fernando Po; Portugal held the islands of Sao Tome and Principe, occupied parts of the coast of Mozambique, and had settlements at Luanda and Benguela on the coast of Angola; Italy held Assab on the Red Sea coast of Ethiopia; Germany had trading posts and settlements on the coast of South-West Africa, Cameroons, Togo and Tanganyika; France was installed in Algeria and Tunisia, and also had trading and military posts in Saint-Louis and Goree on the Senegal Coast and at Grand Bassam, Assinie, Porto-Novo and Libreville, all on the west coast of Africa; Britain had trading posts in the Niger Delta, settlements on the Gambia River, on Sierra Leone, on the coast of the Gold Coast and the Cape Colony in South Africa, and exercised protectorate powers over Egypt and Upper Nile Valley.

The Europeans had also seized important trade networks much earlier on. For example, in 1810 a squadron of four ships with a total of ninety-eight guns, was sent to patrol some 3,000 miles of the West African coast. Its professed mission was twofold: (a) to enforce the British law of 1807 that declared the slave trade illegal;[b] and (b) to "protect" British "legitimate" traders, ie those who did not engage in the slave trade. With the arrival of the fleet, Britain entered an era of gunboat diplomacy to secure profitable trade monopolies. "With gunboats sheltering them, British traders quickly lost their fear of, and respect for, the authorities of Africa's coastal states and principalities... Before long, the British forced unequal trade treaties upon them and insisted that they open the markets of their hinterland to British participation. When African rulers resisted such demands, trade wars and shooting wars erupted."[8]

An incident in 1836 clearly illustrates the modality of the British gunboat diplomacy whose object was the seizure of legitimate African commerce. In 1836, a ship of the British fleet entered the port of Bonny, one of the Niger Delta city-states, and seized a Spanish ship it accused of waiting there for a cargo of slaves. Affronted by such gross interference in the sovereignty of his territory, Alali, the regent of Bonny, imprisoned the British officers involved. The British fleet moved in and threatened to raze Bonny to the ground unless the prisoners were released. Having secured their release, the British contrived Alali's overthrow and his succession by the 20-year-old King William Dappa Pepple. But the latter soon displeased the British by resisting their attempt to dominate the £1 million-a-year trade with Europe. Pepple was deposed and banished, first to the offshore island of Fernando Po, then later to the island of Ascension, and finally to London. The way was open for a British monopoly of Bonny's trade with Europe!

This pattern was repeated on Bonny's neighbours to the east and west. By 1885 Old Calabar's palm-oil trade was worth £½ million a year. The African middlemen decided that they would earn much higher prices by shipping their palm-oil directly to England. The

British consul saw this decision as "insolent" and moved to set a deterrent example. Under the concocted pretext of wanting to rid the land of human sacrifices, he ordered British gunboats to bombard and level a section of the town of Old Calabar. Earlier, in 1851, there had been several interferences in the affairs of Lagos under the guise of stamping out slavery. They threatened naval bombardment of the city, dethroned and banished King Kosoko, and installed another 'king' on the throne. By 1861, they dispensed with control through puppet intermediaries altogether, annexed the City, and proclaimed it a British colony.

Of course, this *modus operandi* was not peculiar to the British. The French acquired land on the estuary of the River Ogowe and in 1843 built thereon blockhouses for "fighting African slave traders". From this beachhead they established trading posts up the valley of the Congo for "legitimate" trade. In this manner, using the suppression of the slave trade as their pretext and employing their naval squadrons to blockade ports, shell towns, and intimidate rulers into co-operative submission, the agents of the European industrial nations began their assault on Africa. This era of Euro-African trade rivalries and gunboat diplomacy served as prelude to the European invasion of Africa that hurried to a climax after 1885.[9]

From these coastal beachheads, armed with the intelligence previously gathered by the Missionaries, the Europeans marched on Africa. By the turn of the twentieth century, the whole of Africa, except Ethiopia was under European domination. Some had resisted gallantly – the Ashantis, for example, withstood the British onslaught for a hundred years, defeating or forcing the British to a draw in six major wars before Kumasi, the capital, was occupied.

When Sahala (Menelik as he called himself later) succeeded to the Ethiopian throne, the British, the French and the Italians were all struggling for a foothold in Ethiopia. It was the Italians, however, who succeeded in signing a treaty with Menelik which gave them complete control over Ethiopia's relations with foreign powers. But Menelik was no fool! He had no intention of selling his country's sovereignty to the Italians. As part of the terms of the treaty, the Italians gave Menelik 38,000 rifles and twenty-eight cannons and loaned him 4 million francs. Menelik soon repaid the loan. Meanwhile, the Italians got a foothold in the north-eastern part of the country and christened the area Eritrea. Menelik shrewdly, and without much fanfare began to mobilise his people. Finally, in 1896, the forces of Menelik engaged 14,500 Italian forces moving towards Adowa. By the time the battle was over, 12,000 Italians lay dead or dying and over 1,000 were prisoners. This great victory ensured an independent Ethiopia to this day.

Elsewhere, by 1900 the entire Continent had been overrun, with Britain, Portugal and France taking the lion's share; Belgium, Germany, Spain and Italy obtained smaller territories. By 1914, the remaining pockets of African resistance had been crushed. European "free trade" monopolies such as the Royal Niger Company, the German East Africa Company, the British South Africa Company, the Compagnie du Senegal et de la Côte Occidentale d'Afrique, and the United Africa Company handed over political power to the direct representatives of the imperial governments of Europe. From thenceforth, the latter were to be responsible not only for the military defence of Europe's interest, but also for its political administration. The former concentrated on what they were best at – the ruthless exploitation of Africa's resources and labour. In contrast to the slaving era, the mines, plantations and other primary industries were now to be brought to Africa's labour source.

Just as the ideology of racism offered justification for the brutal treatment and wanton exploitation of the slave, it developed a justification for the colonisation and ruthless exploitation of Africa and the African. While the social-Darwinist saw the justification of colonisation in 'the law of nature' in which weaker nations must be conquered (and annihilated if necessary, as in Australia and the Americas) for the benefit of the stronger nations, the missionaries saw the justification in Africa's savage and heathen nature. The African had degenerated so far from God, it was claimed, that he had to be rescued from himself. The instrument of this Divine rescue mission was to be the 'civilised' and 'Christianised' Europeans. White people in the goodness of their hearts must take on the 'white man's burden', make self-sacrifices and march on as Christian soldiers to rescue the African from the Devil and bring God's Light to the Dark Continent and its benighted black inhabitants.

The white Christian was going to heed the call of Jesus! Whether she liked it or not, Africa was going to be civilised – European style! The poor benighted black savages had never known even the rudiments of socio-political organisation. How could they? Being naturally inferior, they could never on their own evolve from their barbarism. Europe, in a genuine altruism was going to obey God's command, take on the arduous spiritual task, and bring the benefits of Christianity and civilisation to these unfortunate black devils. The means of achieving such high moral objectives were to be the wanton exploitation of Africa's material and labour resources.

Protestantism had earlier preached the virtue of hardwork as an end in itself. After all, the idle mind is the Devil's workshop! If the African was going to be redeemed, learning the virtues of hard work and industry was a pre-condition of his salvation.

In addition to the spiritual salvation being brought to him, the

African was also going to benefit from the temporal – he was to be patiently taught democracy – European style. Africa was going to be democratised, and the means to achieve this was (yes, you guessed!): a violent despotism, maintained through the power of the rifle and machine gun, under which the disenfranchised African would be slowly, but steadily taught the rudiments of democracy. Democracy by dictatorship? Who cares about the contradictions as long as Europe prospered at the black man's expense?

While most Europeans at home internalised such ideological tripe, some politicians knew better. They were strongheaded enough to need no such justification to salve their consciences. Lord Lugard, conqueror of Uganda and Nigeria, stated the plain truth: "the partition of Africa was, as we all recognise, due primarily to economic necessity of increasing the supplies of raw materials and food to meet the needs of the industrialised nations of Europe".[10]

"Let it be admitted at the outset", he realistically wrote, "that European brains, capital, and energy have not been, and never will be, expended in developing the resources of Africa from motives of pure philanthropy; that Europe is in Africa for the mutual benefit of her own industrial classes, and of the native races in their progress to a higher plane; that the benefit can be made reciprocal, and that it is the aim and desire of civilized administration to fulfil this dual mandate."

To Cecil Rhodes, the choice was quite simple: "I will lay down my policy on this Native question... either you will receive them on an equal footing as citizens or call them a subject race.... I have made up my mind that there must be class (race) legislation.... The native is to be treated as a child and denied the franchise. We must adopt the system of despotism.... These are my politics and these are the politics of South Africa."[11]

Dispensing with the ideological rationalisation, the great French administrator, Marshall Lyantey was equally frank. He "intended to keep Morocco for France until the end, not only as a possession or as a conquered prize, but as a reserve of resources of all kinds for the mother-country."[12]

In a treatise demanding the return of the German colonies taken from them following their defeat in World War I, the German politician, Franz Von Papen wrote in 1933:

"Colonies, I repeat, are an economic necessity for Germany for four reasons:
To feed her own people.
To take care of her surplus population.
To meet her foreign credit engagements, especially her private loans.
To afford her an opportunity of spreading culture and civilization."[13]

The last point was a small concession to the conventional wisdom!

Sir Harry Johnston, the great British administrator was even more blunt: "It somehow shocks the sense of fairness of hard-headed white or yellow people," he wrote in 1920, "that semi-savages should be driving ill-bred sheep, scraggy cattle or ponies hardly fit for polo over plains and mountains that are little else than great treasure-vaults of valuable minerals and chemicals; or that they should roam with their blow-pipes and bows and arrows through forests of inestimable value for the timber, drugs, dyes, latices, gums, oil seeds, nuts, or fruits; be turning this waiting wealth to no use, not allowing it to circulate in the world's market."[14]

Those who held such beliefs, however, were few. The 'moral majority' cocooned themselves in self-delusion, believing the claims of the ideology that the African had reached such a level of degeneracy – spiritually, morally, intellectually – that only the 'civilised' whites, Bible in one hand and gun in the other, could bring him 'salvation'. The ideology of racism, originating in the economic social relationship, co-opted into the cultural relationship, was now firmly entrenched in the political realm! As Peter Fryer states: "...amid all the ramifications of contending schools of racist thought, there was total agreement on one essential point:

> Whether the 'inferior races' were to be coddled and protected, exterminated, forced to labour for their 'betters', or made into permanent wards, they were undoubtedly outsiders – a kind of racial proletariat. They were forever barred both individually and collectively from high office in church and state, from important technical posts in law and medicine, and from any important voice in their own affairs... They were racially unfitted for 'advanced' British institutions such as representative democracy."

From now on 'apartheid' in political institutions was going to be the social practice wherever black people and white people share common citizenship of a geopolitical entity.

The real purpose of the European scramble for Africa, was threefold: (a) to gain unfettered access to, and unrestricted exploitation of, Africa's massive natural resources; (b) to utilise African labour (by force whenever necessary) to plunder African resources for European benefit; and (c) to transplant European surplus population to the most 'suitable' part of Africa. This they proceeded to do with ruthless effectiveness, having first viciously brought the African to heel militarily.

Let us take a look at some of the methods by which the human and material resources of Africa were exploited and plundered. In keeping with Europe's objectives, land had to be appropriated from the conquered Africans and a 'pool' of cheap and/or free African labour had to be assembled to mine the land for gold, diamond, copper, asbestos, tin, iron, zinc, bauxite, manganese, etc., or to farm it for wool, cattle, tobacco, timber, sugar, bananas, coffee, cocoa, cotton, cashews, sisal, palm oil and kernels, rubber, ground-nuts, tea and so on. But, as Chinweizu rightly observes, the Africans were neither willing to be dispossessed of their lands nor motivated to work for the profit of Europeans; such land as the Europeans wanted had, therefore, to be confiscated and African labour compelled. This was achieved by "the adopting by a white ruling race of legal measures designed expressly to compel the individual natives to whom they apply to quit the land, which they occupy and by which they can live, in order to work in white service for the private gain of the white man. When lands formerly occupied by natives are confiscated, or otherwise annexed for white owners, the creation of a labour supply out of the dispossessed natives is usually a secondary object."[15]

Those like the so-called Bushmen of South Africa and some of the Amerindians found untamable were either exterminated or expel-led en masse from their land to make way for the Europeans.

"War, murder, strong drink, syphilis and other civilized diseases are chief instruments of a destruction commonly couched in euphemism 'contact with a superior civilization'. The land thus cleared of natives passes into white possession, and white men must work it themselves, or introduce other lower industrial peoples to work it for them..."[16]

Where expulsion and extermination were deemed unprofitable, other methods were tried. Some were quite ingenious. In Bechuana-land in 1897, for example, a small local riot involving a few drunken "natives" was formented and used as a pretext for expelling 8,000 of the "natives" from lands "inalienably" secured to them by the Bechuanaland Annexation Act of 1805. The rest of the population, 30,000 of them, were forcibly evacuated to other and poorer districts. The land confiscated was turned over to British occupation.[17] This method has reached perfection under the obno-xious system of apartheid in South Africa where black people who constitute 80% of the population are 'allocated' 13% of the total land area of the country and where, by the mid-1980s, between three and four million black people had been forcibly removed from "white areas".

The confiscation of property by the 'civilised' Europeans was not limited to land. After the Matabele War, there was a wholesale confiscation of the cattle of the Matabeles by the British for the purpose of stocking the farms of the white settlers. This provoked further wars, leading to further defeats of the Matabeles, leading to further confiscations of their cattle. "Our cattle is gone", complained the conquered Matabeles in despair, "we have nothing to live for. Our women are deserting us; the white man does as he likes with them. We are the slaves of the white man; we are nobody, and have no rights or laws of any kind."

In Sierra Leone, the British method of compelling labour from the African was by the imposition of a high and burdensome "hut-tax" whose collection was harshly enforced. To earn money to pay this tax which was payable in the white man's currency, the African had to sell his labour to the white men. When the method proved inadequate in producing sufficient cheap African labour, the British introduced the compulsory labour ordinance which made it "obligatory on persons of the labouring classes to give labour for public purposes on being called out by their chiefs or other native superiors." In 1895 a similar ordinance was passed in the Gold Coast to compel chiefs to furnish "Carriers" for the British expedition forces marching northwards against the Ashantis.

In South Africa, in order to meet the insatiable demands of the mines, a more sophisticated 'social engineering' system was contrived to "break up the tribal system which gives solidarity and some political and economic strength to native life; set the Kaffir on an individual footing as an economic bargainer, to which he is wholly unaccustomed, take him by taxation or other 'stimulus' from his locality, put him down under circumstances where he has no option but to labour at the mines."[18]

Some missionaries remonstrated against the breaking up of the tribes, describing it as being immoral. Their protestation died away when they were assured by a magistrate who delivered a scholarly apologia of the system:

> "...the labour question and the land question are indissolubly bound together. In my opinion it is of little use framing enactments to compel unwilling persons to go out to work. It is like the old saw about leading a horse to the water; you can take him there, but you cannot make him drink. In the same way you may impose your labour-tax, but you cannot make your unwilling persons work. Create a healthy thirst in your horse and he will drink fast enough. Similarly create the necessity for the native to work and he will work, and none better. Hitherto, under our commercial-tenure system, there has been little absolute necessity for our young natives to leave their homes to work. The land supplies them with food, and a few shillings will buy a blanket, and as soon as the young man marries he is entitled to receive his lot of arable land; but once this is stopped – and it will be stopped by the survey and individual tenure – a young man before he marries a wife will have to be in a position to support a wife, and to obtain this *he must work*[c] [for the European, that is] and once having married her he must still work to maintain her and himself, and *once the necessity of work is created*[c] there will be no lack of men ready and willing to work."[19]

This ingenious but callous mode of coercing the African to work for the profit of the European by his dispossession from the land and by his impoverishment was not a British monopoly. The Germans enhanced the methodology with greater brutality. After conquerig the people of Tanganyika, they built forts in strategic areas, created white settlements around them, suppressed revolts, exacted taxes, and conscripted African labour for their plantations. The bestiality with which the Germans treated their labour conscripts was so appalling, even by European colonial standards, that some African chiefs, including Kinyasi of Usambara, abdicated their 'client chieftaincies' in order to relieve themselves from the responsibility of supplying African labour to such vicious German planters. So ferocious was the planter regime that all the peoples of southern Tanganyika united in rebellion despite their weak position vis-à-vis the trigger-happy Germans. The ensuing Maji Maji rebellion was to last many years before the Germans succeeded in stamping it out.

The exploitation of human and material resources by bestiality par excellence, however, was attained by the French and the Belgians in French Equitorial Africa and in the Congo 'Free' State respectively. In a vicious method which would have won the warm acclaim of the Nazis, French and Belgian traders who had come to Africa to 'bring law and order and enlightenment to supposedly lawless, disordered, benighted, savage and primitive Africans', settled down to a systematic and beastly orgy of exploitation and genocidal onslaught against 'natives' which must surely rank among the worst of capitalist barbarities.

Rubber had become an important and profitable merchandise in Europe and the French and Belgian factories needed every ounce of the raw material they could lay hands on, preferably at little or no labour cost for procuring. The Congo had been discovered as a natural preserve of the raw material for rubber needed by their factories at home:

"The Concessionaire Companies acquired by their charters *the sole right of possession*^c of the negotiable products of the country. *They became de facto owners*^c of the rubber trees and vines within their respective concessions. This implies, of course, dispossession of the natives. Dispossession of the native implied, in its turn, the immediate cessation of the act of purchase and sale – otherwise trade – between the native population and white men.... The years which followed were to witness the attempt to compel 'by force of arms' some nine million African natives, or as many of that total who could be reached, to submit not only to be robbed, but to spend their lives in the extremely arduous and dangerous task of gathering and preparing india-rubber in the virgin forests, and on behalf of a few wealthy financiers in Brussels, Paris and Antwerp.... The Concessionaires settled down to their work... of forcing as much rubber as possible out of the natives. In the lower part of the French Congo the effect was immediate. Here the native population had been traders with white men... for decades. To their bewilderment they found themselves suddenly faced with a demand for rubber as a 'tax' from the administration, and with a demand for rubber as by divine right from strange white men who claimed to *own* it, and claimed power to compel the real owners to collect it for whatever the former chose to pay. The trading stations where the natives had been wont to carry their produce and barter it... they were forbidden to approach. The natives of the French Congo did what any other people would have done. They declined to be despoiled of their property and robbed of the fruits of their labours. The chiefs appealed to the authorities and asked what they had done to be so 'punished'. Appeals were in vain. Refusal to 'work rubber' was met with attempted compulsion. The natives rose.... In the N'Gunie region no fewer than five military expeditions had been sent against the natives in as many months at the request of the local Concessionaire Company. In the Shari, the Chief of an important tribe had been arrested because his people did not bring in enough rubber and had died in prison. In the neighbourhood of Bengui an official had caused fifty-eight women and ten children to be taken as hostages to compel their male relatives to bring in rubber: in three weeks forty-five of these women and two of the children had died of starvation and want of air, packed tightly in a small dwelling place. At Fort Sibut one hundred and nineteen women and little girls had been similarly arrested, and many had died. An official circular had prescribed that these 'hostage-houses' should be erected in the bush and out of sight of possible travellers.[c] In one of the concessions of the Lower Congo the natives had been forbidden to make salt in order to compel them to buy it from the company, which would only sell it against large quantities of rubber; widespread sickness ensued, salt being an indispensable article of native diet in tropical Africa."[20]

Amidst this rubber-mad orgy

"Of floggings and burning of villages, of rape and mutilation, of natives being used as targets for revolver practice, and as human experiments to test the efficacy of dynamite cartridges; of 'hostage-houses' in which men, women and children perished,"[21]

hundreds of thousands died or were uprooted. In the face of such vile military oppressions, a majority of the natives fled their homes into the rain forests to escape the burning, slaughter, rape and torture. A junior French Congo official who was himself a member of this horde of savages, wrote:

"The dead, we no longer count them. The villages, horrible charnel-houses, disappear in this yawning gulf. A thousand diseases follow in our footsteps.... And this martyrdom continues.... We white men must shut our eyes not to see the hideous dead; the dying curse us, and the wounded who implore, the weeping women and the starving children. We must stop our ears not to hear the lamentations, the cries, the maledictions which rise from every foot of land, from every tuft of grass."[22]

Europe's civilising mission was gathering momentum and proceeding with ruthless efficiency! With the Bible in one hand and the gun in the other, fired with an evangelistic fervour to proselyte the teachings of their Christian God, motivated by European idealism, filled with patriotic desire to spread European civilisation, spurred by an altruistic desire to redeem the poor benighted blacks, the

French, 'with their angelic features', were bringing the Light of God
and the benefits of European enlightenment to the Dark Continent,
or so the ideology of racism tells us!

The Belgians were not to be outdone by their French cousins.
Leopold II, frustrated by the insignificance of his tiny kindgom,
simply declared the Congo 'Free' State his own personal estate: "The
Congo", he wrote in 1906, "has been, and could have been, nothing
but a personal undertaking. There is no more legitimate or
respectable right than that of an author over his work, the fruit of
his labour.... My rights over the Congo are to be shared with none;
they are the fruit of my own struggles and expenditures."[23]

But this personal ownership did not only apply to the land, but to
its black inhabitants as well. Leopold needed rubber, abundant
rubber, and yet more rubber! He was going to get his rubber and if
in the process a few million black people lose their lives, well what is
the value of the lives of these sub-humans anyway? Surely the
satisfaction of the economic needs of white people – the crown of the
white God's creation – must be an end that justifies the means!

And so in a twenty-year period, the black population of Leopold's
personal estate – the Congo Free State – was reduced from over 20
million to under 10 million.[24] Slavery was supposed to have ended,
but who would dare question how Leopold treated his black
properties on his own estate? He wrecked the trade and agriculture
that existed, reduced the inhabitants who were not slaughtered to
de facto, if not *de jure,* slaves and their *raison d'être:* to procure
rubber, rubber, and yet more rubber for Leopold and his cronies.
Such was the degree of brutality of the regime that even one of
Leopold's battle-hardened agents was becoming increasingly de-
spairing. Lieutenant Tilkens wrote a letter:

"Commandant Verstraeten visited my station and congratulated me warmly.
He said his report would depend upon the quantity of rubber which I was able
to provide. The quantity increased from 360 kilogrammes in September to
1500 in October, and from January onwards it will amount to 4000 per
month, which will bring me in a monthly premium of 500 francs. Am I not a
lucky fellow? If I go on like this, within two years I shall have earned
premiums of 12,000 Fcs.... S.S. Van Kerkhoven is coming down the Nile and
will demand 1500 Porters. Unlucky niggers! I can hardly bear to think of
them. I am asking myself how on earth I shall be able to hunt up so large a
number.... Marshes, hunger, exhaustion. How much blood will be shed
because of this transport! Three times already, I have had to make war upon
the chiefs who would not help me to get the men I needed. The fellows would
rather die in their own forests than as members of a transport train. If a chief
refuses, that means war, with modern fire-arms on one side against spear
and javelins on the other! A chief has just been to see me, complaining: 'My
village has been destroyed and my wives have been killed'! But what on
earth can I do? I have often been compelled to keep these unhappy chiefs in
chains until they get for me one or two hundred porters. Very often my

soldiers find the villages empty of men, and then they seize the women and the children.... I see the likelihood of a general uprising. The natives are sick of the regime, of having to work as porters, of gathering rubber, of being forced to provide foodstuffs. Once more I have been fighting for three months with only ten days' interval. I have 152 prisoners. For two years I have been making war in this district, but have not been able to force the natives to submit; they would rather die. What am I to do? I am paid for my work. I am merely a tool in the hands of my superiors, and carry out their orders as discipline demands!"[25]

Edmund Pickard, distinguished jurist and senator, saw the devastating effect of this brutal regime on the Congolese. He recorded what he saw on a journey through the Congo Free State:

"The inhabitants have disappeared. Their homes have been burned; huge heaps of ashes amid neglected palm-hedges and devastated abandoned fields. Inhuman floggings, murders, plundering, and carrying-offs.... The people flee.... A continual succession of blacks, carrying loads upon their heads; worn-out beasts of burden, with projecting joints, wasted features, and staring eyes, perpetually trying to keep afoot despite their exhaustion. By thousands they pass, in the service of the State, handed over by their chiefs, whose slaves they are and who rob them of their wages. They totter along the road, with bent knees and protruding bellies, crawling with vermin, a dreadful procession across hill and dale, dying from exhaustion by the wayside, or often succumbing even should they reach home after their wanderings."[26]

No doubt, the Almighty, Omnipotent, Omniscient, Omnipresent God of Justice was witnessing these severe atrocities by His White Messengers who had come to Africa in response to His call to spread His Gospel and to 'civilise' Africa! One wonders if the Almighty approved the methodology, and if not, why the deafening silence? Or were those days gone for ever, when the Lord intervened in the affairs of men and punished the wicked, as occured at the time of Noah in Sodom and Gomorrah, and in Egypt at the time of the exodus of the Israelites? Or maybe the White God intervenes not in the affairs of men if the victims are black!

Such was the savagery of the Belgian regime on the vanquished Congolese that by 1892, twelve months after the mad demand for rubber began,

"The whole country was transformed. It was as though a tornado had torn across it and destroyed everything in its passage. But the effects were more lasting than any natural phenomenon. Thriving communities had been transformed into scattered groups of panic-stricken folk; precipitated from active commercial prosperity and industrial life into utter barbarism."[27]

In 1903, while on a visit to the Congo, a British diplomat, Sir Roger Casement, had a Congolese villager describe to him the system of payment for rubber-picking:

"Our village got cloth and a little salt, but not the people who did the work. Our chiefs ate up the cloth; the workers got nothing. The pay was a fathom of cloth and a little salt for every big basketful, but it was given to the chief, never to the men. It used to take ten days to get the twenty baskets of rubber – we were always in the forest, and then when we were late we were killed. We had to go farther and farther into the forest to find the rubber vines, to go without food, and our women had to give up cultivating the fields and gardens. Then we starved. Wild beasts – the leopards – killed some of us when we were working away in the forest, and others got lost or died from exposure and starvation, and we begged the white men to leave us alone, saying we could get no more rubber, but the white men and their soldiers said: 'Go! you are only beasts yourselves...!

"We tried always going farther into the forest, and when we failed and our rubber was short, the soldiers came to our towns and killed us. Many were shot, some had their ears cut off; others tied up with ropes around their necks and bodies and taken away. The white men sometimes at the posts did not know of the bad things the soldiers did to us, but it was the white men who sent the soldiers to punish us for not bringing in enough rubber."[28]

The European 'civilising' mission in Black Africa was proceeding according to plan!

This barbarity, twenty nightmarish years of vicious warfare for rubber, left deep scars of social devastation:

"There is not an inhabited village left in four days' steaming through a country formerly so rich: today entirely ruined.... The villages are compelled to furnish so many kilos of rubber every week.... The soldiers sent out to get rubber and ivory are depopulating the country. They find that the quickest and cheapest method is to raid villages, seize prisoners, and have them redeemed afterwards for ivory."[29]

An American missionary, in a report, added to this catalogue of wanton bestiality:

"It is blood-curdling to see them (the soldiers) returning with hands of the slain, and to find the hands of young children amongst the bigger ones evidencing their bravery.... The rubber from this district has cost hundreds of lives, and the scenes I have witnessed, while unable to help the oppressed, have been almost enough to make me wish I were dead.... This rubber traffic is steeped in blood, and if the natives were to rise and sweep every white person on the Upper Congo into eternity, there would still be left a fearful balance to their credit."[30]

An agent of a Concessionaire Company wrote home boasting of his own gruesome deeds amidst this orgy of killings. He had killed, he claimed, 150 men, cut off sixty hands, crucified women and children, and hung the remains of mutilated men on the village fence. "After years of such man-made devastation, in justification of their conduct, Belgian ministers of state presented the Congo Africans to the world as little better than animals, with no conception of land tenure or government, no instinct for commerce or industrial pursuits, a people "entitled... to nothing."[31]

But compare the white man's double standard of morality when a few white people are killed by black people. In 1964, during the height of the Congo crisis, Moise Tshombe's troops, led by white mercenaries murdered several thousand Congolese. The murder of a few white people was used as pretext to involve Belgian paratroopers, dropped by American aircraft. In a news coverage of the killing of Dr Paul Carlson, an American missionary, the American magazine, *Time* wrote, *inter alia,* on December 4, 1964:

"Carlson symbolised all the *white men* – and there are many – *who want nothing from Africa but a chance to help.*[c] He was no saint and no deliberate martyr. He was a highly skilled physician *who, out of a strong Christian faith and a sense of common humanity,*[c] had gone to the Congo to treat the sick. His death did more than prove *that Black African civilization*[c] – with its elaborate trappings of half a hundred sovereignties, governments and United Nations delegations – *is largely a pretence.* The rebels were, after all, for the most part, only *a rabble of dazed, ignorant savages*[c] used and abused by semi-sophisticated leaders.

"But virtually all other black African nations, including all the more advanced and moderate ones, supported the rebels without even a hint of condemnation for their bestialities. Virtually all those nations echoed the cynical communist line in denouncing the parachute rescue as 'imperialist aggression'. When this happened, *the sane part of the world*[c] [the white world! no doubt] *could only wonder whether Black Africa can be taken seriously at all, or whether, for the forseeable future, it is beyond the reach of reason.*"[c32]

One might be tolerant enough to grant that the Editor was wholly ignorant of the fact that the crisis in the Congo at the time had been created by the Belgians, aided by the Americans. Congo (now Zaire) had won its independence from Belgium in 1960. When the Belgians found that the Prime Minister, Patrice Lumumba was an uncompromising nationalist who would not allow the Congolese economy to remain a satellite of the Belgian economy, they intervened to cut out the mineral-rich Katanga from the independent Congo. Under the American-backed puppet regime of Moise Tshombe, a large mercenary force was recruited who, together with Tshombe's undisciplined black soldiers, committed terrible atrocities and murdered thousands of Africans. The fact of these heinous crimes might have escaped the attention of the American magazine, *Time* .

But they surely could not be so ignorant as to be totally oblivious to America's past and recent history! Were they totally ignorant of 300 years of slavery and its attendant white barbarity and bestiality? Were they totally uninformed of the slaughter of black Americans by the marauding white gangs – the Ku Klux Klan – clad in 'white' like the angels, burning the cross (a ritual which was meant to symbolize their 'Christian beliefs')? Were they truly unaware of the grenades that were lobbed into black Churches by white people, killing and maiming innocent black worshippers? Were they totally oblivious to the 'lynching' of innocent black people in the deep South as late as the fifties? Were they so illiterate of historical reality that they did not know that in the history of brutality against man by man, black people could never, even if they wished, come anywhere near equalling the white man's utterly ruthless record of genocidal attacks and cold, callous and efficient killings of millions the world over – Africans, Australian Aborigines, the Carib Indians, North and South American Indians? The black Tasmanians were completely wiped out – became extinct – thanks to the white Australians' killing efficiency. Equally a number of South and North American Indians were wiped out by the murderous horde of Spanish, Portuguese and Americans.

And yet so thoroughly has been the effectiveness of the ideology of racism in influencing the perspectives of its adherents that the American *Times* in blissful ignorance could state in 1964 that the black ignorant savages were beyond the reach of reason. The truth is that under the assumption of the ideology of racism, the wholesale slaughter of black people by white people or the genocide of a whole tribe by white people does not constitute murder or savagery (note that what constitutes murder is socially defined)! After all, who would label the killers of 'animals' murderers? But the murder of a few white persons by black persons arouses moral indignation of such proportion that it shakes the world to its foundations! The black savages are showing their true complexion again! they cry in anger.

Returning to the Congo 'Free' State – King Leopold's private estate – it is instructive to note that the atrocities and holocaust recounted are not the result of the excesses of a few maniacal Belgian (or French in the French Congo) killers. As E.D. Morel has demonstrated, the conduct of these functionaries flowed from Belgian (and French) imperialist policy. The brutality was an expected part of the implementation of that policy. As Morel states:

> The Policy was quite simple. Native rights in land were deemed to be confined to the actual sites of the town or village, and the areas under food cultivation around them. Beyond these areas no such rights would be admitted. The land was "vacant", i.e. without owners. Consequently the "state" was owner. The 'State' was Leopold II, ...as Sovereign of the 'Congo Free State'. Native rights in nine-tenths of the Congo territory being thus declared non-existent, it followed that the native population had no proprietary right in the plants and trees growing upon that territory, and which yielded rubber, resins, oils, dyes, etc.; no right, in short, to anything animal, vegetable, or mineral which the land contained. In making use of the produce of the land, either for internal or external trade or internal industry and social requirements, the native population would thus obviously be making use of that which did not belong to it, but which belonged to...

Leopold II. It followed logically that any third person – European or other –
acquiring, or attempting to acquire, such produce from the native population
by purchase, in exchange for corresponding goods or services, would be guilty
of robbery of 'State property'. [ie Leopold's property] A 'State' required
revenue. Revenue implied taxation. The only articles in the Congo territory
capable of producing revenue were the ivory, the rubber, the resinous gums
and oils; which had become the property of the 'State'. The only medium
through which these articles could be gathered, prepared and exported to
Europe – where they would be sold and converted into revenue – was native
labour. Native labour would be called upon to furnish those articles in the
name of 'taxation'....

In the nature of the case, the execution of this policy took some years before
it could become really effective and systematic. The process called for some
ingenuity and a certain breadth of vision, for a good many issues were
involved. In the first place, the notion that an economic relationship existed
between the European and the Congo native, that the native had anything to
sell, must be thoroughly stamped out. Regulations were issued forbidding the
natives to sell rubber or ivory to European merchants, and threatening the
latter with prosecution if they bought these articles from the natives. In the
second place, every official in the country had to be made a partner in the
business of getting rubber and ivory out of the natives in the guise of
'taxation'. Circulars, which remained secret for many years, were sent out, to
the effect that the paramount duty of Officials was to make their districts
yield the greatest possible quantity of these articles; promotion would be
reckoned on that basis. As a further stimulus to 'energetic action' a system of
sliding-scale bonuses was elaborated, whereby the less the native was 'paid'
for his labour in producing these articles of 'taxation', ie the lower the outlay
in obtaining them, the higher was the Official's commission...

A native army was the pre-requisite [for implementing this plan]. The five
years which preceded the Edicts of 1891-2 were employed in raising the
nucleus of a force of 5,000. It was successively increased to nearly 20,000
apart from the many thousands of 'irregulars' employed by the Concessionaire Companies. This force was amply sufficient for the purpose, for a
single native soldier armed with a rifle and with a plentiful supply of ball
cartridge can terrorise a whole village. The same system of promotion and
reward would apply to the native soldier as to the Official – the more rubber
from the village, the greater the prospect of having a completely free hand to
loot and rape. A systematic warfare upon the women and children would
prove an excellent means of pressure. They would be converted into
'hostages' for the good behaviour, in rubber-collecting of the men. 'Hostage
houses' would become an institution in the Congo. But in certain parts of the
Congo the rubber-vine did not grow. This peculiarity of nature was, in one
way, all to the good. For the army of Officials and native soldiers, with their
wives, and concubines, and camp-followers generally, required feeding. The
non-rubber producing districts should feed them. Fishing tribes would be
'taxed' in fish; agricultural tribes in foodstuffs. In this case, too, the women
and children would answer for the men. Frequent military expeditions would
probably be an unfortunate necessity. Such expeditions would demand in
every case hundreds of carriers for the transport of loads, ammunition, and
general impedimenta. Here, again, was an excellent school in which this idle
people could learn the dignity of labour. The whole territory would thus
become a busy hive of human activities, continuously and usefully engaged
for the benefit of the 'owners' of the soil thousands of miles away, and their
crowned head, whose intention, proclaimed on repeated occasions to an
admiring [European] world, was the 'moral and material regeneration' of the

natives of the Congo.
Such was the Leopoldian 'system' briefly epitomised."[33]

The Africans, as can be expected, resisted such an intolerable and immoral system.

"The natives naturally refused to yield up their ivory stocks; to indulge in the perils of hunting the elephant; to carry out the arduous task of tapping the rubber vines, gathering the flowing latex in calabashes, drying it, preparing it, reducing it generally to a marketable condition, and transporting it either by land or water, often for long distances; unless they received, as before, the value of their produce at current market rates. To be suddenly told that this labour must no longer be regarded as a voluntary act on their part, but was required of them; to be further told that its yield must be handed over as a 'tax' or tribute; that they would get no value for the produce itself because their property in it was not recognised, and only such 'payment' for their labour as the recipients of the 'tax' might arbitrarily determine: this was tantamount to informing the native population inhabiting the part of the Congo which had been in trade relationship with Europeans, either directly or indirectly, from time immemorial, that it was in future to be robbed and enslaved. It refused to submit to the process.... In such parts of the Congo where the natives... appear to have acquiesced, unwillingly enough, with the requisitions when first imposed, hoping that the white man would presently go away and leave them in peace... when they saw that the white man was insatiable, they could only carry out his orders by neglecting their farms and dislocating their whole social life, when they found men of strange tribes armed with guns permanently stationed in their villages, interfering with their women and usurping the position and functions of their own chiefs and elders – they, too, rose."[34]

This led to twenty years of fighting, destruction, devastation, and impoverishment as noted above. Mercifully such degree of European savagery and oppression was not practised uniformly throughout the entire continent. But everywhere on the Continent (apart from Ethiopia), massive exploitation of the African's labour and material resources and systematic destruction of his previous socio-economic organisations were being carried out by the White Colonialists.

A Labour Party Report in 1926 described the result of British 'civilising' mission in East Africa:

"The whole organization, and administration of Government is directed... towards compelling the African inhabitants to work for European masters, and is based on the absolute subjection of the native population. Labour is recruited and controlled by the Government, and every possible device, including actual conscription, is used to force the natives into the labour market. All land, except what has already been sold to Europeans, belongs to the Crown, and, with the exception of one district in Uganda, Africans have only been allowed to occupy certain areas on terms of extreme insecurity. Railways, harbours, mines and factories are owned either by Government or by Europeans."

"What has been the result of a generation of British ownership?" the report questioned.

The answer was surprisingly candid:

> "Parts of East Africa, before Europeans took control, used to export grain. Now it is necessary for the Government to import food into countries which are extraordinarily fertile in every kind of crop. There have been periods of actual famine.
> "Diseases, both those which are native to the country and those which have been brought into it by Europeans, have spread with fearful rapidity, and the population in nearly all parts of East Africa is declining."[35]

Another method by which the European Colonialists obtained raw materials to feed their industries and to restructure the African economy into a satellite of European economy, with devastating results on Africa's ability to feed herself in the future, was the introduction of the 'cash crop' and mono-crop economic systems. European factories and shops needed such agricultural produce as cocoa, coffee, rubber, tea, sugar cane, groundnuts, tobacco, bananas, etc. To ensure constant and cheap supply of such produce, the colonised peoples had taxes imposed on them which were payable in the white man's currency. To obtain such cash, one had to sell a marketable produce. The sale of 'cash crop' became one of the surest ways of obtaining that 'hard European currency'. Moreover, as more varied consumables from Europe flooded the African markets and the African became a 'consumer' of such products, the need for more hard currency to procure such goods, became self-evident. Production of food became secondary to 'cash crop' farming. As marketing techniques such as advertising, became more sophisticated and consumer "needs" for certain European consumer products were created and sustained, more and more acreage of arable lands were cultivated almost exclusively for such 'cash crops' and Africa's ability to feed herself declined in inverse proportion.

We noted in our analyses of the transatlantic slave trade that a number of African kings, chiefs and traders engaged in the shameful trade in human beings. The participation of these Africans in this most inhuman trade, will stand out as one of Africa's most shameful periods in the Continent's history. To their eternal damnation, they conspired, co-operated and colluded with the white slave traders in shamefully and treacherously selling Africa's finest young men and women into slavery in return for such goods as guns, beads, whisky; etc. But they do not stand condemned alone; theirs was not an isolated incident. In the period of colonisation, following the end of *de jure* slavery, there were thousands of African auxiliaries who, out of either cowardice or personal benefit, were prepared to collaborate with, and work for the success of, European colonialism and imperialism. For Europe needed such black soldiers, policemen, administrators, chiefs, interpreters, etc., in order for their continued subjugation and repression of the African to be maintained. Had these auxiliaries been imported from Europe, the cost would have been too exhorbitant to have made the exploitation of Africa a profitable and hence viable capitalist venture. Some of these black soldiers became just as savage and bestial as the white masters who hired, trained and paid them.

The degree of freedom, power and prestige granted to the African auxiliaries varied. For example, it was high in Buganda and northern Nigeria, but low in French Africa and the Belgian Congo. In French Africa a chief was a mere functionary appointed to administer for the French an administrative unit. In contrast with an emir in Nigeria who ruled for the British, a French African chief had no right to any part of the taxes he collected. Officially he had a salary, and if he kept part of the taxes he collected that was technically illegal, though this would normally be overlooked unless the French wanted a pretext to oust him. The African chief in the French-ruled territory had no court, no police, no prisons of his own. Real effective power was in the hands of the prefect, commandant, or ultimately the Governor.

In such situations of powerlessness, the African was dispossessed of the best of his land; compelled to sell his labour cheaply to the colonised peoples had taxes imposed on them which were payable in supply raw materials required by European industries, and generally exploited to the maximum. He found himself, in certain parts of the continent, in the obscene situation in which he was treated like an alien in his own land. As David Livingstone recounts:

"I have myself been an eyewitness of Boers coming to a village and, according to their usual custom, demanding twenty or thirty women to weed their gardens, and have seen these women proceed to the scene of unrequited toil, carrying their own food on their heads, their children on their backs and instruments of labour on their shoulders. Nor have the Boers any wish to conceal the meanness of thus employing unpaid labour. On the contrary, every one... lauded his own humanity and justice in making such an equitable regulation. *We make the people work for us in consideration of allowing them to live in our country.*"[36]

Whether colonial rule was savage as occurred in French Equitorial Africa and in the Congo Free State of the Belgians or comparatively more humane as in Northern Nigeria or Ashanti in the Gold Coast, the colonial powers operated to achieve the objectives of making Europe prosperous by controlling, dominating and restructuring African economies into satellites of European economies.

At the time of 'independence' many African countries had become 'monocrop' economies producing cocoa, coffee, groundnuts, tobacco, tea, sugar cane, etc., to feed European factories at financial returns which by its inequitable arrangement was guaranteed to ensure their steady economic decline. For the price of the African (and the Third World) raw materials would be determined in London, Paris, Washington, or Brussels while European, American and Japanese industrial products exported to Africa and the Third World, are, again, determined by Europe, America and Japan. Analyses of the market prices of most raw materials supplied from Africa and the Third World to Europe, the US and Japan over the past forty years indicate that these have steadily declined in real terms while the prices of industrial goods supplied to the Third World have risen sharply in real terms. Furthermore, large debts incurred by the 'Third World' during the sixties and early seventies, at a time of relatively high economic growth and low interest rates, have now become millstones around the 'necks' of African countries. This has come about through steep and long-sustained increases in interest rates brought about by the deliberate economic policies of the Western nations. Whilst these long-sustained high interest rates have brought enormous profits to Western Bankers and investors, they have wrought devastation on the economic and social development potentials and aspirations of African countries, and have contributed to the syphoning of wealth from the impoverished 'South' to the rich 'North'. For example, in 1985 alone, there was a net transfer of £22,000 million from the former to the latter. This inequitable world economic order is bound inexorably to lead to the continued deterioration in the economic performance of Africa and to the perpetual impoverishment of her people. Hence, while patent colonialism appears to have largely disappeared, neo-colonialism and imperialism still rule supreme!

By the time African demand for independence became militarily and politically irresistable, all Europe had to do was to create a political situation which would ensure that the above economic relationship would be perpetuated; events have shown that they did an excellent job of it. When colonial rule became no longer tenable after the Second World War, the European Powers took steps to ensure that power would be transferred to those African leaders who would maintain the economic order and relationships that Europe had ordained. Wherever possible, they smashed those freedom fighters who appeared to be unamenable to the European grand economic design, and handed power to 'acceptable nationalists' who were more English or more French than the English or the French, respectively.

Contemporary African leaders who dare to challenge such economic arrangements face: (a) overthrow organised by European or American secret agents using local military 'proxies'; (b) direct intervention by a combined force of mercenary and local 'fighters'; (c) overthrow by selfish, ignorant local soldiers who know they can always count on the West after the event; (d) destabilisation by South Africa or by South African-recruited and trained black fighters (where geographically relevant, as in Angola and Mozambique); or (e) joint European/American effort to drive the price of the 'mono-crop', foreign exchange earner, to a level guaranteed to bankrupt the 'offending' country, leading to political turmoil and eventual overthrow of its government.

By these methods, among others, Africa became progressively more impoverished and less capable to deal with such natural disasters as droughts, floods, and so on. Perceived manifest 'reality' pointed to Africa's palpable inability to rule herself or to feed herself, needing White 'aid', Band Aid, Live Aid, Fashion Aid, Sports Aid, etc., to provide the basic necessities of life for her population. (I am not in any way impugning the character, integrity and motive of those individuals and organisations who raise or contribute to such funds. I am saying that the West has so impoverished Africa over the last 500 years that her people need outside charity to survive natural or economic disasters!)

With Africa in such turmoil, the assumptions of the ideology of racism need no constant re-affirmation. It has become 'axiomatic' that black people must be inherently inferior, for they are everywhere socio-economically inferior to white people. Who would take seriously the suggestion that black people in the US, the Caribbean and Europe have been rendered inferior by white people through the process of racial discrimination when 'independent' Africa, the original home of the world's black people, is so impoverished and economically inferior? The ideology of racism operates to ensure that the powers that perpetuate Africa's impoverishment remain invisible while the effect is daily open to observation.

And so, to most people, the claims of the ideology of racism appear on the surface to correlate so closely with perceived reality that they go unchallenged. For how could black people in Africa and the Americas, the Caribbean, Europe and Australia be so palpably and uniformly 'inferior' vis-à-vis white people without some underlying commonly-shared inherent factor which makes the former 'naturally' inferior to the latter? The triumph of the ideology of racism has become unassailable!

Another factor that has led to a toning down, and a more subtle presentation of the ideology of racism was the mass murder of Jews by the Nazis during World War II. As we have shown in our historical analyses of the slave trade and colonial eras, there had been brutal mass murder of black people and Indians in Africa, Australia and the Americas in the past without much protest. But

Hitler introduced a new version of the ideology of racism in which even 'Whites' were graded on the scale of superiority/inferiority ranking order, with the Germans occupying the zenith of human perfection and superiority. The Jews, although white, were lower down the scale of 'whiteness' and could, therefore, be justifiably exterminated. The realisation that the ideology of racism that had justified the murder and enslavement of millions of black people over four centuries could also be used to justify the mass-murder of 'whites', made the presentation of the more crude form of the ideology no longer "acceptable" or "fashionable". A more subtle form of presentation had to be adopted. As a result, a person who strongly believes in the 'natural superiority' of white people or the 'natural inferiority' of black people, would nevertheless take great offence and threaten a libel suit for defamation of character if he was called a racist!

Throughout the above analyses, no evidence has as yet been proffered to rebut the fundamental assumption of the ideology of racism, viz., the assertion of biologically-determined inferiority of the black man relative to the white man. Could not the uniformity and consistency with which the theory has been presented by 'scientists', surgeons, politicians, lawyers, explorers, anthropologists, historians, authors and others over the past four centuries be indicative of the validity of its central claim – a proof that you cannot put down a good theory? After all, the claim made above that the white man, through his power position, deliberately, consciously and systematically rendered the black man inferior is only a hypothesis – at best, another theory. On what solid evidence does one deny or reject the validity of the theory underlying the ideology of racism?

Before we take a closer look at the effect of the ideology of racism on contemporary racial attitudes in general and how it affects in particular the employment opportunities for black people in Britain, I shall address those questions. The validity of the assumptions of the ideology of racism, and the evidence cited as proof, will be subjected to critical analyses to see if they stand the test of established historical facts. To this task, the next three Chapters will be devoted.

Notes

a. *The West and the Rest of Us,* Vintage Books, 1975.

b. Basil Davidson (see *Black Mother,* p.89), Ronald Segal *(The Race War,* p.49), Eric Williams *(Capitalism and Slavery), et. al.,* have shown that the decision to outlaw slavery was not motivated by moral, but economic considerations. Albeit, Britain successfully presented this as a moral and philanthropic act and up to date, still claim it as evidence of Britain's high moral ideals.

c. emphasis mine.

CHAPTER FIVE

Refuting a Myth: Black Egypt – The Origin of Human Civilisation

It was demonstrated in Chapter Three that the overwhelming consensus of opinion among 'scientists' and scholars between the sixteenth and early twentieth centuries was that the black man was naturally inferior to the white man. The evidence to justify this claim, as we noted in David Hume's statement, and the *Encyclopaedia Britannica's* 1884 claims, among others, was that they had neither in the past developed a civilisation on their own as a people, nor had any black, as an individual, demonstrated the capacity to create or invent. At best, black people were imitators who might acquire manual skills, but their limited intellectual capacity precluded them from highly abstract, creative and complex problem-solving activities.

W.S. Jenkins (1935) and C. Putnam (1961), two of the most ardent advocates of the ideology of racism presented what they saw as irrefutable evidence of the black man's immutable inferiority:

> Jenkins: "The social, moral and political as well as the physical history of the Negro race bears strong testimony against them; it furnishes the most undeniable proof of their mental inferiority. *In no age or condition has the real Negro shown a capacity to throw off the chains of barbarism and brutality that have long bound down the nations of that race;*[a] or to rise above the common cloud of darkness that still broods over them... Moreover, *when left alone in his native land, he had never of his own initiative advanced from a state of barbarism to develop a civilization of his own*[a] .... The large continent of Africa stood in plain view as an ever present reminder, a rank wilderness, where the various tribes engaged in incessant attempts to subject each other to slavery.... From the vain search for an indigenous civilization (Cobb drew) the conclusion that the history of the Negro race could not represent a chapter of mere accidents but that it was the fulfilment of manifest destiny.... *The Negro was imitative, but never inventive or suggestive; and by consequence, he could never create a civilization of his own.*"[a1]
>
> "The slaveholder pointed out that on every occasion on which the servile race had gained freedom, after once having been held in bondage, it had inevitably within a time lapsed into barbarism. A most vivid illustration of this tendency was found in the history of Santo Domingo and Haiti. The results of emancipation in this island were a powerful object lesson.... An

official representative of United States in Haiti wrote it was a conviction forced upon him by his observation that 'Negroes only cease to be children when they degenerate into savages.' He was convinced that a short residence there would cause 'the most determined philanthropist to entertain *serious doubts of the possibility of their ever attaining the full stature of intellectual and civilized manhood.*"[a2]

Putnam: "Personally, I feel only affection for the Negro. But there are facts that have to be faced. Any man with two eyes in his head can observe a Negro settlement in the Congo, can study the pure-blooded African in his native habitat as he exists when left on his own resources, can compare this settlement with London or Paris, and can draw his own conclusions regarding levels of character and intelligence which is civilization. *Finally he can enquire as to the number of pure-blooded blacks who have made contribution to great literature or engineering or medicine or philosophy or abstract science*[a].... There is no validity to the argument that the Negro 'hasn't been given a chance'. We were all in caves or trees originally. *The progress which the pure-blooded black has made when left to himself, with a minimum of white help or hindrance genetically or otherwise, can be measured today in the Congo.*"[a3]

"What happens to the Negro even after he has had the advantage of long contact with white men and is then thrown on his resources is well illustrated by Liberia.... A glance at Haiti is also instructive. Although bolstered constantly by help from the United States, Haitian civilization is little above that of Africa. Illiteracy and poverty among the masses are almost universal. The remains of the earlier French civilization have fallen into ruin. Except where restored by American business enterprise, the bridges and roads are nearly impassable. The religion is Voodoo. *Such is the best example available on earth of what a black civilization, led by mulattoes, can accomplish when left to itself.*"[a4]

"...if one searched through all history for the time when the best pure Negro culture, uninfluenced by white help, was at its peak, and then sought the time when the worst pure white culture, was as its bottom, I suppose one might decide that as a white man, one would have preferred to have lived among the Negroes, although I doubt it. I have not heard of any tribal poetry among Negroes comparable to Beowulf or the Nibelungelied.

Of greater importance, it would be well to examine more closely these so-called 'magnificent Negro civilizations' in Africa. At one time, and a very brief one, there were west Sudan Kingdoms with more brilliance than the contemporary one in, say, Scandinavia, but they could not be compared with the contemporary Byzantine Empire or even the troubadour civilization of Provence.

As for the city of Timbuktu, can you mention the Arab-inspired mosque school of that city in the same breath with the University of Paris, also founded in the twelfth century? Which of their medieval professors had the modern influence of St. Thomas Aquinas? Remember also that Timbuktu was ruled by an Arab nobility and a slightly coloured Tuareg upper class. Full-blooded Negroes were at the bottom of the social scale."[5]

The near identical reproduction of the ideology of racism shows the 'originality' of Jenkins and Putnam! Such racial arrogance, stemming from blissful ignorance, was not original; its substance had been monotonously reproduced by several Portuguese, Spanish, Dutch, British and American advocates of racism for four hundred years. Its 'form' or packaging has changed from time to time – after all, ideology, as I pointed out, is dynamic, not static – but the essence has remained unaltered. The ideological imperative, the logic of racism was bound to lead to that conclusion.

To the European mind, the African did not, and indeed could not, have a history prior to the advent of the white man on the African continent. He was benighted; existed in primitive and barbarous state; and had made little progress since his evolution from Homo Sapiens Neanderthalensis (if indeed he evolved that far). Any evidence of civilisation or human advancement in science, art, technology, social organisation, etc, found on the Continent must, as of logical necessity, have been created by Caucasians or by Africans under Caucasian influence and direction. So blinded by the ideology of racism was the European that some of the explanations he offered for the artifacts of human genius found on the continent, were grotesquely absurd!

In this chapter, evidence from established historical facts will be produced to show that: (a) not only have black people, pure, full-blooded black people, created highly advanced civilisations in the past, but that which has been arrogantly termed *Western civilisation* had its foundations laid firmly and incontrovertibly by *black Africans;* and (b) despite a history of the worst, most prolonged, and most barbaric oppression and suppression suffered by any race, many individual black people (as will be shown in Chapter Seven), have manifested the finest human genius, originality and creativity, and have made superb contributions to the understanding and conquest of nature.

The analysis will begin by looking briefly at the ancient African civilisation of Egypt. In Chapter Six, we will focus on the African civilisations of Kush, Zang, Monomotapa, Ghana, Mali and Songhay and, more importantly, we will examine the evidence of the 'race' of the people who were responsible for the development of these civilisations on the African continent.

Ancient Egyptian Civilisation

That the ancient Egyptian civilisation was the oldest, grandest, and most advanced of all known ancient civilisations, there is not the slightest doubt. One of the major stimuli to the beginning of agriculture, leading to sedentary (from nomadic) social life, a pre-condition of civilisation, was the River Nile, the longest in Africa. The River Nile flows 4,127 miles across Africa from lake Nyanza to the Mediteranean. The physical landscape of the area of Africa through which the Nile flows is a vast inclined plane, the highlands of which begin in Central Africa at 3,000 feet above sea level, and rises southward to higher levels, reaching the highest level of 15,000 feet in the Southeastern provinces of the ancient Ethiopian empire, causing the continent to slope down northward. This caused the Nile to flow in the same direction – a tragedy for the black African as we shall soon see.

For its first 3,372 miles through the heart of black Africa, it sank as it cut deep canyons in the soft limestone soil, leaving cliffs at places from a few hundred to a thousand feet high. This means that for over 3,000 miles through the eastern side of the continent, the Nile was collecting the rich soil carried to it by heavy rains and a thousand tributaries. At its last stretch of 750 miles to the Mediterranean sea, the hard sandstone bottom above Assuan (Aswan) causes the Nile to rise and begin its periodic overflow, depositing silt and enriching the soil, making it highly fertile for agriculture.

It was previously believed by some historians that the Ethiopians[b] moved to the Nile Valley, and began cultivating cereals about 8,000 years ago. But there is now evidence to suggest that agriculture began, not in India 9,000 years ago as some Western historians are wont to claim, but in southern Egypt 10,000 years earlier than previously believed. An international team of Egyptian, Polish and US scientists found remants of cultivated barley with a radio-carbon date of 17,000 to 18,300 years ago. During the Nubian salvage campaign (to which I shall later return), numerous agricultural tools dated 14,500 + 490 years old were uncovered, giving further proof of an African site for the earliest known origin of cereal cultivation.[6]

A further migratory movement towards the Nile came from the West. As the Tassili engravings discovered by a team of French scientists confirmed, the Sahara Desert was once a land of flowing rivers and green pastures. However, about 7,000 years ago the Saharan climate became less wet and rivers began to dry up. The Saharan people turned increasingly to rearing cattle and other livestock; and the pressure of more hostile climatic changes led to population movements towards the Nile.

As agriculture expanded, and increased skills and better tools led to better harvest, Upper Ethiopia (later to be called Egypt) became the "Bread Basket of the World", attracting more migrants not only from the Southern and Western regions of Africa, but from Asia as well, a fact which as alluded to above, was to lead to tragic consequences for the Africans. Had the rich fertile Nile Valley been located two thousand miles south of, rather than 750 miles northward towards, the Mediterranean, black African history might have been different – white migrants might have found it much more impenetrable.

The exact period of the 'Asian' migration to Egypt is not known; it should however be noted that the term 'Asian' is used generically to denote white immigrants who were Hebrews, Syrians, Hittites Persians, Babylonians, Assyrians, Turks, Arabs, Indians and so on. These Asians settled along the Mediterranean and by 3,000 BC[c], occupied what came to be known later as Lower Egypt, comprising about a quarter of Egypt.

The fertility of the Nile Valley depended on the annual flooding of the Nile. This natural environmental condition imposed on the Egyptians the need to regulate their whole socio-economic lives around that event. This in turn, led to the need to observe and to establish the regularity and uniformity of the movement of the stars, hence the development of astronomy and the invention of the "calendar". Survival depended on social co-operation and as the Egyptians became more organised so their community became more complex, leading to the rise of central political authority and the institution of 'kingship'. The need for a more precise and equitable distribution of the land after the annual flooding and subsequent boundary locations led to the invention of geometry, etc.

By the end of the fourth millenium BC, an increasingly complex and sophisticated urban society was thriving in Chem or Northern Ethiopia (later called Upper Egypt). The black people had established their capital at Nekheb, with Thebes and Napata being their cultural centres. But tensions between the black people in Upper Egypt and the white people (Asians) in Lower Egypt led to conflicts and wars between them, culminating finally in the victory of King Menes of Ethiopia (also known as Narmer) and the unification of the 'Two Lands' at around 3200 BC. "As the historic period opened in Egypt, it appeared that the Africans were retaking the whole of their country. The Palermo Stone records victory after victory over the Asians. Finally, the great triumph came when the African King, Menes, defeated the Asians decisively, united all Egypt under African rule again, and thus began the historic First Dynasty."[7]

After the defeat of the Asian North, the capital of the Ethiopian empire which now extended from the Mediterranean to the source of the Nile, was moved from Nekheb to Thinis, near Abydos. Menes then set about to construct a new strategic city – Memphis (the city of Menes) was constructed on a site reclaimed by building a great dam at the border between Upper and Lower Egypt in order to divert the course of the Nile; and for "generations, Memphis was almost entirely an all-African city, with white Asian villages slowly growing up around the outskirts."[8]

Hitherto, the name Egypt has been used above, but the name did not in fact exist prior to the building of Memphis, city of Menes. For

Menes, the first 'Pharaoh' of Egypt

Memphis was also call "Hikuptah", or the "Mansion of the Soul of Ptah", the god-protector of the city. The Greek rendition of Hikuptah – "Aigyptos" – later became the name of the "Two Lands", extending from the Mediterranean to the First Cataract.

In a period of peace and tranquility that ensued, agriculture expanded, with vast food surpluses; commercial trade developed; gold, copper and tin were mined; vast stone quarries were opened up. Great prosperity spread through the land and with it, rapid development and advancement. The supreme genius of man was never more in evidence than the first 1,500 years of Egyptian Dynastic rule. The height of engineering skills attained, still confound the twentieth-century man, despite his scientific and technological advancement.

"Within the first 700 years of King Menes' first Dynastic rule, there was enough power and wealth, as well as enough skill and scientific understanding, to build the great Pyramid of Cheops, quickly followed by the almost as imposing Pyramids of Chephren and Mycerinus."[9]

Despite the vandalism of modern white fortune hunting predators, at least recognisable remains of 80 Pyramids can still be found in Sudan and Egypt, of which the greatest is the Great Pyramid. The great Pyramid of Cheops at Giza, first of the seven wonders of the world, built as a tomb, is estimated to consist of over 2,000,000 blocks of well-trimmed limestone, each weighing between 2.5 and 15 tonnes (total estimated weight of some 6 million tons of stone). The square base originally measured 755.43ft., 755.88 ft. and 755.77 ft. on its north, south, east and west sides respectively. The height was 481.4 ft. and the base covered an area of 13.1 acres. Large enough to hold the English Westminster Abbey and St. Paul's Cathedral plus the cathedrals of Florence, Milan and St. Peter's in Rome, the Great Pyramid is so massive that if broken up into 1-foot cubes, it would stretch two-thirds of the way around the equator. And yet the right angles, at each corner of the base, line the walls up almost perfectly with the four cardinal points; with the angles accurate within 0.07°. "It is a fact that half the perimeter of the base divided by the height is 3.1408392; compared to the modern value of pi of 3.1415927, the difference is only 0.0007535."[10]

The degree of scientific knowledge and engineering skills required to cut the stones, transport, and construct such gigantic structures to attain such geometrical precision, boggles the mind. For example, murals found in the tomb of Hatshepsut, a woman Pharaoh (around 1500 BC), show one barge, carrying a 600-ton load of two obelisks, being towed by a fleet of 30 ships. How the 300-ton obelisk was loaded and unloaded is still a mystery. But, in fact, evidence of much larger barges of Queen Hatshepsut have been discovered. These have been estimated at 95 metres in length with a beam of 32 metres and a deadweight of 2,500 tons. The two obelisks transported by these barges were 108 cubits (57 metres) high, each weighing 2,400 tons. One of these barges was hauled by 30 tugboats, manned by almost 1,000 oarsmen.

Hundreds of these obelisks and millions of stones weighing several tons each were transported to build temples, pyramids and palaces. The Egyptians obviously had advanced shipbuilding knowledge and skills. Furthermore, consider the managerial, administrative and organisational skills required to plan, organise workers, co-ordinate numerous engineers, mathematicians, and artisans, procure the necessary materials, food and drink for the thousands of workers, etc. for such large-scale projects.

John Pappademos[11] has catalogued from available research works some of the achievements of the ancient Egyptians in Physics. The Egyptians, he notes, were centuries ahead of Europeans in mining, metallurgy (including metal alloying); metals fabrication (including making wires and rivets); glass-making; medical science (including internal medicine, anatomy and surgery); development of complex irrigation systems and carpentry. There is evidence that they were smelting iron and steel and even welding these metals as early as 1500-1200 BC.

To the Egyptians, Pappademos continues, we owe the concepts of most of the fundamental physical quantities: distance, area, volume, weight and time. Europe is indebted to Egypt for the invention of standards, units, and methods for accurate measurement of all of these quantities. The idea of letting a symbol represent an unknown quantity in algebra is owed to the Egyptians, who used it in solving equations of the first and second degree. The scientific measurement of time started with the Egyptians. Based on their stellar observations, the calendar they developed as far back as 4241 BC is the one we use today, with only two minor modifications. The Egyptian calendar year contained 365 days: 12 months of 30 days each, plus five festival days and has been termed "the only intelligent calendar which ever existed in human history" by Otto Neugebauer,[12] who dismisses the Babylonian and Greek calendars as far inferior.

The practice of dividing the day into 24 hours and starting the day at midnight was devised by the Egyptians who also used sundials and water clocks for measurement of smaller intervals of time. The most ancient sundial known is Egyptian, dating back to the time of Thutmosis III (fifteenth century BC); preceded of course by the invention of the water clock in 2000 BC. The latter was still in use in Europe as late as the time of Galileo, who used one in his experiments on accelerated motion.

The Egyptian knowledge of astronomy is evidenced by their

calendar, tables of star culminations, tables of star risings, and instruments such as the ingenious sundials. Their astronomers were also aware of the precision of the equinoxes, indicated by the successive reorientation of the axes of a number of their stellar temples. Finally, the obelisks which were found all over Egypt, were a symbol of the sun-god Ra, but also had astronomical significance as well. From the shadows cast by the obelisks in the brilliant Egyptian sun, information relevant to timekeeping could be gained: the date of the summer solstice (21st June) when the obelisk casts the shortest shadow, the winter solstice (21st December) when the sun is lowest and the shadow the longest; and the dates of the vernal and autumnal equinoxes, (21st March and 21st September) when the shadows fall along an east-west line at sunrise and sunset. The taller the obelisk, the longer the shadow and the more accurate the measurement. This explains the need for the increasing size of the obelisks over the centuries.

Few modern Egyptologists would deny the enormous contributions made by the Egyptians to the so-called 'Western Civilisation', through the Greeks; although most modern Western scientists and historians, for obvious reaons, would want to look no further than the ancient Greeks. The truth, backed by historical evidence, is that most of the best known Greek philosophers either studied in Egypt, under Egyptian scholars or were taught by those trained in Egypt; among these were Pythagoras, Solon, Archimedes and Erastosthenes. In fact, two-thirds of the Greek scholars are said to have studied in Egypt.

In a highly well researched book, Professor George James[13] asserts categorically that the term Greek Philosophy is a misnomer, for there is no such philosophy in existence. The Greeks, he states, were not the originators of 'Greek Philosophy', but the Black People of North Africa, commonly called the Egyptians. In his book, James argues, with documentary evidence, that not only did most of the Greek Philosophers study in Egypt, but that their basic philosophical doctrines derived directly from the Ancient Egyptian Mysteries which encapsulated the body of organised knowlege in Religion, Science, Mathematics, Music, Logic, Astronomy, Physics, Architecture, etc., possessed by the Egyptian priests and scholars.

Professor James' analyses may come as a shock – an epistemological earthquake – to most Western scholars whose beliefs are firmly rooted in the paradigm, one of the cardinal assumptions of which is that the Greeks laid the foundations of 'Western Philosophy and Civilisation'. But while many may be persuaded by available evidence to accept that it was the ancient Egyptians (not the Greeks) who laid the foundations of 'Western Civilisation', what very few will be prepared to accept is that the true originators of that civilisation were not only Africans but *black Africans*. Western scholars have had no difficulties attributing the remains of past civilisations such as monuments and artifacts to the ancestors of natives of any country. For example, without the slightest hesitation, the Inca civilisation has been attributed to the ancestors of the American Indians of Peru; and the Aztec civilisation to the Mexican Indians. The same can be said of ancient Persian, Chinese, Korean, Indian, Greek, Roman civilisations. In Africa, however, every evidence of past civilisation has been either ascribed to Caucasians or in some cases (believe it or not!) to extra-terrestial beings. The reason for this is simple: the ideology of racism, *ut supra*, operates within a paradigm which assumes that black people are biologically inferior and, *ex hypothesi*, have never created any civilisation of their own in the past; and have not, as individuals, made any contribution to the conquest of nature. Any evidence of past civilisation in Africa, therefore, has to be rationalised within the logic of the ideology's fundamental assumption. Different conclusions can only be reached outside of that paradigm. Like the metaphor of the train and rail lines used above, any change of course outside of the pre-determined direction of the rail tracks, would lead to a derailment of the ideology. This is why most European scholars when faced with incontrovertible evidence of a highly advanced 'black African' civilisation, have to agonisingly seek explanations elsewhere. When the imposing presence of Africa's brilliant past could not be covered up, "European genius" found a 'rational explanation' - the white man was in Africa before the African! The Caucasian was in Egypt before the African! Note that the whites in South Africa today, claim they arrived in South Africa before the 'Bantus'.

The reality, however, is that Africa, the second largest continent in the world, covering 12,000,000 sq. miles, 5,000 miles from north to south, 4,600 miles from east to west, was once known as BILAD AS SUDAN, "The Land of the Blacks". Caucasian presence anywhere on the Continent was a result of immigration from Eurasia.

Since the West attributes 'Western Civilisation' to the Greeks, let us see what the ancient Greeks had to say about the Egyptians whose civilisation developed thousands of years before the former's. Asa Hilliard, Dean of School of Education, San Francisco State University, in the introduction to the 1976 reprint of Professor James' book, op.cit., quotes Herodotus, the "Father of History", describing the Egyptians as "burnt-skinned, flat-nosed, thick-lipped and wooly-haired".[14]

Professor Pappademos, op.cit., states "The Greeks generally viewed Egypt as the seat of scientific knowledge. Socrates, in the

Phaidros, called the Egyptian god Thoth, the inventor of writing, astronomy, and geometry. Herodotus had a similarly high opinion of Egyptian science, stating that the Greeks learned geometry from the Egyptians. It was Democritos of Abdera's boast that his own scientific abilities were unsurpassed in the world, not exceeded by even the Egyptian scholars. The most brilliant of the Greek students of science such as Thales of Miletos (c. 600 BC), Democritos, Pythagoras, and Eudoxos (404-355 BC) travelled to Egypt to study. Seneca tell us that Eudoxos had to go to Egypt to study planetary motion; at that time, Egypt must have been the world's leading centre of astronomy. Pythagoras (c. 6th century BC) spent no less than 22 years in Egypt studying astronomy, geometry and the mysteries."[15]

Pappademos notes that Herodotus characterised the colour of the Egyptians as *black* wherever the question of their colour was mentioned and had no difficulty in seeing close kinship between the Ethiopians and the Egyptians.[16]

Herodotus is further quoted as affirming that the following came into Greece from Egypt: "almost all the names of the gods", astrology, geometry, the correct calendar, and astronomy.[17] On medical science, Herodotus states that "The Egyptians have also discovered more prognostics than all the rest of mankind besides. Whenever a prodigy takes place, they watch and record the result; then, if anything similar ever happens again, they expect the same consequences".[18] On specialisation, he comments that "Medicine is practised among them on a plan of separation; each physician treats a single disorder, and no more; thus the country swarms with medical practitioners, some undertaking to cure diseases of the eye, others of the head, others again of the teeth, others of the intestines, and some those which are not local."[19]

Isocrates also states that Pythagorus introduced Philosophy into Greece after study among Egyptian priests and that his instructions included medicine. He states of Pythagorus's instructors: "and the priests, because they enjoyed such conditions of life, discovered for the body the aid which the medical art affords, not that which uses dangerous drugs, but drugs of such a nature that they are as harmless as daily food, yet in their effects are so beneficial that all men agree the Egyptians are the healthiest and most long of life among men; and then for the soul they introduced philosophy's training, a pursuit which has the power, not only to establish laws but also to investigate the nature of the universe."[20] Isocrates firmly confirms Professor James's contention of the Egyptians being the originators of 'Greek Philosophy'.

Basil Davidson also investigated what the ancient Greeks said about the ancient Egyptians. It is instructive to quote here in full

Professor Basil Davidson's summary of the Greeks' attitude towards the Egyptians:

"But the Greeks had quite different notions about their neighbours across the Mediterranean sea. They trafficked much with Libya and Egypt, since they had trading colonies there. They knew the Egyptians at first hand, and were bound to admire them. For those Egyptians, although their mighty civilization was then well past its peak, were still the leaders of the world in terms of civic order and scientific advance. Built 2,000 years before the Parthenon of Athens, the Pyramids of Gizeh were not only the largest stone buildings ever constructed anywhere; they were also, by their astonishing symmetry, monuments to a mathematical science which the Greeks were only beginning to master.

To the Greeks, moreover, the Egypt of the Pharaohs was the threshold across which innumerable marvel could be glimpsed. Here was the source of spiritual wisdom, because 'the names of nearly all the gods', as Herodotus commented to readers who could have found nothing strange about the statement, 'came to Greece from Egypt'. Yet if Egypt was the source of spiritual wisdom for the Greeks, it was not the origin of the wisdom. This lay further south.

It lay in the lands of the African interior which the Greeks did not know, where dwelt 'the long-lived black peoples' who 'are said to be the tallest and best looking people in the world'. Here, in other words, deviancy from the norm did not grow with distance. On the contrary, because of the belief in Africa's spiritual primacy, it lessened with distance. Those who read Herodotus would have known this already. Homer's Iliad had long prepared them for the information with its tale of how the gods of Greece went every year to 'the Ethiopians' (which we should properly translate as 'black peoples') for an all-god banquet:

> For Zeus had yesterday to Ocean's bounds
> Set forth to feast with Ethiop's faultless men,
> And he was followed there by all the gods.

What was wisest and most ancient came out of Africa. That was the general belief, and it marked the general attitude of the ancient Greeks, the endlessly inquisitive founders of our own civilization. And they set forth this attitude in their many works of art displaying African motifs. Nothing shows it better than a type of two-headed vase, known as kantheros, of which several fine examples have survived.[d] For the Greeks of antiquity, the black peoples were different from themselves, but equal to themselves or even, at times, superior.

Herodotus called Egypt 'the gift of the Nile', a bountiful land made available to men by the flood-laid silt of the famous river, building up its soil year after year. *He and his readers also saw the Egyptians as being absolutely African in origin and nature.*[e] Here along the Nile, Egyptians had fashioned the highest civilization any where, and this civilization, for the Greeks, was African. In support of this they proceeded to add historical explanations to the mythology of the Iliad, and some of their explanations reveal an extraordinary prescience.

Writing in about 50 BC the Sicilian Greek historian Diodorus summarized the specialist views of his time. By then the Ptolemies, kings of Greek origin, had been ruling Egypt for almost three centuries, and Greek knowledge of that region of Africa was correspondingly capacious. The black peoples, wrote

Diodorus, 'were the first of all men, and the proofs of this statement, historians agree, are manifest'.
He recorded another agreement among historians. This was that 'the Egyptians are colonists sent out by the Ethiopians (the black peoples of the African interior) and the most part of Egyptian customs are Ethiopian, with the colonists still preserving their ancient manners'. Manners and beliefs, that is, concerning the divine appointment of kings, life after death, the value of consulting oracles, or, in more humdrum terms, the customs of everyday life.
Later European attitudes lifted the Egypt of the Pharaohs entirely out of African history, and either added it to the history of western Asia or assigned it to a mysterious isolation. Diodorus and his colleagues, as we have seen, thought just the reverse, and modern science, notably over the past 30 years or so, has gone far to show that Diodorus was right."[21]

Professor Davidson concludes:

"to summarise these findings about the inner African origins of Pharaonic civilization: the earliest population movements into the valley of the Nile were predominantly from the south and west; the earliest state-forming influence moved in the same direction – not from the north to the south, but the reverse; in modern terms, the Egypt of the Pharaohs was first and foremost the product of black initiative and progress."e[22]

Dr Diop also reaches the same conclusion and states emphatically:

"*Ancient Egypt was a Negro civilization.... The Ancient Egyptians were Negroes.*"[23]

Many black and white scholars such as W.E.B. DuBois, C.de Volney, Abbe Emile Amelineau, had come to similar conclusions. Dr Cheikh Anta Diop, historian, physicist, philosopher, and the first black African Egyptologist, in a book entitled *The African Origin of Civilization, Myth or Reality,* notes the reaction of one of the first French scholars to visit Egypt and that of the later Western Egyptologists. He quotes Count Constanti de Volney (1757-1820) reporting on the Copts, the Egyptian race that had produced the Pharaohs:

"...all have a bloated face, puffed up eyes, flat nose, thick lips; in a word, the true face of the mulatto. I was tempted to attribute it to the climate, but when I visited the Sphinx, its appearance gave me the key to the riddle. On seeing that head, typically Negro in all its features, I remembered the remarkable passage where Herodotus says: "as for me, I judge the Colchians to be a colony of the Egyptians because, like them, they are black with wooly hair..." In other words, *the ancient Egyptians were true Negroes of the same type as all native-born Africans.** That being so, we can see how their blood, mixed for several centuries with that of the Romans and Greeks, must have lost the intensity of its original colour, while retaining nonetheless the imprint of its original mould. We can even state as a general principle that the face is a kind of monument able, in many cases, to attest or shed light on historical evidence on the origins of peoples."

After illustrating this proposition by citing the case of Normans who still resembled the Danes 900 years after the conquest of Normandy, Volney adds:

> "But returning to Egypt, the lesson she teaches history contains many reflections for philosophy. What a subject for meditation, to see the present barbarism and ignorance of the Copts, descendants of the alliance between the profound genius of the Egyptians and the brilliant mind of the Greeks! *Just think that this race of black men, today our slaves and object of our scorn, is the very race to which we owe our arts, sciences, and even the use of speech!" Just imagine, finally, that it is in the midst of peoples who call themselves the greatest friends of liberty and humanity that one has approved the most barbarous slavery and questioned whether black men have the same kind of intelligence as Whites!"[24]*

Abbe Emile Amelineau (1850-1916), a great Egyptologist, archaeologist and Professor of the History of Religions, excavated at Om El'Gaab, near Abydos, and discovered Osiris' tomb at Abydos, proving that Osiris was not a mythical hero, but an historic personage, an initial ancestor of the Pharaohs, a black ancestor, as was his sister, Isis. Amelineau concluded in his theory of the race of the Ancient Egyptian:

> "....It clearly follows from what has been stated earlier: *Egyptian civilization is not of Asiatic, but of African origin, of Negroid origin,* however paradoxical this may seem. *We are not accustomed, in fact, to endow the Black or related races with too much intelligence, or even with enough intelligence to make the first discoveries necessary for civilization.* Yet, there is not a single tribe inhabiting the African interior that has not possessed and does not still possess at least one of those first discoveries."[25]

But, wait a minute, this is revolutionary thought! It threatens to overthrow by sheer force of factual, incontrovertible evidence the central plank on which the ideology of racism was constructed. After all, black slavery was at its peak. What would happen if black people were to learn that contrary to the claim that they were the most inferior of all races – incapable of developing a civilisation of their own – that white people (their enslavers!) in fact owed their civilisation to the black ancestors of Egypt? And what would be the effect on white people who had legitimised the most barbaric slavery on the assumption that black people were sub-human and therefore could not be expected to be treated as 'normal' human beings? Would there not be widespread condemnation of the slavery system and immediate mass demands for its abolition? What would then happen to the plantations and the whole economic system on which European prosperity depended? This is treasonable and seditious talk!

After the initial shock following this bombshell, the ideology of racism quickly reasserted itself. Dr Diop observes that,

"Egyptologists were dumbfounded with admiration for the past grandeur and perfection then discovered. They gradually recognised it as the most ancient civilization that had engendered all others. But imperialism being what it is it became increasingly inadmissible to continue to accept the theory – evident until then – of a Negro Egypt. The birth of Egyptology was thus marked by the need to destroy the memory of a Negro Egypt at any cost and in all minds. Henceforth, the common denominator of all the theses of the Egyptologists, their close relationship and profound affinity, can be characterized as a desperate attempt to refute that opinion. Almost all Egyptologists stress its falsity as a matter of course. Usually these attempted refutations take the following form:
    Unable to detect any contradiction in the formal statements of the Ancients after an objective confrontation with total Egyptian reality, and consequently unable to disprove them, they either give them the silent treatment or reject them dogmatically and indignantly. They express regret that people as normal as the ancient Egyptians could have made so grievous an error and thus create so many difficulties and delicate problems for modern specialists. Next they try in vain to find a White origin for Egyptian civilization. They finally become mired down in their own contradictions, sliding over the difficulties of the problem after performing intellectual acrobatics as learned as they are unwarranted. They then repeat the initial dogma, judging that they have demonstrated to all honourable folk the White origin of Egyptian civilization."[26]

Dr Diop's analysis confirms our contention of the potency of an ideology and its capacity to triumph even in the face of objective factual evidence, contradicting its fundamental assumptions.

From the above historical evidence and analyses, we can confidently state that: (a) what has been termed "Western Philosophy", "Western Civilisation", mathematics, physics, medical science, geometry, astronomy and many other branches of science derived not from the Greeks, but from the Egyptians; (b) the Egyptian civilisation was the most ancient, the grandest, and most advanced of all ancient civilisations; (c) the originators of this – the world's first recorded civilisation – were black Africans; (d) the civilisation built in Egypt by these black Africans had its origins from the African interior, ie, contrary to Western belief, the Egyptian civilisation moved northwards from the African interior and *not* southward from the Mediterranean; and (e) the later falsification of the available historical and archaeological evidence was to preserve the integrity of the ideology of racism.

Point (d) above requires further analysis and elaboration. The acquisition of complex knowledge and/or skills are never instantaneous, but gradual, progressive, incremental, cumulative. Before a child can learn to run, it must first learn to crawl, to stand erect and to walk. These skills are acquired progessively, as intricate muscular movements and control, and limb manipulation are, through the process of trial and error, learned, stored in the brain and habituated by countless repetition. The development of the sciences and the various ingenious inventions and discoveries, such as mathematics, astronomy, the calendar, religion, agriculture, technique, engineering, sculpture and architecture, followed a process of progressive and cumulative development of knowledge and experimentation. Let us take a look at the construction of the pyramids as an example.

If the white people (Asians) who occupied Lower Egypt, along the Mediterranean, were responsible for their construction, we would expect to find evidence of earlier, less complex, architectural structures either in the region they occupied or the part of the world from whence they migrated. If, on the other hand, the Ethiopians (note that "Ethiopian" is the Greek rendering of black or the "sun-burnt" people), ie black Africans, were the architects and builders of these pyramids, the evidence would lie on the migratory route northward from the African interior.

Chancellor Williams informs us that

> "The time continuum in the history of the blacks is highly important in reference to the state of civilization from which the invading groups came during the first thousand years of Black ascendency in Egypt and Southern Ethiopia (the Sudan). The record is quite clear that the incursive groups [the Asians] were largely tent-dwelling nomads. They had no tradition of great cities with imposing temples, obelisks, pyramids or, indeed, stone masonry at all. In particular, one should note the number of centuries after Thebes and Memphis before their ancient cities were founded:

Nowe (Thebes)	Prehistory
Memphis	3100 BC
Rome (Village)	1000 BC
Rome (Town)	250 BC
Athens (Village)	1200 BC
Athens (City)	360 BC
Antioch	400 BC
Jerusalem	1400 BC
Babylon	2100 BC

> In short, what great contributions did these roaming nomads have to make to an already highly developed black civilization? Since even Jerusalem was not in existence, what people in Lower Egypt came from a country with a city as great as Thebes or Memphis?"[27]

Before the pyramids of Gizeh, there were the great temples of Thebes and Napata; before Memphis, the city of the black king Menes, there was Thebes (Nowe), the most ancient and most important city of black civilisation. Indeed, all Upper Egypt was variously once called: (a) Thebald after its greatest city, Thebes, and its people – the black Thebans; (b) Ethiopia which means 'The Black Land'; and (c) Chem which also means 'The Black Land' (not 'black soil' as Pliny was later to suggest). The process of designing and constructing had, therefore, been long and progressively learned and mastered, before they designed and built the pyramids; and the evidence *all* lay in the south, towards the African hinterland, *not*

north, towards the Mediterranean, nor east along the Isthmus of
Suez, the points of white entry into Africa!
The historical evidence of the different stages of experimentation
and development, leading to the true pyramid, has been analysed by
Beatrice Lumpkin. The designers, organisers, and builders of the
Pyramids did not come suddenly on the Egyptian scene and perform
a series of miracles. The miracle, if there was a miracle, observed
Lumpkin, lies in the genius of the Egyptian people. "Pyramid
building 'developed directly from crude brick construction', according to Lauer. Thus the basic technology for pyramid building came
from the genius of the common people, the unknown inventors who
progessed from mud-daubed red huts to shaping the Nile mud into
bricks to bake in the sun for more comfortable, durable housing."[28]

The first pyramid was designed for King Zoser (a Black Pharaoh)
at Saqqara by Imhotep, the world's first multi-genius (of whom we
shall have more to say), who was undoubtedly a *black* man.
Imhotep's successful design followed a five-stage scientific experiment.

> "The first step was to build a large stone mastaba, resembling the huge mud
> brick tombs of earlier kings, but built in lasting stone. Mastaba is the
> modern Arabic word for the benches built outside of peasant homes which
> have the same shape as these tombs. Then the base was enlarged. Taking
> advantage of the strength of the stone blocks, Imhotep made a further
> innovation. He added, on top of the mastaba, a series of three other mastaba,
> each smaller than the one beneath. The base was enlarged again and
> additional layers added to make a total of 6 steps, all made of stone from the
> nearby quarries. The step pyramid which resulted was then encased with
> fine limestone quarried from the Tura and Masura hills across the river and
> ferried to the west bank.
> Almost as impressive as the pyramid itself was the stone wall which
> enclosed the pyramid, 30 ft. high and 990 ft. by 1,785 ft. in its length and
> width, with 14 imitation gates cut into the stone. The burial chamber itself,
> for such was the purpose of the pyramid, was in a chamber cut out of the rock
> beneath the pyramid and reached by a passageway outside of the pyramid.
> Although relatively small stones were used in the basic construction, a 3-ton
> granite plug sealed the hole in the ceiling of the burial chamber."[29]

The knowledge and experience gained from the step-pyramid
became an indispensable input to the design and construction of
later pyramids. The proceeding pyramids showed the steps becoming progressively smooth-sloping. The use of larger, more massive
stones which had the advantage of greater stablility and required
less cutting labour were introduced as the technological know-how
of transporting massive stones increased.

> "At Meidum a 7-step pyramid was built. Then the steps were filled in until
> the sides sloped like a true pyramid. A final casing of good limestone finished
> the first true pyramid. The angle of inclination was similar to that of Zoser's,
> 75°. But this angle proved too steep for a pyramid at Dashur, one of the first
> designed originally as a true pyramid.
> The famous Bent Pyramid of Dashur was started with an incline of 54°31′.

Supporting timbers, still in place, indicate that structural weaknesses developed. The angle of incline was abruptly decreased to 43°21' and the reduced pyramid was finished in haste. This experience possibly led to excessive caution in building the nearby Northern Stone Pyramid of Dashur, the earliest tomb completed as a pyramid. Its angle of inclination is only 43°40' instead of the 52° used in the subsequent pyramids, resulting in a lower pyramid.

This record of experimentation in pyramid-building provides the background for appreciating some of the Egyptian mathematics which has come down to us. Very likely we know only a fragment of the mathematics of these ancient Africans, but it is a very interesting fragment."[30]

With no shred of evidence of such architectural evolution in Lower Egypt, how could the building of the Pyramids be attributed to the Asians?

One of the arguments previously used by most European historians to deny the black African origin of Egyptian civilisation was that the social institution of "divine kingship" was not an African invention. Kingships and kingdoms, they asserted, originated from the Middle East, were introduced to Egypt by the migrating Caucasians (Asians), and from thence, spread southward to the rest of Africa. Evidence from archaeological excavation dealt a decisive and fatal blow to this theory.

The building of the Aswan Dam in the 1960s meant that an area, believed to be rich in unexcavated sites, was going to be flooded. An International Nubian Rescue Mission began excavation to salvage as much as possible before the flooding. A team of Egyptologists headed by the late Keith Seele from the Oriental Institute of the University of Chicago was assigned a site of an ancient cemetery at a place called Qustul in ancient Nubia, inside the modern Republic of Sudan. Quantities of artifacts were found, catalogued and assessed and the results were published by Bruce Williams of the Chicago Institute. To the Euro-centric historian, the evidence was dynamite, for it blew sky-high the assumption that the Egyptian civilisation had originated in the north of Egypt and spread south. "For here was strong evidence for a succession of 12 kings who had ruled in Nubia – in Ta-Seti, the 'Land of the Bow', as it was called then – long before the rise of the first historic Egyptian dynasty. Here was highly recognisable 'divine kingship' and correspondingly advanced political organisation, established in the distant south, several generations before it was clearly fashioned in the north."[31]

So, here in Ta-Seti was clear evidence that the Egyptian civilisation had not burst on the Nile Valley scene suddenly and mysteriously, but had been the result of a process of evolutionary development, originating in the south and moving northwards. Here, at least 360 years before the first Pharaonic dynasty was established by the Ethiopian king Menes, was a relatively well-advanced black civilisation. The art of writing, contrary to previous belief, had been invented in Ta-Seti and carried over to Egypt. Surely, if the Egyptian civilisation was the product of a Caucasian race, it would be absurd to suggest that they left a benighted Asian or European homeland, crossed the Mediterranean or the Isthmus of Suez into Africa and, ignoring the lush, fertile Nile valley, trekked thousands of miles south into the African interior; and finally started a slow movement back to their point of entry into Africa, spreading evidence of a developing civilisation only on their return journey!

The evidence of a black-initiated Egyptian civilisation, on the other hand, is entirely consistent with archaeological, linguistic[f] and ancient historical evidence. The Tassili pictures and handbuilt pottery of the eastward migrating Africans; the artifacts of Tasian, Badarian (circa 7471 BC), Amratian (circa 6500 BC), protodynastic Blacks; the evidence unearthed by the International Nubian Rescue Mission; the evidence from the prehistoric black city of Thebes (Nowe); the fact that the plants and animals represented in the hieroglyphics are found in Nubia, the African interior, and not in Lower Egypt; all attest to a civilisation originated by black Africans from the South (and to a lesser extent, from the West), migrating to, and settling in the Nile Valley. This conclusion is firmly supported by the ancients who insisted on the anteriority of Ethiopia to Egypt and the fact that the latter was merely a colony of the former; as well as the claims of the ancient Ethiopians themselves. Indeed, throughout Antiquity, the Meroitic Sudan was even believed to be the birth place of humanity. As Cherubini, Champollion-Figeac's travelling companion observed:

"The human race must have been considered there as spontaneous, having been born in the upper areas of Ethiopia where the two sources of life – heat and humidity – are ever present. It is also in this region that the first glimmerings of history reveal the origin of societies and the primitive home of civilization. In the earliest Antiquity, before the ordinary calculations of history, a social organization appears, fully structured, with its religion, laws and institutions. The Ethiopians boasted of having been the first to establish worship of the divinity and the use of sacrifices. There, too, the torch of science and the arts was probably first lighted. To this people we must attribute the origin of sculpture, the use of written symbols, in short, the start of all the developments that make up an advanced civilization.[32]

"...They boasted of having preceded the other peoples on earth and about the real or relative superiority of their civilization while most societies were still in their infancy, and they seemed to justify their claims. No evidence attributed to any other source the beginning of the Ethiopian family. On the contrary, a combination of very important facts tended to assign it a purely local origin at an early date."[33]

"Ethiopian was considered as a country apart. From this more or less paradisiacal source, the beginnings of life, the origin of living beings, seemed to emanate...

Except for some particulars furnished by the Father of History on those Ethiopians known as Macrobians, there was a rather hazy idea that Ethiopia produced men who surpassed the rest of humanity in height, beauty and longevity. One nevertheless recognized two great indigenous nations in Africa: the Libyans and the Ethiopians. The latter included the south-ernmost peoples of the Black race; they were thus distinguished from the Libyans who, occupying the north of Africa, were less tanned by the sun. Such is the information that the Ancients have provided. . ."[34]

"It is reasonable to assume that nowhere else on earth could we find a civilization whose progress would seem more certain and present such unquestionable evidence of priority. . . Consistent with the original monuments, the writings of scholarly philosophical antiquity authentically testify to this anteriority. In the history of primitive societies, perhaps no fact is supported by more complete and more decisive unanimity."[35]

Despite the abundant evidence and the categoric statements of the very scientists and philosophers who have transmitted present-day civilisation to us – from Herodotus to Diodorus, from Greece to Rome – that they borrowed that civilisation from black Ethiopians of the Nile Valley (the Egyptians), Cherubini and Champollion-Figeac, like Champollion the Younger before them, and many archaeologists, Egyptologists, and historians after them, sought to defind the indefensible by seeking to reinterpret the facts to prove that the original Egyptians were Caucasians. As Diop's analyses of their works show, their efforts only led to a quagmire of contradic-tion, illogicality and absurdity.

Faced with the unanimous testimony of the ancients that, first the Ethiopians, then the Egyptians (who were of Ethiopian orgin), created and raised to an extraordinary stage of development all the elements of civilisation, while other peoples, especially the Eura-sians, were still deep in barbarism; baffled by the constant reference to the Egyptians by the ancient Greek historians and philosophers as being black-skinned (using 'melanochroes', the strongest word in Greek to express blackness); confronted by the fact that the Egyptians used the word 'Khem' – black – to refer to themselves and 'Kemit' – land of the blacks – to refer to their country; confused by the knowledge that the Egyptians painted their gods coal-black; the white adherents of the ideology of race resorted to a most agile intellectual acrobatics to undo the past, to obliterate history.

Champollion Figeac, in a critique of Volney, op.cit., states:

"To support his opinion, Volney invokes that of Herodotus who, apropos the Colchians, recalls that the Egyptians had black skin and woolly hair. Yet these two physical qualities do not suffice to characterize the Negro race and Volney's conclusion as to the Negro origin of the ancient Egyptian civilization is evidently forced and inadmissible."[36]

"In a textbook for pupils in cinquieme (eighth grade), we read: 'A Black is distinguished less by the color of his skin (for there are Whites with black skin), than by his features: thick lips, flat nose, etc."[37]

As incredible as it may appear, white genius has transported us to the zenith of absurdity – to a topsy-turvy world – where white men have black skin and, by logical corollary, black men (men with black skin, but without flat nose and thick lips) are white men; so white is black and black is white! This is the extent to which the ideology of racism would go to prove the validity of its assumptions.

Today, such absurdities constitute an integral part of most of the literature, films and drama on Egyptology. Let us take a look at an example from a book by Penelope Davies and Philippa Stewart entitled *Tutankhamun's Egypt*. The authors reproduce on page 16 a portrait of Queen Tiye's head with the following comment:

> "*A powerful queen.* Scholars argue about who Tutankhamun's parents were. Some believe that Amenophis III and his wife, Queen Tiye, were his parents. Others think they were his grandparents. But we do know that Tiye was still very powerful during the reigns of Akhenaten and Tutankhamun. As you can see from this portrait head, she was not Egyptian. She probably came from Nubia. This shows just how clever she was. It was most unusual for a foreigner to achieve a powerful position in Egypt."

The comment clearly confirms that: (a) "scholars" agree that Queen Tiye is either Tutankhamun's mother or grandmother; and (b) Queen Tiye (as the portrait clearly shows) is a *black* woman. However, the assumption throughout the book is that the Egyptians were not Black. Faced with the contradiction between their assumption and the portrait of Tutankhamun's mother (or grandmother), they proceed to inform the reader: "As you can see from this portrait head, she was not Egyptian. She probably came from Nubia."

One may readily forgive the authors' ignorance of the historical fact that the ancient Egyptians, Ethiopians (Nubians) and Greek historians had all stated without equivocation that the Egyptians originally came from Ethiopia (Nubia or present-day Sudan) and hence, except those mixed with the migrant Asians, would all be the same colour as the Nubians.

Where one cannot pardon the authors is that they present evidence on pages 68 and 69 of the same book which totally contradicts their initial assumption, but being totally blinded by the ideology of race, they could not perceive that obvious contradiction. Against a painting of Ramses II in battle against the Syrians, they comment as follows:

> "CAPTURING A CITY – Ramses II was another fearless and warlike pharaoh, but his campaigns were not always successful. He failed to drive the Hittites out of northern Syria, although all the accounts of this campaign make out that it was an Egyptian success! Here he is about to kill the general of a besieged Syrian fortress. The prisoners are led by the neck before him as

Queen Tiye. Historians agree she is either the mother or the grandmother of Tutankhamun

Portrait of Tutankhamun

Ramses II, "a fearless and warlike pharaoh"

Portrait of Ramses II

Ramses II, viewing the spoils of war

he stands on the backs of two others."

The authors appear to be wholly oblivious to the fact that Ramses II
and the Egyptian soldier with him are obviously painted in different
colours from those of the Syrians who are portrayed as white.
Rather than assuming that Queen Tiye was not Egyptian because
she was black, the paintings of the Pharaoh Ramses II and his
Egyptian soldier vis-à-vis the Syrians should have led the authors to
deduce the obvious: that the original Egyptians were black people.
Where the ideology of racism reigns, the *obvious* becomes *obscure* if
it produces facts which contradict the assumption of "black
inferiority".

Finally, three other important factors must be noted here: (a) the
real source of Egyptian wealth was in the South (Upper Egypt). The
gold mines, the vast stone quarrying, copper and tin mining were all
located there. The papyrus plants from which black people invented
paper and built the first and finest boats, were grown in the South.
From the South came ivory and the then highly-prized ostrich
feathers.

(b) The priestess of Amon at Thebes, the Egyptian holy site par
excellence, could not be other than a Meroitic Sudanese.[38] When
Herodotus argued that "... by calling the dove black the Dodoneans
indicated that the woman was an Egyptian" he was seeking to
demonstrate the profound influence of Egypt, especially in religion.
He sought to prove that the Oracles of Amon (in Libya) and that of
Dodona (in Greece) were of Egyptian origin and were founded by
black women kidnapped from the capital of Upper Egypt, Thebes. It
would make no sense for the indispensable qualification of every
potential priestess of the holiest site of white worship to be a black
woman. It would be tantamount to a requirement, for example, that
the Archbishop of Canterbury has to be a black woman.

> "... the Pharaoh Merneptah resided in Memphis by military necessity, but,
> like almost all Egyptian Pharaohs, he was to be buried at Thebes. Even when
> a Pharaoh died at Memphis, in Lower Egypt, they took the trouble to
> transport the corpse to Upper Egypt and bury it in the sacred Theban cities:
> Abydos, Thebes, Karnak. In those towns of Upper Egypt, the Pharaohs had
> their tombs next to those of the ancestors; there they always sent offerings,
> even if they resided in Memphis."

As we noted earlier, Thebes (the date of construction of which was
prior to recorded history) was the most ancient and most important
city of the black people and all Upper Egypt was called, among other
names, Thebald and its people the 'black Thebans'. Thebes (Nowe)
was once called "The Mother of Cities", "the City of a Hundred
Gates", the "City Beautiful", "The Two Cities", "The City of the
Living" and "The City of the Dead", "the City of Amon, king of the

Gods". On the East Bank of the Nile was the City of the Living where the magnificent palaces and mansions were concentrated. The City of the Dead was on the West Bank of the Nile and here were cited the mortuary temples of kings and queens along with the various religious cults, and houses of priests, craftsmen, soldiers and the masses. The West Bank was also the centre of industrial and commercial activities. Both the Cities of the Living and the Dead had numerous Temples, many of which were, in reality, seats of learning. Here scholars from foreign lands came to study, and from here religious ideas and architectural designs spread abroad. This was the City of Amon, the King of the Gods, and of his wife, the great goddess, Mut.

Thebes, then, was truly the centre of gravity of the black people in Upper Egypt. It is inconceivable that the Pharaohs of Ancient Egypt, if they were white people, would have been buried in the cultural and religious centre of the black people, when their people (the 'white' Asians) were concentrated mainly along the Mediterranean in Lower Egypt.

The next critical question we have to address, then, is how did what was once an all-black Egypt become a virtually all-white Egypt? It is beyond the scope of the present work to go into the details of the ethnological changes that occurred gradually over the millenia. We shall, therefore, take a bird's-eye view of the major events. Readers interested in further details of this rather intriguing period of Egyptian history, may consult Chancellor Williams, op.cit., Chapters II and III and Cheikh Anta Diop, op.cit., Chapter X.

We have already noted that with the unification of the Two Lands by Menes (3200 BC[g]), the capital of the united kingdom was transferred from Nekheb to Thinis. The first two Pharaonic dynasties – The Thinite dynasties – lasted from 3200 BC to 2778 BC. By the Third Dynasty (2778-2723) centralisation of the monarchy was complete, significant social reforms had been brought about, and a complex and sophisticated administra-tive system had been instituted.[39]

Socially, all Egyptians – men and women – had equal rights and marital power, and paternal authority no longer existed; all families except the king's were strictly monogamous, and the wife could dispose of her property without the husband's authorisation. Administratively, bureaucracy had replaced the old hereditary feudal system. A large corps of civil servants appointed and paid by the king, rigorously classified and hierarchically structured with promotion dependent on experience through the ranks, were operating. Justice, dispensed exclusively in the name of the king, was entrusted to royal tribunals. Cities enjoyed devolved autonomous power, though they were integrated within the general

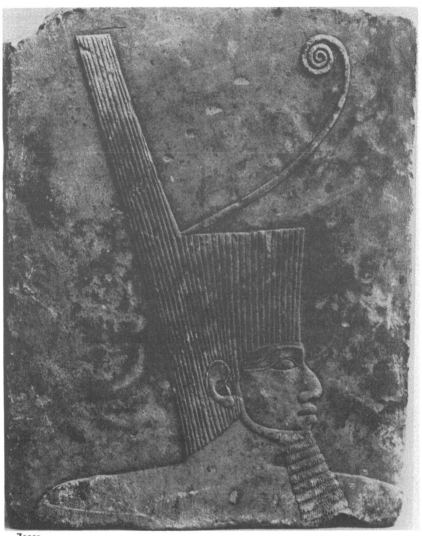

Zoser

Portrait of Khafre, Pharaoh of the Third Dynasty who initiated the building of the pyramids

administrative system of the country.

The first pyramid, as noted above, was built in the Third Dynasty, but the great pyramid builders were the Pharaohs of the Fourth Dynasty. The Great Pyramid was built by Khufu (later called Cheops), 2590 – 2567 BC. His nephew Khafre (later called Chephren by Europeans) built the second Great Pyramid as well as the Sphinx depicting his unquestionable Negro features – flat nose, thick lips and all! From the First to the Fifth Dynasty, Egypt, under its great Black African kings, reached the zenith of its development. Great leaders such as Menes, Athothes, Peribsen, Khasekhem, Imhotep, Zoser, Sneferu, Khufu, Khafre, Userkaf, Neferefre, among others, brought peace, prosperity and progress. It was 750 years of glorious and ingenious development and achievement; it would be two thousand years before another civilisation would come anywhere near achieving similar levels of intellectual, scientific, engineering and technological feats – and they, the Greeks, were trained by the black Egyptians. Even today, those achievements continue to excite the most informed intellect.

But by the end of the Fifth Dynasty, serious cracks had occurred within the elaborate social, administrative, economic and political structures. The enormous cost of maintaining the pomp of the royal court, royal buildings, religious structures, and the large administrative organisation, led to crippling taxation. New privileged classes had arisen to supplant the social ideal of equality: access to many top positions in the administration, priesthood, provincial and city governments had all become hereditary. Feudalism was creeping back everywhere. Lands allocated to remunerate the great officers of the crown (which went with the post and passed on to the new postholder on the incumbent's promotion, resignation, retirement, or death) now became private property, because the post was now inherited. A class of landed aristocracy emerged, whilst the masses were increasingly becoming poorer.

The country plunged into anarchy; insecurity reigned; and taking advantage of the general chaos and the concomitant diminishing central authority, the 'Asiatics' mounted increasingly regular raids. At the same time several jobs intended for Egyptians in the various workshops and urban building yards, were now monopolised by the 'Asiatics'. Thus the Old Kingdom (First to the Fifth dynasties) ended with Egypt ripe for social revolution.

During the Sixth Dynasty, the impoverished, wretched masses of Memphis, capital city and sanctuary of royalty, revolted, pillaging the city, robbing the rich and driving them into the streets. The revolution spread to other cities, one of which, Sais, temporarily set up a self-government led by a group of ten notables. The following account graphically depicts the anarchy that reigned:

Portrait of Mentuhoptep I, founder of the Eleventh Dynasty

"Thieves become proprietors and the former rich are robbed. Those dressed in fine garments are beaten. Ladies who had never set foot outside, now go out. The children of nobles are dashed against the walls. Towns are abandoned. Doors, walls columns are set aflame. The offspring of the great are thrown into the street. Nobles are hungry and in distress. Servants now are served. Noble ladies flee ... [their children] cringe in fear of death. The country is full of mal-contents. Peasants wear shields into the fields. Man slays his own brother. The roads are traps. People lie in ambush until [the farmer] returns in the evening; then they steal whatever he is carrying. Beaten with cudgels, he is shamefully killed. Cattle roam at will; no one attends them. . .

Each man leads away any animals he had branded... Everywhere crops are rotting, clothing, spices, oil are lacking. Filth covers the earth. The government stores are looted and their guards struck down. People eat grass and drink water. So great is their hunger that they eat the food intended for the swine. The dead are thrown into the river; the Nile is a sepulcher. Public records are no longer secret."[40]

Williams notes that most of the chaos, anarchy and social disintegration occurred during the reign of Pepi II in the Sixth Dynasty. The expansion of "white power" from the Delta into Upper Egypt (which had been virtually all black) increased remorselessly. "Whites" had been appointed in various capacities as ministers, court officials of various kinds, trade commissioners, army officers and soldiers, mercenaries and so on. But during the record-setting ninety-year reign of Pepi II, "white" influence became even greater. The first fifty years of his reign had been marked by strong leadership, but during the last forty years, he became too old to govern or even to know what was going on in the country. A period of chaos ensued and, during the course of the Sixth Dynasty, Memphis, the capital, was sacked by rebels. The black royalty took refuge, as was to be repeated many times in the future, in Upper Egypt, the ancestral home of the black people.

"This happened repeatedly in Egyptian annals. Whenever the nation was threatened by an invasion of Whites from Asia or Europe via the Mediterranean, whenever such incursions disrupted national life, the political power migrated to the south, towards its ancestral habitat. Inevitably, salvation, in other words, the reconquest of political power, reunification, and national rebirth were achieved through the efforts of the legitimate Black dynasties indigenous to the south."[41]

During most part of the 'Middle Kingdom' of Egyptian history, from the end of the Sixth Dynasty onwards, there was disintegration everywhere. There were simultaneous dynasties of Asian, Libyan and Theban Pharaohs and several different capitals. The Eighth, Ninth and Tenth Dynasties were characterised by so many short "reigns" that many of their names are unknown.

But salvation again came from the black south. In 2200 BC, before the end of the Tenth Dynasty, strong rulers among the line of African kings who had ruled most of Upper Egypt from Thebes, began to emerge and lay strategies for the reunification of Egypt. This, the Eleventh Dynasty of the great Mentuhoteps achieved after nearly two centuries, in 2065 BC[h], by overcoming the other powerful Asian dynasty which was centred at Heracleopolis.

The second reunification ushered in another 'golden age' in black history. African ships of commerce sailed the seas again, nation-wide reconstruction was pushed and the revival of learning, science, the arts and crafts marked the Eleventh and Twelfth Dynasties. Administrative centralisation of the Third Dynasty, was also revived.

Probably the greatest of the Eleventh Dynasty Pharaohs was Mentuhotep II who undertook to settle the white Asian problem forever by reversing the policy of racial integration and expelling them from Lower Egypt. Although historians of the period suggest that he expelled the Asians from the Delta in 2040 BC this was an exaggeration, for it was now impossible to expel the Asians en masse as they then constituted a substantial proportion of the Egyptian population. A considerable intermarriage between the races had also taken place by then, compounding the problem for Mentuhotep II. What he succeeded in doing, however, was to put the parallel 'white' government to flight, along with its army and other known supporters. Little did Mentuhotep II know (although many non-integrating black people in the South had known this and revolted against the central government during periods of weak kings precisely on this very issue) that such was the shifting ethnological balance in Egypt that the fate of the black people had been sealed a thousand years earlier.

The era of unity and prosperity, following the second reunification, lasted only three centuries before Egypt was suddenly invaded by marauding Asiatic hordes (the Hyksos) in 1730 BC. The Hyksos – Hebrews – occupied only the eastern region of the Delta, with Avaris as their capital and formed the Thirteenth and Sixteenth Dynasties. "Their barbarism", according to Diop, "was indescribable".[42] Chancellor Williams, quoting the historian Josephus, notes that the Hebrews were "ruthless and aimed at nothing less than the extermination of the Egyptian people and their replacement by the Israelites".[43] During their rule, immigration by their fellow-tribesmen, the Semites, accelerated, further increasing the Asian population in Egypt, a factor which acted as a magnet in the future, inviting further invasions by their Asiatic kinsmen in Asia.

During the reign of the Hyksos ruler, Apophis, the black dynasty of Upper Egypt mobilised the people once again against the "Semitic-Aryan" invaders. Kamose, the last Theban king in the Seventeenth Dynasty launched a full-scale war of liberation against the Hebrews, defeated the Hyksos Dynasty, and expelled many of

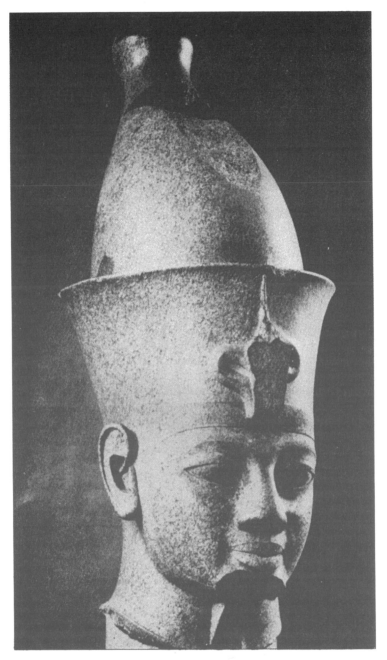

Portrait of Thutmose III, son of a Sudanese woman

them en masse in 1580 BC.[i] This brought about the third reunification and introduced the glorious Eighteenth Dynasty. This dynasty boasted of a great and immortal line of Kings and Queens such as Ahmose I, Nefertari, Amenhotep II, Thutmose I, Thutmose II, Queen Hatshepsut the Great (one of the greatest rulers of Black Egypt), Thutmose III, Amenhotep III, Akhnaton (Amenhotep IV), the "Great Reformer", and Tutankhamun.

The reign of Hatshepsut was particularly remarkable; she was a Queen absolute, ruling alone as a King, even often dressing in royal male attire, including the false beard and ring of the Pharaohs. She expanded foreign trade, international diplomatic relations, strengthened national defences, undertook vast public building programmes, strengthened the unity of the political structure of the North and South, and built a great navy for both commercial and military purposes.

Meanwhile, her son-in-law, Thutmose, son of a Sudanese woman, was waiting impatiently to succeed her as Pharaoh. The longer Hatshepsut reigned, the more frustrated Thutmose became, and the more frustrated he became, the more his resentment and hate for his mother-in-law grew. When she died and he finally assumed the throne, his hatred for his late mother-in-law was most intense and, as a prelude to what Asians and Europeans would later do to "blackout" the black African history of Egypt, Thutmose sought to obliterate her completely from Egyptian history. Her name was erased from all the monuments and temples she had built; documents bearing her name were destroyed; all sculptured likenesses, paintings, etc., were smashed up. "Also as later Europeans and Asians were to do to all recognised Blacks, Thutmose III had his own and that of his brother engraved where Hatshepsut's had been chiselled out, thus taking credit for all of her achievements in addition to his own outstanding works"[44]

Thutmose III felt that black Egypt had suffered enough invasions from western Asia to merit a decisive reponse. The period following the routing and expulsion of the Hyksos was deemed a propitious time to launch a counter-offensive and Thutmose accordingly launched an imperialistic drive to 'pacify' the Asians.

"He overpowered all the States of Western Asia and the islands of the Eastern Mediterranean, reducing them to the status of vassals compelled to pay annual tribute. This was the case with Mitanni (an Indo-European state on the Upper Euphrates), Babylonia, Cilicia, the Hittite State, Cyprus, Crete, etc. Syria and Palestine were simply integrated into the Egyptian kingdom...

In any case, Egypt was then the foremost technical, military and imperial power in the world. Foreign vassal rulers vied with each other in submissiveness; each tried to use the most obsequious formulas in addressing the Pharaoh: 'I am your footstool. I lick the dust from your sandals. You are my sun,' a Syrian vassal wrote to Amenophis IV. After the Eighteenth Dynasty, the Egyptians acquired the habit of holding as hostages the sons of vassal rulers of Asia and the Mediterranean, training them in the Pharaoh's court in the hope that they might govern their countries as good vassals. This was one of several causes of the extensive, profound and almost exclusively Egyptian influence on Western Asia and the Mediterranean."[45]

This process of the imposition of Egyptian ideological and political hegemony, and its influence on Eurasian development would of course be conveniently 'forgotten' or, when acknowledged, the rulers and people of Egypt had already been 'bleached' white by European genius so that it would be seen as colonisation by one group of Caucasians (Egyptians) against another group of Caucasians (Asians and Mediterraneans). To add insult to injury, not only would Euro-centric historians and Egyptologists 'whiten' Thutmose III of the Eighteenth Dynasty, the son of a Sudanese woman, but that he would be given the title "Napoleon of Antiquity", when, in reality, he became an emperor three thousand years before Napoleon. It is Napoleon who should be known as Thutmose III of the eighteenth century AD. Thutmose III and his ancestors from Menes, Athothes, Peribsen, Khasekhem, Zoser, Sneferu, Khufu, Khafre, Userkaf, Neferefre, Queen Nefertari, to Hatshepsut, etc., would turn in their graves and weep uncontrollably (were it possible) to hear their descendants referred to as people so inherently inferior, intellectually, that they could not create a civilisation without Caucasian intervention and direction!

During the Eighteenth Dynasty, administrative centralisation and a host of social reforms were re-introduced. Administrative posts, once again, ceased to be hereditary; agrarian reform was introduced so that although in theory the land was the property of the Pharaoh, the people had sufficient access to it to continue their economic activities. Although paying tax on the land, it could be sold or bequeathed. Access to land meant that virtually everyone worked for himself. "Except for the conquered Indo-Europeans, systematically enslaved and branded to prevent their escape, Egypt, unlike Greco-Roman and feudal societies, had no servile labour force."[46]

But there were also the beginnings of capitalism. Business classes emerged who rented land in the countryside and hired workers to cultivate it, the produce being sold for profit. "The same business practices were carried on in the cities: interest-bearing loans, renting or subletting personal property or real estate for the purpose of financial speculation."[47] However this 'primitive' capitalism was peripheral, not central, to the Egyptian economic system and the mode of production. "The alienation of the worker in the Egyptian countryside never had more than minor importance. The State was responsible for organising production and achieving the optimum yield from the soil. So the division of labour on the administrative level was extremely sophisticated. It is hard to imagine today the technical efficiency that the Egyptian state organisation had attained. Facing the threat of the Asiatic hordes and Indo-European barbarians, for a long time Egypt was saved by the headstart it had made in the field of organisation. This enabled it to recover with surprising speed after an invasion or a period of anarchy."[48]

It was also in the Eighteenth Dynasty that Amenophis IV (Amenhotep IV) or Akhnaton attempted his great religious reform by seeking to impose the concept of the One and Only Almighty God, Creator of the Universe, preceding the monotheism of Genesis by several centuries. His religious reform failed, but his 'absolutist' policy survived and was consolidated in the Nineteeth Dynasty with the deification of Ramses II. The perennial problems of over-taxation, excessive bureaucracy and impoverishment of the masses began to rear its ugly head again towards the end of Amenophis's reign.

Horemheb sought to stem the tide by introducing several laws designed to improve the lot of the masses and to punish government employees, soldiers and judges guilty of theft or fraud against ordinary people. His efforts, however, had limited effect and the privileged classes continued to enjoy their unfair prerogatives based on heredity, rather than on meritocracy.

The Nineteenth Dynasty, from 1320 BC, saw the Age of the Ramses. While this Dynasty (1320-1200 BC) did not equal the 'glorious' Eighteenth, it was nevertheless a period of outstanding leadership and achievements, continuing into the Twentieth Dynasty, 1200-1085 BC.

The Twenty-First, Twenty-Second, and Twenty-third periods, 1085-730 BC, were once again periods of national fragmentation and disintegration with several simultaneous or parallel dynasties all over the land. There were feudal lords, war lords, priests, and pretenders declaring their geo-political areas of interest 'independent' and setting themselves up as 'pharaohs'. In reality, these were 'nomarchies' or local kingdoms only. Chaos and disunity was the order of the day. By the beginning of this period (1085 BC), "the Asian population was so vast... that new Asian dynasties were relatively easy to establish almost anywhere north of the First Cataract. During one of these periods, 70 kings in 70 days are reported."[49]

It is important to note here that as early as the reign of Pepi I, Egypt began to import white women from Asia[50] some of whom ended up in the King's harem and others used as prostitutes. The Phoenicians are known to have engaged in white slavery – buying or kidnapping white women from Greece and selling them in Egypt.[51] Add to this the fact that there was a substantial white Asian population in Lower Egypt, leading to a widespread miscegenation between the races, creating a large mulatto offspring in Egypt as a whole. In fact, many of the Pharaohs during the predominantly Black Dynasties (The Six, Eleventh, Twelfth, Eighteenth and Nineteeth) were of mixed African/Asian parentage. The end of the reign of Ramses II and that of Merneptah, saw determined and systematic effort by a coalition of white people to take over all Egypt once and for all from the black people, aided and abetted by the 'whites' of Lower Egypt and many Egyptians of mixed parentage. Chancellor Williams suggests that the 'mulatto problem' was one of the decisive factors, turning an all-black Egypt to 'brown' and 'white' Egypt,[52] for the former, whose size in the population became significant over the centuries, sided with the latter against the Blacks.

Although most of these invasions were successfully repulsed, each one shifted the racial balance, as many white captives were given to the temples to be used as soldiers or slave labour on the farms. In 1229, the first large coalition of Indo-Europeans comprising of Libyans, Shardana, Siculans, Achaeans, Lycians, and Etruscans, led by Merirey, king of Libya, were routed by Pharaoh Merneptah, killing thousands of them, capturing 9,000 soldiers and swords and pieces of armour, and a great booty.[53] Tradition has it that the Etruscans led by Aeneas later settled in Italy after the defeat of the 'white' coalition. Later, Merneptah sent out an expedition to 'pacify' Palestine where a large migratory wave of "sea peoples" had arrived, and successfully subdued them.

Thanks to superior organisation, the Egyptian armed forces scored a dual victory, on land and sea, over that second alliance. The fleet of the 'Peoples of the North' was entirely destroyed and the invasion route through the Delta was cut.[54] Ramses III destroyed a third coalition force of Indo-Aryans in Libya very soon after, and in 1191, he annihilated a fourth coalition. The last two wars in particular, produced largely white captives.

"Meanwhile, the Libyans in the western part of the Delta, were organising still another coalition, the fifth directed against the Black Egyptian nation by the Indo-Europeans. Ramses III defeated them at Memphis in 1188 B.C. After that date the white Libyans never again revolted against Egypt, but they tried by every possible means to infiltrate peacefully and to settle there as serfs or semi-serfs, working at various kinds of manual labour, as farmers or artisans, especially in the Delta. They were also employed in the army as an auxiliary foreign corps called Kehek."[55]

Thereafter, Ramses III succeeded in bringing about stability in

the political, economic, and administrative realms. From Ramses III
to Ramses XI, Egypt enjoyed a century of tranquility and uneventful
succession of kings.

Following the anarchy of the Twenty-Second and Twenty-third
Dynasties, Libyan and Achaean "freedmen" (whites) who held
military posts of any importance, set themselves up as chiefs or
"princes". There was such chaos that the Libyan usurper, Osorkon,
tried to force his son on Thebes as an Amon King. This was
sacrilege, for only Black Nubians may hold such post! The clergy
fled to Nubian Sudan and sought the aid of the king of Sudan,
Piankhi. This was a challenge the Blacks could not fail to respond
to. Piankhi mobilised his forces... "the country was divided into two
camps: in the north, the coalition of White rebels, former slaves; in
the south, the authentic Egyptian nation solidly behind the
Sudanese King. In the eyes of the clergy, the guardian of tradition,
the fullblooded Black from this land of the ancestors was monarchi-
cal legitimacy incarnate."[56]

The black holy city was now in the hands of the Libyan (generic
term for the white people of the Delta) coalition, led by Tefnakhte
and Bocchoria. They had control of all Thebald (Upper Egypt),
except the great city of Heracleopolis, where the black people still
held out. The battle was joined at Heracleopolis, where Piankhi put
Tefnakhte and his court to flight. The Asian armies were driven out
of Thebes and the city was re-established as the capital city of the
North.[57] The siege of Hermopolis was led by Piankhi himself. He had
trenches dug around the town and wooden towers constructed from
which catapults hurled projectiles on the city. Nimrod sent his
diadem and a tribute in gold to Piankhi as a sign of surrender.

In the meantime, Tefnakhte, with 8,000 infantry men and
marines, set up defences at Memphis. Piankhi attacked from the
river, through the port, smashed through their defences, penetrated
the city, and put the defenders to flight. Piankhi then moved on to
Heliopolis, where he was crowned Pharaoh of Upper and Lower
Egypt. Piankhi finally pushed onto Athribis, where the last white
usurpers and pretenders to the Pharaonic throne surrendered. For
the fourth time in Egyptian history, black power had swept from the
South and pushed up to the Mediterranean to claim their ancestral
land, their civilisation, their national (African) integrity.

The Twenty-Fifth and last black Dynasty in Egypt had begun.
But this dynasty which ended three centuries of fuedalistic anarchy
and a steady increase of the white population in Egypt (and,
incidentally, the only dynasty admitted by all white Egyptologists
as being all-black), was doomed right from the start. It appears that
the anteriority of their magnificent civilisation to all other societies;
the splendour of their human and material achievements; the

ingenuity of their scientific achievements; the brilliance of their technological and engineering attainments, when most other societies around them were steeped in barbarism, had lulled the black Egyptians into a mood of unjustified complacency. The Temehou (white Libyans) had settled to the west of Egypt, threatening the Tehenu or black Lebou (the original black inhabitants of Libya); nomadic whites had been pressing on them from the east and, later, from the North across the Mediterranean; and yet, the black Egyptians seemed too pre-occupied with spiritual, scientific, social and economic progress to worry too much about the threat pressing on them from all sides. Had they applied their considerable scientific, engineering, and technological know-how to producing armaments and building a strong national defence, the history of the black man might be entirely different!

Another factor that contributed to the black man's loss of Egypt was his tendency, at that period, to put self, rather than national interest, first. The strength and survival of a nation depend on, among other things, a strong sense of nationalism and patriotism, and a willingness of its citizens to put the unity and survival of the nation first, particularly, in times of national crisis and/or threat from external aggression. The perpetual drive towards individual aggrandisement at the expense of the poor, the weak and the masses in general; the willingness to put national unity at risk in the quest for personal power; the preference for short-term personal gratification, against the long-term interest of the nation; and the astonishing readiness to ally even with aliens against his own kind in order to win personal advantage, irrespective of the cost to the nation, has been repeated with deplorable regularity throughout the history of the black man. These, among other social weaknesses, made Piankhi's victory a temporary check to the inexorable white drive to conquer Africa and to subjugate the African.

This notwithstanding, the Twenty-Fifth and last Black Pharaonic Dynasty was to last a century. Piankhi had, for the fourth time in black Egyptian history, brought salvation from the Black south. But Piankhi returned to the capital city of Napata in the black "Heartland" before Lower Egypt was brought under complete control. The task of complete reunification and reconstruction, therefore, was left to his brother and successor Shabaka. At the time of his coming to power in 706 BC, Bocchoris had replaced his father Tefnakhte at the head of the 'white' rebels in the Delta. Shabaka routed them at Sais and put Bocchoris to death. Peace ensued and with it, a powerful movement of cultural revival and national resurgence was born. Like the black Pharaohs before him, Shabaka felt the need to transfer his administrative capital from Napata to Memphis (and later to Tanis), in order to forestall conspiratorial attempts by the whites and mulattoes in Lower Egypt to usurp the throne. When Shabaka died in 701, his nephew Shabataka became Pharaoh.

Shabataka was soon locked in battle with the Assyrian forces over Palestine. The invading Egyptian forces, commanded by Taharqa (the Biblical Tirhakah), youngest son of Piankhi, were repulsed, following their betrayal by the white people of Lower Egypt. But a strong resurgence of black nationalism swept through the country: artisans and shopkeepers from the Delta cities volunteered to form a militia which decisively routed the Assyrians.[58] Shabataka was assassinated on the orders of Taharqa who ascended the Pharaonic throne in 689 BC. Peace once again ensued and the black people, as in the past, brought about strong economic, cultural, intellectual and spiritual revival. This was, in particular, a period of strong architectural renaissance and its achievements include the Temple of Mout (Queen of Sudan) erected in honour of Pharaoh Taharqa's mother; monuments such as the Column of Taharqa in Karnak; and the statues of Mentuemhat and Amenardis.

Taharqa sought to revive Egypt's imperialist past by intervening in Asia. Once again, the white vassals betrayed the black Pharaoh; the Assyrians successfully marched into Lower Egypt and made it an Assyrian province. Taharqa fled to Thebes for sanctuary, as many of his predecessors had done and here, he enjoyed the support of the governor of Thebes and the "divine spouse of Amon". In 669 BC, he recaptured Memphis and remained there till 666 BC when he was once again betrayed by the white feudal lords of the Delta. He fled to Napata where he died two years later.

Sabataka's son Tanutamon succeeded him to the throne of Napata and was acclaimed in Thebes as the legitimate heir of the Pharaohs by the clergy and the divine spouse of Amon.[59] Tanutamon marched up north against a new coalition of white feudal lords, among them Necho, son of Bocchoris who had been executed by the Pharaoh, Shabaka. Tanutamon defeated the white alliance and captured Memphis; but in a display of surprising political naivety, he restored all the feudal lords to their previous posts except Necho of Sais who was killed in battle, and Psammetichus, son of Necho who remained loyal to Assyria and fled to the court of Nineveh.

But the victory of Tanutamon was to be ephemeral; his failure to deal decisively with the 'white' Egyptians who were determined to rid the country of its legitimate and indigenous black rulers, to usurp all black achievements of Egypt, to fraudulently declare themselves the originators of that grand civilisation, to plagiarise black literature on science, mathematics, technology, the arts and religion, is inexplicable with the benefit of hindsight. To leave in charge of provinces in Lower Egypt as feudal lords, these

Taharqa, Sudanese Pharaoh of the Twenty-fifth Dynasty

conspirators who were continually colluding with their people from Asia and elsewhere to take over Egypt, was to say the least, political idiocy. Tanutamon's failure to purge Egypt of these cancerous elements (as was the failure of his predecessors of the Eleventh, Eighteenth and Twenty-Fifth Dynasties), was to have drastic consequences for the destiny of the black race for over two thousand years.

In 661 BC, Ashurbanipal attacked Egypt and pillaged the city of Thebes, that great prehistoric "Mother of Cities", built by black people, which symbolised their intellectual, spiritual, and cultural achievements, destroying it and with it, the black leadership of world civilisation. The symbolic 'soul' of the race was extinguished, marking the inexorable decline of black political, scientific, intellectual, technological and spiritual supremacy in Antiquity. This tragedy of Thebes was to be followed by the destruction of Napata in 690 BC by the Assyrians and Greeks. Napata, as noted above, was the second of the great sacred cities of the black people in Antiquity.

The destruction of the cities of Thebes and Napata marked the end of an era; from thence, black people were never to attain the heights of civilisation brought about by their own ingenuity, for almost all succeeding attempts to rise to the zenith attained in Egypt would be destroyed by Caucasians.

Tanutamon fled to Napata and Psammetichus inaugurated the Twenty-Sixth Dynasty (663-525) which ended with the Persian conquest of 525 BC, led by Darius the Great. From then on Egypt was to be under almost permanent occupation by foreigners and the racial structure of its people was to change irreversibly. After the Persians came the Macedonians under Alexander the Great (333 BC); the Romans under Julius Caesar followed (50 BC); the Arabs and Turks were next, in the seventh and sixteenth centuries AD respectively; and finally, the French under Napoleon and the English at the end of the nineteenth century. Each of these conquests was to contribute to the destruction and looting of Antiquity's greatest civilisation and its artifacts, and the systematic attempt to obliterate its Black origin. Many sculptures were either systematically destroyed or had their unquestionably negroid noses and lips chipped. Millions of pounds worth of artifacts were to end up in Museums and Royal Courts in Europe and Asia. The plunder and loot of Egyptian artifacts by the Persian, Cambyses, the "Vandal", in the sixth century BC, with an estimated value of $100,000,000, was only one of hundreds of 'scavenging' expeditions by Asia and Europe. Large amounts of sculptures and statues bearing unequivocal testimony to the black origin of Egyptian civilisation, as noted, were callously and criminally destroyed. The ideology of racism marshalled its intellectual exponents to formulate theories that ascribed Egyptian civilisation to Caucasians; and finally the genius of European intellect carved out Egypt from Africa altogether and located it in the "Middle East", in spite of the contrary geographical reality. The ideology of racism had achieved one of its greatest triumphs!

Notes

a. emphasis mine.
b. Ethiopians as used here are not the same as modern Ethiopians (Abyssinians), but were the black inhabitants of modern Sudan.
c. Cheikh Anta Diop disputes this date and puts the white (Asian) presence in large numbers, more than 1,500 years later.
d. The 'Kantheros' was a two-headed vase showing two female heads: one African, the other Greek, juxtaposed.
e. emphasis mine.
f. see Cheikh Anta Diop, op. cit., Chapter VII.
g. 3,000 B C according to C. Williams.
h. Chancellor Williams gives 2040 B C as the date of the second reunification, while C.A. Diop suggests 2065 B C.
i. Note that this expulsion of the Hebrews from Egypt took place nearly six centuries before the Biblical story of Moses and the captivity.

CHAPTER SIX

Refuting a Myth: Black Civilizations: Central, East, South & West

It was imperative to devote considerable space to the origin, development and achievement of the Egyptian Civilisation, and more significantly, the racial identity of the builders of that civilisation for a number of reasons: (a) it was anterior to any other known civilisation; (b) the grandeur of its achievements were unsurpassed by any other society for millenia; (c) their influence on other civilisations – particularly Greek and hence 'Western Civilisation'; (d) the attempt by Western scholars and historians to deny the black origin of Egyptian and hence 'Western Civilisation'; and (e) the importance of the race of the ancient Egyptians to the debate on the truth or falsity of the main plank of the assumptions of the ideology of racism.

Having effectively rebutted the assumptions of the ideology by demonstrating the anteriority of black civilisation to all others, and its incredible achievements, we shall look very briefly at some of the geographically representative African civilisations of the past, built by black initiative and progress.

Kush

The kingdom of Kush was founded in Nubia around 800 BC following the national disintegration in Egypt after the Twenty-First Dynasty. We have already noted that the black Pharaohs took refuge in the South during periods of external aggression. The large increase of white people in Egypt led to many black people moving southward; and the many battles fought made the need for a more secure nation, less accessible to the white invaders, a necessity.

Egypt, the daughter of Ethiopia (Nubia), had outshone the mother-country in almost every field of human endeavour. In her

heyday, Egypt had influenced Nubia considerably, after being
launched on her extraordinary development by Nubia. Now, with
white people in ascendancy and the whole of Egypt under threat of
being completely overwhelmed by foreigners, Kush made a bid for
economic and political leadership of black peoples in that region of
Africa.

In a period of peace, the Nubians brought about agricultural and
industrial development, increased national prosperity, advancement in science and technology and social progress. The economy
was primarily agriculture-based – mainly crop cultivation and
stock-breeding – but although there was more arable land then than
there is today (the Sahara was yet to spread its catastrophic
destruction of vegetation of modern proportion to this part of
Africa), cultivable acreage and the richness of the soil did not equal
that of the Nile Delta. Moreover, rainfall was erratic and unreliable;
in some cases, there was not a spot of rain in places for a number of
years. To counter such climatic disasters, the black people constructed a system of national reservoirs, strategically located
around the capital, at Musawarat, Naga, Hordan, Umm, Usuda, in
the Gezira region, at Duanib, Basa, and doubtlessly at other sites
not yet excavated.[1]

The African, as we noted above, had discovered the process of
smelting iron and steel and even welding these metals as early as
1500-1200 BC. This knowledge was, however, kept a closely
guarded secret amongst a select few. Their failure to exploit the
weaponry potential of this metal was to cost them very dearly, for
centuries later, the Assyrians produced superior weapons from iron
which helped them sweep the black people out of Egypt. That
mistake was not repeated in Kush. At their great capital, Meroe, an
important iron-smelting industry was developed and, even today,
heaps of slag at the ruins of the city attest to the signficance of this
industry.

But the Kushite prosperity was not built only on agriculture and
industry; there was long distance trade with most of the then
'civilised' world along the Red Sea and across the Indian Ocean.

The height of civilisation attained in Kush's one thousand-year
history is, even today, still evidenced in the great monuments and
ruins of Elephantine island, Musawarat, Meroe, Naza and many
other sites all over modern-day Sudan. The architectural excellence
of the pyramids and temples of Meroe, though smaller, are no less
impressive than those of Egypt. For example, two of the greatest
temples of Antiquity were built in Meroe by Aspalta, King of Kush
(593-568 BC). They were the "Sun Temple" and "Temple of Amon".

The Kushites pioneered the training of elephants for war and
other purposes. These trained elephants became formidable war

'machines' in those days. Legend has it that after the conquest of Egypt, Alexander the Great attempted to invade the kingdom of Kush. A large fighting force was mobilised, commanded by the famous Queen Candace. Alexander decided that the risk of being defeated by a woman leading a force with many mounted on these trained elephants, far outweighed the gains of conquering Kush. It has also been suggested that the war elephants of Hannibal, the great black General who in 218 BC annihilated the Roman army at Lake Trasimene and Cannae, were trained by the techniques pioneered and perfected by the Kushites at Musawarat.

The African had invented the art of writing in Ta-Seti (in Nubia) at least three centuries before King Menes, the "Theban" (as the Greek historian Erathosthenes called him) founded the Pharaonic Dynasty of black Egypt.[2] And here in Kush, they invented perhaps the first (or at least one of the earliest) alphabetic writing. "The Kushites were... one of the earliest peoples anywhere to develop a purely alphabetic script. And their way of writing, however surprising this may be to those who have imagined that Africans were never able to invent such things, was as effective as the alphabetic script developed by the Greeks."[3]

The Kushite alphabet had twenty-three characters or letters – four vowel signs, seventeen consonants, and two signs of the syllable. It was far more flexible than the hieroglyphics, and new concepts or special words could be easily introduced. Clarity and ease of reading was assured by measured spacing between words. A system of numerical symbols for mathematics were also developed.[4]

If the African invented the art of writing, how did he lose these skills? The same question could, of course, be asked about how the Egyptians lost the ability to read and write hieroglyphics and it was left to the Europeans – The Champollions et al. – to decipher and to unlock the key to the mystery of Ancient Egypt. The answer lies in the fact that in these earlier civilisations, writing was confined to a small professional class, the scribes. "All books, scrolls, inscriptions, letters, etc. were written by them. Therefore, in any society where the scribes were either captured or disappeared from it for whatever reason, the art of writing in that society died. In view of the developments in black Africa, the disppearance of writing is not a mystery at all."[5]

In 350 AD the forces of the kingdom of Axum attacked and destroyed Meroe. But new kingdoms formed and thriving civilisations continued, albeit on a declining scale. The Kingdoms of Nabadae, Makuria and Alwa arose from the ruins of Kush. One of these, Makuria, was powerful enough to inflict on the Arabs "the most devastating defeat ever suffered by an Arab army", according to an Arab historian of the time.[6] The Arabs invaded Makuria in

643 AD following their successful conquest of Egypt in 642 AD. Their defeat on the plains of Makuria at the hands of the black people was so decisive that eight years elapsed before the Arabs attempted another invasion in 651 AD. After an initial setback, King Kalydosos courageously resisted the Arabs and created a military stalemate, leading to an armistice and a peace treaty that was to last 600 years.

The Zanj Empire –
A Swahili Civilisation

Long before the Europeans developed inter-continental trading links, the East Africans had developed a complex and highly prosperous maritime trading network which extended across the Indian Ocean and as far as India, Malaysia, Indonesia and China. The name Zanj was used by medieval Arabs for East African peoples, but this was a rendition of an earlier name "Azania" which appears in a much earlier account by a Greek Captain of Roman Egypt, who referred to the East African coast as the "seaboard of Azania". But medieval Arabs had also called this coastland "swahili" or shore. Although the people were African, the acceptance of the Islamic religion after 700 AD made its civilisation increasingly Muslim. They spoke their own Bantu language, but borrowed useful words from their Arab visitors. A consequence of this linguistic influence was that they began to call themselves the "Swahilis" – the people of the coastland.

In fact, the Chinese knew of the Empire of Zanj as early as 202 BC.[8] As we have noted above, the African had always engaged in international trade from the Egyptian period through the Kush civilisation. But it appears that the economic base of the Zanj civilisation, unlike earlier African civilisations, was built principally on international trade rather than on agriculture. African countries of the interior produced gold, ivory, rhinoceros horns, peppers, herbs, fruits and other produce. From inland came caravans of commerce bearing these commodities. From the Indian Ocean came ships from many countries carrying cotton, silk, porcelain, copper, and many luxury goods for the people of Africa. Several trading settlements were built along the East African coast by African middle-men to facilitate the exchange and to make profits for themselves. A complex system of taxation on imports and exports ensured regular revenue for the State. These trading ports became large and prosperous cities, forming the Zanj Empire of the Swahilis.

But the Swahilis were not just rich mercantilists or market middle-men; they were sea captains, sailors, boat and ship builders.

"Their own entrepreneurs travelled far in both directions, sharing in the caravan trade with the kingdoms of the Zimbabwe culture, and also sharing in the maritime skills of the region. Like the Arabs and Indians, the Swahili had the sailing and navigating expertise – learned initially from the Chinese – to voyage out of sight of land for long distances; and they possessed these skills many years before such things were in Atlantic waters. It was done by a combination of lateen-rigged sails – capable at least to some extent of 'boring into the wind' – and the use of the magnetic compass, together with position-fixing by reference to the Pole Star and its 'guards'".[9]

"The Swahilis enjoyed a wide reputation in the Medieval world. The Arab historian al-Idrisi stated that the Swahili exported iron 'to all the lands of India'."[10]

"Swahili kings exchanged ambassadors with distant monarchs, and sent ambitious gifts. In 1414 the city of Malindi even managed to present a giraffe to the Emperor of China, notwithstanding the enormous problems of transporting such an elongated creature and keeping it alive on the long sea journey. This particular feat of diplomacy also had an interesting sequel. In 1417 the Chinese high-seas admiral Cheng Ho began a series of western voyages that took him as far as Malindi in that year, and, on a second occasion some years later, to other Swahili harbours."[11]

Note that the date of the first European voyage to India by Vasco da Gama was 1497-9.

The Swahilis built cities along the East African coast from modern Somalia to ports more than 3,000 km to the South. Harbour cities such as Rhapta (known to the Greeks of Roman Egypt), Manda island, Pate, Malindi, Mombasa, Mafia, Sofala and Kilwa were famous among the merchants of Africa, Arabia, Persia, India and China. Malindi and Mombasa to the north grew into powerful and wealthy city states whose rich inhabitants lived a life of great luxury. But perhaps the richest and most famous was Kilwa.

The world renowned fourteenth century Arab traveller, Ibn Battuta visited Kilwa in 1331:

"We spent a night on the Island [of Mombasa] and then set sail for Kilwa, the principal town of the coast, the greater part of whose inhabitants are Zenj of very black complexion. Their faces are scarred, like the Limin of Janada.... Kilwa is one of the most beautiful and well constructed towns in the world. The whole of it is elegantly built..."[12]

Vasco da Gama and his Portuguese sailors were equally impressed:

"His astonished crew sailed past city after city, each rivalling the next in the splendour of its buildings, the wealth of its inhabitants, and the number of trading vessels thronging its harbours. But the inhabitants were not impressed by da Gama and his cheap trading goods. 'When we had been two or three days at this place,' da Gama wrote in his log, 'two gentlemen of the country came to see us. They were very haughty, and valued nothing which we gave them. One of them wore a tonca, with a fringe embroidered in silk, and the other a cap of green satin..."[13]

A few years later, another Portuguese traveller, Duarte Barbosa, visited Kilwa and wrote that it was a town

"with many fair houses of stone and mortar, with many windows after our fashion, very well arranged in streets, with many flat roofs. The doors are of wood, well carved, with excellent joinery. Around it are streams and orchards and fruit-gardens with many channels of sweet water. It has a Moorish king over it. Of the Moors there are some fair and some black, they are finely clad in many rich garments of gold and silk and cotton, and the women as well, also with much gold and sliver in chains and bracelets, which they wear on their legs and arms, and many jewelled earrings in their ears."

Barbosa also visited Mombasa:

"Along the coast towards India, there is an isle hard by the mainland, on which is a town called Mombasa. It is a very fair place, with lofty stone and mortar houses, well aligned in streets after the fashion of Kilwa. The wood is well fitted with excellent joiner's work. It has its own King, himself a Moor. The men are in colour either tawny, black, or white[a] and also their women go very bravely [finely] attired with many fine garments of silk and gold in abundance."

Barbosa continues:

"This is a place of great traffic, and has a good harbour, in which are always moored craft of many kinds and also great ships, both of those which come from Sofala and those which go thither, and others which come from the great kingdom of Cambay [India] and from Malindi; others which sail to the Isles of Zanzibar, and yet others of which I shall speak anon."

This was a land of abundance as Barbosa observed:

"There are found many very fine sheep with round tails, cows and other cattle in great plenty, and many fowls, all of which are exceeding fat. There is much millet and rice, sweet and bitter oranges, lemons, pomegranates, Indian figs, vegetables of diverse kinds, and much sweet water. The men ...carry on trade with them, bringing thence great store of honey, wax and ivory."[14]

So here was a highly developed African civilisation built on mercantilism, forming a commercial bridge between rich and powerful kingdoms of the African interior and the civilised nations of the East, going back to the period before Christ. Its level of development and sophistication; its wealth and splendour; the availability and abundance of food supplies – all surpassed that of most of Europe at the time. But the Swahilis were then 'inferior' to the Europeans in two ways: (a) they did not possess guns and cannons (or at least not in the same quantity); and (b) they were not

as barbaric, bestial and ruthless in warfare. The arrival of the Portuguese spelt doom for this black civilisation.
As Basil Davidson notes,

> "The Swahili cities suffered even before those of India. On his second voyage, da Gama told the king of Kilwa that he would burn the city to the ground unless homage and tribute were paid to the king of Portugal. Ravasio followed suit at Zanzibar. Saldanha stormed Berbera, Soares wrecked Zeila, d'Acunha assaulted Brava where, in Barbosa's contemporary report, the Portuguese slew many people and took great spoil in gold and silver. But none of the coral cities suffered as sorely as Kilwa and Mombasa, the richest on the cost."[15]

In 1505 Francisco d'Almeida stormed Kilwa with eight ships, unleashing a murderous onslaught against its prosperous, but peaceful inhabitants. When the slaughtering was over, they called for their priests (the Christian God's messengers on earth!) and "The vicar-general and some of the Franciscan fathers came ashore carrying two crosses in procession and singing the Te Deum. These went to the palace, where they set up a cross and the Admiral prayed. Then everyone started to plunder the town of all its merchandise and provisions."
The same fate befell Mombasa after they had put up a strong initial resistance.

> "D'Almeida fired the town with burning arrows shot into the thatch roofs, following with an assault in force." Hans Mayr, a German aboard d'Almeida's flagship wrote that after the town was taken "the Admiral ordered that Mombasa should be sacked, and that each man should carry off to his ship whatever he found, so that at the end there would be a division of the spoil. Then everyone started to plunder the town and search the houses, forcing doors with axes and bars."

Not satisfied with the loot of that day, they plundered the town again a day later. The king of Mombasa who survived the massacre, wrote to his neighbour in Malindi that his people,

> 'On returning to their city after the raiders' departure found 'no living thing in it, neither man nor woman, young nor old, nor child however small. All who had failed to escape had been killed and burned'."[16]

A great African civilisation of several centuries duration had been most viciously and brutally annihilated! And yet, a few years later, the European, without a bat of an eyelid, nor a twitch of conscience, was to declare unashamedly that he had come to Africa to bring the poor benighted African savage, the benefits and blessings of European 'civilisation'!

The Empire of Monomotapa

As early as 300 BC several small states had formed and were engaged in a wide range of diversified economic activities in the area which was to be brought together to form the Monomotapa Empire. The development of the economies of these small states was to lead not only to widespread inter-state trade, but foreign trade over the Indian Ocean as well.[17]

Increasing exploitation of mineral resources led to the growth of large scale mining activities and the spread of related craft industries. "Over four thousand ancient mining sites have been discovered, and no one claims that these are all." Gold, iron, copper and tin were mined and goldsmiths, blacksmiths, coppersmiths and tinsmiths became an important part of an increasingly sophisticated economy.

> "By 1200 AD, production and international trade had already reached the high level of affluence that was to attract Arabs and Europeans to this land. Gold was the leading export commodity, although there was also a great demand in India for the superior type of ironware processed in Monomotapa. The African smelting process and type of iron ore peculiar to the region enabled them to produce the best swords, spears and other weapons that could be found anywhere."[19]

Indeed, such was the sophistication of African metallurgical know-how in that region that the method they used was technologically superior to any developed in Europe until the mid-nineteenth century. In a report published in the September 22, 1978 issue of *Science*, Donald H. Avery, Professor of Engineering and Peter Schmidt, Assistant Professor of Anthropology, both of Brown University, USA announced to the scientific world that "as long as 2,000 years ago Africans living on the western shores of Lake Victoria had produced carbon steel in preheated forced-draft furnaces..."[20]

> "We have found" [announced Schmidt] "a technological process in the African Iron Age which is exceedingly complex. To be able to say that a technologically superior culture developed in Africa more than 1,500 years ago overturns popular and scholarly ideas[b] that technological sophistication developed in Europe but not in Africa."

Historical Anthropologist Peter Schmidt had, over a nine-year period made several visits to Tanzania where he had been studying the history of the Haya, a Bantu-speaking people who live along the western shore of Lake Victoria. Schmidt was taken to a site where he was told an ancient king had climbed a pillar of iron to ascend to heaven. Archaeological investigation confirmed that steel had been produced at the site as long as 2,000 years ago. Tests on slag found at these early Iron Age sites showed that it had been formed at temperatures of 1350° to 1400°C (about 2500°F). Schmidt enlisted the help of metallurgist Avery for further investigation.

The Haya, although no longer practising the craft, had nonetheless an intimate knowledge of the technique of carbon steel production based on oral tradition, transmitted from generation to generation for two thousand years. In 1976, Schmidt persuaded some elderly Hayas who last practised the craft during their youth fifty to sixty years earlier, to construct a traditional furnace. The furnace which they built looked roughly like an inverted ice cream cone and was begun by digging and lining a 'bowl' in the ground with mud made from the earth of a termite mound. "Termite mud," explains Avery, "turns out to be a very good refractory material. Termites have made their hills of material that won't absorb water, so they make them of bits of alumina and silica, grain by grain."[21] The five foot shaft, or cone, was also made from refractory slag from previous iron smelting site and termite mud. Eight blowpipes, or tuyères, about two feet long were inserted to varying depths at the base of the furnace and eight drum bellows covered with goat skins were used to force air into the tuyères.

The tuyères, being inside the furnace, preheat the air passing through them, thus enabling much higher combustion temperatures to be attained in the furnace, as well as achieving better fuel economy. The *process of smelting* resulted in the 'growing' of "perfect crystals of iron" *which was entirely unique.*[c] This process of smelting was different in two respects: (a) the preheating of the air draft through blowpipes (tuyères); and (b) the formation of iron crystals, rather than by "the sintering of fine, solid particles" as in European smelting. As Avery commented: *"It's a very unique and original process[c] that uses a large number of sophisticated techniques. This is really semi-conductor technology – the growing of crystals – not iron-smelting technology."*[22c]

One year after the reconstruction and successful re-enactment of this sophisticated African process of smelting, Schmidt excavated thirteen early Iron Age furnaces at Kemondo Bay on the coast of Lake Victoria, very similar to the one reconstructed by the Haya elders, confirming the oral history which had been passed down without major alteration for 2,000 years. "Schmidt suggests that similar furnaces were used by neighbouring cultures – in Uganda, for instance – and that this level of technological complexity was not limited to East Africa."[23]

There is little doubt that this metallurgical know-how was widespread among the neighbouring craftsmen of the region which was to become Monomotapa. In addition, there were great architects and stone-masons as the ruins of over 200 stone-built 'zimbabwes' (royal courts) attest. So, by the end of the thirteenth century, all the socio-economic ingredients of a powerful nation were present – a strong and growing economy, a highly multi-skilled entrepreneurial community, a growing and profitable intra- and inter-state as well as international trade; a network of trading posts scattered throughout the region and beyond – to the Indian Ocean – and a well developed administration. All that was required was the political element: a strong leadership to weld the many states into one great empire. That task was taken on by the Vakaranga king, Mutota.

The Vakaranga, led by their Rosvi chiefs, immigrated into the region in 1400 (circa). Essentially a cattle-breeding people, the Vakaranga found the indigenous people more highly advanced than themselves. However, the immigrants had a greater vision of the need for, and the virtues of, a large, unified political entity and began to formulate a grand strategy to bring this about. In 1440 AD[d] Mutota the Great embarked on the mission of empire building. By 1450, "all [the] territory between the Limpopo in South Africa to the Zambesi had been brought under imperial rule".[24] When Mutota died in 1450, the task was far from complete and the mantle fell on his son Maptope,[e] himself a young military commander, to complete the grand design. Aided by two of his father's great generals – Changa and Togwa – Matope carried on the expansion until the Empire of Monomotapa extended from below the Limpopo River in South Africa, encompassed modern Zimbabwe, and stretched north-ward beyond the Zambesi River in Zambia, and over Mozambique to the Indian Ocean. In 1480, Emperor Matope died, having achieved his father's objective, and was succeeded by his son Nyahuma.

But Nyahuma was a 'political pygmy' occupying a throne previously ruled by 'political giants'. Under his leadership, the history of Egypt began to repeat itself. Factionalism, disunity, pursuit of self-interest at the expense of national interest, began to undermine the sovereignty and integrity of the great Empire. The ageing Changa, king of Guniuswa – now known as Changamire, following the conferment of the Arab title of Amir on him – rebelled against the Emperor Nyahuma. A bitter civil war ensued, leading to the death of Nyahuma in battle in 1490. The rot had set in and the fragmentation of the Empire had begun. This was the state of the Empire when the marauding Portuguese arrived on the east African scene in 1498.

Following their murderous onslaught against, and the complete destruction and plunder of, the wealthy Swahili port cities, they turned their attention to the declining but still powerful Empire of

Monomotapa. They knew that the Empire was the source of the great gold and ivory trade along the Swahili coastline and were intent on seizing the gold mines. Their pretext, as was often the case, was that they were bringing Christianity to the poor, benighted savages of the Dark Continent of Africa whose barbarism cried for divine intervention. If ever a people deserve to be damned for dishonesty, surely the European missionaries and explorers ought to be on the top of the 'Christian God's' list!

"On 23 January 1569 an assembly of ecclesiastics took as a pretext the assassination of a Portuguese missionary in order to authorise a war against the people who opposed the propagation of the true faith. The King of Portugal was authorized to 'build fortresses and send armed men into the ten kingdoms and domains of the Monomotapa.... If the Kaffirs and other peoples in the conquered countries do not wish to allow the entry of the said ministers, or to permit them to teach the Gospel with all the precautions indicated, or oppose violence to the hospitality and to the trade that are the common right of men, the captains and the vessels of the King will very rightly take all measures of defense with all. necessary moderation'. The King was also enjoined 'to abrogate the tyrannical laws' and pernicious rites [of the Monomotapa]. The Portuguese expeditionary corps that landed on the African coast opposite the Island of Mozambique found its work cut out for it... The soldiers were decimated by disease and lost their way along paths that proved to be blind alleys. It took them five years to reach the approaches of the Rhodesian plateau, where they soon realized the illusory character of their plan for an effective military conquest.... They found the defenders fanatically brave and after five years they had only established a few beach-heads.... The Portuguese finally had to be satisfied with a few points of support in the Zambesi valley (Tete and Sena) without developing the slightest political and religious sphere of influence.... In the last analysis the military means at the disposal of the [Portuguese spearhead of the] western powers proved to be just as inadequate as their political and religious means [for] the conquest of the world in general and of Africa in particular.... Not only did the Monomotapa display remarkable military prowess, but they showed above all an unflagging devotion to their customs, whcih were founded on a coherent system of relations between the individual and the universe both visible and invisible."[25]

So even in its weakened state, the Portuguese found the Empire of Monomotapa powerful and defiant opponent. Failing to conquer them militarily, the Portuguese set about to strangle them economically by closing off their trade routes to the coast. In the next century, the Portuguese increased their stranglehold along the East African coast by gradually increasing their settlements and encroaching upon the territories of Monomotapa.

By the early seventeenth century, the combined effect of prolonged religious assault and economic strangulation had paved the way for cultural and political hegemony; Emperor Mauura acknowledged the King of Portugal as his Overlord and became his vassal. In a behaviour which must surely be almost completely unique to the African and his descendants, the Emperors of Monomotapa, like the Christianised rulers of Angola and the Congo, the Islamised Africans before them and the many Christians and Moslems after them, were ready to abandon their African names and to adopt the names of their oppressors.[f] Subsequent Emperors became Sebastios, Philippes, Domingos, Affonsos, etc. The Indians, Chinese, Arabs, Amerindians, and Mexicans were also colonised and some enslaved, but with few exceptions held tenaciously on to their native names.

The Empire of Monomotapa was down, but certainly not out! Towards the end of the seventeenth century (in 1693), the original centre of the Empire, still under the leadership of a continuing line of Changamires, brought former separatist kingdoms together and launched a war of liberation against the Portuguese. "The Portuguese suffered heavy casualties and fled to the comparative safety of their fortified settlements nearer the coasts. The Changamire armies reconquered most of Monomotapa and a vigorous anti-Portuguese policy was adopted."[26]

But their victory was, tragically, only a temporary check to the inexorable advance of the insidious European powers who were, with the Portuguese and French, already engaged in the most brutal slave trade the world had ever known, on the West coast of Africa. The British and the Dutch had already penetrated southern Africa from the Cape and were setting up 'republics' and thereby completing the encirclement of Africa: the North was completely in the hands either of the Arabs or European powers who had, or were in the process of invading the Arabs; the whole of the West was being subjected to the vicious, systematic, and debilitating attack of the slave trade, softening it for the impending 'scramble' for complete takeover; the East had experienced the bestial destructive force of Portuguese 'civilising' assault; and now the South was being claimed for 'Christianity' and the establishment of the most advanced form of the ideology of racism: *Apartheid*!

But there was an even more immediate threat to the Empire of Monomotapa. Shaka had also become aware of the threat posed by the British and the Dutch to the Zulus, and the need for a unified force to repulse these foreign 'canker-worms'. As Shaka expanded his Zulu Empire, many tribal states fled northward and eastward, spreading death and destruction among those who would stand in their path. Among the leading groups to reach the Changamire kingdoms first were the Ndebele, Swazi and the Shangana who crossed the Limpopo in 1830 and swept on to the Zambezi, bringing to an end a great African civilisation whose foundations were laid three centuries before Christ and reached its zenith in the fifteenth century. Of course, no great empires and Emperors were to replace

it – the superior fire power of the British and Dutch were soon to
smash the military might of the great Zulu King and General,
Shaka, as well as the smaller Kingdoms of the Matabele and Barwe.
A partition agreement was reached between the British and the
Portuguese and, following the Boer war, all the whites soon patched
up their differences and shared up the spoils of African land, wealth
and peoples between them. Relentlessly and insidiously, the
holocaust brought on Africa from the fifteenth century had, like
cancer, spread through the entire body of the great Continent!

Monomotapa, like many past civilisations in Africa, left evidence
of its past – a history of progress and development; of power and
grandeur; of the African's ingenuity, but also of his frailty; of how
far the African had retrogressed from his past achievements.
Monomotapa left over two hundred sites of ruins of great architectural structures: great royal palaces, temples and artifacts manifest-
ing magnificent artistic talent and skill, dating back to 1100 AD or
earlier.

Of the 200-plus ruins of stone complexes found in the area,
including the sites of Dhlo Dhlo, Khami, Mtoko, and Chisvingo, the
greatest, and the one that has excited the imagination most and
stimulated the fiercest debate, is "The Great Zimbabwe". Sited
seventeen miles south of the modern Zimbabwean city of Nyanda, it
is a massive stone complex exceeded in Africa only by the pyramids
of Egypt and Sudan, and the Bigo Ruins of Uganda. The ancient
plan of Great Zimbabwe was in two parts: the hill complex (now
commonly called the Royal Enclosure); and the valley complexes
which comprised of nine separate stone sites including the Imba
Huru, Great Enclosure.

Among the many enclosures within the hill complex were the
ritual enclosure, the smelting enclosure and the iron-keeping
enclosure.

> "The valley complexes", [observed Molefi and Kariamu Asante], "are
> dominated by the Imba Huru, Great Enclosure. The wall is 250 metres long
> and it utilizes 15,000 tons of granite blocks. We estimated that within a
> section one meter long, from top to bottom, two meters thick, there were
> approximately 4500 stone blocks. The height of the main wall of the Imba
> Huru was nothing more than a shell of stone. But even so in its bewildering
> become so symbolic of Zimbabwe. To build any of these complexes took skill,
> will and industry. Yet, the Imba Huru demonstrates administrative and
> social achievement by bringing workers together on such an elephant scale
> to erect the complex. Peter Garlake (1982) estimates that over 10,000 people
> lived in Great Zimbabwe, making it one of the largest cities of its day."[27]

The first European to see the Great Zimbabwe was the German,
Karl Mauch, followed by Willi Posselt, Theodore Bent and scores of
others. With complete disregard for aesthetic value, the Europeans

plundered the contents with the instinct of scavengers. Priceless gold artificats were melted down and turned into gold bars; those relics which did not meet the same fate, eg the 'Shiri ya Mwari', the Bird of Gold, ended up in the South African Museum, the Paul Tishman collection of New York, the British Museum and the Museum Fur Volkerkunde of Berlin.

> "The site [noted Asante and Asante], "has withstood successive raids by European treasure hunters, souvenir seekers and plunderers. In 1892 the Imba Huru and other buildings were ransacked by the English Royal Horse Guards. Sixty men gutted the insides of the great building taking everything that was light enough to be removed. When they left the scene the Imba Huru was nothing more than a shell of stone. But even so in its bewildering emptiness it remained an impressive example of African workmanship."[28]

There were also acts of mindless vandalism which sought to destroy the remains of the structure rather than to search for treasure.

But the greatest destruction and vandalism committed by these Europeans was intellectual rather than physical – the attempt to distort, destroy and obliterate black ownership and history. Confronted with such massive, magnificent, and incontrovertible evidence of a great civilisation, five hundred miles into the African interior, the ideology of racism summoned its great 'ideologues' to theorise on the racial origin of the builders, the firm assumption being that black people were absolutely incapable of accomplishing such outward manifestation of civilisation. As H.L. Duff had observed in 1903: "Nothing could more forcibly illustrate the difference between extremes of racial character than the picture thus conjured up – the European engineer forcing with incredible toil his broad and certain way, stemming rivers, draining marshes, shattering tons of earth and rock; and, on the other hand, the savage, careless of everything but the present, seeking only the readiest path, and content to let a pebble baulk him rather than stoop to lift it."[29]

And hadn't another Englishman written with conviction bordering on religious faith: "By their own unaided efforts, I doubt whether the Negroes would ever advance much above the status of savagery in which they still exist in those parts of Africa where neither European nor Arab civilization has yet reached them.... The Negro seems to require the intervention of some superior race before he can be roused to any definite advance from the low stage of human development in which he has contentedly remained for many thousand years."[30]

The search for the builders of the Great Zimbabwe outside of such a mental framework was inconceivable!

European 'genius' came out with one theory after another about the identity of the builders of the Great Zimbabwe. One theory held that it was built by the Persians for the worship of Ashtar. Were this true, modern Zimbabwe would be teeming with Persians, for as we noted above, there were over 200 such sites and Great Zimbabwe alone is estimated to have had a population of 10,000. Another theory suggested that it was the land of 'King Solomon's mines'; while other theories ascribed them to the Phoenicians, Portuguese, Arabs and Chinese.

I have noted above that had these ruins and artifacts of civilisation been found anywhere else other than Africa, they would have been ascribed, without the slightest difficulty, to the ancestors of the inhabitants (unless there was overwhelming evidence to the contrary). Asante and Asante rightly point out that "The question of the origin of the Great Zimbabwe would probably never have occurred if the structure had been found on a continent other than Africa. Few writers have ascribed the building of Teotihuaucan to people other than the Aztecs or Chichen Itza to other than the Mayans or Macchu Picchu to other than the Incas."[31]

Two further illustrations of the potency of the ideology of racism can be seen at work. The Ife civilisation of the twelfth century produced, among other things, sculptors of great skill and talent. When Europeans came into contact with the highly artistic skill and remarkable works of the sculptors and the life-like realism of the Ife sculptures, the ideology of racism precluded any explanation that attributed such achievement to black people. A German researcher, Leo Frobenius who visited Ife in Nigeria and obtained a number of terracotta sculptures, suggested to his audience in Europe that they were the products of the people of the lost civilisation of Atlantis, which, naturally, was assumed to be Caucasian!

The other example relates to the Dogon of Mali in West Africa. The astronomer-priests of the Dogon had apparently amassed a wealth of knowledge of the universe which not only shook the scientific world to its foundations, but galvanised the race ideologues into an urgent search for "rational" explanation. These Dogons, it turned out, knew about,

"The rings of Saturn, the moons of Jupiter, the spiral structure of the Milky Way Galaxy, in which our planet lies. They knew a billion worlds spiralled in space like the circulation of blood within the body of God. They knew that the moon was a barren world. They said it was 'dry and dead, like dried blood'. They knew also of things far in advance of their time, intricate details about a star which no one can see except with the most powerful of telescopes.

Bronze head representing a Benin Queen

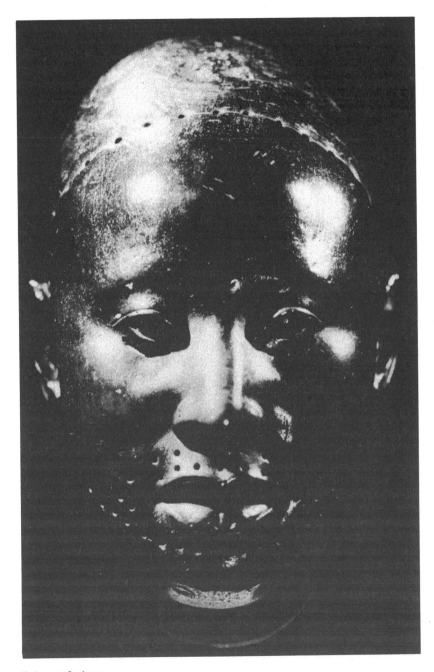

Ife bronze Sculpture

They not only saw it. They observed or intuited its mass and nature. They plotted its orbit almost up until the year 2,000. And they did all this between five and seven hundreds years ago."[32]

The remarkable astronomical knowledge of the Dogon was brought to light by two French anthropologists, Marcel Griaule and Germaine Dieterlen who lived among the Dogon from 1931 to 1956. They were initiated into this level of knowledge after sixteen years of 'education' by the Dogons. As they were to learn, the Dogons had an intimate knowledge of, and a preoccupation with, a star within the Sirius star system. Every sixty years, when the orbits of Jupiter and Saturn converged, the Dogons had a ceremony to Sirius. This ceremony, however, was not to Sirius, the brightest star in the sky, but to its companion, Sirius B, 'a star so small, so dense, so difficult to perceive, it is truly amazing that any medieval science was aware of it'.

"The Dogon knew that this star, although invisible to the naked eye, had an elliptical orbit around Sirius A that took 50 years to complete. Modern science confirms this orbit. The Dogon drew a diagram... showing the course and trajectory of this star up unto the year 1990. Modern astronomical projections are identical with this. The Dogon say that this tiny star is composed of a metal brighter than iron and that if all the men on earth were a single lifting force they could not budge it. Modern science confirms that this is the nature of that type of star – 'a white dwarf' – a star so compacted that its mass may be many times greater than a star which appears many times larger."[33]

In view of the basic assumptions of the European about the African, what was the reaction of the white scientific community to this information? Robert Temple, a member of the Royal Astronomical Society of Great Britain in his book, 'The Sirius Mystery', speculated that "space-beings" from the Sirius star-system must have brought this marvellous knowledge down to the Africans. Carl Sagan of the TV series, Cosmos, suggests that some 'clever European' traveller preceded the French anthropologists and imparted this knowledge to the Dogon. The latter's information to Griaule and Dieterlen was, therefore, a mere parrot-fashion reproduction of European knowledge. The problem which Carl Sagan has to address, though, is that the Dogon ceremony to Sirius B goes back 700 years – several centuries before Europe knew of its existence.

Kenneth Brecher of the Massachusetts Institute of Technology, in an article titled "Sirius Enigmas" in the December 1977 edtion of *Technology Review*, summarises the problem neatly: "The problem for us, therefore, is how the Dogon could have known a host of astronomical facts, all of which are invisible to the unaided eye". In an apparent frustration, he adds: "They have no business knowing any of this".[34]

Had these Euro-centric scientists accepted the fact that the world's first calendar, still in use today, after minor modification, was invented by black Africans of Egypt in 4241 BC and that the science of astronomy was invented in Africa by the black Egyptians, the "problem" posed would be non-problematic.

It is from this type of Euro-centric perspective then that Europeans encountered Great Zimbabwe. Of course, expert investigators from David Randall-MacIver in 1905, Gertrude Caton-Thompson in 1929 to researchers of the 1950s: Kenneth Robinson, Roger Simmers, Peter Garlake *et al.*, have since dismissed the 'theories' of the racial ideologists. Every evidence found amongst the Zimbabwe ruins has pointed to a Shona origin. But notwithstanding the available facts, even today the overwhelming majority of white people in Zimbabwe and South Africa cannot accept this historical reality. In their blissful ignorance, they are still firmly convinced that without Caucasian intervention black people could never create a civilisation.

The Ghana Empire

The Arab geographer and historian, al-Bakri had visited the ancient West African empire of Ghana sometime after 960 AD and described it as a vast country of fertile fields with rivers and lakes, woods, and green plains, of busy villages, towns and "cities of stone".[35] And yet, when Bonnel de Mezieres, a French district officer went in search of the site of its capital – the twin city – Kumbi-Kumbi, all he saw as far as the eyes could see was a wasteland of rocks and sand.

Was ancient Ghana an African mythology? Had the Arab geographers, travellers, and scholars who claimed to have visited it, conspired with the Africans to create an imaginary African civilisation? If not, where is the evidence to substantiate the claims of African oral history that this was the site of Ghana's ancient capital? The archaeologists commenced digging with healthy scepticism, but were soon rewarded by the unearthing of the ancient city which for centuries had been entombed by the Sahara sands.

"Ghana's actual history", Williams observes, "goes far back beyond its known record. That record listed forty-four kings before the Christian era and this alone would extend Ghana's known history beyond the 25th Dynasty when the last black pharaohs ruled Egypt (seventh century BC)."[36]

When West Africa's Iron Age began in about 500 BC[37] greater opportunities for creativity and industry, division of labour and the development of new skills, the creation and accumulation of wealth, led to steady social, political, and cultural advances so that by the eleventh century AD,[g] a large and prosperous African empire had been formed. The extent of the wealth of the Empire is evidenced in the account of the royal stables of the king of Ghana at the end of the seventh century given in the Tarikh-el-Fatash, one of the two old histories of the Sudan, published in Timbuktu:

> "None of the one thousand horses slept except upon a carpet, nor was he tied except by a silken rope round his neck and to his foot. Each of them had a copper pot into which he urinated. No drop of urine should fall except into the receptacle, were it night or day. One would never see beneath these horses the slightest droppings. Each horse had three persons attached to his service and seated near him. One took charge of his food, the second his drink, and the third took charge of urine and droppings."[38]

Ghana was known to people of the medieval period as Awkar, according to al-Bakri and the title given to their king by the foreign visitors was Ghana – leader or head of the State – and, in time, the empire came to be known as Ghana. The empire had expanded territorially by both conquests and peaceful alliances with neighbouring countries, including dependencies such as Sama, Garantel, Gadiaro, Galam (present day Northern Ghana area), Diara, Soso and Tekrur. The desert tribes of Berbers were made tributaries – the Zenaga, Lemtuna, Goddala, Messufa, *et al.* At the height of its power, the empire was comparable to most European states at that time and surpassed many others in social organisation, military power, economic wealth, and in the promotion of higher education.

Although the Ghana Empire was known as the "Land of Gold" because it controlled the greatest source of gold for both Europe and Asia, its economy was quite diversified. Agricultural products included wheat, millet, cotton, corn, yams, animal husbandry – cows, horses, goats, camels and sheep. Mining and smeltering played an important role in the economy and numerous crafts were organised as guilds: goldsmiths, blacksmiths, and coppersmiths. Other guilds included stone-masons, brick-masons, carpenters, cabinet-makers, furniture makers, weavers, dyers, sandal-makers, and potters. The empire engaged in a large international trade, exporting chiefly gold, ivory and slaves and importing wheat, salt, textiles, cowrie shells, brass, dates, figs, pearls, fruit, raisins and honey. Both imports and exports, according to al-Bakri, were taxed and the Emperor apparently operated a complex network of internal revenue collection throughout the realm.

Ghana had a well-established educational system, although as was the case with most ancient civilisations, only a proportionally small élite had access to its education. The most famous schools were at the capital, Kumbi-Kumbi (which was also known as

Kumbi-Saleh) and Djenne. The world renowned University of
Sankore was at Timbuktu.

When Tunka Manin came to the throne in 1063, the Ghana
Empire was prosperous and powerful. Al-Bakri informs us in his
'Book of the Roads and Kingdoms' published in 1068 that the
imperial army numbered 200,000 of which 100,000 were mounted
and 40,000 of them were archers. He describes the majesty of the
Emperor:

> "When the King gives audience, or hears grievances against officials, he sits
> in a domed pavilion around which stand ten horses covered with gold-
> embroidered clothes. Behind the King stand ten pages holding shields and
> swords decorated with gold; and his right are the sons of the vassal kings of
> his country, wearing splendid garments with gold plaited into their hair. At
> the door of the pavilion are dogs of an excellent breed, and these hardly ever
> leave the place where the King is. Round their neck their wear collars of gold
> and silver."[39]

One wonders how many European Kings of the eleventh century
rivalled such wealth, pomp, pageantry, grandeur and splendour!

In 1076, Ghana's capital fell to Almoravid invaders from Morocco.
These were Berber nomads who hated settled life and destroyed
without rebuilding. The destruction of the capital, the drying up of
the Wagadu river, regular raids by Berber and Arab desert nomads,
caused a mass flight of Ghanaians towards the forests southwards
and westwards towards the coast. Decline set in and with it, the
weakening of central authority. By 1200 AD rulers of parts of the
Empire saw their chance to throw off the Soninke rulers of Ghana
and make a bid not only for independence, but to build a rival
empire. Kangoba, a small kingdom of the Mandinka people,
southern neighbours of the Soninke, were the ones to successfully
challenge the Ghana rulers and usher in the famous Mali Empire.

The Mali Empire

The struggle for leadership of the region following the decline of
Ghana began with two rebelling provinces of Ghana – Kaniaga and
Diara – making bids for supremacy. These were, however, defeated
by the nearby Kingdom of Tegrur whose King, Sumanguru captured
Kumi-Saleh, the capital of Ghana in 1203. His attempt to rebuild
the empire foundered and in 1240, his army was defeated by the
Mandinka king, Sundiata Keita at the Battle of Kirina.

The emergent Mali Empire was built on solid political foundation
thanks to strong leadership under Emperors Sundiata Keita and his
successor Mansa Uli who systematically and effectively re-
organised, consolidated and expanded the old Ghana Empire. By the

time Mansa Musa ascended the throne in 1312, Mali had become
"one of the largest states and one of the richest systems of tax and
tribute in the world west of India and China. It enclosed most of the
western plains of the Sudan, and, on the reckoning of an experienced traveller, who lived for 35 years in Mali during the first half
of the fourteenth century, was 'four or more months' journey in
length, and as much in width".[40]

As I noted above, even an extreme bigoted racist like Putnam had
admitted that at one time ancient West African Kingdoms'
"brilliance" exceeded that of contemporary Scandinavia. The Mali
Empire became even more wealthy and powerful than the old
Ghana Empire it replaced. The Syrian writer Ibn Fadl al-Umari,
then a resident of Cairo, wrote of the now legendary pilgrimage to
Mecca through Cairo, by the Emperor Mansa Kankan Musa: "This
man flooded Cairo with his benefactions. He left no courtier nor
holder of a royal office without the gift of a load of gold. The
Cairenes made incalculable profits out of him and his suite in
buying and selling and giving and taking. They exchanged gold
until they depressed its value in Egypt, and caused its price to
fall."[41] According to al-Umari, 12 years after the Mali Emperor's
visit, the price of gold in Cairo had still not recovered.

When the Arab scholar and traveller Ibn Battuta visited Mali in
1352-1353, Suleyman Mansa had succeeded Mansa Musa. He
describes audiences granted by the Emperor:

> "On certain days the sultan holds audiences in the palace yard, where there
> is a platform under a tree, with three steps; this they call the pempi. It is
> carpeted with silk and has cushions placed on it. Over it is raised the
> umbrella, which is a sort of pavilion made of silk, surmounted by a bird in
> gold, about the size of a falcon. The sultan comes out of a door in a corner of
> the palace, carrying gold skull-cap, bound with a gold band which has narrow
> ends shaped like knives, more than a span in length. His usual dress is a
> velvety red tunic, made of the European fabrics called mutanfas. The sultan
> is preceded by his musicians, who carry gold and silver two-stringed guitars,
> and behind him come 300 armed slaves. He walks in a leisurely fashion,
> affecting a very slow movement, and even stops from time to time. On
> reaching the pempi he stops and looks around the assembly, then ascends it
> in the sedate manner of a preacher ascending a mosque-pulpit. As he takes
> his seat the drums, trumpets and bugles are sounded. Three slaves go out at a
> run to summon the sovereign's deputy and military commanders, who enter
> and sit down. Two saddled and bridled horses are brought, along with two
> goats, which they hold to serve as a protection against the evil eye. Dugha
> stands at the gate and the rest of the people remain in the street, under the
> trees...."[42]

In complete contrast to the assertions by the proponents of the
ideology of racism and the wild claims by the *Encyclopaedia
Britannica* in 1810, Ibn Battuta witnessed at first hand a highly

civilised society in which social order and respect for the law was taken for granted; a society whose high moral standard and ethical values was unsurpassed by any other society which Battuta had visited – and he had travelled widely in Africa, the Middle East, parts of Europe, India, China, etc.

Among the admirable qualities of the ancient people of Mali, he noted the following:

1. The small number of acts of injustice that one finds here; for the Negroes are of all peoples those who most abhor injustice. The sultan pardons no one who is guilty of it.

2. The complete and general safety one enjoys throughout the land. The traveller has no more reason to fear brigands, thieves, or ravishers than the man who stays at home.

3. The Blacks do not confiscate the goods of the white man [ie, of North Africans] who die in their country, not even when these consist of big treasures. They deposit them, on the contrary, with a man of confidence among the whites until those who have a right to the goods present themselves and take possession.[43]

How many Western societies today can boast of that level of order, respect for the rights, persons and properties of others, as well as a greater sense of ethics and morality and, above all honesty? And yet, compare Ibn Battuta's account with that of the medical officer for the African Company, James Houston, quoted above, who stated of the West Africans: "their natural Temper is barbarously cruel, selfish, and deceitful, and their Government equally barbarous and uncivil; and consequently the Men of greatest Eminency among them are those who are most capable of being the greatest Rogues". It would appear that the medical officer was suffering from the classic psychological case of projection in which one attributes to others the very things that one is worried about in oneself. Indeed I will challenge any historian to identify a single European country in the fourteenth century in which a greater degree of law and order prevailed, or one in which a higher standard of ethical and moral behaviour amongst the populace obtained!

We noted above that Putnam acknowledged that 'at a brief period' there were West African Kingdoms whose brilliance surpassed contemporary Scandinavia, but went on to state that Timbuktu was rulers of Ghana reigned over the Berber-Tuareg and Aoudaghost, class. Full-blooded Negroes, he claimed, were at the bottom of the social scale. Let us examine the available historical record and see if they bear out Putnam's assertion.

Firstly, it is a well known fact that the Ghana, Mali and Songhay Empires included strong Arab and Berber tribal states under their

rule.[44] But these desert tribes were made tributaries.[45] "Thanks to
Arab chroniclers of the Middle Ages, it is known that the Black
rulers of Ghana reigned over the Berber-Tuareg and Aoudaghost,
who paid them tribute."[46]

Secondly, from the seventh century AD, Arab, Berber and
Tuareg Muslims controlled all Northern access to the coast of
Africa, from Morocco to Egypt. They therefore came to control West
Africa's import and export trade with Europe, the Middle East and
the Far East. The trans-Saharan caravan route, especially, became
vulnerable as Muslim Nomadic tribes mounted increasingly effective raiding attacks against the merchants. Given the conditions of
the Saharan desert, the armed guards were powerless against the
guerilla tactics adopted by the raiders. Economic necessity, therefore, forced many Black kings and leaders to embrace Islam as a
way of preventing or minimising such attacks against their citizens.
"One solution of the problem, it was believed, was for Black kings to
become Muslims. Embracing Islam became not merely a policy of
expediency wherever Arab and Berber Muslims gained a dominant
foothold in Black Africa, but it became a compelling means to
economic survival."[47]

It would appear, however, that the Islamic religion had little
impact on the socio-cultural and ethical lives of the African
masses, at least up to the eighteenth century: "Islam had come to
West Africa over 500 years earlier, with the caravan merchants of
the eighth or ninth century, but it had been slow to take root. Not
until the eleventh century did West African kings and courts begin
to find it useful to accept Islam as one of their faiths, while
conserving their respect for the ancestral shrines and the beliefs of
the peoples over whom they ruled. For many years after that – well
into the eighteenth century in most parts of West Africa – Islam
remained a religion only of the towns while country folk worshipped
their own gods as before."[48]

Of course, as the kings, chiefs, scholars, merchants, etc. accepted
Islam, even if as a marriage of convenience, so they adopted Islamic
names. Many Europeans were to later assume these Kings and
Emperors to be Arabs or Berbers as a consequence. For example the
Soninke scholars, Mahmud Kati who wrote Tarikh-al-Fatash, or
Chronicle of the Seeker and Raham as Said, author of Tarikh-Al-
Sudan and the biographer and lexicographer Ahmad Babo, who
authored a comprehensive dictionary and forty other works[49] were
assumed by many to be Arabs. Equally many contemporary black
Americans who have achieved brilliance in many fields of human
endeavour are either wrongly assumed to be white or their race is
deliberately and conveniently omitted from the literature, leaving
people to assume them to be white.

Thirdly, Ibn Battuta contrasted his account of the wealth and high level of civilisation he found in Mali, with certain cultural practices (despite the influence of Islam), that quite shocked him and which leaves the reader in no doubt that the ancient Mali rulers were neither Arabs, Berbers, nor Tuaregs.

> "These people" [he complained], "have some deplorable customs.... Women servants, slave women and young girls go about quite naked, not even concealing their sexual parts. I saw many like this during Ramadhan; because it is the custom with the Negroes that commanding officers should break their fast in the Sultan's palace, and they are served with food which is brought by women slaves, twenty or more of them who are completely naked.
> "Women go naked into the Sultan's presence, too, without even a veil; his daughters also go about naked. On the twenty-seventh night of Ramadhan I saw about a hundred women slaves coming out of the Sultan's palace with food, and they were naked. Two daughters of the Sultan were with them, and these had no veil either, although they had big breasts."[50]

Nudity, as is well known, is one of the recurring 'proofs', cited by the European proponents of the ideology of racism, of the black races' uncivilised status. But nudity in most parts of Africa was due to the unavailability of textile products – like ancient Egypt, nudity in ancient Mali existed side by side with the availability of the finest quality garments! Today, nudist beaches and camps are fashionable throughout the Western world. Indeed in the USA and some European countries, actual explicit 'copulation' takes place on stage in front of large paying audiences, but no one cites these as evidence of the 'uncivilised' nature of Western societies.

Finally, as far as the West African Empires were concerned, Ibn Battuta, the Tangier-born Arab, left us in no doubt of their racial identity. From the above quotation he tells us that the inhabitants of the Mali Empire were Negroes. Putnam had claimed as we noted above that these Blacks were ruled, however, by Arab nobility and slightly coloured Tuareg upper class. Let us see what Ibn Battuta, who had met the King in person as well as many members of the aristocracy, had to say about their race:

> "Our merchants stood in his presence and he addressed them through a third person, though they were standing close to him. That showed how little consideration he had for them and I was so displeased that I bitterly resented having to come to *a country whose inhabitants show themselves to be so impolite and evince such scorn for white men.*"[51]

This was a misunderstanding of African custom, of course! The Emperor had meant no disrespect to the white foreigners; African Kings speak through a 'linguist', indicating the fact that they speak not on their own behalf but on the people's behalf. Even where there is no language barrier, the linguist would repeat the king's statement to the person addressed and repeat back his or her response to the king. The cultural misunderstanding aside, Ibn Battuta leaves us in no doubt that the Mali Emperor Suleyman Mansa (as well as his predecessors) were *black Africans!* And furthermore, that the Ghana and Mali civilisations were the undisputed product of *black* initiative and progress. I challenge any historian to prove otherwise!

From 1400 onwards, internal disunity and strife led to the gradual decline and splintering of the Mali Empire and by the end of the fifteenth century, a new and powerful black Empire had relegated what was left of Mali into a third-rate Kingdom. That new black Empire was Songhay.

The Songhay Empire

Songhay was a small African state between Gao in present day Mali and Agades in Niger with its capital at Kukya. Its history under a long line of dias (kings) can be traced back to the seventh century. The 16th ruler, Dia Kossoi was crowned at Gao early in the eleventh century and moved the capital there from Kukya. Gao, a city-state had been captured from the Sorko people in the seventh century.[52]

Gao was of strategic importance economically, for it dominated the commerce of the central regions of the Western Sudan, controlling the flow of gold and ivory from the southern forests and the precious salt trade from the Taghaza mines in the northern desert. The temptation to take control of such a commercially strategic city was economically and politically irresisitible. So in 1325 the Mali Emperor Mansa Musa sent an invading force to bring Gao and other Songhay territories into his empire. The defeated Songhay pretended loyalty to Mansa Musa while strategically planning, rebuilding, and restructuring the institution of monarchy by abolishng the rule of dias and introducing a new system of leadership with the title of sunni.

During the reign of the second sunni of the new line, Sulieman-Mar, Songhay felt strong enough to declare its independence in 1375. The expected military reaction from Mali did not materialise and Songhay, after a relative period of calm, began an expansionist policy when Sunni Ali came to the throne in 1464 and at a time when the Mali Empire was in a steep decline. Sunni Ali built Songhay into a powerful empire politically, economically and militarily. He became a nominal Muslim for the same economic reasons as his predecessors, but his successor in 1492, Sunni Baru, refused to compromise with Islam and was deposed.

He was succeeded by his chief minister and greatest General who, in contrast to many previous West African kings and Emperors, was an ardent and sincere Muslim. Muhammad Ture became Emperor in 1493, with the military title of Askia. During his reign, he expanded the empire eastward over the Hausa States in Northern Nigeria, northward over the Sahara beyond the Taghaza salt mines, and westward to the Atlantic Ocean, and earned the name 'Askia the Great'. His contribution to Songhay Empire and civilisation was not just political and territorial; under his rule Songhay thrived economically and, most especially, intellectually.

The two principal seats of learning in the Ghana and Mali Empires, Timbuktu and Djenne, had been incorporated into the Songhay Empire in its northward and westward expansion. Together with Gao, these three educational centres developed into centres of academic excellence whose reputation spread far beyond the borders of the empire. The world famous University of Sankore at Timbuktu was at the head of these three centres of scholarship, and its students came from near and far.

The University structure, according to Williams,[53] consisted of a (1) Faculty of Law; (2) Medicine and Surgery; (3) Letters; (4) Grammar; (5) Geography; and (6) Art ('Art' as used here encompassed practical training such as manufacturing, building, and other allied crafts). Among the thousands of students from West Africa and abroad, were a 'large number of scientists, doctors, lawyers and other scholars'.[54] More importantly, Williams observes that though the literature is silent, there must have been a number of elementary and secondary schools in West Africa 'without which there could not have been a University of Sankore with such high standards of admission'.

The basic language of instruction was Arabic. We have noted above that politico-economic necessity had led to many West African kings adopting Islam. But Arabic, the language of Islam had importance not only because it was the language of religion and learning, but also because it was the language of trade and commerce. And the latter made its use more widespread among the black people than it would otherwise have been. Black scholars in West Africa used Arabic as the basic language of Academia whether they were Muslims or not. This factor led to the assumption that the West African civilisations were Arab or Muslim originated and inspired. But this is far from the truth.

The fact that Arabic was the language of scholarship is no more proof that the West African civilisations were Arab-inspired than that Western intellectual development after the Dark Ages was caused by Islam, for as Williams has observed:

"It may not be without significance that the renaissance in Africa occurred at the same time it developed in Europe – between the 15th and 16th centuries, and that both in Europe and Africa Islamic sources were the catalysts. For the Arabs, like the early Greeks, had advanced their civilization by systematically drawing heavily on the cultures of pre-existing civilizations with which they came in contact as they spread out from the deserts of Arabia to distant lands. They enriched and expanded their own langauge in a well organized enterprise in copying the most important literature they could find. The most important classical manuscripts had disappeared from Europe entirely during the so-called 'Dark Ages'. The only sources extant were those copied and preserved by the Arabs – and without which, 'scholars generally agree' the great European Renaissance could not have occurred."[55]

Askia the Great was deposed in 1528 at the age of 80, by his eldest son, having ruled Songhay for thirty-five years. He died ten years later. But again, as was the case in previous black Kingdoms and Empires (as was also the case in history of peoples everywhere), weak leadership led to decline and tendency towards fragmentation. In 1582 the Hausa States, a powerful neighbouring Kingdom to the south, resumed their attacks against Songhay. The Sultan of Morocco, Mulay Ahmad saw this as a propitious time to capture the salt mines of Taghaza and the gold of Songhay. "Armed with guns and cannons – then unavailable to African armies – the Moroccans met the Army of Songhay under Askia Issihak at Tondibi in 1594. Spears and arrows had to give way to gunfire. Thereafter the Songhay forces split up into small units to harass enemy garrisons and outposts in surprise attacks. These attempts to dislodge the invaders lasted over 70 years. But the Songhay of glorious memory was no more. The armies of Islam continued their triumphant march in Africa, destroying its basic institutions wherever they could do so."[56]

We began Chapter Five of our analyses of the ideology of racism by restating its basic assumption, viz., that the black man was naturally inferior to the white man. We noted furthermore that the evidence proffered to support this basic premise was two-fold: (a) that blacks, as a people, have never in the past created a civilisation of their own without Caucasian intervention or direction; and (b) that blacks have, as individuals, made no contribution to the conquest of nature, ie, that in the field of science and technology, no individual black has made a contribution.

As far as proposition (a) is concerned, I have demonstrated from available historical data that the foundation of the ideology of racism was constructed not on *FACTS*, but on *FICTION*; not on *REALITY*, but on *MYTHOLOGY*; not on *TRUTH* but on (often deliberate) *falsehood*; not on sound *CONCLUSIONS* derived from observations and analyses, but on *ILLUSIONS* created by the figment of European *IMAGINATION*; not on the results of an honest quest for *KNOWLEDGE*, but on a deliberate and often ingenious effort to *FALSIFY* and to *DISTORT;* not on *SCIENCE* but on *WISHFUL THINKING;* not on an attempt to understand the biological and social phenomena of the diversity of human races, but on a calculated racist attempt to demonstrate the 'superiority' of white people and the logical corollary of the 'inferiority' of black people.

Having, it is hoped, accomplished an effective rebuttal of proposition (a), we are going to produce *facts* to demolish proposition (b) in the next Chapter.

Notes

a. Note that the Swahilis were black Africans, but at the time the Portuguese arrived, towards the end of the Fifteenth century, the Africans had been trading with Arabians, Persians, Indians and Chinese for centuries and many merchants and sailors from these countries had settled among the Africans. The proponents of the ideology of racism tell us that the Arabs completely controlled the East African trade, which is arrant nonsense.

b. For "popular and scholarly ideas," read: *the ideology of racism.*

c. emphasis mine.

d. Basil Davidson suggests 1425 as the year when Mutota began the process of empire building.

e. Unlike most African societies of the period, the Vakaranga had become patrilineal.

f. This author is no exception to this disgraceful deculturation.

g. Cheikh Anta Diop suggests that the Ghana Empire was probably founded in the third century A D (see *The African Origin of Civilisation,* p. 163).

h. emphasis mine

CHAPTER SEVEN

Refuting a Myth: Black Scientists and Inventors

"The choice of historical topics and figures found in current physics and physical science texts has the effect of reinforcing the racial stereotypes that denigrate the intellectual and scientific abilities of non-whites. A survey of seventeen representative texts published since 1970 shows that 'not once is a scientific discovery or discoverer identified as being of African origin. No black scientist is pictured in any of these books nor is a single black credited with any contribution'."[1]

That was the summary of the findings of a survey conducted by Dr John Pappademos, Professor of Physics, University of Illinois at Chicago Circle, to ascertain the extent to which textbooks on physics and the physical sciences reflect the contribution of non-whites. The textbooks, which had been selected at random except for the requirement that their date of publication be post-1970 for reasons of currency, were being used at university and high school levels.

Pappademos found that 'the choice of pictures of people which appeared in the various texts, the references to the contributions of whole peoples (races, nations, or continents)' were calculated to omit the contribution of peoples other than whites. For example, 'out of the 17 books surveyed, although there were 94 different scientists appearing in 186 pictures of scientists, Asian scientists were pictured only eight times, including Chandrasekhar, Raman, Yukawa, Ting, and three that were unidentified'. Pappademos found 'not a single Black or Latino scientist pictured in any of the books'. He found that the text-books presented a Eurocentric perspective of the world in which 'little or no acknowledgement is made of the basis laid by the peoples of Africa and the Near East for the later European achievement in science'. He observes that 'the results of this survey clearly support the view that currently used US physics and physical science texts do indeed tend to reinforce racial stereotypes'. He concludes from the results of the survey that "by neglecting the contribution of non-white people (particularly black people) the 17 texts belittle their contributions and effectively promote the view that the progress of physics owes little or nothing to the intellectual ability and labour of other than white people".[2]

Pappademos's findings are only the tip of a very large iceberg as we shall see. But before we examine the role of the ideology of racism in creating and covering the iceberg, let us look at some black individuals who, through genius, hard work, tremendous persever- ance in the face of multi-variate racist hurdles, and dedicated desire to apply the principles of science for the betterment of humanity, have contributed to the understanding and exploitation of nature for the benefit of mankind.

Imhotep − "The Father of Medicine"

Since the Egyptians invented 'science', it is only appropriate that we begin our analysis of individual black contribution to the develop- ment of science in Egypt. The term "science" is used here to denote knowledge ascertained by observation and experimentation, criti- cally tested, systematised and brought under general rules.

When black American doctors in the 1950s were organising various conferences to address racial discrimination in American hospitals, they called the events "Imhotep Conferences" in order to demonstrate the iniquitous state of affairs in which the first physician known to antiquity was black and yet entrance to the profession in modern America was being severely restricted to black people.

Imhotep, the world's first multi-genius, is now acknowledged by many medical historians as the "Father of Medicine", not Hippo- crates as the Euro-centric presentation of history would have us believe. Imhotep lived about 2980 BC during the reign of Pharaoh Zoser of the Third Dynasty. He was a member of the Pharaoh's court and was an architect, scribe, priest, administrator and a physician.[3] We have already noted that the first Pyramid (the step pyramid at Saqqara) was designed by him. So great was his influence in the field of medicine that the ancient Egyptians erected shrines and temples in his honour to which Egyptians in need of healing flocked. By 525 BC he had become a full deity and an inscription to him read. "Turn thy face towards me, my lord Imhotep, son of Ptah. It is thou who dost work miracles and who are beneficent in all thy deeds."[4]

"Medical historians generally recognise the importance of Imhotep but do not comment on his race. According to Osler, he was 'the first figure of a physician to stand out clearly from the mists of antiquity'. Sigerist introduces Imhotep as the architect of the step pyramid of Saqqara: 'It is the oldest monument of hewn stone known to the world, and it was built by a man of genius, Imhotep, the first universal scholar, architect, engineer, statesman, sage, and physician'. Ackerknect also acknowledges the priority and importance of Imhotep but, like Sigerist, makes no mention of his race."[5]

This conspiracy of silence on the race of Imhotep did not involve the Ancients. The Greeks knew Imhotep as Imouthes and identified him with their later god of healing, Aesclepios (we have already noted that Herodotus has affirmed that nearly all the names of Greek gods came from Egypt). Early Christian Rome acknowledged his healing ability, identified him with Jesus, and more importantly, represented him as black. Later, Jesus replaced Imhotep as Massey writes:

> "Jesus, the divine healer, does not retain the black complexion of Iu-em-hetep in the canonical Gospels, but he does in the Church of Rome when represented by the little black bambino. A jewelled image of the child-Christ as a blackamoor is sacredly preserved at the headquarters of the Franciscan order... to visit the sick, and demonstrate the supposed healing power of the Egyptian Aesculapius thus Christianized."[6]

To appreciate the immense contribution to the development of medical science by Egypt in general and Imhotep in particular, let us take a brief look at the state of the 'art' in ancient Egypt. We have already noted the statement by Herodotus that the 'Egyptians have discovered more prognostics than all the rest of mankind besides', and his comment on the medical specialisation among the practitioners, the only nation in antiquity to have done so, according to Finch. Homer also says in the Odyssey, "In medical knowledge, Egypt leaves the rest of the world behind". It is a well known fact that the city-state of Athens as well as the kingdoms of the Near East used to import Egyptian physicians.[7] Wilson, Saunder, Luth Ghalioungui, and others have noted the strong influence of Egyptian medicine on the development of Greek medicine.[8]

The Egyptians, according to Sigerist were writing medical textbooks 5,000 years ago, but of the hundreds of thousands of medical papyri that must have been written, only ten are extant of which the most important are the Ebers and Edwin Smith Papyri.[9] The latter (original 2600 BC) is kept at the New York Academy of Medicine. In addition to a considerable share of magic and religion, it contains notes on anatomy, herbal pharmacology, pathology, physical diagnosis, and what today would be called scientific medicine. The Ebers papyrus (1500 BC) contains chapters on intestinal disease, helminthiasis, ophthalmology, gynaecology, obstetrics, pregnancy diagnoses, contraception, dentistry, and surgical treatment of abscesses, tumours, fractures, and burns.[10]

> "A study of ancient Egyptian diagnostic methods" [observes Finch], "reads disconcertingly like a modern textbook on physical diagnosis. A physician summoned to examine a patient would begin with a careful appraisal of the patient's general appearance. This would be followed by a series of questions to elicit a description of the complaint. The color of the face and eyes, the

quality of nasal secretions, the presence of perspiration, the stiffness of the
limbs or abdomen, and the condition of the skin were all carefully noted. The
physician was also at pains to take cognizance of the smell of the body, sweat,
breath, and wounds. The urine and feces were inspected, the pulse palpated
and measured, and the abdomen, swellings, and wounds probed and
palpated. The pulse taking is worth noting because it indicates that the
Egyptians knew of its circulatory and hemodynamic significance. Percussion
of the abdomen and chest was performed and certain functional tests we still
use today were done, ie, the coughing test for hernia detection; the
extension-flexion maneuver of the legs to test for a dislocated lumber
vertebra. Sometimes, the case required more than one consultation and the
physician might, as is done today, embark on a 'therapeutic trial' to ascertain
the efficacy of treatment. It also seems that the Egyptians practiced a form of
socialized medicine. All physicians were employees of the state and medical
care was available to everyone."[11]

The medical papyri show that the Egyptians had an extensive
knowledge of anatomy and physiology. They understood the importance of pulsation and 4,500 years before William Harvey (1578-
1657) and Caesalpinus, knew of the structure and function of the
cardiovascular system. They knew that the heart was the centre of
this system, had names for all the major vessels, knew the relation
between heart and lung, and knew the distribution of the vessels
through the limb.[12] They were well-versed in many pathological
syndromes, identifying diseases through methodical and painstak-
ing clinical observation. Egyptian physicians understood the origin
of paraplegia and paralysis from spinal chord injuries and recognised the traumatic origin of neurological symptoms such as
deafness, urinary incontinence and priapism. They knew and
described many syndromes of cardiac origin; recognised the significance of heart palpitations and arrythmias; and gave a highly
perceptive and precise definition of angina pectoris: "If thou
examinest a man for illness in his cardia and he has pains in his
arms, in his breast, and on one side of his cardia... it is death
threatening him."[13]

It is evident: (a) that the ancient Egyptians had developed a
highly complex medical knowledge and practice; (b) that they
heavily influenced the development of Greek medical science; and
(c) that the man who originated and stimulated the further
development of this knowledge and pratice, was the deified black
multigenius Imhotep, the true Father of Medicine. Had Imhotep
been white, I have little doubt that newly qualified medical doctors
would be taking the "Imhotepic" rather than the "Hippocratic" oath.

There is no doubt that the great achievement and high magnificence of the Egyptian civilisation boasted of many great individual
scientists, political scientists, administrators, teachers, military
strategists, etc. Likewise, the civilisations of Kush, Zanj, Monomotapa, Ghana, Mali, Songhay, et al. all produced many talented and

brilliant individuals who made great contributions to their society's adaptation to their environment, and their understanding, and utilisation of nature's resources for the betterment of their peoples. The development of science and technology has obviously had a long, chequered history as the achievements of Egpytian, Babylonian, Chinese, Indian, Greek, Roman, etc. civilisations testify. But the last three centuries, and in particular the last 100 years, has seen unprecedented acceleration of human knowledge and understanding of the universe. As our knowledge of the laws, regularities and uniformities of nature increase, so do our inventive capabilities. This knowledge, inventiveness and our technical and organisational abilities to exploit these inventions have led to a vastly changed environment and freed humanity from many of the limitations previously suffered. We have succeeded in breaking the umbilical cord which bound us to our earth and gone to the moon and successfully returned; we can travel round the globe in a few hours at twice the speed of sound; through the application of microtechnology we can not only build and operate completely automated production systems, but we can also solve highly complex mathematical and engineering problems within minutes, and process literally thousands of data by mainframe computers within seconds; we have designed and built machines which, in turn, design and build other, more complex, machines themselves; we have increased tremendously our destructive capabilities by producing powerful, sophisticated and guided weaponry systems that can cause severe devastation within minutes; the understanding of nuclear physics has led to the obscene proliferation of nuclear weapons which can obliterate life from the earth with fifty-plus overkill capacity; today so advanced has medical knowledge and practice become that the transplant of human organs such as kidney, heart, lung and liver have become routine procedures; 'test-tube' babies and 'surrogate motherhood' have lost their novelty and become commonplace; information technology has reached such an incredible level of sophistication that we can transmit large volumes of data as well as television pictures via satellite from one part of the globe to the other, almost instantaneously; there are exciting new developments in the bio-chemical, electronic, medical, engineering and space technology fields. The scope and pace of man's scientific and technological progress and advancement is truly breath-taking.

In looking at the relatively more recent contribution by individuals of different races to this tremendous scientific development of mankind, it is crucially important to identify the conditions necessary for scientific work. Successful development of scientific work presupposes at least three conditions: (1) the creation of surplus wealth which frees some individuals from full-time pressures for personal survival; (2) freedom of thought and speculation, and the freedom to challenge existing beliefs and assumptions without fear of retribution from the powers that be; and (3) a stimulating cultural environment.

Black contribution to the recent development of science and technology has been limited compared to their achievements in antiquity. The reason is not due to diminishing inventive capabilities among black people, but to the fact that the period of most rapid scientific advancement coincided with the era of slavery and colonisation. It would be unrealistic and unreasonable to expect black people to make equal contribution under a system of slavery which punished those who made any attempt towards intellectual development. The slavery system was calculated to turn its victims into dehumanised, depersonalised, degraded, and intellectually stunted 'sub-human work-machines'. The only degree of intellectual requirement was that these 'sub-human work-machines' be capable of understanding and executing orders without arguing. Those who were fortunate to operate above this intellectual threshold, did so because it suited the economic interest of the master to allow them so to do. Otherwise, any display of intelligence beyond the master's requirement was viewed as a threat to the system and had to be ruthlessly dealt with.

As far as the non-enslaved Africans were concerned, we have shown that colonialism ensured that any progress by, and for the benefit of, the African was checked and African economies were structured to serve as satellites to Europe's economies. Not only does the colonial impoverishment of the African continue to persist today, but that the current inequitable world economic order, combined with disastrous climatic conditions on the Continent, have reduced most African economies to the level of mere subsistence.

During the slavery and colonial eras, the very survival of such vicious servitude, oppression, suppression and deprivation was an eloquent testimony to the greatness of the spirit of the survivors. It required a high degree of human greatness to maintain sanity and rationality under such severe brutality and psychological trauma as black people endured under slavery. But what human genius anywhere in the world could surpass those black people who not only remained sane and rational but rose above slavery and racism – from the depth of an ocean of oppression, suppression, exploitation, dehumanisation, deprivation, degradation and denigration – to make some of the finest contributions to human progress and achievement? Let us take a look at some of these black people who, in spite of the severe limitations and handicap placed on them by a hostile and racist society, and despite the almost non-existent conditions necessary for scientific work, nevertheless surmounted these obstacles and made constributions to human progress and advancement in the field of science, technology and industry.

Jededia Buxton

In 1788 the *Gentlemen's Magazine,* a mouthpiece of British racism, reported the information it had received about Jededia Buxton, a slave and a 'prodigy of calculation', whose arithmetical powers were superior not only to his own people, but to most white people also. The magazine thought this was most extraordinary since *'it is somewhere remarked that few of the race of wooly-headed blacks can go further in the art enumeration than the number 5'.*[a] As an example of Buxton's mathematical talent, the magazine reported an incident in which he was asked how many seconds a man of seventy years, some odd months, weeks and days had lived. In a minute and a half he gave the answer. His questioner, after making the same calculation but with the aid of pen and paper, said that Buxton was wrong. "Stop, Massa" replied the mathematical 'wizard'. "You forget the Leap Years". His white questioner, after including them, found that Buxton was precisely right.[14]

I deliberately chose the story of Buxton not because he made a contribution to the development of mathematics. I chose him firstly, to pay tribute to the man's genius – for an illiterate (forbidden access to education by his white enslavers), his was a manifestation of magnificent, genuine inherent talent and an indomitable spirit to overcome his dehumanisation. It is an excellent example of the African spirit which 6,000 years ago showed mankind the path to civilisation and human progress. Secondly, Buxton's story graphically illustrates the ignorance, arrogance and utter lack of sincerity of the early proponents of racism. With the greatest of ease they unashamedly quoted an unidentifiable source as remarking that only a few black people could count beyond five. Thirdly, Buxton's contribution was that he gave an opportunity to the racists to confront the falsehood of their assumptions of black inferiority. That the racists were incapable of questioning the basic premise of their ideology in the face of reality, was not his fault but a warning to those who would seek to combat racism of the futility in seeking to change racist attitude by presenting facts which oppose their beliefs.

In discussing relatively recent contributions by black people in science and technology, one is compelled to concentrate on the United States, either because most of the contributions have come from there, or data of such contribution is most readily available from there.

Prior to the end of the American Civil War, inventions by black people were not numerous. For most black people, almost all intellectual resources were deployed towards personal survival – escaping from slavery, finding ways of buying oneself out of 'ownership', or in some cases avoiding being murdered by a drunken or psychopathic owner at times of 'diminished' responsibility, etc. But even in that pre-Civil War era, whenever black people were allowed participation in the craft and inventive occupations, they helped to produce artifacts to increase productivity or to lessen human toil and monotony, although these would generally not be attributed to them. However, bits and pieces of historical evidence have shown that black people whose slave labour was used to run the plantation systems and the mechanical industries, designed and built simple tools to lessen the burden of their daily toil.[15]

These inventions, though, could not be patented by black people because in 1858, the US Attorney General, Jeremiah S. Black, ruled that 'since a patent was a contract between the government and the inventor, and since a slave was not considered a United States citizen, he could neither make a contract with the government nor assign his invention to his master'.[16] Thus the credit for many black inventions went to white people. And here, one can see clear evidence of the situation I analysed earlier in which white people, through their power position, declared black people inferior and adopted measures to prevent black people proving their proposition false.

For example,

> "Jo Anderson, a slave on the plantation of Cyrus McCormick, is said to have made a major contribution to the McCormick grain harvester. Yet he is only credited in the official records as being a handyman or helper to McCormick. In 1862, a slave owned by Jefferson Davis, President of the Conferderacy, invented a propeller for ocean vessels. With a model of his invention the slave showed remarkable mechanical skill in wood and metal working. He was unable to get a patent on his propeller, but the merits of his invention were reported in many southern newspapers. The propeller was finally used in ships of the Confederate Navy."[17]

Fortunately, because the ban on patents for slaves did not apply to "Free Persons of Colour", James Forten (1776-1842) who perfected a new device for handling sails, was able to obtain a patent for it. In 1834 Henry Blair received a patent for a 'seed planter' and in 1836, his second patent for a corn harvester. In both cases, the patent records described the inventor as "A Colored Man", but from thence the US Patent Office stopped indicating the race of the inventor.

However, two inquiries to the Patent Office led to the search for information on black inventors. In 1900 the United States Commission which was preparing an exhibit on black Americans for a fair in Paris; and the Pennsylvania Commission, planning a Freedom Exhibit in Philadelphia in 1913, had made respective requests for information. The Patent Office sent a circular to thousands of patent lawyers, large manufacturing firms, and to various newspapers edited by black people.

> "The replies were numerous. The information showed that a very large number of blacks had contacted lawyers. Even so, many were unable to get patents because they lacked the necessary funds to apply for them. Some had actually obtained them but the records of most lawyers were poorly kept and so the names and inventions of many blacks were lost. Patents were often taken out in the name of the lawyer. A large number of black inventors allowed this because *they felt that the racial identity of the inventor would lower the value of a patented invention.*" Yet more than a thousand patents were fully identified by the name of the inventor, date, patent number and the title of invention as being owned by black people. These patents represented inventions in nearly every branch of industrial arts such as household goods, mechanical appliances, electrical devices and chemical compounds."[18]

Before we take a more detailed look at a small sample of these individual black scientists and inventors from the Nineteenth to the Twentieth Centuries, two comments are called for: (a) the records show that despite an environment of cruel oppression, odious racial discrimination, and denied opportunities (even for basic education in most cases), individual black people in America not only maintained their sanity and rationality but rose above almost impossible barriers to display marvellous talent, intellect and, in many cases, real genius; and (b) the immense emotional and psychological damage done to black people of whatever class or ability. How many white inventors were denied patents for their inventions because they were slaves and, therefore, assumed to be non-persons? How many white inventors have had to adopt the names of people of other races in order that the value of their inventions might not be down-graded because of their race? How many white people have ever suffered such soul-destroying indignities in which people of creative abilities have had to hide their true identities because those identities are deemed inferior? White inventors who made original and/or significant innovative contributions to science and technology received recognition, fame, fortune, accolade and the knowledge that their names would live on indefinitely. Many black inventors of similar status hid their true identity because of racism whilst others never attained the same recognition and rewards that their white counterparts enjoyed.

Elijah McCoy (1843-1929)

The end of the American Civil War and the Reconstruction period which followed, saw a rapid increase in machine inventions. Many of these machines were complicated devices with many moving parts which had to be oiled regularly to prevent damage due to wear and tear caused by friction. Every time the machines needed oiling, production had to be halted – a most costly and inefficient waste of time. McCoy's genius was the invention of a 'drip cup' which enabled industrial machines to be oiled while in operation.[19]

Elijah McCoy was born in Canada in 1843. His parents had been slaves who had fled from their master in the State of Kentucky. As a boy, McCoy had been fascinated with machines and tools, and when he came to the United States after the Civil War, he worked in a machine shop near Ypsilanti, Michigan where he had settled. In 1870 he began to work on the problem of oiling machinery which was in motion. His basic invention which earned him his first patent on July 12, 1872 was an oil-filled small container with a stop cock to regulate the flow of oil to the innards of moving machinery. It was later to be described as a "key device in perfecting the overall lubrication system used in large industry today". Large machinery no longer needed to be stopped or shut down in order to apply the needed lubrication.

Major industries using heavy equipment quickly adopted it; and so popular did this lubrication system become that persons inspecting new equipment would inquire if it contained the "real McCoy". The measure of the significance to industry of this invention is that the phrase "the real McCoy" is now part of the English language and is symbolic of high quality, genuine product or parts as opposed to 'cheap' imitation.

McCoy set up the Elijah McCoy Manufacturing Company in Detroit, Michigan, to develop and market his inventions. He was to receive 25 patents for different types of lubricators for different equipment between 1872 and 1899. He worked with such intensity that he often patented two or three new devices a year. On April 20, 1915, McCoy received a patent for a 'Graphite Lubricator'[20] which he invented for use on railway locomotives with superheated engines. This provided a continuous flow of oil without clogging the engine. His other inventions included an ironing table, lawn sprinkler, steam dome, and dope cup.

I wonder how many people, including purveyors of the ideology of racism, who use the phrase "the real McCoy", know that they are affirming the significant contribution to industry by a black inventor, a self-taught mechanic, and the son of a fugitive black slave couple!

Garret A. Morgan (1875-1963)

An explosion in a tunnel 228 feet below Lake Erie and the Cleveland Waterworks on July 25, 1916, was to thrust Garret Morgan into the public lime-light.[21] No one knew whether there were any survivors among the over two dozen men trapped by the explosion, and since the tunnel was filled with smoke, natural gases, dust and debris, it was impossible to mount a rescue operation. At 2.00 am with the situation looking hopeless, someone recalled that a chap called Garret Morgan had been demonstrating a gas inhalator in an effort to interest manufacturers.

Morgan rushed to the site on being informed of the disaster. With his brother and two volunteers, they donned the inhalators and descended down the dark, gas-filled tunnel. Eventually over a score of the workmen were brought out alive. Morgan, deservedly, became a hero and was awarded a solid gold medal by the City of Cleveland for the heroic rescue. The inhalator had previously won him first grand prize at the Second International Exposition of Sanitation and Safety in 1914. Many manufacturers and fire departments became interested in his breathing device, and he was requested to demonstrate it in many towns and cities.

To demonstrate his inhalator in the Deep South, Morgan had to employ a white man. "Orders began to pour into Cleveland as many municipalities purchased the Morgan inhalator. *However, the orders soon stopped when the racial identity of the inventor became known*[a].[22]

Undaunted by such blatant racism, Morgan returned to the drawing board and in 1923 achieved another first: he created "a device which makes possible the orderly movement of the millions of automobiles in today's cities and towns – the automatic stop-sign."[23] Morgan sold the rights to the stop sign to General Electric for the sum of $40,000. Morgan, who had moved to Cleveland, Ohio, penniless from Paris, Tennesse where he was born, also invented a belt fastener for sewing machines.

Another black person had blown sky-high the mythical assumption of the ideology of racism that black people are imitators – never creators – by virtue of their limited intellectual capacity.

Jan Ernst Matzeliger (1852-1889)

In 1876, a 24-year-old young man arrived in Lynn, Massachusetts, poor and friendless, having been for two years a sailor. When he died thirteen years later, his name was known not only in Massachusetts, but wherever inventors gathered.[24] Matzeliger laid the foundation of the shoe industry in the United States, revolutionised the method of shoe-making, and made Lynn, Massachusetts the shoe capital of the world.

Before Matzeliger, the efforts of hundreds of inventors and thousands of dollars research investment had failed to make possible the manufacturing of a complete shoe by machinery. Crude shoe making machines had been developed by inventors such as Thompson, Mckay and Copeland, but the final problem of shaping the upper leather over the last and attaching this leather to the bottom of the shoe had remained 'the missing link' of mechanical shoe production. This problem created an aristocratic occupational group in the shoe industry – the 'hand-lasters' – with unchallenged industrial muscle. Though highly paid, they deliberately restricted the volume of production to between forty to fifty five pairs per hand-laster.

As Matzeliger worked in shoe factories around Lynn, he heard it stated repeatedly that it was impossible to last shoes by machine. He took on the challenge and began experimenting in secret, first on a crude wooden machine he built and later on a model he built out of scrap iron. When news of his attempt reached the public, there were jeers of derision – how could a black man succeed where white people had failed? But Matzeliger persisted doggedly.

Finally, in 1881 Matzeliger felt he had solved the 'impossible technical problem' and submitted an application to Washington for a patent. The diagram accompanying his application was so complicated, the patent reviewers could not understand it. An official was sent to see the model itself, after which, on March 20, 1883, he was granted patent number 274,207. At last, the mass production of shoes by automated method had become a reality! Sadly, six years later, Matzeliger died of tuberculosis at the young age of 36.

There is a social irony to this story of a genius which must be told. There is little doubt that the greatest economic benefit from Matzeliger's invention went primarily to white industrialists and yet, in his days of loneliness, he had sought but was denied membership in several white churches. Matzeliger had been born to a black Surinamese mother and a Dutch father, and as was the practice then, and still is in several churches in America today, white people would not worship with black people nor 'mulattoes' – an ecclesiastical apartheid. A little digression here to look at the implications of this ecclesiastical phenomenon will not be inappropriate.

Jesus had said that all the laws of the Old Testament could be reduced to two, namely: love the Lord thy God, and love thy neighbour as thyself. Indeed he went on to say that the genuine adherence to the former is evidenced by manifestation of the latter, for how can one love God whom one cannot see if one is incapable of loving one's neighbour? One of the cardinal tests of the validity of Christianity must surely be the effect that it produces on the social behaviour of its adherents. And yet the history of social relationships between black and white people has demonstrated time and time again that the most bigoted racists, have also been among the most devout and ardent 'Christians'.

It takes very little imagination to envisage a scenario in 'heaven' where black and white Christian faithfuls from, for example, South Africa, the United States of America, Britain, France, Portugal, Spain, etc., arrive after death. Are these white people going to be able to co-exist with and accept their black 'brothers and sisters' in heaven after they have treated them on earth as inferior products of God's creation? Or is God going to 'bleach' black people to become as white as snow (like the angels) to prevent racism re-emerging in His Kingdom? But surely the last question presupposes, like the monogenetic theory, that God is 'white'. If so, why did a 'white' omniscient God, who knows the end from the beginning and should have foreseen the racial intolerance and oppression that would result, create black people who would suffer so much injustice and indignity on earth, only to be 'bleached' white after death to co-exist with their white oppressive 'brethren' in heaven?

Unable to reconcile this and many other theological problems with socio-political realities that a black person is daily confronted with, I decided after several agonising years of 'soul-searching', to repudiate Christianity and to opt out of 'heaven', determined not to be bleached white nor to endure another existence elsewhere under the obscenity of racism. I am positive that a 'Black Satan', the Supremo of Hell (as the racist would have us believe), will not put me through the indignity of changing my race in order to make me acceptable as an equal to white people.

Granville T. Woods
(1856-1910)

"Granville T. Woods, the greatest colored inventor in the history of the race, and equal, if not superior, to any inventor in the country, is destined to revolutionize the mode of street car transit", declared 'The Cincinnati', Ohio *Catholic Tribune* in an article on January 14, 1886. On April 1, 1887 the same paper stated: "Mr. Woods, who is the greatest electrician in the world, still continues to add to his long list of electrical inventions."[25] Although these claims may be considered an extravagant tribute to a local scientist and inventor, it nevertheless reflected the genius of this prolific black engineer.

Born in Columbus, Ohio on April 23, 1856, Granville Woods attended school until he was ten and then worked in a machine shop. With the basic mechanical knowledge gained from the latter, Woods took up jobs with the Missouri railroad in 1872, a Springfield rolling mill in 1874 and in 1876, enrolled for a course in mechanical engineering in an Eastern college. Following his college training, Woods obtained a job as an engineer on *Ironside*, a British steamer, and later, a job with the D & S Railroad. His inability to advance in these jobs led Woods to start his own company, the Woods' Railway Telegraph Company to market his telegraph and other inventions.

Woods, who was sometimes called the "Black Edison",[b] held over 35 patents on electro-mechanical devices which he sold to American Bell Telephone, General Electric and Westinghouse Air Brake. Among these inventions were a steam boiler furnace (1884), an incubator (1900) and the automatic air brake (1902).

While he patented more than a dozen inventions for electric railways and many more for electrical control and distribution, improvements in telegraphy, telephone instruments, automatic cut-offs for electric circuits and electric motor regulators, perhaps his most significant invention was the "Induction Telegraph", a system for communicating to and from moving trains. Electrical engineers were searching for solutions to reduce the number of train accidents and collisions which were causing increasing concern to both the railway companies and the public. Woods invented the 'Synchronous Multiplex Railway Telegraph' for the purpose of: (a) 'averting accidents by keeping each train informed of the whereabouts of the one immediately ahead or following it; (b) communicating with stations from moving trains; and (c) promoting general social and commercial 'intercourse'. Woods' works attracted universal attention from technical and scientific journals throughout the world.

Lewis Howard Latimer (1848-1928)

"The collective contribution of Black Americans to science and inventions is so extensive that it is not possible to live a full day in any part of the United States, or the world in general, without sharing the benefits of their contribution. Yet, the genius of the Black American imagination, that influences every aspect of life in the United States is generally unknown to most Americans." So began John Henrik Clarke in an article on Lewis Howard Latimer – Bringer of the Light.[26]

Lewis Latimer, draftsman, poet, inventor, musician, author and artist, was the son of a fugitive slave. His father had escaped from slavery in Virginia and found his way to Boston where abolitionists including William Lloyd Garrison, and Frederick Douglass, raised funds to purchase his freedom. Latimer was born in September 1848 in Chelsea, Massachusetts. When he was ten years old his father disappeared suddenly, leaving his mother with four children to look after. He was sent to a Farm School where his brother Williams later joined him. The two boys escaped from the school and returned to Boston to work to support their family. During the Civil War, Lewis, then fifteen years old, joined the Union Navy and saw action on the James River, while his brothers were fighting with the land forces.

Lewis returned to Boston at the end of the war and after many difficulties finally found a job as an office boy in a firm called Crosly and Gage. He saw draftsmen at work and knew that was the career he wanted. Young Lewis bought a set of second-hand drafting tools and began reading every book he could find on the subject. When he, at last, approached his boss and asked to do some drawings, he was not taken seriously; but after persistent requests, he got his chance, made the best of it, and was given a desk and a pay rise.

It was while he worked for Crosly and Gage that Lewis met Alexander Graham Bell who was a teacher in a nearby school. Bell's father had invented the sign language that enabled deaf and dumb people to communicate and he had come to America to teach his father's 'language'. In an effort to invent a device which would enable his deaf mute wife to hear him, Bell perfected a machine which he called the telephone. He asked his close friend Lewis Latimer to make a drawing of his invention so that he could apply for a patent. Latimer had to draw each part of the device and describe how it worked – a job he did excellently. Bell obtained his patent in 1876.

Latimer himself had patented his first invention, a "Water Closet for Railroad Cars" on February 10, 1874. In 1879, while doing odd jobs for a machine shop in Bridgeport, Connecticut, he met Herman Maxim, Chief Engineer and Electrician for the United States Electric Lighting Company who was also the inventor of the machine gun. Maxim was impressed by the 'first black draftsman' he had ever seen, and hired Latimer as a draftsman and secretary. Under Maxim's guidance, he learned all he could about the then young electric industry. Thomas A. Edison had, by this time, just invented the incandescent electric lamp.

Latimer began experimenting in order to improve some of the electric devices of his day. In 1881, he invented and patented (September 13, 1881) the first electric lamp with a carbon filament – the first practical electric light bulb. More importantly, in January of 1882 he received a patent for his new invention – a "Process for Manufacturing Carbons". This was a cheap method for making filaments. "His innovations and lighting were a sensation for his day and some of his inventions are now on display at the Smithsonian Institute in Washington DC."[27]

Lewis Latimer became one of the great pioneers in the development of electricity; the only black member of the 'Edison Pioneers' – a group of distinguished scientists and inventors who worked for Thomas Edison – and the one to whom goes the honour of solving the problem of transforming the electric current into light. He also supervised the installation of electric lighting of streets for New York, Philadelphia, London (England) and several other cities in the 1880s. In 1890 he wrote the book *Incandescent Electric Lighting: A Practical Description of the Edison System*, the first textbook on the Edison electric system. Towards the end of his career, Latimer was chief draftsman for the companies, General Electric and Westinghouse. He was assuredly one of the most distinguished of the pioneers who started with Thomas Edison. On May 10, 1968 a public school, the Lewis H. Latimer School, in Brooklyn, New York, was dedicated to his memory.

Norbert Rillieux (1806-1894)

Norbert Rillieux had been born a slave in New Orleans, studied and taught in France, and returned to Louisiana to become the state's most famous engineer. When assigned to reorganise a sugar refining plant, he was given many special privileges including a fine house, complete with servants for his exclusive use. He was one of the most important men of the state, but could not take part in its affairs except by invitation. He tolerated this State ambivalence whereby he was regarded and treated as a most important personality, and yet excluded from many state affairs because he was black. But when the state required that he carried a pass, that was the last straw – Rillieux left Louisiana for ever in 1854.[28]

Until 1846, the process by which sugar cane juice was transformed into sugar was a slow and costly method known as the 'Jamaica Train'. Two scientists, Howard and Degrand, had developed vacuum pans and condensing coils which imperfectly utilised heat in evaporating the liquid portion of the sugar cane. But "...it remained for Rillieux, by a stroke of genius, to enclose the condensing coils in a vacuum chamber and to employ the vapour from this first condensing chamber for evaporating the juice in a second chamber under higher vacuum".

Rillieux's process greatly reduced production cost, produced superior quality sugar and was immediately hailed by sugar manufacturers as a revolution in the manufacturing of sugar. Mexico and Cuba followed the US in adopting the Rillieux process. However when Rillieux tried to interest European manufacturers on his return to France following his self-imposed exile from Louisiana, they were lukewarm. He gave up trying and, for ten years, worked with the Champollions deciphering hieroglyphics.

Eventually, when Europe adopted his process for sugar manufacturing, Rillieux returned to invention. He applied his process to the sugar beet and cut production costs in half.

'King Sugar' was one of the most important economic commodities which had contributed to Britain's capital accumulation, making possible the industrial revolution in the eighteenth century. It is highly significant to note that not only did Europe depend entirely on black slave labour to produce the sugar cane, but that in the nineteenth century, the scientist who invented the most effective and efficient method of processing sugar, was a black genius. And yet, the ideology of racism, in order to justify the barbaric treatment and ruthless exploitation of black slave labour, had given as justification, the inherent intellectual inferiority of black people which makes them incapable of work other than of menial nature.

Daniel Hale Williams (1858-1931)

From the age of twelve, Dan Williams had to fend for himself. He worked as an apprentice shoemaker, a roustabout on a lake steamer, and barber, but his aspiration all along was to be a medical doctor. When he drifted from Pennsylvania, his birthplace, to Janesville, Illinois, he met a white physician who encouraged him to enter medicine. With the aid of friends, Williams completed his medical studies at the Chicago Medical College in 1883 and opened his office on Chicago's South Side. His extraordinary skill earned him a post with Chicago Medical College as a surgeon and demonstrator in anatomy.[29]

Dr Dan, as he was affectionately known, felt a need to do something about the appalling situation at the time in which no hospital in Chicago would allow Negro doctors to use their facilities. Black doctors had to perform operations on couches and kitchen tables in the crowded tenements of Chicago's South Side. The degree of inhumanity which racism can lead even professional people such as doctors to descend to, is indicative of the power of racial ideology on its victims. The Hippocratic oath had little effect where the ideology of racism held sway!

In 1891, against great odds and almost single-handed, he created Provident Hospital for the use of all physicians without regard to colour. It was here that an incident in 1893 raised Dr Williams from a relative obscurity to a position of national renown as the first successful heart surgeon and one of America's greatest surgeons.

In a brawl, a young street fighter named James Cornish was stabbed in an artery a fraction of an inch from the heart. The state of knowledge in the art of medical practice at the time meant that heart wounds or even wounds in the thoracic cavity inevitably led to the patient's death. X-rays, sulfa drugs, blood transfusions – now absolute necessities – were unknown medical tools. Caught between the desire to save the patient's life on the one hand, and the unavailability of facilities to save him, Dr Dan decided he had nothing to lose by taking a gamble. He would open Cornish's chest and operate on the heart – an operation no other doctor had attempted before. He called six of his colleagues on the staff of the struggling Provident Hospital in Chicago and operated successfully. Dr Dan had peformed the impossible operation "... Sewed up his heart", a Chicago newspaper headlined. Dr Dan's skill as a surgeon spread and physicians from far and near came to Provident to see the wizard of the scalpel perform.

In 1894, Dr Williams was invited to head Freedmen's Hospital in Washington, a collection of six old pre-Civil War buildings, with medical facilities equally as primitive. He successfully organised Freedmen's into departments, brought in a staff of twenty volunteer specialists, and created the beginnings of the first nursing school for black people. In 1898 he returned to Chicago and became the first black person to hold a post at St. Luke Hospital and Northwestern

University. At his death Dr Dan bequeathed part of his estate for the advancement of Negro physicians and part to the National Association for the Advancement of Coloured People (NAACP).

Today, so advanced has medical science become that heart transplant, heart-lung transplant, open heart surgery, etc. have become routine and are taken for granted. Black people have contributed towards this progress by producing the earliest physicians, medical knowledge, medical literature and, despite the most brutal history of slavery, oppression and denied opportunities for personal development, the world's first successful heart surgeon. Before Dr Williams, the human heart had been regarded as off-limits for surgery. Removing this taboo was a necessary first step for the eventual successful heart transplant.

Charles Drew (1904-1950)

Death brought tragically to an end the life of a man of 46 years of age who had achieved excellence in virtually every pursuit he set his mind on and who, no doubt, would have continued to contribute to human progress in a remarkable way. Whether on the track cinders, in the operating room or in the research laboratory, Charles Drew brought talent, determination and the pursuit of excellence.

A native of Washington D.C., Dr Drew had been the captain of the track team and an outstanding halfback on the football team at Amherst where he had been an undergraduate. He received the Mossman trophy for having brought the most honour to the school over a four-year period. At McGill University in Canada, Dr Drew won first prize in physiological anatomy and set track records which stood for years. He won the Spingarn Medal from the NAACP in recognition of his contribution to Negro progress.[30a]

The greatest achievement of Dr Drew's short life, though, was his pioneering work in blood plasma preservation which saved hundreds of lives during World War II. Before Drew, there was no efficient way to store large quantities of blood plasma for use during emergencies or for use in wartime where thousands of lives depended on the availability of blood for blood transfusions. Dr Drew solved this problem by discovering ways and means of preserving blood plasma in what are commonly known as blood banks.

Beginning his research into the properties of blood plasma at Columbia University, Dr Drew became an authority on the subject and was asked by the British to set up a plasma programme for them. He later did the same for the United States in 1942.

One night in 1952, he fell asleep at the wheel of his car and was killed in a crash. At the time of his death, Dr Drew was chief surgeon and chief of staff at Freedmen's Hospital. The world was robbed of a star athlete, scholar, scientist, surgeon, a highly intelligent and brilliant man who no doubt had so much more to give at the age of 46.

Percy Julian (1899-1975)

"Education's investment in him has been returned manyfold in the magnificence of his service to mankind." That was the citation on one of Dr Percy Julian's many honorary degrees. The greatest single scientific contribution of this brilliant black chemist brought relief to millions suffering from the excruciating pain of arthritis – from the soybean, he extracted an ingredient to relieve inflammatory arthritis.[30]

Until the late thirties, Europe had a monopoly on the production of sterols, which were extracted from the bile of animals at a cost of several hundred dollars per gram. Dr Julian's immense contribution was to substitute sterols from the oil of the soybean (which was until his time just another bean) and thereby reduce its cost to less than twenty cents a gram. This made cortisone, a sterol derivative, available to the needy at reasonable cost.

Dr Julian also found a way to mass-produce the drug physostigmine used for treating glaucoma, and perfected the mass production of sex hormones which led the way to birth control pills.

Dr Julian, the son of a railway clerk, worked his way through DePauw University, graduating in 1920. After spending several years teaching at Fisk and Howard Universities and West Virginia State College, Julian attended Harvard and then took a doctorate at the University of Vienna. He taught at DePauw for several years, became Director of Research and Manager of Fine Chemical at Glidden Company, and later formed his own company, devoted mainly to the production of sterols. In 1961 his company merged with the huge Smith, Kline and French Pharmaceutical Company in an agreement which paid Dr Julian several milions of dollars. Dr Julian died of liver cancer in 1975.

Frederick   McKinley   Jones
(1893 - 1961)

Today, all over the world, there are thousands of refrigerated trucks moving large quantities of frozen and chilled foods from factories to warehouses and supermarkets. The person who invented the first practical truck refrigeration which revolutionised the food transport industry in America was a black man – Frederick McKinley Jones. Jones had earlier invented a portable refrigeration unit which was used on the battlefields of Europe during World War II and helped to save many lives, since blood serum for transfusions, medicines and foodstuffs could be kept readily available under a cooling system.[31]

Born in 1893, Jones was an orphan for most of his childhood and was educated only to eighth grade level. As a teenager, he worked as an automobile mechanic, built racing cars, and served in World War I where he studied electricity and electronics. Jones went to live in Hallock, Minnesota after the war and worked first as a farm machinery mechanic and later as a technician for a company that manufactured motion picture film equipment.

Jones' work on truck refrigeration began in the 1930s when he learned one day that a friend of his boss who was in the trucking business, had lost a consignment of poultry when the ice blocks which kept the chicken chilled during transportation, had melted before reaching its destination. Jones went to work to design and build a cooling system for trucks. He succeeded and on July 12, 1949, received a US patent for his air cooling unit.

At the time of his death in 1961, Jones had been awarded more than 60 patents, 40 of which were for refrigeration equipment alone. His other patents were for special parts for his air cooling machines; X-ray machines and sound equipment techniques for motion pictures; the self-starting gasoline engine that turned his cooling units on and off; the reverse cycling mechanism for producing heat or cold; devices for controlling air temperature and moisture, etc.

By the age of 50, Jones was one of the truly outstanding authorities in the field of refrigeration in the US and in 1944 was elected to membership of the American Society of Refrigeration Engineers. This black man whose formal education did not go beyond the eighth grade, was nevertheless sought after by University-graduated scientists and engineers who welcomed the opportunity to work with, and to learn from, a true genius. During the 1980s he was called to Washington to advise on problems to do with refrigeration and was a consultant to both the Defense Department and the United States Bureau of Standards.

Today, there is hardly anyone in the West, and many parts of the world for that matter, whose life is unaffected by Jones' inventions. And yet, as we shall show in the following Chapters, purveyors of the ideology of racism, even today, explicitly and implicitly perpetuate the myth that black people have made no contribution to the development of science, technology and industry.

Meredith Gourdine (1919-   )

Electrogasdynamics technology – a process concerned with the interaction of charged particles with a moving gas stream which can produce very high voltage from a low voltage originally generated – is a phenomenon which has been known by scientists since the late 1700s. The problem was that no one could figure out how to harness the principle to generate enough electricity to make it practical – especially for modern needs.[32]

The solution to this problem was found through the inventive genius of a black physicist and systems engineer, Meredith Gourdine who pioneered the development of electrogasdynamics systems and the practical application of the energy conversion process. The US Department of Interior's Office of Coal Research awarded Gourdine over $600,000 in 1966 to perfect a model generator that used a low grade coal to directly generate 80,000 volts of electricity. The generator had no moving parts and did not use steam.

Born in Livingston, New Jersey in 1919, Gourdine received his Doctorate Degree in Engineering Science from California Institute of Technology after which he worked for the Aeronautical Divison of Curtiss-Wright Corp. It was here that he rediscovered the eighteenth century energy conversion method and from it developed his pioneering work in the field of electrogasdynamics. When he failed to sell his generator to his employer, he raised $200,000 and founded his own research and development firm, Gourdine Systems Inc.

His firm has moved from research and development in electrogasdynamics to four major application areas in energy conversion, paint spraying, air pollution control, and printing. Gourdine's direct high voltage electricity generation using pulverised coal and air in a combustion chamber located at the mouth of a mine, is set to bring in a new source of cheap electrical power.

Gourdine's electrogasdynamics technology research has been

used to deal with problems related to non-contact printing processes. The control of air pollution in urban areas have been affected
using Gourdine's direct energy conversion process. This has involved the ionising and driving of dust particles by a moving air
system to a collection point. The system has been used by Gourdine's
company to develop methods for control of industrial, residential,
automotive and diesel exhausting into the atmosphere. In paint-
spraying, Gourdine's 'electradyne coating or painting system uses a
gun to emit particles by an applied potential of 6kV. A portion of the
kinetic energy in the moving air stream or in the particles
themselves is utilised to raise the particles to high potential. The
charged particles apply themselves to the nearest ground plane
which is the work piece to be coated'.

In an era of increasing energy demand, escalating energy cost,
and dwindling energy resources, Gourdine's method of generating
cheap electrical power through the electrogasdynamics process,
holds great promise of a more efficient utilisation of our finite
energy resource.

Otis Boykin (1920-   )

Otis Boykin was born in Dallas, Texas in 1920. His inventive talent
was discovered while he was working as parcel post clerk in 1941.
He attended Fisk University and the Illinois Institute of Technology.

Boykin, who since 1964, has been a private research consultant
for several American companies and three firms in Paris, is credited
with devising the control unit used in artificial heart stimulators;
inventing a tiny electrical device used in all guided missiles and
IBM computers, plus 26 other electronic devices, and an oil filter.
Thirty-seven resulting products from Boykin's inventions are now
being manufactured in Paris and distributed throughout Western
Europe.[33]

George Carruthers (1939-   )

We noted at the beginning of this section of our analysis the Survey
undertaken by Professor Pappademos, which found that of the 17
physics textbooks examined in the US "not once is a scientific
discovery or discoverer identified as being of African origin. No

black scientist is pictured in any of these books nor is a single black credited with any contribution." And yet, the reality is that several black American physicists, engineers and inventors are making significant contributions to the latest endeavours in space sciences, despite racial discrimination which still greatly impacts differentially on black people with regards to access to opportunities in American society. Dr George Carruthers[34] is one of these contributors.

Carruthers was born in Cincinatti, Ohio, on October 1, 1939. He showed early interest in science fiction and participated in science fairs at predominantly white schools, despite racial jeers. In 1957, George entered the College of Engineering, University of Illinois where he earned a B.Sc. in 1961, M.Sc. in 1962 and Ph.D. in 1964 in the area of aeronautical and astronomical engineering, with a thesis on 'experimental investigations of atomic nitrogen recombination'.

Upon graduation, Carruthers was awarded the highly prestigious National Science Foundation's Fellowship to join the rocket astronomy group at the Naval Research Laboratory (N.R.L.) in Washington, D.C., and two years later (1966) became a full-time research physicist at the E.O. Hulburt Centre for Space Research (N.R.L.). In 1967 he published his first scientific paper on "An Upper Limit on the Concentration of Molecular Hydrogen in Inter-Stellar Space," and in 1968 followed it with "Far Ultraviolet Spectroscopy and Photometry of some Early Type Stars". These two essays clearly established Carruthers as a brilliant Astrophysicist.

On November 11, 1969, Carruthers was granted Patent no. 3,478,216 for an "Image Converter for Detecting Electromagnetic Radiation Especially in Short Wave Lengths". He had filed the application as early as July 27, 1966 at the age of 26; this means that perhaps as young as 24, Carruthers was an inventor. In the same year that he obtained his patent his article on "Magnetically Focussed Electronographic Image Converters for Space Astronomy Applications" appeared in Applied Optics.

Dr Carruthers' Apollo 16 Far Ultraviolet Camera/Spectograph "is perhaps the most significant single contribution in recent years relating to our knowledge of the world's physical structure", according to James Spady.[35] The equipment enabled space explorers for the first time to study and record planetary and astronomical phenomenon from the moon. Asked by Spady if he knew Carruthers, the Astronaut, John W. Young, Commander of Apollo 16 flight to the moon stated:

"I have known Dr Carruthers for a long time. He was the Principal Investigator at the Naval Research Laboratory and had this telescope built that we used on the moon. It was the very first telescope that we have ever had operating from another celestial body. He was in charge of the whole business. I think new knowledge coming from Astronomers like him will revolutionize the way we think."

Carruthers' camera was set up in the shadow of the lunar module by the Apollo 16 crew to photograph the earth and selected celestial objects in ultraviolet light of wavelengths shorter than 1600 angstroms; and in mid-May 1972 the Manned Spacecraft Centre in Houston released the photographs with some of the first scientific results from Apollo 16.

A highly advanced and complex piece of equipment, Carruthers' semi-automatic device is a combination spectograph and camera, with an electron intensifier. 'A Schmidt optical system focuses an image on a potassium bromide cathode that emits electrons in proportion to the number of ultraviolet photons striking it. A 25,000 volt potential accelerates the electron toward a special photographic film. The focusing magnet surrounding the camera ensures that the electron image accurately reproduces the ultraviolet images. Thereby a 10-20-fold reduction in exposure time results from his electronic intensification process'.

In a highly illuminating essay – "Space Astronomy in the Shuttle Era" – explaining the advantage of using his Far Ultraviolet Camera/Spectograph and future ones based on his prototype, Carruthers writes:

"The far ultraviolet, below the atmospheric cut off 3000°A, and extending down to the soft X-ray range below 100°A is of great importance to the astronomer because it allows the detection and measurement of common elements (hydrogen, oxygen, nitrogen, carbon, and many others) in their cool, unexcited condition ("Ground state" of the atom or molecule), a task which is difficult or impossible in the ground-accessible wavelength range. This allows more accurate measurements of the compositions of interstellar gas, planetary atmospheres, etc. The ultraviolet also conveys important information on solid particles (dust) in interstellar space and elsewhere, and provides for much more accurate measurements of the energy outputs of very hot stars – that is those stars having temperatures in the range 10,000-100,000°K for our sun, which emits most of their radiation in wavelengths below 3000A...

"In the infrared, the improvement of sensitivity afforded by space observations, and the elimination of terrestrial atmospheric emissions and absorptions, will allow greatly improved measurements of the cool states of cosmic material – dense concentrations of interstellar gas and dust, stars in the process of formation, and planetary atmospheres."[36]

In a period of 12 years, Carruthers has authored or co-authored 63 major scientific papers, in such major journals and volumes as *Astrophysical Journal, Science, The Interstellar Medium* (Holland, 1974). *Apollo 16 Preliminary Science Report, NASA SP-315* (1972), and the *Society of Photo-Optical Instrumentation Engineers' Instrumentation in Astronomy* (1973). His pioneering "Television Sensors for Ultraviolet Space Astronomy" in *Astronomical Observations with Television-Type Sensors* was published by the prestigious Institute of Astronomy and Space Science at the University of British Columbia, Canada.

The black ancestors of Ancient Egypt created the science of Astronomy. Thousands of years later, we were told by the proponents of ideology of racism that "the full-blooded black is incapable of highly abstract thinking – only whites have such capability". Dr Carruthers and many black people who have managed to defy the barriers to opportunities in the scientific fields, erected by white racist societies, have demonstrated the falsehood of the premise.

George Washington Carver (1861 - 1943)

"Dr Carver was, as everyone knows, a Negro. But he triumphed over every obstacle. Perhaps there is no one in this century whose example has done more to promote a better understanding between the races. Such greatness partakes of the eternal." That was the tribute of the *New York Herald Tribune* following the death of Dr Carver.

"A Negro, born into slavery, George Washington Carver became a scientist of undisputed genius and an artist whose paintings were prized by museums the world over. He never looked for fame, but presidents and princes sought his advice. He could have gained great riches, but he chose instead to give his discoveries – now widely in use – to anyone who asked for them. He felt the wounds of discrimination, but he would not allow himself to hate. His basic belief: the world is 'the garden of God'. To read his extraordinary story is to renew one's faith in mankind." That was how the *Reader's Digest* began its article on Dr Carver's life and enormous achievements in its July 1965 issue.[c]

But who was this black man of "undisputed genius", one of America's greatest biologists? To fully appreciate the brilliant contribution of Dr Carver to humanity, it is essential to take a more detailed look (than we have hitherto done with the other black scientists and inventors) at his early life in order: (a) to fully comprehend the almost impossible odds that he had to overcome; and (b) to visualise his achievements against the backcloth of a life of misfortune and disadvantage. For his was a life of opposites: a manifestation of sheer, genuine, indisputable genius, humility and humanity on the one hand, and a catalogue of misfortune, suffering, continual illness, humiliation and appalling discrimination on the other. It is a lesson not only of a magnificent intellectual display in the face of severely discouraging environment, but also one of humanity in its purest form of selflessness, devotion to a life of service to others, friendliness, kindliness, philanthropy, honesty, integrity and hard work. ·

George had been born in Diamond Grove, Missouri to Mary, the only slave of Moses Carver. Moses Carver was one of the few white people who had opposed slavery; he had run his farm, unlike other Missouri farmers, without the benefit of slave labour. However, as his wife Susan got older and found it harder to cope with the household chores, he was persuaded to buy Mary from his neighbour for $700. Mary had three children before being widowed – Melissa, Jim and George.

One bitterly cold night in 1862, in the severe winter of the American Civil War, the 'night raiders' – masked bandits who terrorised Missouri, stealing livestock and kidnapping slaves to sell at highly inflated wartime prices – attacked Moses Carver's farm. In a previous raid, Moses had successfully hidden Mary and her three sons in a cave, but this time only Jim could be saved. George had suffered from a rasping cough from birth and Mary could not bring herself to take the baby out in the blustering and biting wind without warm clothing to cover him. She desperately searched for something warm for the baby, ignoring Moses Carver's protestations and order to follow him to the cave.

The raiders seized Mary and her children, Melissa and George and charged southward on their horses. Moses could not live with his conscience and hired John Bentley, who was rumoured to have once ridden with the raiders, to ransom Mary and her children. Six days later, in a cold driving rain, Bentley rode into the farmyard with a small, dirty and damp bundle under his coat. He had pursued the raiders all the way to Arkansas before losing their trail. Believing the sick and frail baby to be worth nothing, they had given Mary's little baby to some womenfolk on the way and that was how Bentley came to rescue and return George to Moses Carver. When Bentley handed the filthy parcel to Susan she found the boy's lips and eyelids were tinged with blue, and he lay still in her arms 'like a new-born sparrow that had died in the nest'. She ran to heat milk, then knelt with the child by the fire, stripping the wet homespun from his tiny body. Moses brought her the milk, with a pinch of sugar, and she held a spoonful to the infant's lips. At first the milk trickled down his chin. Then he choked, cried feebly, and sucked for more.

His first few years were a tremendous battle for survival, as

George clung tenaciously and precariously to life, falling victim to every childhood illness. The unending cough tore his vocal chords, so that his voice was like the chirp of a frightened bird, and some traumatic memory knotted his tongue and left him with a pitiful stammer. But through Susan's nursing and some 'mysterious' toughness within himself, he survived. The war ended and so did slavery, at least in theory, but Jim and his brother had nowhere else to go and stayed on with 'Uncle' Moses and 'Aunt' Susan. Jim was soon sturdy enough to help Moses on the farm but George was still fighting for a firm hold on life, rarely straying far from the kitchen.

He followed Aunt Susan all day long, and began to help with chores such as sweeping and dishwashing. Before long, George was learning how to tan hides and spin flax and cure bacon. The boy's extraordinary intelligence soon began to show when, to Aunt Susan's surprise, he taught himself to knit, using turkey feathers from the yard and an old unravelled mitten. But George's real interest lay in the woods where his curious and inquisitive mind began to watch and study the crawling insects and wild flowers, distinguishing which of the latter sought the sun and those that managed in the shade. He would spend hours in the woods examining beetles, rocks, tobacco worms and lizards and felt a strong yearing to understand this complex world. What made rain fall? he would ask, and why were some roses red, and others yellow?

One summer afternoon, he heard a next-door neighbour, Mrs Baynham, complaining about her roses. George went to her garden and found the problem to be lack of adequate sunshine. He moved and watered them and went in to explain what he had done. While in Mrs Baynham's house, he saw pictures hung round the room, beautiful paintings of forests and flowers, and portraits of bearded old men. George was rewarded with a nickel, but as he went home, all he could think about was paintings. That evening he squeezed the dark juice from some berries and began painting with his fingers on a flat rock; after that day he was always making pictures, scratching faces on a stone with a piece of tin, or tracing the outline of a flower in any smooth place on the ground.

Meanwhile Mrs Bayham's roses bloomed and she sang George's praises wherever she went. Other neighbours came to George with their gardening problems. Soon, although still a boy, people took to calling him a plant doctor and throughout the area it was said that Carver's George could heal the ailments of anything that grew.

George one day discovered that a cabin not far from the farm that served as the community's house of worship was also used as a school during weekdays. With excitement, he ran to Uncle Moses and asked if he could go to school the next day. Moses was forced to inform the boy that black kids were not allowed to attend that school. George was stunned. The realisation cruelly dawned on him that he was not only different from others in terms of skin pigmentation but that society evaluated him on that basis – access to opportunities, certain privileges, services, facilities and, indeed, basic human rights were determined by, among other things, the colour of one's skin. This was a bombshell, a psychological trauma of severe proportion; he rushed to hide in his secret glade and wept bitterly!

But he refused to abandon his dream. Aunt Susan dug out an old spelling book from her trunk and taught him the alphabet and within a few weeks, he had memorised every line in the book, and could rattle off the spelling of each word. Aunt Susan guided his fist until unaided, he could write his name.

One morning, during a visit to Neosho, eight miles away, George made a startling discovery. He could not wait to tell his brother Jim that he had found a school for black people. It was soon evident that so resolute was his determination to go to school, he could not be persuaded to the contrary. When asked how he hoped to pay for his board and lodging, George replied: "I c-can cook and s-sweep and t-tend fires." And so one autumn morning in 1875, at the age of 14, he set off.

Mariah Watkins and her husband Andrew, a childless black couple in Neosho, found George sitting patiently on a fence on Saturday waiting for the school to open. Mariah recalled years later that when asked what he hoped to learn, he had replied that he had come to Neosho to find out what made hail and snow, and whether a person could change the colour of a flower by changing the seed. The couple took him to their home and on Monday morning George set off for school. When asked under what name he was going to register, he replied: "Carver's George".

"You can't go calling yourself Carver's George any more!" Mariah told him. "You're a person, hear? From now on you're George Carver".

George duly reported himself to the young black teacher at the tumbledown shack known as Lincoln School for Coloured Children. That winter, he was plagued by numerous colds and tormented himself over missing lessons every time he was unable to go to school. To distract him, Mariah would sometimes tell about her slave days. She had lived on a large plantation where only one Negro could read. Frequently those who could read and write were suspect and apt to be sold downriver; but, secretly, those who could, taught others their words and sentences.

"And that's what you must do," Mariah told George. "You must learn all you can, and then go out into the world and give your learning back to our people."

The next winter, George again lost several days from school through illness, but it did not really matter, for George had learned all he could from that school and felt a change of environment might improve his health. He heard that a family down the street was moving to Fort Scott in Kansas, nearly 75 miles away, and asked if they could take him along. They agreed and on a bitterly cold January morning in 1877, George bade goodbye to Mariah and Andrew Watkins.

For ten years, George wandered the western country, attending one school till it could teach him no more, and then moving on to the next school. The cost of accommodation (in most cases decrepit and ramshackle), food, and school textbooks was always a problem. He cooked, chopped wood, tended gardens, cleaned rugs, dug ditches, hammered nails, swabbed outhouses, whitewashed fences – whatever anyone wanted done – to raise money for his bare essentials. He applied himself studiously after classes, reading everything he could lay hands on.

While in Fort Scott, George had another traumatic experience – one night a mob of wild-eyed white men built a great bonfire in the village square, dragged a Negro from the jail, drenched him with oil and threw him into the leaping flames. Trembling with uncontrollable fear, George packed up his belongings and left Fort Scott for ever. He roamed all through Western Kansas, wherever he could find a school for the 'Coloured'. During the summer, he would hire himself out, bounding wheat from farm to farm. Somewhere in his wanderings, he lost the stammer for ever.

In Olanthe, Kansas he was taken into the home of Christopher and Lucy Seymour, an elderly Negro couple. In 1880 the Seymours journeyed west to Minneapolis and there George at last entered secondary school. As he neared the end of his schooling, he received a letter from Aunt Mariah, informing him that his brother Jim had died from smallpox. He felt extremely saddened and, for a while, desperately lonely. But then he received another letter. In reply to his application for admission, George had been accepted by a small Presbyterian college called Highland, in the north-east corner of Kansas, commencing with the autumn term on September 20, 1885. The letter was signed by the Rev. Duncan Brown, D.D. (Doctor of Divinity), Principal.

For the rest of the summer, George consoled himself with the opportunity and excitement of going to College. On September 20, he caught a train to .Highland and duly presented himself for enrolment. But there was a surprise waiting for him: the principal had assumed he was white; on seeing George, he told him to get the hell out of his office as the college did not accept Negroes. He was alone again and, after spending his money on the train fare, almost penniless. He slept in a barn and the next morning found work on a fruit farm with a family named Beeler and there, for months, pruned trees and mended fences, building up capital.

In 1886, he moved into the Kansas plain and laid claim to a 160-acre homestead and built a sod house, where for two years he battled against the furious blizzards in the winter and scorching heat of the summer. Gradually, the passing seasons and the solitude healed his spirit, and he began to read again, and to paint. In the early summer of 1888, he mortgaged his homestead, headed east and crossed into Iowa where he found a job as a cook in a hotel in the village of Winterset.

He joined the Baptist Church choir and one Sunday morning a white woman, Mrs. Milholland, the choir leader asked Dr John Milholland, if George could be invited to their home for singing lessons. George became a great friend of the Milhollands and the warmth of their friendship helped him to overcome the fears he had carried with him from Fort Scott. Eventually, Mrs Milholland encouraged him to apply to Simpson College in Indianola 'which had been endowed by a Methodist bishop named Matthew Simpson, a friend of Abraham Lincoln and a firm believer in the equality of men'. George was accepted immediately and on September 9, 1890, he arrived at Simpson College. "It was at school that I first learned what it meant to be a human being", he said later, "and at Simpson that I could truly believe I was one."

At Simpson he studied etymology, composition, mathematics and his favourite subject, art. To pay his way, he set up a laundry in a small house off the college grounds.

As an exercise, George had painted a picture of a cactus-grafting experiment he had devised and Miss Etta Budd, his art teacher was very impressed by it. She showed it to her father, a professor of horticulture at the Iowa Agricultural College at Ames who suggested George should be studying agriculture at Ames. He accepted the invitation and arrived at Ames in May, an inauspicious time. The College year followed the planting season, February to November and with the term well begun, there was no room available for the new student. But a member of the teaching staff, Professor Wilson, asked that George be sent to him. He cleared his desk and moved up to the first floor, ordered a camp-bed and a chest of drawers to be brought to his old office and asked the astonished and grateful George to move in.

This kindness, however, was contrasted by an incident that occurred shortly afterwards. He was told that he could not eat in the canteen with the white students; he would have to take his meals in the basement with the kitchen staff and field hands. When Professor Budd wrote to his daughter about the affair, Etta Budd was furious, but she could not leave her art classes in mid-term. Instead she talked to a friend, Mrs Liston, who had known George, and agreed to visit him. George was surprised to see her, but he spent the day showing her round and introducing her to his teachers. Then, at dinnertime, Mrs Liston insisted she was going to eat in the basement with her friend. When they pleaded with her pointing out that the Dean would not be pleased, she snapped back, saying that they should have considered that when they arranged Mr Carver's dining facilities.

At breakfast the next morning, George was invited to join the students at Table 6. He became a favourite of his school mates and within a week, had devised a table game that swept the dining-hall and remains an institution at Ames to this day. Each dish had to be asked for by its scientific name. For example, if a student remembered *Triticum vulgare,* he could fill up on bread, but if he forgot the words *solanum tuberosum,* he would not get potatoes – unless he sat next to George. A boy who had forgotten the formula for sugar and could not stand his tasteless porridge would whisper to George who would whisper back: C twelve, H twenty-two, O eleven".

George immersed himself in his studies with all his characteristic enthusiasm for learning, enrolling for botany, geometry, chemistry, zoology, bacteriology and entomology. As always, he worked to support himself: a handyman in North Hall, waiter, greenhouse and laboratory caretaker.

In 1894, George received his long-sought Bachelor of Science degree. A few days after his graduation, Dr Louis Pammel, a professor at Iowa State University and an eminent botanist sent for him in response to his application for a job as an assistant botanist at the College's experimental station. He was put in charge of the greenhouse and began to concentrate on mycology, the branch of botany which deals with fungus growth. Soon his collection contained some 20,000 specimens, and his skill at hybridising rendered whole families of fruits and plants resistant to fungus attack. Scientific journals began to cite G.W. Carver as their authority.

He earned his MA degree in agriculture and bacterial botany in 1896. George had never been more content in his life, but was painfully aware of the fact that across the land millions of black people starved and stultified; was he serving them as a role model of what a black person subject to all the social disadvantages could achieve, or did he belong among them, sharing the knowledge he had acquired through his arduous struggles?

About this time, 800 miles away in the Alabama town of Tuskegee, Booker T. Washington, the acknowledged spokesman of the American black people, was struggling to set up an institute of learning for black people. Washington reasoned that the most urgent task of his institute was to teach his people to farm, but it was a subject that he had no knowledge of. He had heard that there was a noted agriculturalist, a black man at a school in Iowa, and so on April 1, 1896 Washington wrote him a letter:

> "I cannot offer you money, position or fame. The first two you have. The last, from the place you now occupy, you will no doubt achieve. These things I now ask you to give up. I offer you in their place work – hard work – the task of bringing a people from degradation, poverty and waste to full manhood."

George knew upon reading the letter that this was his destiny. After a farewell party at Ames during which Professor Wilson presented him with a magnificent microscope, he boarded a train and headed down south with all haste. On the way, he saw what nothing in his experience could have prepared him for. It was harvest time and he was entering the realm of King Cotton. Men, women and children – all who had the strength to raise a hand – were out in the fields picking cotton. These were his people – the people he had come to help! His heart sank at the enormity of the task. The tyranny of King Cotton and of its capitalist landowners was brutally apparent everywhere.

On arriving at the grounds of the Tuskegee Normal and Industrial Institute, he could not believe he had reached his destination. In all directions, there was only sand and bare yellow clay, scarred by rain gullies so deep that a man – a horse! – could be lost in them. Numbly, he walked down the main road. It lay ankle-deep in dust and would, he knew, run with a river of mud whenever it rained. He passed a pathetic collection of shacks, an occasional larger building, and one of brick, called Alabama Hall. In the sky behind it vultures circled, taking it in turns to swoop down on the kitchen garbage. There was no sewage system.

"What do you think of our school?" Booker T. Washington sked when Carver was shown into the principal's plain, sparsely furnished office.

"There seems much to be done," was Carver's reply.

Washington told him that a site had been chosen for the agricultural building, but for the moment a single room was all that could be spared and it would have to serve as his living quarters as well. "Your department exists only on paper," Washington said. "And your laboratory will have to be in your head."

"I will manage," said Carver. And he set to work.

One morning, he led the 13 students of his first agricultural class to the school junk heap on a reclamation expedition. To the amazement of his students, Carver directed the collection of a startling array of bottles, rusted pans, fruit-jar lids, saucepan handles, wire and odd bits of metal. No one had the vaguest notion what he was up to, but when they had exhausted the possibility of the school dump, he directed them to the town, scavenging rubbish in black alleys and knocking on doors to ask for rubber, old kettles and china jars.

But their curiosity was soon to be rewarded, for as they watched in awe, a makeshift laboratory soon took shape from the materials scavenged from the rubbish tips. Having set up the laboratory, George turned his students' attention to the 20-acre school farm which students and teachers alike agreed was the worst soil in Alabama. In a three-year agricultural experiment, George persuaded the principal, Washington, to buy several hundred pounds of phosphates. When the students had spread it, they were ready to plant a crop, but George had other ideas. He led his students to a dump to extract the kitchen waste – vegetable peelings, barn sweepings etc. – from which a big compost heap was made and by the spring, this had rotted to a rich, black humus. George had the compost spread on the 20 acres.

'King Cotton' ruled the South and the students quite naturally expected they were going to plant cotton. They were flabbergasted when Carver decreed that their first crop was to be cowpeas. Had all this back-breaking work been done to plant such an economically insignificant crop? The teacher patiently explained to his students that most plants drained life-giving nitrogen from the soil, and cotton was among the worst consumers. But legumes such as cowpeas absorbed nitrogen from the air and fed it back to the soil. So, an essential fertilizer ingredient, worth one and four-pence a pound commercially, could be gained at no cost. At the end of the first year the produce from the farm provided the Institute's canteen well into November, and showed an overall profit. In the spring, they planted sweet potatoes and experimented with legumes. The sweet potato yield was 265 bushels per acre – more than six times the usual harvest.

When eventually Carver planted cotton, farmers, black and white, came to stare in amazement. The yield was an incredible 500-pound bale per acre. So rich a crop had never been grown in that part of the land. So, how could a Northerner, a teacher who had never seen cotton until he was a grown man, best those who had devoted a life-time to raising it? they asked.

But this was only the beginning for Carver. He landscaped the College grounds, grading and terracing, planting young trees, shrubbery, grass and flowers so that, in time, the once barren field became transformed into a great natural garden. The new agriculture building was built with Carver designing the interior. In the autumn of 1898 he persuaded his old friend, Professor Wilson, now

Secretary of Agriculture to come and dedicate it.

The scene was now set for Carver to settle down to a quiet, deserving, long academic life. It was then that an incident occurred which was to bring out the real genius in Carver. During his many wanderings, he had learned to play the piano and now on Sunday nights he would sit down at the ancient upright piano in Alabama Hall. One Sunday, the school treasurer, Warren Logan, suggested that he go on a concert tour. Carver dismissed the idea, but he had at this time been seeking ways of raising money to add 15 acres to the school farm. Soon, circulars announcing a Carver piano tour were sent to towns and hamlets in Alabama, Georgia, Louisiana and Texas. When he returned to Tuskegee five weeks later, he had several hundred dollars raised.

While on the tour, the degree of deprivation experienced by black people in the deep South was brought home forcefully to Carver. Wherever he went, there were emaciated, hunger-haunted Negroes, often ten or more in each squalid shanty home, pigsties at their very door. The soil was scorched and poor, but it could be made rich. The despotism of 'King Cotton' could be ended. There could be good food for his people, and opportunity for their children if they could be shown how! What contribution could he make to improve the lot of his hungry people?

Carver decided that on the third Tuesday of each month he would invite the farmers from the surrounding country-side to the immaculate new agriculture building. For two hours, he would talk to them about their land. He urged them to plant a kitchen garden. Fresh vegetables, he argued, would break the tyranny of the meat, meal and molasses diet that had made pellagra a deadly caller in nearly every home. Dramatically, Dr Carver would cut into a ripe red tomato – generally regarded as poisonous at the time – and, to the horror of his audience, eat it with obvious relish.

In time, the farmers coming to the Institute grew to over 50. But out where the roads ended, in the thickets and the swamps, were thousands of Negroes who had never heard of Tuskegee, and Carver was determined to reach them! He wheeled a wagon and a mule, and with a few tools, packets of seeds, and some boxed demonstration plants, he set forth after classes, at weekends and every moment he could spare, seeking isolated farms, covering groups at fairs and on street corners.

Some men were sceptical – "How come you're smarter'n me? You just as black" – but others listened and asked questions. He urged them to save five cents every working day; and at the end of the year, they would have enough to buy three acres of land and a small reserve fund left over. There was no other way of breaking the grip of the landlord and the overseer, he told them. Soon, all over the area, coins were being hoarded in jars, tins and hollow stumps. Slowly and doggedly, he began to change the eating habits of the South. He taught the farmers how to cure pork so that even in the hottest weather it would not spoil. He distributed packets of seed and showed the men how to plant the vegetables. But their wives had little clue of what to do with the produce. Carver would go to their stoves and with sleeves rolled up, show them how to flavour and cook the greens and beets and potatoes.

As word about the Tuskegee wagon spread, Dr Carver began attracting Saturday-afternoon crowds to the town squares. At first white people were uneasy at such an arrangement and some broke up the meetings. "We don't want uppity niggers round here," they said. Their real motive, however, was that they did not want black farmers outproducing white ones. But before long, the white people stopped grumbling and edged close to hear what the "nigger teacher" was saying. Carver was pleased to have them, for black and white people faced similar agricultural problems in the South.

The "wagon school" started a revolution in soil conservation, all but eradicated pellagra, and went on to become a world-wide institution. Requests from other communities poured into Tuskegee, all seeking assistance in launching their own mobile schools. The idea spread overseas and visitors from Russia, China, Japan, India, Africa, Australia and South America came to listen to the lanky, unassuming professor recount his experiences in the rural South and to his suggested techniques for putting them to use in other lands. To his dying day, Carver insisted that the wagon school was his most important work.

Throughout these years, Carver had been urging farmers to diversify from the mono-crop production of cotton, but without much success. His plea that they should grow cowpea and sweet potato fell on deaf ears. He experimented with the soya bean and showed how it can be easily transformed into flour, meal, even milk, but the farmers were unimpressed.

In 1915, Dr Carver found a most persuasive ally. For years, he had warned the farmers that the insidious spread of the boll weevil, a rapacious beetle that feeds on cotton, could not be stopped. The plague of 1915 was one of the most devastating agricultural scourges of modern times. The boll weevil ravaged cotton fields across Louisiana, Mississippi and Alabama and drove thousands of farmers into bankruptcy and despair.

Around this time, Dr Carver had been examining an odd little vine that produced a peanut. It was considered worthless, but a few farmers had planted a few patches of peanuts, mostly because their children liked to crack the double-humped shells and eat the nuts. "Burn off your infected cotton," Carver now told the stricken farmers, 'Plant peanuts'!

To dramatise his campaign, he invited nine influential local businessmen to lunch at the Institute. The meal, prepared under Carver's direction, consisted of soup, mock chicken, a pureed vegetable, bread, salad, ice cream, sweets, biscuits and coffee. The businessmen noted that each dish had a unique zesty flavour and when Carver informed them that they had eaten nothing but peanut prepared in nine different ways, they broke into applause.

Slowly pushed by the boll weevil and pulled by Carver's entreaty, the farmers began to do as he said. Where there had been random peanut patches, now 20 to 40 acre fields began to bloom. In time, whole communities abandoned cotton, and peanuts became one of the most important crops in a great farming belt that ran from Montgomery, Alabama, to the Florida border.

Then one October afternoon, an old woman knocked at Carver's door. She was a widow, she informed the professor. She had followed his counsel and turned the farm to peanuts. There had been a bumper harvest and after setting aside all the peanuts she could use for the year ahead, she still had hundreds of pounds left over. What was she to do with the surplus? Who would buy them?

Carver had no answer and was quick to grasp the calamity. He had been so busy trying to break the mono-crop economic system, he had not thought through the full implications of his proposed alternative. A hasty tour of the countryside revealed the enormity of his blunder. Barns were piled up high with the surplus and still more peanuts were rotting in the fields. He returned to his laboratory racked with guilt that he had thought the problem only half-way through. Not only must the people be freed from the economic tyranny of cotton; they had to have a cash crop as well. If there were no markets for peanuts, then he would have to create some.

Inside his laboratory, Carver closed the door, put on an apron and shelled a handful of peanuts. All that day and night, he literally tore the nuts apart, isolating their fats and gums, their resins and sugars and starches. Spread before him were pentoses, pentosans, legumins, lysin, amido and amino acids. He tested these in different combinations under varying degrees of heat and pressure, and soon his hoard of synthetic treasures began to grow: milk, ink, dyes, shoe polish, creosote, salve, shaving cream and, of course, peanut butter.

From the shells, he made a soil conditioner, insulating board and fuel briquettes. Binding another batch with an adhesive, he pressed it, buffed it to a high gloss – and held in his hands a light weather-proof square that looked precisely like marble and was every bit as hard. For two days and two nights he worked, dismissing the worried students who tapped at his door, enquiring if he was all right.

By the time the wearied professor stepped out into that chilly, October morning in 1915, the world of synthetics and the discipline of agricultural chemistry were born! As news of his startling discoveries circulated around the country, Dr Carver was called to Washington to report on his findings before the House Ways and Means Committee. For over one hour, the gentle Doctor pulled from his bags, item after item and convinced sceptical congressmen that "King Cotton" need not continue to hold the southern region in its tyranny.

Carver had made it possible for men to use every peanut harvested, and that if the crop trebled – as it was to do in a short space of four years – every farmer would still find a ready buyer in the market-place. By the end of the First World War, the infant US peanut industry was worth 80 million dollars a year. By the time Carver died, there were well over 300 by-products, scores of factories had been built to make them, and their range staggered the mind – mayonnaise, cheese, chili, sauce, shampoo, bleach, axle grease, linoleum, metal polish, wood stains, adhesives and plastics; and the value of the peanut crop continued to grow to a point where by 1981 the value of the peanut production in the US reached $1,069,526,000. Although the total area under cultivation had been significantly reduced by 1983, the value of production was still just under $800 million.

Booker T. Washington, the founder of Tuskegee and Carver's close friend for almost 20 years, died on November 14, 1915. Carver was greatly saddened and sought to fill the incalculable void with work, the only solace he had ever known. Five years earlier, the Tuskegee trustees had voted to build a new Department of Agricultural Research with Carver in charge. Relieved of all but a few classes, he concentrated on what he called the "creative sciences". He continued to contribute to a broad spectrum of human knowledge – in agronomy, nutrition, chemistry, genetics, mycology, plant pathology – but more and more his interests were turning to the creation of useful materials from the waste products of agriculture and industry.

There are those who feel that this concept, still the subject of widespread research, was Carver's most important gift to humankind. Never before had anyone advocated the use of agricultural products for anything but food and clothing.

Some of his ideas took decades to materialise. He had made paper from the southern pine – and 25 years later his process led to a major new paper industry. He made synthetic marble from peanut shells and food wastes, and these discoveries presaged the fabrication of plastics from all sorts of vegetable matter. Substituting cellulose for steel, US car manufacturers would, in time, be building 350 pounds of agricultural products into every car.

From the sweet potato, Carver devised 118 products, ranging from wartime flour to inexpensive gum for postage stamps and laid the foundation for still another industry. He discovered during the First World War that he could reduce 100 pounds of sweet potatoes to a powder that fitted into a compact carton, kept indefinitely and could be instantly reconstituted by the addition of water. Today the dehydrated-food industry is worth billions of dollars, as are frozen foods, a first cousin; the food industry owes his genius a debt of gratitude.

Carver's discoveries knew no limits. From the Osage orange, he extracted a juice that tamed the toughest cut of beef – one of the first meat tenderisers. He showed that the giant thistle – ranted at by farmers – contained medical properties, as did 250 other weeds he examined. When chemists learned to synthesise rayon and other artificial fibres, it seemed that the era when Southern farmers could sell as much cotton as they produced was at an end. But Carver's brilliant mind soon produced alternative solutions and in a few years the farmers were flourishing again, their markets spurred by the use of cotton in plastics, paving stones for roads, car tyres and fertiliser. He extracted paints and colour washes from the clay hills. Another Carver experiment led to the now-standard use of soya bean oil as the base for car spray paints.

Any one of his discoveries could have made Carver a man of fabulous wealth. But all his life he refused to accept payment for a single discovery. He had scant regard for money and, forty years after his arrival at Tuskegee, he was still earning the $125 a month first offered him by Booker T. Washington, having refused all offers of increased salary. Indeed the treasurer had to plead with him regularly to cash his salary cheques, which were always stuffed in his pockets, so that the school could balance its books. On many occcasions, he gave them away to pay the bills of many boys – black and white – in their times of need. Virtually every-one who knew him remembers at least one such instance.

He was constantly besieged by businessmen willing to pay handsomely for his advice. A group of peanut farmers in Florida sent a 100-dollar cheque and a box of diseased specimens; if the professor could cure their crop, they would put him on a monthly retainer. Carver sent back a diagnosis of the disease, and the cheque. "As the good Lord charged nothing to grow your peanuts", he wrote, "I do not think it fitting to charge anything for curing them."

When a dyestuffs firm heard that he had perfected an array of substitute vegetable dyes, the owner offered to build a laboratory for

Carver, and sent him a blank cheque. He sent back the cheque, together with the formulas for the 536 dyes he had found to date. To the industrialists, this was a welcome substitute to the aniline dyes formerly imported from Germany. When he declined a princely sum to join another company which had adopted his process for making garden furniture out of synthetic marble, the company literally came to him – moving factory and machines to Tuskegee – and got the benefit of his advice at no cost at all. He was invited by Thomas Edison to come and work in the latter's laboratory at a minimum annual salary of $100,000. Carver declined the offer, as he had all the others.

"But if you had all that money", he was once challenged, "you could help your people."

"If I had all that money," Carver replied, "I might forget about my people."

Carver's reputation travelled far and wide and so many letters poured in from across the world, some simply addressed to the 'Peanut Man'. He also became affectionately known as "The Wizard of Tuskegee". He received a steady stream of visitors seeking his advice on all kinds of problems and his door remained always open. He was a friend of presidents and kings and princes, scientists, inventors, and government officials journeyed to see him. The crown prince of Sweden studied under him for three weeks, gleaning information on the use of agricultural wastes. In an extended correspondence with Ghandi, Carver prescribed for him a vegetable diet, and detailed the food values in plants that could easily be grown by the Mahatma's hungry people.

But Carver's most frequent and best known guest was Henry Ford. They met in 1937, became firm friends, and agreed to get together at least once a year. Carver went to Ford's home in Michigan, or to his Georgia plantation. Later, when Dr Carver's health began to fail, Ford came regularly to Tuskegee. Carver's most significant work with Ford was in the fabrication of rubber. Fields of golden rod covered the Georgia plantation and from this unlikely harvest Carver extracted a milky liquid that could be synthesized into a material with rubber-like characteristics. Thus an exciting start was made in the long search for a synthetic substitute for rubber.

During the fortieth-anniversary of Dr Carver's arrival at Tuskegee, the college commemorated his work by an exhibition. The remarkable achievement of Carver's life-time was truly fantastic. There were thousands of products shaped from peanuts, sweet potatoes and weeds; these were all gathered into a display that was later made permanent in a museum in a separate building, dedicated by Ford and called the George Washington Carver

Museum.

In 1938 Carver donated $30,000 of his life's saving to the establishment of the George Washington Carver Foundation and, shortly before his death, willed the remainder of his estate to the Foundation whose purpose is to discover uses for agricultural wastes and to develop food products from common agricultural products with the aim of creating new markets for them.

On January 5, 1943 Dr Carver died at the age of eighty-two. The simple epitaph on his grave gave an eloquent testimony to a true intellectual giant – a great human being in the truest meaning of the term:

"He could have added fortune to fame, but caring for neither, he found happiness and honour in being helpful to the world."

Today there is hardly anybody in the industrialised world whose life is unaffected by the discoveries of Dr Carver. Born into slavery, orphaned, having struggled throughout his childhood for survival against numerous illnesses, having endured untold hardships, sorrow, deprivation, soul-destroying racial discrimination and the most awful social disadvantage, Carver's invincible inner self gave him the mental strength which his physique lacked, to overcome the worst that a racist society could throw at him. His brilliant intellect led him to a lifetime of achievements that mark him as one of the greatest scientists of all time.

In Carver, we can see a specimen of the African genius which 5,000 years ago, in the African plains of Nubia and the Nile Valley, led the world of barbarism into a world of civilisation and human progress. Up to the age of 14 he had not been able to start formal education despite his desperate craving for learning; for him there was no "public school" or "grammar school"; there was no "Oxford, Cambridge, Harvard or Yale"; there was no Foundation scholarships, nor special grants for research; there was no finely equipped laboratory and well-stocked libraries – his initial laboratory was his head.

His contribution to the poor, the hungry, and the peasant farmers of the American deep South both black and white; his original contribution to the development of science and to our understanding of plant life; his magnificently practical mind which found solutions to many human, social, agricultural and industrial problems; his kindness and generosity which made the hundreds of his discoveries freely available to anyone on request (the overwhelming majority, no doubt, to the white race which enslaved, oppressed and deprived his people!); these and more make him a superb scientist and humanist, unsurpassed by any of his contemporaries.

I challenge anyone to produce evidence of a scientist of greater stature, intellectual magnificence, prolific discoveries and inventions, and more varied contribution to the needs of humankind. *And he was a blackman, a full-blooded blackman.*

Apart from the above individuals; the 1,000-plus known patents by black inventors by 1913; the large number of black inventors who, for reasons of racial discrimination, had to patent their inventions in the names of their white lawyers, or to deliberately obscure their racial identity in order to give their invention a commercial viability, there were many others such as Benjamin Banneker, a self-taught black mathematician and surveyor who helped to lay our Washington D.C., USA, and made the first clock constructed in the USA, did work in astronomy which attracted the attention of astronomers on both sides of the Atlantic, and through the use of mathematics, plotted the cycles of the 17-year locust and thus helped farmers to anticpate them; Oneissimus who developed an effective antidote for the dreaded smallpox in 1721; James Derham, a slave who is generally regarded as the first trained black physician in the USA and in the 1780s became one of the most prominent physicians in New Orleans; Edward Bouchet who in 1876 earned a Ph.D. degree from Yale University for work on "Measuring Refractive Indices"; Dr. Charles Turner of St. Louis, Missouri who wrote at least 47 academic treatises in the field of biology. Other black inventors were producing such things as rotary engines (A.J. Beard, 1892), pianolas (J.H. Dickinson, 1899), railway switches (W.H. Jackson, 1897), printing presses (W.A. Lavalette, 1878), electric railways (W.B. Purvis, 1894), refrigerators (J. Standard, 1891), corn husking machines (Washington Wade, 1883), and a host of others.[37]

More recently there have been notable scientists such as Dr Lloyd Quarterman, a nuclear scientist, a flouride chemist and a spectros-copist. He is author and co-author of dozens of original scientific papers. He is a member of the most distinguished scientific bodies – The Society of Applied Spectroscopy, the Society of Sigma XI, the Scientific Research Society of America, the American Chemical Society and the American Association for the Advancement of Science. Dr Quarterman is one of six black scientists who worked on the 'Manhattan Project' – the code-name for the Atom Bomb research for which he received a certificate of appreciation from the US Secretary of War, for his contribution to the production of the Atomic Bomb.

On July 1, 1946, he joined the Argonne National Laboratory where he worked with the team of scientists who made the first reactor for the *Nantilus,* the atomic powered submarine. Dr Quarterman was a leading member of a team which did pioneering work in flouride chemistry.

"They led the world in flouride chemistry. For a period of time they were the greatest fluoride chemists on earth. When Quarterman was going to school there were no 'compounds' of zeon or argon or krypton. These were known as the 'noble' gases, since they were thought to stand sovereign and alone, reacting with nothing. But Quarterman and his team made them react with the flourine atoms. They made zeon tetrafluoride – zeon difluoride – zeon hexafluoride. They led the world in this and on top of that, Quarterman took zeon difluoride and incorporated it in other experiments, making a whole series of new compounds."[38]

Dr Quarterman wanted to study something in hydrogen fluoride, the world's greatest solvent, a compound so corrosive that it would dissolve glass, or all known metals. His solution was the invention in 1976 of what came to be known as "the diamond window" which enabled a spectroscopist to study, through the electro-magnetic beam, compounds dissolved in HF (hydrogen flouride) and to gain an understanding of the structures, from the vibrations of the molecules in the solution.

He also pioneered work on "synthetic blood" in the early '60s. But when he presented papers to his superiors, the project was shelved on the grounds that "they didn't have a budget for it". This is a field of research in which the Japanese are now thought to be well advanced.[39]

Whilst Albert Einstein propounded the theory of relativity, the quantum theory was developed over a thirty-year period through the efforts of many scientists. But it was left to a black scientist in the US, Elmer S. Imes, to establish definitely that the quantum theory could be extended to include rotational states of molecules. In a doctoral dissertation on "Measurements of the Near Infrared Absorption Spectra of Some Diatomic Molecules", one of two known publications by Imes, and which appeared in the *Astrophysical Journal*, 1919, Imes "initiated the field of high resolution spectral studies".[40]

In 1973, Professor S. J. Cyvin of the Institute of Theoretical Chemistry, University of Tronheim, Norway said of Imes' work: "The infrared spectrum of hydrogen fluoride polymers is reported probably for the first time by Imes".

In 1974, Frederick S. Simmons, author of an article on "Infrared Spectroscopic Study of Hydrogen-Fluorine Flames" said of the effect of Imes' work on Aeronautics and Astronautical Space studies: "In regards to Dr Imes' thesis work on HF vibration-rotation, it certainly does qualify as a pioneer effort. The consequences of his work are important today in two areas of technical concern: thermal radiation from rocket engines using fluorine compounds as oxidizers, and radiation from chemical lasers based on hydrogenfluorine reactions."[41]

And so the list goes on – in the field of information technology, including fibre-optics technology; micro-computers; the invention of 'foil electrets', used to convert sound into electrical signals in hearing aids, portable tape recorders, lapel microphones, and 'smart' information terminals, such as the phone-with-a-memory manufactured by Bell Laboratories, black people have been involved in both pioneering and significant innovation work.[42]

Black people have also been involved in space science. For example, the test pilot who field-tested and sold the ground-based microwave landing system to the Airport Association (a system in which Britain unsuccessfully competed), was a black man. Major Frederick Gregory, scheduled to be the first black space 'shuttle' pilot, has flown more than 40 different aircrafts and holds several patents for aircraft cockpit modifications. He designed the 'Single-hand Sidestick Throttle Controller' (SSTC) that combines both throttle power control as well as control over roll and pitch which, if introduced, will give pilots a much more precise control of the aeroplane with one hand thus freeing the other hand for managing the other critical systems. He also has the major responsibility for redesigning space 'shuttle' cockpits.

The Director of Dryden's Flight Research Centre at Edwards Air Force Base in California which is responsible for the performance of the space shuttle's critical approach and landing tests, is a black man – Isaac Gillam. Gillam was also previously head of two of NASA's most important missile-launch programmes, Delta and Scout. "Under his direction, Nasa put into orbit satellites for RCA, Comstat and Western Union, as well as companies in France, Germany, Italy, Indonesia, Canada and Japan. His role in the foreign satellite launch programme earned him the Distinguished Service Medal, NASA's highest award."[43]

Also among the many black contributors to America's space science programme is Robert Shurney, the man who designed the tyres used on America's 'Moon Buggy'. NASA set a specification with three requirements for the moon buggy tyres: (a) they had to be extraordinarily lightweight; and yet be (b) strong enough to hold the weight of the astronaut and the laboratory of instruments he would carry with him; and (c) although much lighter, they would need to have as good a traction as that of the rubber tyre used on Earth. Shurney's design was found most suitable.

Black people, therefore, have shown themselves as ingenious, talented, creative, innovative and resourceful as anybody else when given equality of opportunity and access to society's facilities, resources, support, stimulus to creativity, privileges and responsibilities. Indeed, we have shown that many creative black people have made their contribution despite being denied these facilities by white racist societies.

But for every one such successful black inventor or scientist, there were scores of equally capable and talented black people who, for numerous reasons, could not break through the 'prison walls of institutionalised racial discrimination' and the denial of access to opportunities for education, personal advancement, and contribution to human progress.

Those who broke through the barriers constructed by white racist societies have given the lie to the claims of the ideology of racism that no individual black person has ever made (and by implication, could ever make) any contribution to mankind's conquest, and understanding of nature. The second major evidence cited by the ideology of racism as proof of its central premise (viz., that black people are inherently inferior to white people), was, like the first major proof, based not on facts, but on fiction and very often, deliberate falsification of 'reality'. Black scientists, inventors and technologists are either presented in such a way as to imply that they are white people, or altogether omitted from textbooks and scientific/academic treatises. The consequence is that, even where it is not explicitly stated, the implicit impression, through default, is that all human progress is due to the caucasian and a few Asians – black people have not and cannot make any significant contribution.

Notes

a. emphasis mine.
b. Note that white people are always the "standard of measurement" – black people are rarely judged in their own right, eg. the Black Pharaoh, Thutmosis III was referred to by later Historians as "Napoleon of Antiquity" when he preceded Napoleon by over 3,000 years, and should, by right, have been the "standard" by which Napoleon was measured.
c. I am indebted to the *Reader's Digest* for most of the material on Craver's life and works.

CHAPTER EIGHT

Psychology, IQ, and Black Inferiority; Old Wine in a New Bottle

I have demonstrated in Chapters Five, Six, and Seven, the falsehood of the basic premise of the ideology of racism by demolishing the evidence proffered to support the premise. I have also shown that the doctrine of immanent black inferiority on which the ideology of racism was founded was nothing more than a mythical edifice, constructed to justify European exploitation, brutality and bestiality against African slaves and, later, colonies. The early adherents of the ideology imbibed the assumption with its stereotypes, imagery, and discourse out of ignorance. Later adherents who had opportunity to invalidate the ideology's basic premise through personal contact with the African, did not challenge the ideology, because: (1) many of them found the assumption too comfortable to take the risk of falsifying. To be told that one is born to a "superior" race who occupy the apex of humanity's racial hierarchy, is an ego-boosting thought which many were only too glad to cling to – true or false; and (2) the European had, through his power over the African, so systematically and effectively rendered him socio-economically inferior that even the sceptics have been persuaded by the overwhelming, openly available evidence. Perceived reality, therefore, correlated the ideology's basic assumptions and discourse.

At any rate, it is vital to grasp the fact that in social relationships, the validity of the assumptions of an ideology is not a necessary condition for the acceptance of the ideology. Social *reality* is socially constructed, externalised, objectified and then internalised and experienced as *reality*. Whether the ideas underlying the construct have any validity or truthfulness may be irrelevant. Two examples from religion and social law may help to illustrate this social phenomenon.

Let us imagine a scenario in which a respected member of a village community claiming to be possessed by a spirit, persuades the villagers, who were suffering from drought, to build a giant concrete eagle (or any object you care to imagine) on a hilltop;

construct a shrine over it; call it the "God of Rain", and name the mountain the "Holy Mountain of the Rain God". This 'spiritual leader' develops an elaborate theory about the nature of the God of Rain; his power and control over rainfall; how and when people might worship, sacrifice to, and communicate with him. He further persuades the desperate farming community to make sacrifices of sheep, goats, cows, or whatever, to the Rain God, who would in His mercy, and if satisfied with the 'sacrifice', let the rain fall. The villagers obey the 'spiritual leader', offer sacrifices to the Rain God on the Holy Mountain, and in seven days time get their first rainfall for a year, followed by many days of rain, leading to a bumper harvest.

The social practice of pre-planting season pilgrimage, sacrifices and supplications to the Rain God on the Holy Mountain, and the offering of farm produce as thanksgiving after harvest, become well-established annual events. The role of the spiritual leader becomes established as the 'High Priest' of the Rain God; and he develops elaborate discourse, liturgy, ritual incantations, procedures for worship and the offering of sacrifices; the role, responsibility and privileges of the High Priest , and the procedures for his succession.

If drought occurs in future, this would not falsify the assumptions of the theory – the High Priest would explain that the villagers have violated the commandments of the Rain God, defiled his Holy Mountain or committed some terrible sin. Further sacrifices would be called for, and so on.

In time, the worship of the Rain God becomes a well established religion; the discourse is transmitted and diffused throughout the community and becomes embodied in the pattern of social behaviour and permeates social institutions and practices; and, as the original reason for the birth of this social practice becomes obscure with the passage of time, so the practice acquires the status of a profound mystery, spiritual wisdom and truth.

If in future, members of the cult of the Rain God should be exposed to the science of meteorology and come to understand the natural elements, conditions and processes that lead to cloud formation and rainfall – insolation, relative humidity, cloud formation and precipitation – they could still claim that such elements as air pressure, temperature and humidity are still controlled by the Rain God who, therefore, indirectly still controls rainfall. The integrity of their belief could still remain intact in the face of contrary evidence. The validity of the assumption that rainfall is controlled by the Rain God who sits on top of the Holy Mountain is hence, not a necessary condition for the belief in the ideology of the cult of the Rain God!

Another example can be cited from the field of jurisprudence.

Laws are socially constructed and imposed on the populace by the dominant group within a geo-political boundary. To be effective as an instrument of socio-political control, however, the role of ideology is indispensable, because if a people refuse to obey the law, social control becomes impossible in complex societies. If motorists, for example, refuse to stop when the traffic lights are showing red, traffic law and order becomes impossible. Massive police and even armed forces might be deployed but, if drivers refuse to be cowed by tanks and machine guns, the law becomes meaningless. The introduction of draconian repressive measures under the state of emergency, introduced by the racist minority regime of South Africa, has not, for instance, succeeded in achieving its objective of suppressing the black demand for their legitimate rights. By the end of 1986, over 2000 black people (including children and babies) had been killed, most of them by the police, in a two-year period of resistance against apartheid; but the resistance against the 'Law' and oppression continues unabated.

Effective social control, therefore, depends on the consent of the majority to abide by the 'Law'. This concensus is obtained through an ideology which teaches that the Law was designed to protect all and must be obeyed even if specific aspects of it are perceived by a section of the community to be repressive. The Law itself prescribes the procedures by which changes may be introduced. The Law is framed in such a way as to ensure the maintenance of the status quo and the dominance by the ruling class since they create or strongly influence the creation of the laws.

But through the process of socialisation and ideological hegemony, most people in most societies come to accept the Law as sacrosanct. 'It must be obeyed – sanctions or no sanctions!' If the Law is repressive or perceived to be unjust, it must nevertheless be obeyed while changes are sought through the procedures prescribed by the Law. 'The Law is the Law, is the Law, is the Law!' 'We cannot pick and choose which parts to obey and those to be disobeyed', etc. The Law is fundamentally just, hence if I cannot obtain justice from the law, perhaps my concept of justice needs re-examining, for the Law defines what constitutes Justice, and there are learned Judges, QCs, Barristers and Solicitors, trained in, and authorised by, the Law to interpret the Law.

Particular aspects of the Law may be designed to curtail my freedom, to deny me certain basic human rights, to control my behaviour and to allow my domination by the dominant class, but once I accept the basic ideological proposition that the Law is the Law and must be obeyed irrespective... then even unjust and repressive laws must be obeyed, because they are an integral part of the 'Law'. People relate to the Law as if they were made for the Law!

Through ideology, people come to accept the fact that the primary
purpose of the Law is to protect ALL citizens alike, rather than the
reality that the Law is primarily designed to protect the interests of
the ruling and dominant classes.

It can be seen then that in the realm of both religion and the Law
man conceptualises, creates, externalises, objectifies and internal-
ises 'reality' and lives by that reality. We can create 'reality' in the
abstract and set it outside of ourselves, objectify and concretise it,
and operate according to, or be entirely dominated by, that *reality,*
be it a God or the Law. This process applies not only in religion and
social laws, but in virtually all social practice.

This being the case, the fact that the assumptions of the ideology
of racism can be demonstrably shown to be palpable fantasy, will
not and cannot destroy racism. In social relationships, 'perceived
reality' is more important than 'objective reality' in shaping
attitudes from which behaviour derives. Hence the racists will
continue to perceive 'reality' constructed by the ideology of racism
as *the* 'reality'. The impoverishment of black people through the
concentration of power in the hands of white people who control the
allocation and distribution of resources, is only an additional bonus
to the triumph of the ideology of racism, for surface reality is made
to correlate with, and hence is seen as reinforcing the reality of, the
ideology of racism. Black inferiority is seen then, not as a figment of
European imagination, but as an axiom – a self-evident truth.

By the 1940s the ideology of racism had become a deeply
ingrained and entrenched belief in European, American, Dutch and
Australian attitudes. Its influence had become so pervasive and
widespread that there was no major social institution – economic,
political, or cultural – which was immune. It had become an integral
part of their language; an elaborate discourse with its imagery,
symbolism, and folklore had become well established and embodied
in social consciousness. The belief in black inferiority was taken for
granted; it knew no class or religious boundaries.

Christianity proclaimed "all men to be created equal", but the
deeds of its adherents which 'spoke' louder than their words, were
proclaiming: "but white people are more equal than black people".
The constitutions and the laws of Europe and America, etc, were
proclaiming the equality of all men, whilst the enforcement of the
law, respect for human rights, access to social rights, privileges,
opportunities and responsibilities, depended, *inter alia,* on the
colour of one's skin. Employment selection criteria were piously
claimed to be determined purely by merit and ability to do the job:
"we employ the best person for the job". In practice, application
forms from black people were screwed up and consigned to the
rubbish bins. The principle of political representation and participa-

tion were enunciated as forming the cornerstone of democracy. In reality white people were contriving to prevent black people sharing power – black people had become unelectable except in a few 'ghetto' or 'slum' constituencies where they might form a majority. "And rightly so", the racial ideologues would nod with satisfaction, "for how can 'inferiors' govern or make laws for their 'superiors'?" In all areas of social relationships, therefore, the triumph of the ideology of racism had become unassailable. Who cares whether in theory black people were not, in reality, inferior to white people so long as they can be rendered inferior in practice and thus be palpably seen as 'inferiors'?

Data reinforcing such racial attitudes were readily accepted and assimilated. Contrary information, such as the evidence that black people created the ancient Egyptian civilization or that the monuments of the ancient civilisation in Zimbabwe were built by black people, are either ignored, treated as rare exceptions, or in some cases, feats of mental acrobatics are performed to explain away the evidence. We have noted above, for example, that Champollion-Figeac et al., in an attempt to rebut the claims by the ancient Greeks that the Egyptian civilisation was the product of black initiative, claimed that black skin and woolly hair did not characterise the Negro, "for there are white men with black skin". The claim of Frobenius that the Yoruba terracotta sculptures he acquired in Nigeria were the work of a long lost Greek colony or even possibly the work of the people of the legendary continent of Atlantis; and the claims of Robert Temple, member of the Royal Astronomical Society, in his highly acclaimed book, The Sirius Mystery, that space-beings from the Sirius star-system must have brought the 'marvellous knowledge of Sirius to the Dogon in Africa', are but a few examples of the agility of the mental acrobatics that the white mind would perform to explain away evidence that disproves the doctrine of inherent black inferiority.

Indeed, so pervasive had the influence of the ideology of racism on white perception and attitude become that UNESCO (United Nations Educational, Scientific and Cultural Organisation) at its Fourth General Conference, approved a resolution calling upon its Director-General: "1. To collect scientific materials concerning problems of race; 2. to give wide diffusion to the scientific information collected; 3. To prepare an educational campaign based on this information."

Dr Jaime Torres-Bodet, the then Director-General of UNESCO assigned the task to UNESCO's head of Social Sciences, Dr Arthur Ramos, who invited ten scientists from New Zealand, Mexico, Poland, USA, Britain, India, France, Brazil and Sweden to meet at UNESCO headquarters in Paris on the 12th-14th December 1949.

The scientists were mainly anthropologists, sociologists and psychologists.

After two statements had been produced, debated and amended, a third draft 'statement on race' was sent to other scientists in the field of genetics, general biology, social psychology, sociology and anthropology, as well as experts in labour-management relations. Following this consultation, *The Statement on Race* was issued in Paris in July 1950. A second committee comprising seven physical anthropologists and five geneticists met in Paris from 4th - 8th of June 1951 and issued a 'Second Statement'. A much more expanded third committee of twenty-two members, including representations from Nigeria, Germany, Japan, the USSR, Canada, Venezuela, Belgium, Senegal and Czechosovakia met in Moscow in August 1964 and issued *The Third UNESCO Statement on Race*. And, finally, a fourth committee met in Paris between 18th and 26th September 1967 and produced *The Fourth UNESCO Statement on Race*.

Extracts from the August 1964 *Third UNESCO Statement on Race* is presented in Appendix A. *The Fourth UNESCO Statement on Race,* in particular, was highly perceptive in its bold grasp of the social causality of racism, the relevant issues involved in the debate, and prescriptions for its eradication. The full text is reproduced in Appendix B.

However, this bold statement has had little perceptible effect on the attitudes of white racists. As we noted above, the crude form of the ideology's manifestation and pronouncements have given way to a more subtle and sophisticated form of presentation. The need for constant reaffirmation, moreover, has been rendered unnecessary, for white power has ensured that palpable evidence will continue to reinforce the unstated assumption. A successful assault on the ideology will only come about, therefore, through an attack on the structured racial inequality. That task, though, cannot be attempted in this book since this treatise offers a theoretical analysis of the phenomenon rather than a prescription for its solution.

The scene is now set for the analysis of the effect of the ideology of racism on attitude-formation, through socialisation, of both black people and white people in Britain, and other multi-racial societies. But no analysis of racism can be complete without taking a look at Psychology, IQ tests and the race debate – the latter-day scientific racism.

Psychology, IQ Tests and the Race Debate

It is outside the scope of this book to attempt a major critique of the nature/nurture, geneticists/environmentalist debate on this complex topic. It is, however, imperative to cite some of the salient features of the polemic for two main reasons: (a) to demonstrate the contribution of one school of thought to, and reinforcement of, the ideology of racism; and (b) the effect of the debate on the education and employment opportunities for black people.

It has been said that 'in the universe, there is nothing great but man; in man there is nothing great but mind'. Man's large and complex brain containing some 10-12 billion nerve cells and his consequent high intelligence – his capacity for learning – is one of the factors that distinguishes man from the lower animals. Man's ability to create civilisations and complex cultures; to analyse and solve complex problems, both concrete and abstract; to discover and understand 'natural laws' through observation, experimentation, critical analysis, and the organisation and systematisation of the knowledge gained through this process, and to communicate such knowledge to others, etc., has set us apart from all other animals. This ability is attributed to our higher intellectual capacity.

Within the human species itself, one of the most important factors by which the individual is evaluated is intelligence. The test of intelligence which is mistakenly closely tied to the concept of intelligence, and its evaluative effect on the individual's life-chances in the educational system as well as the selection process in many jobs, is well known. The intelligence debate, however, is one of the most controversial in psychology. The issues of heredity/environment as determinants of the level of individual intelligence, and the racial differences in intelligence, particularly black-white differences, have provoked highly emotive public controversy and debate not only in intellectual circles but in the social and political arenas as well.

We have already noted that the racial ideologues had at a very early stage of the ideology's development asserted, with the certitude of omniscients, that black people, as a group, were naturally endowed with lower intelligence than white people. Indeed, the claim of white inherent superiority is related more to intellectual capacity than to any other human characteristic. White people could not seriously claim, for example, that they were superior to black people physiologically, nor in physical strength – the theory would have been smashed to smithereens by white/black performances in such human endeavours as athletics, boxing, and many other physically demanding sports. Moreover, the claim that blacks have never as a people created a civilisation without Caucasian intervention, nor, as individuals, made any contribution to man's conquest of nature, was made to offer evidence of the black man's inherent intellectual inferiority.

However, as scientific knowledge increased, the fallacy of the mere speculative treatise offered by 'scientific racism' to explain the alleged black inferiority became apparent, particularly to those who could perceive the 'naked' use of power to render black people socio-economically inferior. A more concrete empirical evidence obtained by rigorous 'scientific' methodology was called for, if the invincibility of the theory underlying the ideology was to continue to be maintained. Attempts were made by craniologists, *ut supra*, to prove differences in black/white cranial capacity by measuring the size and volume of skulls of skeletal remains of black and white people. 'Proof' was found to show that black people had lower cranial volume and hence, lower intellectual capacity. It was, unfortunately for the craniologists, not long before this 'theory' was falsified. But the racial ideologues were a persistent lot; the search for 'scientific evidence' of black intellectual inferiority was on and was to be relentlessly pursued.

Some of the subsequent 'scientific theories' were so audacious that one was left wondering, given their obvious lack of any grain of truth, whether their proponents could be done the honour of being labelled 'fraudulent' and pathological liars, or (as seems more plausible) they were incorrigible imbeciles. So determined were these racial ideologues to 'scientifically' prove the black man's intellectual inferiority relative to white people that they appeared to have lost all sense of objectivity, rationality, and honesty. The black man was alleged to have a smaller brain, thicker skull, a less convoluted brain, etc.

"*Investigation has proved*",[a] *The Star* proclaimed in South Africa in 1957, "that the smoothness of the brain and pigment of the skin go hand in hand. There are exceptions to this rule, but they are in the minority. *Mental activity has the effect of convoluting the brain and the greatest number of convolutions are found in the brains of individuals of the races with the lightest skins;*[a] growing less through the gamut of pigments to the black, at which stage the brain has a smooth surface."[1]

Of course not all the 'scientific works' were as crude and blatantly imbecilic. Some were quite sophisticated, using such statistical tools as multiple regression analysis, co-efficient of correlation, factor analysis, and so on.

One of the earliest and most serious attempts to scientifically measure innate intellectual ability, was that of Francis Galton, a cousin of Darwin, in the 1860s. Galton, described by Eysenck as an all-round genius, firmly believed that mental ability was inherited. He founded the eugenics movement, whose avowed purpose was to improve the human breed by encouraging the genetically superior people to produce more children while discouraging or preventing the genetically inferior from reproducing at all. In time, the earth could be entirely inhabited by geniuses! Social selection was going to attempt to do what natural selection had failed to accomplish.

But to achieve the objective of eugenics, one needed a valid and reliable method of measuring intelligence so that the genetically superior and inferior could be identified. The early attempts to measure intelligence adopted laboratory methodology, taking precise measurements. For example, a person would be asked to press a telegraph key at the sound of a buzzer; his reaction time would be measured to a fraction of a second, the assumption being that quickness in mental reaction was related to quick-wittedness or to intelligence.

"It soon became apparent, however, that precisely measured performances in such laboratory tasks did not even correlate with each other – far less with school grades, or other assumed indices of intelligence. The experimental tests inspired by Galton's interest in eugenics came to a dead end."[2]

The first 'successful' general measure of intelligence was constructed by Alfred Binet (1857-1911), a French doctor, and his colleague Theodore Simon in 1905. The Ministry of Public Instruction in Paris wanted to be able to identify school children who were likely to have difficulty in school and who could benefit from special programmes. Binet saw his test as a 'diagnostic instrument' which would make it possible to pick out children whose intelligence was not developing properly, who could then be given courses in what he called "mental orthopaedics". The objective of such courses would be to *increase* the intelligence of children who had scored low on IQ tests. Note that Binet's intention was not to measure "innate" or "inborn" intelligence. Indeed he firmly repudiated those who believed that "the intelligence of an individual is a fixed quantity, a quantity that one cannot augment... We must protest and react against this brutal pessimism".[3]

Binet's assumption was that intelligence would increase with age and that older children would be able to solve more and complex items on a test. Those children who were dull and retarded would score below the average of their age group, ie, their scores would be more like those of much younger children and consequently the higher their actual age, the greater their degree of retardation.

Binet proposed the concept of mental age to measure a child's intelligence. Several tests were devised, tested and validated. If a child's intelligence were normal, he would be able to pass all the items on an intelligence test that a majority of others of his age passed. The lower the score, the lower the mental age and, conversely, the higher the score, the higher the mental age. Binet's 1905 tests were revised in 1908 and 1911. There was, however, one major problem to the tests – they were too dependent on a child's actual, ie chronological age. The tests did not account for the child who performed well on items at a level above or below his actual age-group; for example, one could not differentiate between a child of ten years who successfully completed test items at level ten, and a child of eight who passed at level twelve.

This problem was overcome with the introduction of a new concept – intelligence quotient (IQ). This was a procedure instituted by Lewis Terman of Stanford University in 1916 which demonstrated the relationship between mental growth and chronological age.[4] The formula for calculating the mental ratio (obtained by dividing mental age by chronological age) was:

$$IQ = \frac{MA \times 100}{CA}$$

For example, if a child with a chronological age of 10 had a mental age of 7, then that child's

$$IQ = \frac{7 \times 100}{10}$$
$$= 70$$
$$IQ = 70$$

A score of 100 was considered 'average', 80-90 'dull' and 70-80 'feebleminded'. An IQ below 70 was thought to be 'deficient' while a person with an IQ of 170 or higher was regarded as a genius.

Binet's intelligence test was like 'manna from heaven' to the eugenics movement and the racial ideologues. Having failed to develop a valid mental test themselves, they seized on Binet's test, distorted the original purpose and findings of the test, and incorporated it into their armoury to demonstrate white intellectual superiority to non-white people in general and black people in particular. Thus Lewis M. Terman, unlike Alfred Binet, believed even before data had been collected, that intelligence had to be largely hereditary. He wrote that IQs in the 70-80 range were "very, very common among Spanish-Indian and Mexican families of the Southwest and also among Negroes". He continued:

> *"Their dullness seems to be racial,*[a] or at least inherent in the family stocks from which they come... *The whole question of racial differences in mental traits will have to be taken up anew,*[a]... The writer predicts that when this is done there will be discovered *enormously significant racial differences in*

general intelligence,[a] differences which cannot be wiped out by any scheme of mental culture.
"Children of this group should be segregated in special classes[a]... *They cannot master abstractions,*[a] but they can often be made efficient workers. There is no possibility at present of convincing society that they should not be allowed to reproduce, although from a eugenic point of view, they constitute a grave problem because of their unusally prolific breeding."*[5]

Terman firmly believed that: (a) differences in IQ scores of different racial groups were produced by genetic differences between the races; and (b) IQ score differences within a particular racial group were also determined by genes. Members of the upper socio-economic classes possessed superior genes which they passed on to their children.

Equally, the late Sir Cyril Burt had approached the subject of mental testing with his mind firmly made up; prior to conducting any scientific study, he was a convinced hereditarian and a disciple of eugenics. In 1903, while an undergraduate student at Oxford, he is quoted as writing in his notebook. "The problem of the very poor – chronic poverty: Little prospect of the solution of the problem without the forcible detention of the wreckage of society...preventing them from propagating their species."[6]

With this firm conviction of the validity of eugenics, Burt began the search for 'evidence' to 'prove' his belief. In 1909, he administered a set of crude tests to two very small groups of school children in Oxford. The children at one school were the sons of Oxford dons, Fellows of the Royal Society, etc., while at the other school, they were the children of ordinary townspeople. Burt maintained that the children of higher social class did better on the tests and that this demonstrated that intelligence was inherited. By 1912, Burt was claiming with a conviction bordering on religious faith that "evidence for the inheritance of mental capacities was conclusive."

By the end of World War II, the influence of both Cyril Burt and IQ testing in Britain had become unassailable. Burt was Professor of Psychology; he was knighted by King George VI; and he won the Thorndike award from the American Psychological Association. With such impressive credentials, Burt was considered an academic 'heavyweight'. On the strength of his enthusiastic argument that a test to a child at the age of 11 could measure its "innate intelligence", an educational policy of far-reaching consequences was introduced in which the result of tests administered to 11-year-olds was used to "stream" children into one of three separate – and far from equal – school systems.

"Intelligence", Burt evangelically proclaimed in 1947, "will enter into everything the child says, thinks, does or attempts, both while

he is at school and later on... If intelligence is innate, the child's
degree of intelligence is permanently limited.^{a} No amount of
teaching will turn the child who is genuinely defective in general
intelligence into a normal pupil."[7]

Binet's purpose of devising a test that would enable the identifica-
tion of children whose intelligence was not developing properly so
that remedial courses could be developed and implemented for
them, had been completely abandoned. Binet's work had been
hijacked, but the objective and findings had been unashamedly
jettisoned. "Capacity," Burt stated in 1961, "must obviously limit
content. It is impossible for a pint jug to hold more than a pint of
milk, and it is equally impossible for a child's educational attainments to rise higher than his educable capacity permits." Totally
contrary to Binet's findings, Burt was claiming that an IQ test could
accurately measure a child's capacity for education and that it was a
waste of effort to try to impart more education to the child than his
score indicated he was capable of assimilating. This firm conclusion
derived from several years of scientific investigation which Burt
claimed to have undertaken spanning a twenty-three-year period –
from 1943 to 1966.

The Heredity/Environment Polemic

The question of whether intelligence is largely determined by
heredity or environment is one of the most controversial topics in
psychology. It is empirically demonstrable that there are individual
differences in terms of scores on IQ tests. Furthermore, IQ scores
tend to run in families: parents with high IQs tend to have children
with high IQs and parents with low IQs tend to have children with
low IQs. Children of different socio-economic classes have different
average IQs, e.g. children of professors, doctors, executives, etc.
have higher average IQ scores than children of manual workers.

The fundamental question is *why* the Hereditarians believe that
the observed differences in IQ scores are due to differences in
heredity, whilst the Environmentalists assert that they are due to
differences in environment. The term *environment* in this context is
defined as "anything which takes place from the moment of
conception and which makes an impact on the life of the individual.
It will be concerned with both the pre-natal and post-natal periods of
the organism's life, and will include such factors as the cytoplasm of
the cell, protein deficiency in the mother which may cause brain
deficiency in her child, and types of emotional and social environments. Environmental factors may even cause mutations to take
place in the genes themselves. All these factors have some

implications for the development of human intelligence."[8] The environmentalists' argument, in short, is that differences in IQ scores between different individuals are caused mainly by differences in experiences.

It can be seen then that much of the controversy revolves around the concept of 'heritability'. It is important to explain what is technically meant by the concept of 'heritability'. If one asserts, for example, that the heritability of IQ is 0.80, one is not claiming that 80 per cent of a person's IQ is inherited, while 20 percent is due to environmental influence. Rather one is claiming that in a particular population, in a particular set of circumstances, at some point in time, 80 per cent of the IQ score differences among individuals are determined by genetic differences. IQ heritability of 100 per cent means that the differences in IQs are totally due to genetic differences, whilst if differences have nothing to do with genetic differences, heritability would be 0 per cent. As Professor Kamin points out, the heritability of two-eyedness in human populations, for instance, is close to zero. That does not mean that the possession of two eyes is not determined by our genes. It means rather that the differences between those with two eyes and the vast majority of those born with one or no eyes, is determined not by variations in transmitted individual genetic make-up, but by environmental accidents to the latter.

But even where high heritability of some human trait (eg IQ) is found in one population, situation, and time, it does not mean that differences in that trait in other populations, other situations, or other points in time must also be largely due to genetic differences. Professor Kamin notes that "the heritability of a trait is not some 'law of nature'. It is a population statistic, rather like the death rate in Madagascar during the fourth century – which tells us nothing about the death rate in North America today."[9]

To prove the heritability of IQ, the hereditarians point to the fact that identical twins score more closely on IQ tests than fraternal twins, for example. The environmentalists counteract by showing that identical twins are far more likely to share the same experiences than fraternal twins. If the heriditarians could empirically demonstrate that separated identical twins, raised in environments materially and significantly different, could nonetheless achieve near identical scores (as those not separated would do), they would have largely won the argument. Cyril Burt, among others, sought to prove this when he began his studies of separated monozygotic (identical) twins.

Monozygotic twins (MZ) are differentiated from dizygotic (DZ) twins in that the former are the result of the fertilization of a single ovum by a single sperm. A split of the zygote in early development results in the mother bearing two separate individuals – always the same sex. The members of a pair of MZ twins are the only human individuals whose genes are literally identical. The latter (DZ twins) result from two separate sperms fertilizing two ova at about the same time. The mother bears two individuals, but the two are genetically no more alike than are ordinary brothers and/or sisters. They may be of the same or different sexes and their physical resemblance is about the same as that of ordinary siblings. Because MZ twins are genetically identical and score about the same on IQ tests, if they are separated and grow in materially (socio-economically) different environments and yet, after several years of such separation, they were to be given identical IQ tests and they scored identically or near identically, the case for heritability of IQ would be overwhelming.

In a paper in 1943, Sir Cyril Burt claimed that he had studied 15 pairs of separated identical twins and their IQ correlation on a test (not specified), was 0.77. By 1966 Burt reported that his sample size had reached 53 with correlation still at 0.771. Burt also claimed to have studied between 1955 and 1966, 83 pairs of MZ twins reared together and had found a correlation of 0.944 in their IQ scores. Burt was by now being hailed as an eminent scientist. Hereditarians, on the basis of Burt's studies, were confidently claiming IQ heritability of 80 per cent.

Meanwhile, across the Atlantic, Professor Arthur Jensen argued in the *Harvard Educational Review* in 1969 that American 'compensatory education' programmes, had failed. Jensen contended that the failure was inevitable, because Cyril Burt had indicated that 80 per cent of the variation in white people's IQs was genetic. He concluded that the difference in average IQ between black and white people (said to be about 15 per cent[b]) was caused by genetic inferiority of black people (where did we hear this argument before?) and being heritable, could not be eliminated by environmental treatments such as compensatory education. A similar argument was advanced by Richard Hernstein, a Harvard Professor of Psychology in 1971. It appeared, by the beginning of the 1970s, that the heriditarians had made a strong case for the heritability of IQ.

However, from 1972 they were to receive shattering blows to their scientifically impressive evidence from which they are yet to recover! Doubts about Burt's study was first expressed by Professor Kamin in a review of the former's work in 1972, 1973, and 1974. Kamin discovered "absurdities, contradictions, evasions, ambiguities and dishonesties scattered throughout Burt's work". More damningly, he observed that despite the increasing number of pairs of twins studied by Burt over the years, the statistical correlation between the IQ scores of his monozygotic twins remained the same to the third decimal place. Thus, as stated above, the first 15 pairs of separated identical twins that Burt claimed to have studied showed an IQ correlation of 0.77. By 1955, the sample size had increased to 21 pairs and the correlation was said to be 0.771. By 1958, Burt claimed the sample size had increased to "over 30", but the correlation remained 0.771. Burt's research associate, Conway, reported by late 1958 that the sample size had reached 42 pairs and the correlation was said to be 0.778. When Burt reported on his latest separated MZ twins studies in 1966, the sample size had reached 53 pairs, but supernaturally (yes, you guessed!) the correlation had returned to an incredibly consistent 0.771!

Burt claimed to have also studied MZ twins reared together in their own families. In 1955, he claimed to have studied 83 such pairs and observed an IQ correlation of 0.944. In his 1958 report, Burt again was claiming a correlation of 0.944 for his identical twins reared together. In a miraculous synchrony with her report on separated identical twins, Conway observed in her 1958 studies, a trivial change in the identical twins reared together. Conway's result was 0.936 compared to Burt's 0.944. As Kamin observes, "There is considerable measurement error involved in IQ testing, and it is doubtful whether if the same group IQ test were to be given on two separate occasions to the same set of people, a correlation that high would be observed between scores on the two occasions."[10] And yet Burt was achieving such remarkably high correlation with so many different pairs of twins at different places and at different periods in time! Such incredible stability is simply not achieved in the real world from data collected by 'real' scientists.

The miracle of Burt was that his third study was showing the same incredible consistency as the other two studies, thus his "sample of siblings reared apart increased from 131 to 151 pairs between 1955 and 1966, but correlations remained identical to the third decimal place. The Burt sample of fraternal (not identical) twins reared together, mysteriously decreased by 45 pairs between the same two years. But no matter: correlations remained the same to the third decimal".[11]

The second 'seismic' shock to the hereditarian position came in 1976 when the London *Sunday Times* medical correspondent Dr Oliver Gillie (himself a geneticist) attempted to locate Burt's research associates – Misses J Conway and Margaret Howard. These two women were the ones who, according to Burt, had actually tested the twins and other relatives about whom he had written so extensively. They had themselves published in collaboration, but separately, in the psychological journal that Burt edited. Dr Gillie could find no documentary evidence of the existence of these

two research associates; none of Burt's associates in the university
had ever seen them nor had his secretary or housekeeper. Burt had
previously claimed in response to enquiries that they had emigrated
to Australia, but the date he gave was *before* the time they were
supposedly undertaking field tests of separated twins in England.
Dr Gillie's front-page article in 1976 was unequivocally damning:
Burt was 'guilty of a major scientific fraud'. This conclusion was
supported by two of Burt's most distinguished former students, Alan
and Ann Clarke.[12]

Faced with a crumbling epistemological foundation, the hereditarian heavyweights wheeled out their big guns: professor Jensen
wrote to *The Times* complaining that Kamin had "spearheaded the
attack... to wholly discredit the large body of research on the
genetics of human mental abilities. The desperate scorched-earth
style of criticism that we have come to know in this debate has
finally gone the limit with charges of 'fraud' and 'fakery' now that
Burt is no longer here to... take warranted legal action against such
unfounded defamation".[13]

Jensen's frustration is entirely understandable, for in 1971 he had
described Burt as "a born nobleman whose larger, more representative samples than any other investigator in the field has ever
assembled, would secure Burt's place in the history of science".[14]

"If Burt was trying to fake the data, a person with his statistical
skills would have done a better job. It is a political attack. The real
targets are me, Hernstein and the whole area of research on the
genetics of intelligence", Jensen bitterly complained in 1976.[15]

Hernstein agreed! The suggestion of fraud "is so outrageous", the
Harvard Professor complained, "I find it hard to stay in my chair.
Burt was a towering figure of twentieth century psychology. I
think it's a crime to cast doubt over a man's career."[16]

Hans Eysenck, Burt's former student and successor to Burt's
professorial chair of psychology at London University, was equally
indignant, describing Burt as "Britain's outstanding psychologist
for many years, who had been knighted for his service to education,
and who had achieved world fame for his contributions..." The
allegations against Burt, Eysenck insisted, contained "a whiff of
McCarthyism, of notorious smear campaigns, and of what used to be
known as character assassination."[17] Eysenck's indignation was
predictable, for as he had himself indicated, he had drawn "rather
heavily" on Burt's work, citing "the outstanding quality of the
design and the statistical treatment in his studies".

But holy indignation or not, the seismic activity was continuing,
the structural damage done by Kamin and Gillie seemed irrepar-
able, and Burt's theoretical edifice was about to collapse like a pack
of cards. The third and most devastating blow was gathering

momentum and the shock wave was unstoppable. Professor Hearn-shaw was an admirer of Burt's and had delivered the eulogy at the latter's memorial service. Hearnshaw had been commissioned by Burt's sister to write Burt's biography, with complete access to all his diaries, letters, and papers. Like Dr Gillie before him, Hearn-shaw could find no trace of Miss Conway, Miss Howard, or any of the identical twins studied. He unearthed evidence of dishonesty, of evasion and of contradiction in Burt's written replies to correspon-dents who had asked questions about his data. The conclusion was crystal clear: "...Burt had collected no data at all during the last 30 years of his life, when most of the twins were supposedly studied." Hearnshaw found the case proven against Burt. His critics were "in their essentials valid" and that Burt had "fabricated figures" and "falsified", Hearnshaw's 1979 biography confirmed. Indeed from all the available evidence, Professor Kamin concluded that "it is reasonable to suggest that perhaps Burt never tested a separated twin, or calculated a genuine correlation between relatives, in his entire life".[18]

Burt's work, which was by far the strongest and clearest in the entire field, had collapsed and had to be completedly discarded for purpose of 'scientific' investigation or debate. So complete had the scholastic fraud been, that not a piece of 'debris' could be salvaged from the 'ruins' of Burt's work for 'scientific' evidence.

The question that lay-persons (non-scientists) like this author would like to ask amidst the rubble is: How could the scientific community, with all its eminent scholars and, no doubt, its fair share of geniuses, have all been fooled for all the time between 1943 and 1966? If they were not all fooled before Kamin's intervention, there must have been a conspiracy of silence; if there was a conspiracy of silence in the face of fraud and fakery (with all the damage done to the life-chances of millions of British school children who had been streamed into unequal education opportuni-ties on Burt's advice), then what confidence can we have in their 'Eminencies' when they produce 'realities' for us on the basis of their 'scientific enquiries'?

N.J. Mackintosh in a 1980 review of Hearnshaw's biography in the British Journal of Psychology summed it up neatly:

"Ignoring the question of fraud, the fact of the matter is that the crucial evidence that his data on IQ are scientifically unacceptable does not depend on any examination of Burt's diaries or correspondence. It is to be found in the data themselves. The evidence was there... in 1961. It was, indeed, clear to anyone with eyes to see in 1958. But it was not seen until 1972, when Kamin first pointed to Burt's totally inadequate reporting of his data and to the impossible consistencies in his correlation coefficients. Until then *the data were cited with respect bordering on reverence, as the most telling proof of the heritability of IQ.*[c] It is a sorry comment on the wider scientific community that *'numbers... simply not worthy of our current attention'... should have entered nearly every psychological textbook*[c]*..."*[19]

And yet, it has been on the basis of the 'expertise', testimony, and 'reputation' of men of such 'scientific stature' that millions of black people have been consigned to the 'scrap heap of intellectual inferiors'. These 'brilliant scientists', accorded recognition, distinction, honour, fame and power, appear to have been no more than a rabble group of incompetent 'scientists' on whom had been conferred a status of respectability which they did not deserve by a fraction. The Emperor had been shown to be naked! The heavyweights of hereditarianism had been exposed for what they were: "scientific racists reincarnated". Their wanton claim of black intellectual inferiority was not drawn from the conclusions of scientific enquiries – they were convinced by the claims of the ideology of racism and sought scientific evidence to support their belief. If the available evidence could not support the ideology, they would invent, fabricate, or fake one. The ideology of racism must be given scientific authenticity and demonstrability!

A brief look at Burt's pedigree will confirm his ideological credentials. Professor Karl Pearson, one of Burt's teachers, had founded in 1925 a new journal, *Annals of Eugenics,* now known as *Annals of Human Genetics.* In an article in the first issue entitled: 'The problem of alien immigration into Great Britain, illustrated by an examination of Russian and Polish Jewish children', Pearson and Moul, with 144 tables and 46 figures in 127 pages, showed immigrant Jewish children in east London to be inferior to the native English as regards teeth, tonsils, adenoids, visual acuity, cleanliness of hair, body and underwear, conscientiousness and intelligence, to have more TB, heart disease, ear disease and eye disease, and to display a tendency to breathe through their mouths. For such poor specimens, Pearson wrote, "there should be no place... They will develop into a parastic race". He admitted, "some of the children of these alien Jews from the academic standpoint have done brilliantly", but added: "No breeder of cattle, however, would purchase an entire herd because he anticipated finding one or two fine specimens included in it..."
Pearson was in no doubt that the inferiority of these alien Jews was genetic:

"In the case of the Russian and Polish Jews there has been more or less continuous oppression, nay a veritable selection... Such a treatment does not necessarily leave the best elements of a race surviving. It is likely indeed to weed out the mentally and physically fitter individuals, who alone may have had the courage to resist their oppressors."[20]

Natural selection, rather than favouring the intelligent Jews had instead favoured the dull ones; the intelligent ones, over the years, would have resisted the Tsars and been exterminated, leaving the inferior residue to survive and to emigrate to Britain and elsewhere. Hitler would award 'distinction' marks to a thesis of such scholastic and 'brilliant' analysis!

Professor Eysenck, like the faithful grandson, was reverently following in the path laid by Pearson (Pearson-Burt-Eysenck, like grandfather like grandson?). In his book *Race, Intelligence and Education,* 1971, Eysenck wrote:

> "When we turn to intelligence, it may seem paradoxical that selection should ever favour the less intelligent, and consequently it may be difficult to reconcile the theories presented above with the possibility of any given racial group having lower genetic potential than others. Yet it is easy to consider such possibilities. If, for instance, the brighter members of the West African tribes which suffered the depredations of the slavers had managed to use their higher intelligence to escape, so that it was mostly the duller ones who got caught, then the gene pool of the slaves brought to America would have been depleted of many high-IQ genes. Alternatively, many slaves appear to have been sold by their tribal chiefs; these chiefs might have got rid of their less intelligent followers. And as far as natural selection after the shipment to America is concerned, it is quite possible that the more intelligent negroes would have contributed an undue proportion of 'uppity' slaves, as well as being much more likely to try and escape. The terrible fate of slaves falling into either of these categories is only too well known; white slavers wanted dull beasts of burden, ready to work themselves to death on the plantations and under those conditions intelligence would have been counter-selective. Thus there is every reason to expect that the particular sub-group of the negro race which is constituted of American negroes is not an unselected sample of negroes, but has been selected throughout history according to criteria which would put the highly intelligent at a disadvantage. The inevitable outcome of such selection would of course be the creation of a gene pool lacking some of the genes making for higher intelligence."[21]

Such is the stuff that 'geniuses' are made of! First we are told that the intelligent Africans evaded capture while the dull ones were captured. The logical extension of such 'scientific deduction' is that all prisoners of war are dull; all kidnap victims are dull; all apprehended criminals are dull; perhaps, only dull fighter pilots get shot down – the intelligent ones evade the enemy's air-to-air missiles as well as ground-to-air missiles; it is plausible, nay, indeed entirely rational to argue that only dull soldiers fall in battle – the clever ones make sure they are not aligned with the enemy's gun sights! If a soldier is cut down in a hail of bullets in an enemy ambush, he must be dull to have fallen into such an ambush! Such absurdity is not unusual: scientific racists have been trotting them out for five hundred years!

Secondly, having captured and brought all these millions of "dull beasts of burden who were ready to work themselves to death" for the greater profit and capital accumulation of the slave-master, we are told that the more intelligent ones escaped to the north, hence the IQ differences between the offsprings of the slaves in the Northern and Southern states of America. Hold it!... I thought only dull ones were captured and shipped to the USA. Where did these "uppity niggers" suddenly appear from? May be what Eysenck meant to say was that the captured dull Africans had IQs ranging from 60-80 (or was it 50-70?). All those with IQs of 70-80 managed to escape from the South, travelling hundreds of miles; evading capture which, because of their dullness, they had failed to do in Africa in a more familiar environment; surviving all the potential dangers en route and the threat of starvation; to successfully reach the North! But, surely, those with such low IQ levels would be better described by Eysenck as "the less dull" slaves rather than the "more intelligent" slaves? Anyway, how come the offsprings of the less dull slaves who had escaped from slavery in the South to the North, achieved higher average IQ scores than the average IQ scores of white people in some Southern States? Had natural selection, by some strange coincidence, consigned those white people (who were duller than the "uppity niggers" of the North) to those Southern States?

Great minds think alike, or so they say. In March 1970, Professor Jensen wrote in the *Bulletin of the Atomic Scientists:*

"Since much of the current thinking behind civil rights, fair employment, and equality of educational opportunity appeals to the fact that there is a disproportionate representation of different racial groups in the various levels of the educational, occupational, and socio-economic hierarchy, we are forced to examine all the possible reasons for this inequality among racial groups in the attainments and rewards generally valued by all groups within our society. To what extent can such inequalities be attributed to unfairness in society's multiple selection processes? ('Unfair' meaning that selection is influenced by intrinsically irrelevant criteria, such as skin color, racial or national origin, etc.) And to what extent are these inequalities attributable to really relevant selection criteria which apply equally to all individuals but at the same time select disproportionately between some racial groups because there exist, in fact, real average differences among the groups – differences in the population distributions of those characteristics which are indisputably relevant to educational and occupational performances?"[22]

The good Professor goes on to argue that the mental inferiority of the black Americans are not due to their deprived environment and, to demonstrate his non-racist perspective, cites the case of the American Indians (who, as the reader will recall, were nearly made extinct by white America) who despite their impoverished status, he claims, score higher on IQ tests than the black people. In other words, from Jensen's analysis of the psycho-social circumstances of white and black Americans, the selection criteria that determine the various levels of the educational, occupational, and socio-economic hierarchy are essentially fair.

It is really unpardonable if Professor Jensen is totally ignorant of the history of his own country and is completely oblivious to the racist structure of American society. Here is a society that: (a) had built its wealth on black slavery; (b) had created an elaborate ideology to justify the brutal exploitation of, and blatant discrimination against black Americans, the basic assumption of such ideology being the inherent inferiority of black to white people (and to all other races); (c) had institutionalised racism into its state laws; (d) had operated 'apartheid' (called 'segregation' in the American context) for centuries and, in the case of the South, perpetuated this system until the late 1950s; (e) had denied black people access to decent, well-equipped, well staffed, high standard educational institutions which were designated "whites only" and provided instead schools with poor facilities, ill-equipped, inadequately re-sourced and demotivated staff, in inner city environments, some of which offered no intellectual stimulation whatsoever; (f) created an educational curriculum which falsified history and taught black and white people alike that all human progress and civilisation has been due to white initiative – black people have not and cannot make any contribution by virtue of their natural inferiority; (g) set up the 'Jim Crow' system to ensure that there would be no competiton between black and white people for jobs; (h) reserved all the best paying occupations to white people; (i) exluded black people from all the desirable suburban residential areas although some could afford to purchase or rent properties in these areas; (j) prevented most black people in the South from registering to vote despite the rights conferred by the American Constitution; (k) denied black people access to political representation and power; (l) brutalised, lynched, and raped black people with near impunity. The list could go on and on, and yet to Jensen these denials of human rights and blatant racial discrimination in the past had no influence on the educational and socio-economic attainments and life chances of black people vis-a-vis white people.

Such naivety would be unforgiveable even when displayed by a semi-literate eighth grade drop-out! But such socio-political myopia is not limited to Jensen. Eysenck wrote in 1980: "But blacks, it is important to note, reverse the usual pattern in the US; they are the only racial group who do comparatively better on tests of crystalli-sed ability than on tests of fluid ability, which suggests that their education has not handicapped them in relation to whites."[23]

At any rate, with the exposure of Burt as a fraud who had faked

scientific evidence on which most of the Hereditarians' case rested,
one would have thought that they would abandon their theory on
grounds that it has been conclusively falsified. Such optimism,
however, would be completely misplaced: there were more geniuses
where Burt came from!

In Chapter Nine of the book, *Intelligence: The Battle for the Mind,
HJ Eysenck versus Leon Kamin,* Eysenck tells us that his previous
analysis had been largely concerned with statistical proofs, but now
he was about to offer the world a 'biological measurement of IQ'
which *"provides the most convincing proof"* to date of the correctness
of the genetic model of intelligence".[24]

There are two approaches to psychophysiological measurement of
IQ, one favoured by Jensen, and the other by Eysenck. Let us take a
brief look at what they are, their underlying assumptions, the
methodologies they adopt, and the results they have produced.

The first of these researches was reported by Jensen and involved
the measurement of reaction times, ie the speed with which a person
can react with a simple movement, such as pushing a button, to a
simple stimulus, such as a light flashing on. The assumption is that
a person's level of intelligence could be measured by the speed with
which they process information, make decisons and react to a
stimulus or a problem. The method involves the use of a light
console which has a set of eight lights and eight buttons. When a
light flashes, the subject must at once turn it out by pressing the
button associated with it. The interval between the light flashing
and the button being pressed constitutes the reaction time. There
are two other formats: 'the probe type' and 'same or different?' but
they are essentially variations on the same theme.

In 1975, Jensen reported that he had tested groups of black and
white people who had been matched for having the same average
IQ. The subjects were asked to press the relevant button as soon as a
signal light flashed on. "When the task involved responding to only
one light, there was no difference in the speed with which blacks
and whites were able to press a button next to the light. When the
task was to respond by pressing a button next to one of several
possible lights, whites were said to respond more rapidly than
blacks. The superiority of the whites increased as the number of
possible alternative lights increased." These remarkable data
supposedly demonstrated that whites could "process information"
more efficiently than blacks, even if the individuals involved had
been matched on standard IQ measures.[25] These results were then
said to have been found to highly correlate with intelligence as
measured by traditional IQ tests. Thus psychophysiological measurements have given convincing proof to the statistical proof
demonstrated by IQ tests.

Verily, verily, such palpable fantasy is not worthy of a discipline which lays claim to the status of a science! The relentless efforts by these hereditarian scholars/scientists/researchers, have to be based on something much more factual than the science fiction which they keep presenting to the world as 'reality'. It appears that twentieth century scientific racism has made little progress compared to that of the eighteenth century.

If the speed with which an individual reacts to complex stimulus is a reflection of the level of intelligence possessed, then it would be logical to expect black people to be under-represented in those occupations and activities which generally demand fast response to complex visual stimulus. Boxing, for example, is one sport in which tip-top reflex action is essential for success – the boxer with slow reflex action could face defeat after defeat and even death at the hands of a fast and strong opponent. A good boxer must not only be capable of delivering effective punches with speed, but must also be able to avoid a counter-punch delivered with speed from the opponent.

No observer of the sport over the last three decades would suggest that white boxers are superior to black boxers in terms of the speed of their reflexes. Black people have shown themselves masters of the 'art'. Names like Muhammed Ali, Sugar Ramos, Sugar Ray Leonard, Marvin Hagler, Larry Holmes, the Spinks brothers and Mike Tyson are synonymous with fast reflex action in the game. In fact, in the heavyweight division, except for a brief period when Ingemar Johannson in 1959 defeated Floyd Patterson, who in the return fight, defeated Johannson in 1960 and the brief reign of Gerry Coetzee of the World Boxing Association championship though not World Boxing Council, there has been no white heavyweight champion of the world. That is thirty years of black domination – 1956 to 1986 – at the top division of the game. There have been many futile searches for a "Great White Hope" to dethrone the black dominance at the top of boxing; the evidence, however, provides little optimism for aspiring white world heavy-weight champions.

The impartial observer who has watched the game of basketball will see the absurdity of the Jensenian 'evidence' of black inferiority vis-a-vis whites in reaction time. Basketball is a game which requires rapid forwards, backwards and sideways movements, agility, fast reflex action and a combination of both speed and precision for scoring and passing the ball to one's team mates. Harlem Globetrotters, a black American basketball team are the undisputed top team in the world of basektball. The speed with which these physical giants handle basketball is truly amazing; there are few human activities which could demonstrate faster reaction time to complex visual cues, including the speed, height and direction of a ball in motion; the number, position and direction of movement of the players – both team mates and opponents – in the immediate vicinity of the ball; the ability to twist and turn very quickly and in several directions with split-second precision when opponents are bearing down on one; and the ability to correctly estimate the precise position of the basket (or goal post), as split-second decisions have to be made as to whether a particular moment is opportune to attempt a score even when one's back is to the goal post.

The final example is a game called "double barrel" (also known as "double Dutch") which is normally played to a fast-rhythm music. It consists of two persons holding one end each of two skipping ropes. The ropes are swung in opposite directions – one clockwise and the other anti-clockwise. While the skipping ropes are being thus swung, one, two or even three other persons skip. For those who have seen black girls either in Africa, Britain or the USA playing this game, it is no ordinary 'traditional' skipping game which one might observe any group of kids playing on any playground. It is exceedingly fast moving – so fast in fact that one cannot follow the movement of the ropes which give an illusion of one 'loop' being swung around in a fast movement. The two operators of the ropes have to be fast, rhythmic and absolutely precise in the synchronisation of their movements. But what is even more amazing is the reflex action of those who have to skip. Theirs is a demonstration of truly amazing fast reflexes, perfect timing and complex muscular control. To see them in action is to see a perfect display of mind and body in absolute harmony. When there is more than one 'skipper', of course, the complexity increases because of the need for perfect synchronisation. The reason for this arises from the fact that the two or three 'skippers' enter and leave the 'loop' not together, but in sequence so that while the skippers might skip in absolutely precise unison, the individual skipper could break the game by failing to synchronise perfectly while entering or leaving the 'loop'.

I challenge Professor Jensen to select and train any group of white kids and match them against the best black girls to see whether they could demonstrate greater reaction time in a game of 'double barrel'! Such a competition would, of course, be open to spectators. The situation in which a lone white professor, determined to prove the inferiority of black people, closets himself with a small group of white and black people with light consoles, records some data, runs a spurious statistical exercise, and emerges, like Moses from Mt. Sinai, to announce to the world that he has found a most convincing proof of black intellectual inferiority has got to be challenged and challenged most vigorously! This is a disgrace to true scientific methodology.

In an article in 1974 in which he admitted, following Kamin's review of Burt's work, that the latter's statistical data were useless, Professor Jensen wrote of the obligation on scientists to make their raw data available for re-analysis to other interested scientists. Following the publication of the findings of his reaction time studies, which, as demonstrated above, is at variance with observable social reality in the field of sports, Professor Kamin wrote to Jensen for the raw data, promising to defray all expenses. Despite repeated requests, Kamin reported in 1981[26] that Jensen had refused to provide the data. One can deduce why: could it, perhaps, be that the venerable Professor is worried that his reaction time studies might go the way of Professor Sir Cyril Burt's separated identical twins studies?

The second psycho-physiological measurement of IQ (favoured by Professor Eysenck) is known as evoked potentials and is measured on the electroencephalograph (EEG). Evoked potentials is said to tell us something about what is going on inside the brain when information is being transmitted. The assumption underlying the technique is that a sudden stimulus, such as a flash of light or a sound delivered through earphones, will give rise to activity in the brain which will register as a characteristic set of waves on the EEG. As Eysenck observes: "The kind of electrical brain activity which the EEG traditionally charts is not very closely related to intelligence. Evoked potentials on the other hand are."[27]

The Canadian psychologist J. Ertl is said to have discovered that dull subjects produced slower (more widely-spaced) waves than bright ones. What Eysenck does not tell his readers is that "Ertl himself has not been able to repeat these specimen results; nor have others. We are not told that Ertl cited his 'massive research data' in promotional literature for a business firm of which he was president. The firm attempted to sell Ertl's 'brain wave analyzer' to school systems as a culture-free intelligence test. The cost of Ertl's brain wave analyzer, in 1976, was $8,500 – with a 'low-cost service contract available thereafter', and with per test fees negotiable, based on number of children to be tested."[28]

Indeed so palpably useless has this machine been (although Eysenck tells us it is one of the two most convincing proofs of the genetic model of intelligence) that no less a person than Jensen wrote the following about it in 1980: "... a thicket of seemingly inconsistent and confusing findings, confounded variables, methodological differences, statistically questionable conclusions, unbridled theoretical speculation... John Ertl, the field's chief innovator, received the brunt of the most highly publicized criticisms... There have also been a number of failures that seem hard to explain...

quite different, even contrary, results... The directions of correlations also seem to flip-flop... It appears that measurements of this
complex phenomenon have not yet been brought completely under
experimental control... The state of the art can hardly be regarded
at present as more than exploratory...".[29]

Professor Eysenck's interest in psychophysiological factors as a
measure of IQ has, in fact, had a long history. In 1971 he wrote:
"...thus it is repeatedly reported that African negro children (and
American negro children as well) show highly precocious sensorimo-
tor development, as compared with white norms. Thus most of the
African negro babies who were drawn up to a sitting position could
keep head erect and back straight from the very first day of life;
white babies typically require six to eight weeks to sustain these
postures!... The observed precocity lasts for about three years, after
which time white children overtake the black ones. These findings
are important because of a very general law in biology according to
which the more prolonged the infancy, the greater in general are the
cognitive or intellectual abilities of the species. This law appears to
work even in a given species; thus sensori-motor precocity in
humans, as shown in so-called 'baby-tests' of intelligence, is
negatively correlated with terminal IQ.[d]

"This early advantage in sensori-motor co-ordination is not
preserved by negroes; there is much evidence to show that at later
ages they are on the average inferior to whites on many diverse
tests involving this ability and other related ones."[30]

Watch out, parents! That fast developing child of yours who, you
thought was very clever – walking at 9 months or earlier, playing
games that required complex muscular manipulation and control,
etc. at the age of two – is terminally going to be intellectually
inferior to the child who is a year or so behind in similar
sensori-motor development. Maybe that is why black people are so
inferior in athletics?

It appears that to Eysenck, black people can never win. He tells us
that the black child is more precocious than the white child, but
quickly cites this early advantage as a further proof of black
inferiority. The child who learns to walk at the age of five is a true
genius in the making – idiots, imbeciles, and morons, perhaps are
able to walk at the age of five months, six months and seven months,
respectively?

Eysenck cites another research evidence which confirms this
psychophysiological black inferiority to whites. In a study carried
out by Noble, he tested children who were asked to follow the
movement of a metal disc superimposed on a round, rotating
gramophone turntable with a metal stylus, the score being the
length of time they manage to keep the stylus on target, ie in

contact with the metal disc. "The results show a very marked difference for the right hand and a very small difference for the left, which is of course much less capable than the right; even so, the negroes do less well with the right than the whites with the left."[e31]

With such massive research evidence available to him, Professor Eysenck threw away the last vestige of pretence and rejected his own earlier speculation that perhaps not the entire black race is intellectually inferior to white people and that the black Americans (and perhaps the Westindians?) might represent the dull Africans who had not been intelligent enough to have escaped from the white and black slave predators. In 1981, abandoning all caution, Eysenck returned into the mainstream of scientific racism's paradigm. He wrote:

"Studies (by whom? we are not told) using IQ tests have been carried out in Uganda, Jamaica, Tanzania, South Africa, Ghana and elsewhere, with similar results; blacks on the whole tend to have IQs between 70 and 80, even though many investigators selected children of higher than average socio-economic status and education, rather than random samples. Studies of black children in England have tended to give results comparable to those carried out in the U.S. There seems little doubt about the facts."[32]

Professor Eysenck had written in 1971 that "University students in this country (Britain) have an average IQ of 125 or so; anyone with an IQ below 115 or so is not likely to get into a university in the first place, and he is certainly not likely to graduate even if he should surmount the admission hurdle. Nor is he likely to enjoy his stay".[33]

If the average IQ of the small proportion who are able to attain the requisite academic standards to enter British Universities is 25 per cent above the average IQ (100) for the population as a whole, then applying the same principle, the top class of equivalent black population would have average IQ of 87.5 to 100 since Eysenck tells us that the average for the black population is 70 to 80. It logically follows then, that the very best equivalent proportion of black population, anywhere in the world, given identical educational opportunities, can still never reach the level of academic attainments necessary to enter and successfully complete a course of University education in Britain. And yet, I know that despite lower educational provision, due to poorer national economies (caused in part, as shown above, by unbridled exploitation by the West), thousands of African students have attained high 'GCE' passes or equivalent and gone on to achieve good honours degrees; some have gone on further to attain Masters and Ph.D. degrees in British, French, German, Russian, American, and Canadian Universities. British, Westindian and American black people given favourable conditions have done the same. Even the relatively small numbers who get into American Universities under 'Affirmative Action', once admitted, succeed or fail on the basis of the same criteria applied to white people. Those who fail to attain the required standards are not awarded degrees. According to Eysenck's evidence, black people from around the world should not have the intellectual ability necessary to complete a course of study in a British (or any white) university.

Eysenck concludes that black inferiority cannot be blamed on poor socio-economic factors:

> "Over the past 20 years blacks in the US have made strides economically and socially, even in the deep South. Discrimination and segregation have been enormously reduced by long-overdue government action and various Supreme Court rulings. Compared with conditions at the time of the First World War, the difference is even more dramatic. One would have expected these advances to reduce the IQ discrepancy between whites and blacks, but McGurk, summarising investigations into these differences, concludes that the gap in IQ has not been closed, nor even narrowed. 'Intellectually', he writes, 'the Negro of today bears the same relationship to the contemporary White as did the Negro of the World War I era to the White of that time... It seems clear that there has been no measurable improvement in either the absolute or the relative intelligence of the Negro."[34]

Let the reader judge, on the basis of the evidence presented about the history, motive, methodology, and results of the hereditarian psychologists' works, whether we are not dealing with latter-day scientific racists whose pedigree is traceable to the 17th, 18th, and 19th Centuries – centuries-old vintage wine presented in a new bottle of scientific discourse.

Hitherto, our analysis of the IQ debate may have given the impression that: (a) the definition of 'intelligence' is non-problematic; and (b) that nearly all eminent psychologists support the hereditarian paradigm, including the assumption of inherent black mental inferiority. Neither impression, if conveyed, is meant.

Firstly, it is important to note that psychologists have not been able to agree on what the precise meaning of the concept of intelligence is; of what it is composed?; how it is formed?; to what extent it is determined by genetic or social factors?; and most importantly, how it may be objectively measured? Some psychologists have argued that there is a single general ability which underlies all intellectual performances; others, that several abilities contribute to intelligence. For example, J.P. Guilford suggests that there are as many as 120 different intellectual factors, while others suggest intelligence refers to a relatively small number of abilities. The Wechsler tests, for instance, distinguishes between verbal IQ and performance IQ, while Thurstone postulates seven primary mental abilities.[35]

The second factor to note is the question of IQ and what it measures. Does IQ measure innate "capacity" or "potential", or does it measure acquired knowledge? Many psychologists will tell you it is the former, others, that it is the latter. Tests of general information are commonly included in IQ tests, the assumption being that everyone has had a roughly equal opportunity to acquire such information. If this assumption is correct, then those who know more correct answers, must be better able to learn and remember. There is, in fact, a further assumption that given equal opportunity, everybody will be motivated to learn the same information.

An experiment was conducted in the USA in which two different sets of test questions were constructed and given to a sample of urban and rural children to answer. The following are examples of three questions taken from each test:

Information Test A
1. What are the colors in the American flag?
2. What is the largest river in the United States?
3. What is the freezing point of water?

Information Test B
1. Of what is butter made?
2. Name a vegetable that grows above ground.
3. About how often do we have a full moon?

The result demonstrated that the assumption that all chlldren should have had the opportunity to have been exposed to similar information and, therefore, that differences in intellectual abilities can be ascertained by giving tests based on that information or knowledge is fallacious. Urban schooldren were found to score much higher on Test A than rural children, while the latter scored significantly higher on Test B than the former. "Analyses of the 25 items on each test indicated that there were many questions for which the direction of the bias could not be predicted by looking at the content of the question. Nevertheless, the two tests yield radically different pictures of rural and urban performance.

"This study demonstrated that items on intelligence tests can be biased in subtle ways in favour of one or another part of the population. Similar results have been obtained in other studies. Such findings indicated how difficult it is to make sure that 'everyone has had an equal opportunity to acquire the information needed to pass the test." [36]

Indeed, the notion that a so-called intelligence test can somehow measure innate capacity or potential was considered and explicitly rejected in 1975 by a committee of testing experts appointed by the American Psychological Assocation's Board of Scientific Affairs. 'The Cleary Committee' declared:

> "A distinction is drawn traditionally between intelligence and achievement tests. A naive statement of the difference is that the intelligence test measures capacity to learn and the achievement test measures what has been learned. But items in all psychological and educational tests measure acquired behaviour... An attempt to recognize the incongruity of a behavioural measure as a measure of capacity is illustrated by the statement that the intelligence tests contain items that everyone has an equal opportunity to learn. This statement can be dismissed as false... There is no merit in maintaining a fiction."[37]

Bourne and Ekstrand (1979) state: "There is no test that is truly 'culture-free', because the selection of items necessarily involves assumptions about what experiences people do in fact have. The critical point is that, if people have had unequal exposure to certain experiences assumed in a test, differences in their scores cannot conclusively be attributed to differences in their ability to learn from these experiences."[38]

As far as (b) above (ie that all eminent psychologists are hereditarians) is concerned, many psychologists in the environmentalist paradigm have written copiously to refute the geneticists' position, offering alternative theoretical orientation in which the environment plays the major role in influencing the development of a person's 'intelligence'.

In fact, one of the most damning indictments of the geneticist position came from a later study undertaken by one of the arch-exponents and (in the absence of Burt) perhaps the contemporary 'High Priest' of Hereditarianism – Professor Arthur Jensen (discussed above). In a study reported in the journal *Development Psychology* and quoted by *Time* on August, 8, 1977,

> "Jensen studied 1,479 children, both black and white, in a dirt-poor town in southeastern Georgia. He compared the scores of pairs of siblings in order to test the thesis that environmental factors can produce a decline in IQ scores. His findings: 'unlike the blacks in relatively affluent Berkeley, whose IQs remained stable with increasing age, *the rural Georgia blacks on the average showed a decrease of one IQ point each year between ages 5 and 18*'. There was no significant decrease with age in the scores of whites, who were generally from less impoverished families.'
> "Though Jensen does not believe these results undermine his genetic theory, he thinks it proves the case for some environmental damage to black children. Says he: 'You have to conclude that something is happening to those kids while they are growing up'. Jensen, in fact, claims he has done a better job proving environmental damage than the environmentalists themselves. Says he: 'This is one of the first rigorous studies of IQ deficit. The

environmentalists just took it for granted. They never did a really careful study'."[39]

Among the stalwarts who have challenged the latter-day scientific racists has been Professor Kamin, op.cit., who first exposed Burt. Another is psychologist, Jerome Kagan, who compared five questions taken from the Wechsler IQ test with five designed by Dove specifically for poor urban blacks:

WECHSLER TEST	DOVE'S TEST
1. Who wrote Hamlet?	1. In C.C. Ryder what does C.C. stand for?
2. Who wrote the Iliad?	2. What is a gashead?
3. What is the Koran?	3. What is Willy May's last name?
4. What does audacious mean?	4. What does "handkerchief" mean?
5. What does plagiarise mean?	5. Who did "Stage Lee" kill in the famous blues legend?

Kagan concluded that it was unreasonable to maintain that scores on either test have anything to do with basic mental capacity.[40]

Professor Eysenck informs us that "Jews have usually done better on IQ tests than any other group tested both in the US and Great Britain". But Thomas Sowell (1977) in a study whose findings Eysenck must be presumed to be aware of, examined the IQ scores of different ethnic groups in the US from a historical perspective. He concluded that European immigrant scores during the 1920s (based on a nation-wide sample of over 70,000 school records) were virtually identical to black scores today.

Immigrants from southern and eastern Europe – such as Italians, Greeks and Poles – generally had IQ scores in the 80s and occasionally in the 70s. Individuals of Polish or Russian ancestry, *about half of whom were Jewish* consistently scored at or near the bottom of the scale for European ethnics. Sowell also found a relationship between average IQ and the position of an ethnic group in the social stratification system.[41]

The only plausible interpretation of Sowell's findings, from the hereditarians' paradigm, must be that emigration from Europe to the US produced per se genetic mutations in the migrants (so that European 'dimwits', simply by crossing the Atlantic became highly intelligent after a few years sojourn in the US, passing on their newly acquired superior genes to their offspring), a position that even Eysenck could not plausibly defend. The charge that IQ tests are designed by white middle class psychologists and that people from working class backgrounds in general, and black people in particular, do not score high (relatively) on such tests because they are not exposed to the same sub-cultural environments assumed by the testers, becomes glaringly obvious.

Professor Sandra Scarr of Yale University in a report to the American Psychological Association, of a study of adopted children (undertaken with Richard A. Weinberg while she was a Professor at the University of Minnesota), concluded: "the tests I have been able to make indicate that there are no substantial genetic differences between US blacks and whites in IQ, personality, or any other behaviour". In the study of black and mixed-race children adopted by 101 white, working-class-to-upper-middle-class familes, the adopted children averaged 110 on IQ tests, well above the average of 90 generally scored by black children in the North Central United States.

School achievement score provided by the children's school districts, which were scattered throughout Minnesota, also showed that in vocabulary, reading and mathematics, the adopted children not only scored above the average scores of black and inter-racial children in the state's public schools, but "were scoring above the national average for white children".

She explained that such above-average performance is consistent with the fact that by their desire to adopt children and by meeting the various criteria required by adoption agencies, the adoptive families "are a better-than-average" group in terms of parental IQ, income, education, occupational standing, and desire to rear children.

The lack of a racial explanation for the usual 10 to 15-point difference between black peoples' and white peoples' performance on IQ tests also was demonstrated, she indicated, by a study of 104 white familes who adopted white children. These adopted children, who were 16 to 22 years old when tested, had average IQ score of 106 – very close to the 110 scored by the adopted black children, whose average age was 7.

Another study revealed no racially-based difference in intelligence. The study used blood groups to estimate the proportion of African and white ancestry in a group of black people, with the estimates based on the frequency and concentration of various blood components. The study showed, she said "that having more or less African ancestry was not related to how well one scored on cognitive tests... Blacks with greater amounts of white ancestry did not score better than other blacks with more African ancestry".[42]

In spite of the considerable body of evidence against the claim of inherent black inferiority in intelligence, hereditarians such as Burt, Eysenck and Jensen have made significant contribution to the reinforcing of the ideology of racism, particularly among the less bigoted. They have consequently done incalculable damage to the reputation of black people in the last three decades.

Sight must not be lost of the fact that the 'geneticists' have the enormous advantage of operating in a psychological field, ploughed and 'fertilised' by the ideology of racism for three hundred years. Any seed whose embryo contains the assumption of "black inferiority", will germinate, grow, blossom and bear fruit. The bigoted adherents of the ideology of racism, of course, do not need the 'proof' of IQ tests, for their belief predates IQ testing by at least three hundred years. 'Confirmation' of their belief by the hereditarians, is warmly received, although the net effect, like preaching to the converted, is the reinforcement of the belief already held – not the conversion of new disciples. The falsification of the hereditarian 'theory' by the environmentalists has had little effect on the "believers", for their belief is not predicated on the findings of the Burts, Eysencks, Jensens and Hernsteins of this world, but on a deeply entrenched white ideology. The 'toxicity' of their theory is the effect it can have on the non-racists or doubters.

More importantly, Burt and Eysenck have made tremendous contribution to the development of a particular school of thought in psychology which, as a discipline, has had a great deal of influence on the British educational system, with dire consequences on black pupils. Moreover, the educational system, as we all know, plays a major role in the process of socialisation!

Notes

a. emphasis mine.
b. The fact that the original data, obtained from a US Army administered "intelligence" test for officer selection, had shown that the average IQ of black people in some Northern States was higher than the average IQ of white people in some Southern States, are either ignored by the hereditarians, or countered by arguing, without evidence, that genetically superior black people had selectively migrated from Southern to Northern States.
c. emphasis mine.
d. The eminent Professor offers no evidence of this negative correlation.
e. Could this shed any light on why Blacks dominate boxing at the top?
f. emphasis mine.

CHAPTER NINE

The Effect of the Ideology on Contemporary Social Attitudes

From the analyses in the previous chapters, it can be seen that racism, as defined in the introduction of this treatise, is ubiquitous in British social consciousness, institutions, discourse and attitudes. In fact, very few serious socio-political observers would deny the racist nature of British society. In a BBC 1 *Panorama* programme – 'Race Against Time' – broadcast on July 18, 1983, Commander Richard Wells of Hendon Police College, said "racial prejudice is endemic in [British] society". The 1984 survey of British social attitudes indicated that racial prejudice and intolerance, rather than improving, is indeed worsening. The survey found that 91% of those interviewed believed that the British are racially prejudiced, 33% admitted being personally prejudiced, and 40% believed racial prejudice was getting worse.

Into such a racist society, white British children are born and socialised. There is no evidence whatsoever to indicate that racial prejudice is instinctive, ie that it is a pattern of behaviour that is biologically fixed and universal for the human species. Instead, racial prejudice is assimilated by the child through the process of socialisation and from a variety of agencies of socialisation which include the family, peer group, schools and colleges, the media, work organisations, the Church, and so on. There is considerable empirical evidence supporting the claim that racial prejudice against black people develops at an early age, in some cases as early as three or four years of age.[1] The degree of early racial prejudice transmitted to, and assimilated by, the child depends upon how bigoted the family and peer groups are.

The realisation that differences between people of different colours or races are not just skin deep is experienced by the white child during the early formative years. The child learns, for example, that the term 'cow' refers to a certain species of farm animal who, apart from other variations, have different coloured hides; brown, black, white, or a combination of two or more colours. No qualitative or 'value' differences are attached by society to cows on the basis of the differences in colour. Differences in their colour are, therefore, perceived literally as 'skin deep'. The child learns similar 'reality' about horses, dogs, cats and so on.

In the human species, however, the child soon learns that differences in skin pigmentation connotes differences in quality and acceptability. These differences are perceived or learned through: (a) comments from parents, siblings and peers – some blatantly racist, others in the form of much more subtle nuances; (b) nursery rhymes and children's stories; (c) television programmes (comedies, documentaries, children's programmes, etc.); (d) television news coverage in which, for example, crime committed by a black person is given much greater prominence than a similar crime committed by a white person. An example of such racially biased reporting in the media occurred in the summer of 1985 when two cases of child battering and murder were being tried in the courts in London and Liverpool simultaneously.

The facts of the two cases in terms of the horrific and heinous nature of the crimes were almost identical – both involved biting and battering the child and the Liverpool case additionally involved burning the child. The basic difference was the colour of the perpetrators of the crimes – the parent in the London trial was black and the one in Liverpool was white. The London trial was the first news item for five consecutive days with a detailed account of every conceivable element of the atrocity, while the Liverpool trial was briefly reported on the first day and almost disappeared from the screens until the final day of the trial. The case involving the black parent has since become a cause célèbre, with numerous subsequent documentaries made by the different channels over the past six months or so. Among the many newspaper headlines reporting the sentencing of the black parent to prison was: "The Animal gets Life!" Needless to say, the white parent in Liverpool was not equally honoured with such 'accolade'. There have also been several white children battered to death by their parents in similar circumstances, with frightening barbarity, over the past twenty-four months. But none has received the same prominence in the media.

The reporting of the 'riots' in Handsworth, Brixton and Tottenham in 1985, need little analysis. The 'riots' were daubed "black riots" although 40 per cent of those arrested in Brixton were 'white'; many of those arrested in both Handsworth and Tottenham were white, including the person charged with the alleged murder of the two Asian brothers in Handsworth and one of those charged with the murder of the police officer in Tottenham. Among the many titles given to the "Black Rioters" were: *animals, hyenas, mob, bloodlust,* and *ratpack.* In fact, until the intervention by the Press Council, it was the practice in the Press to identify black offenders by their race when race was irrelevant for the purposes of the report. This was not done for white offenders.

Another pertinent example relates to an experience I encountered in November/December of 1985. Two letters were printed in the *Milton Keynes Mirror* on November 14 & 28, 1985 as a contribution to the continuing debate in that paper on apartheid and economic sanctions. The letters in question argued in favour of apartheid on the grounds of the threat to stability, order, and democracy that would ensue in the event of an ANC (African National Congress) victory. The author of the article raised a number of issues which were either blatantly racist or factually false; and cited, *inter alia,* a catalogue of some gruesome atrocities committed by 'barbaric African tribes' following independence; and the fact that South Africa was surrounded by 'Marxist' states whilst the states further north were almost all dictatorships.

I wrote to the *Mirror* challenging the premise of those two letters, pointing out that the worst atrocities known to man were committed by whites. A list of many of these major atrocities involving tens of millions of victims, from the slave trade, the genocidal onslaught against the Australian black people and American Indians, to the casualties of World Wars I and II, including the roasting alive of hundreds of thousands in Hiroshima and Nagasaki, was provided. I posed the question whether democracy and human rights could be denied Europeans because of those atrocities. If not, how could it be argued that 25 million black people should be denied basic human and democratic rights in South Africa because of atrocities committed by other Africans elsewhere on the continent? The Editor did not print a single sentence of the evidence I provided about atrocities by white people and also removed most of the strongest arguments raised. To the Editor of the *Milton Keynes Mirror,* it was perfectly legitimate to print the most uncomplimentary and negative statements about black people, but totally unacceptable to print the same about white people.

Through the power possessed by many editors, they decide what the public should know and these powers are used, among other things, to reinforce racism daily, while alternative information and opinions are *censored!* In such a social climate, racism thrives and becomes more deeply entrenched.

Following the tragedy in Colombia (1985) in which the town of Armero was flattened by volcanic mud, leading to the death of an estimated 25,000 people, a British reporter sent in a report showing the plight of survivors who were homeless, but were being prevented by government troops from heading for the capital, Bogota. Several clips were shown depicting the socio-economic problems faced by the masses. Not a single one of these scenes showed a black person until the reporter started talking about rising crime. The scene that accompanied the narrative on rising crime showed three suspicious-looking black men. It is plausible to suggest that the only black people amongst scores of people shown in that report came to be coincidentally associated with the narrative on rising crime, but the evidence suggests that this was no mere coincidence.

The way crime is reported and discussed in the media in Britain (as well as other multi-racial societies in Europe and the Americas) tends to imply that black people have a greater propensity towards criminality. Most people who follow current affairs in Britain will be aware of the annual ritual of the last few years over the report of the Commissioner of Metropolitan Police. For example, 3 million crimes were reported in England and Wales in a particular year. 3% of these were said to relate to 'mugging' in which black people were alleged (not convicted or even arrested) to have been responsible for two-thirds of these incidents reported to the police. That issue became the focus of attention in parliament, in the ensuing media analysis, and the general debate in the country over rising crime. Note that one third of the reported 'muggings' were alleged to have been committed by white people and the overwhelming majority (both in absolute and proportionate terms) of the remaining 97% of the 3 million crimes, were also committed by white people, but the debate left a clear impression that black people were largely responsible for the rising crime rate in Britain.

Nor was the remaining 97% of the crimes any less serious than 'mugging'. There were several vicious murders and rapes, some involving the barbaric murder and mutilation of very young children. Other cases involved the savage assault on, or the murder of, very elderly and, in some cases, crippled people. There were brutal murders of unarmed security personnel during robberies. Why, in the face of all these serious crimes, was 'mugging' selected and social 'search-light' focused on it to the exclusion of the others?

The deliberate obfuscation of the issues served at least four purposes: (a) it obscured the failure of a Conservative government, elected on a 'law-and-order' platform, to hold static, let alone to reduce, the level of crime; (b) it directed attention away from the incompetence of the police force to prevent or detect crimes despite enormously increased resources, both human and material and despite massive increase in wages to the forces, well above the national norm; (c) it provided a convenient scape-goat of a 'group' not regarded as a part of 'us'; and (d) more relevant to our current analysis, it confirmed the stereotypes of the ideology of racism which portrays black people as lay-about buffons who have a natural propensity to criminality. This helps to shift the blame away from the racist nature of British (American, etc.) social structures, placing it instead on the victims of such racism.

I am not in anyway condoning or justifying crimes committed by black people. All crimes[a] are condemnable whoever commits them. My concern here is the efforts of a racist society to 'criminalise' black people (consistent with the tenets of the ideology of racism), by citing the crime committed by an infinitesimal proportion of black people as evidence of the 'natural-bent' of the majority towards criminality.

In parallel with the presentation of negative images of black people are the positive images projected of white people. I have already presented abundant evidence of it in Chapter Three. Let me cite one more example in this context. 'Tarzan' is a film character produced and screened for decades. The simple, consistent and unambiguous message transmitted to its audience, particularly children, is that of a 'superior' white orphan, brought up by an ape, able to communicate with and command the obedience of the most ferocious of animals; a powerful man full of courage, but yet gentle and imbued with the highest sense of morality. This powerful superman, full of goodness, is perpetually pitting his strength and intellect against a rabble horde of dim-witted, child-like, black savages. The outcome is, of course, inevitable – our white hero is always the winner! The black savages have always lived with the wild animals in the jungle, but have not learned to communicate with them, let alone to summon them to their assistance against an external aggressor. A few of the stories may be designed to show Tarzan fighting against white hunters to protect some 'native' black people, but the central theme is unequivocal: the story of a white superman triumphing over all that is fearsome in the jungle, including hundreds of strong but dim-witted black warriors. Have you ever seen a black Tarzan?

So deeply entrenched in white social consciousness is this assumption of white superiority that its exponents are most of the time unaware of projecting that belief. A television reporter, reporting of a young Welsh choir-boy who had recorded a commercially successful record, talked not only of his beautiful voice, but his 'angelic features'. Not surprisingly, the boy had blonde hair and blue eyes. Yes! white people are assumed not only to be superior earthly beings – they also share the 'features' of celestial beings "the Angels" of God – a White God!

All these and many, many more, form part of the ingredient of social perception, value systems, beliefs, ideologies, and stereotypes transmitted daily to the child.

From the age of five, in addition to the influences of parents, siblings, relations, peers, and the media, the white child becomes exposed to much wider socialising agencies. The child learns to read and unconsciously absorb the racism embodied in textbooks. Despite the recent efforts made by certain schools and educationalists not to stock the more blatantly racist textbooks, there are still many books throughout the entire strata of British education which project very negative images and stereotypes of black peoples the world over. As the child's reading skills develop, he becomes exposed to much wider influencing and opinion-forming information sources including the press, many of whose editorial practices, as shown above, are well known organs of racism.

The more insidious but much less obvious influence on the child is the school and college curricula which give the impression – explicitly and implicitly – that all progress in most fields of human endeavours (scientific, technological, economic, political, educational, etc.) are due to the caucasian race. As shown above, black contribution is alleged to be non-existent. All 'experts' in all disciplines are white.

In the *Interim Report* published in June, 1981, by the Committee of Inquiry into the Education of Children from Ethnic Minority Groups, headed by Anthony Rampton, the Committee quotes two typical examples of racist books and teaching materials used in British schools:

(i) "perhaps she could finish her father's unfinished work. He had been interested in savages and backward races. *Africa was the best place to find such people* [b]... Mary would go to Africa. She could go among the wildest savages she could find. She would spend her life studying cannibals. (*Reading on Red Book I,* 7th edition 1968. An English reader for primary children.)"

(ii) "To the conquest of nature through knowledge the contributions made by Asiatics have been negligible and by Africans (Egyptians excluded) non-existent. The printing-press and the telescope, the steam-engine, the internal combustion engine and the aeroplane, the telegraph and the telephone, wireless broadcasting and the cinematograph, the gramophone and television, together with all the leading discoveries in physiology, the circulation of the blood, the laws of respiration and the like, are the result of researches carried out by white men of European stock. (H.A.L. Fisher's *History of Europe* 1945 edition. First published 1936, but still in use in many schools.)"

The historical reality that the child will very rarely, if ever, be exposed to will be the following statement by Shapiro (1944):

"Our debts have not made us humble. We behave as if we had created our civilization singlehanded and had occupied a position of leadership from the beginning of civilization itself. Actually we are not only the inheritors of a varied complex tradition, but the present protagonists of western civilization are merely *the latest of mankind to become civilized*[b]... All during the prehistoric ages North-Western Europe represented a backwater.

Into these remote regions came the stone age innovation, after they had been invented elsewhere. Similarly the Neolithic techniques and the use of bronze and iron only slowly were diffused to Western Europe centuries after this discovery in Egypt and Mesopotamia. *So wild and barbarous were the regions inhabited by the ancient Britons, the Scandinavians and the Germans that the Greeks never knew of their existence.*[b] And to the Romans the inhabitants of these far distant corners were uncouth barbarians unfamiliar with the amenities of civilization. In fact, up to the time of the Renaissance the North-Western Europeans could hardly claim parity by any objective standard with a civilization such as the Chinese of the same epoch, or the native civilizations of Mexico or Peru, where substantial achievements in social organisation, architecture and art far surpassed contemporary European productions."[2]

So convinced is the European of his 'natural superiority' that such historical facts are almost completely excised from their presentation of history. History, Geography, Science, Philosophy, Art, Music, and so on are all presented from a Eurocentric perspective. Contributions by non-caucasians in general and black people in particular, are excised from the literature. A white person can hardly come out of such institutions of socialisation without being a racist (ie without believing that white people are naturally superior to all non-white people on a scale of gradations with black people being the most inferior vis-à-vis white people).

The Swann Report[c] came too late for me to do a critique for the purpose of this book. The Committee clearly falls into the same analytical fallacy as most race relations analysts in Britain. In a chapter entitled "Racism: Theory and Practice" which was supposed to set the framework for their investigation into the educational needs and attainments of children from ethnic minorities, they trace the roots of racism in Britain to the immigration into this country by black people and Asians in the 50s and 60s. This as we have demonstrated above, is palpable nonsense! Their understanding of the social causality of racism is, therefore, quite defective. Despite this fallacy, however, the Committee appears to have produced a very good report within the constraints of 'political acceptability'.

The report cites the findings of some of the main research studies into teachers' attitudes towards ethnic minority pupils. For example:

"Brittan's study (1976) revealed a high degree of consensus of opinion concerning the academic and social behaviour of pupils of West Indian origin, with *more than two-thirds of the teachers in the sample indicating unfavourable opinions of West Indians*"[d]

Stewart's study (1978) showed the teachers interviewed as having *a positive stereotype of the Asian pupils as industrious, responsible, keen to learn and having none of the behaviour problems associated with West Indian pupils".[d]

"Tomlinson's study (1979) showed that the heads interviewed were more likely to respond at length about West Indian pupils and to have generalised views about them than in the case of Asian pupils. The heads expressed strong feelings that the learning process was slower for West Indian pupils, that they lacked long term concentration and they would tend to under-achieve and be remedial."

"The broad consensus of the findings of the studies reviewed by the NFER was that some teachers did have stereotypes of the West Indian pupil and the Asian pupil, that these stereotypes were quite different – that of the former being generally negative and that of the latter generally positive – and the stereotypes of West Indian pupils tended to be more uniform, more firmly established and more strongly held."[3]

In another reference to a research study to investigate the extent to which an awareness of the multi-racial nature of Britain today had influenced the thinking of schools which themselves had few or no ethnic minority pupils, the Report states:

"The project revealed widespread evidence of racism in all areas covered ranging from unintentional racism and patronising and stereotyped ideas about ethnic minority groups combined with appalling ignorance of their cultural backgrounds and life-styles and of the facts of race and immigration, to extremes of overt racial hatred and 'National Front-style' attitudes.... Many of the pupils had little or no direct contact with ethnic minorities on which to formulate their own views, and *the major influence on their outlook appeared to be the attitudes of their parents and local community[d]*... Other major influences were the media[d] – television, for example in its coverage of the Brixton 'disturbances', and in its portrayal of ethnic minority characters in comedy programmes, and the local press, some of which was clearly biased against 'immigrants'[e] – and the school curriculum – especially history and geography lessons and textbooks which emphasised an Anglocentric and Imperialist view of the world as well as portraying developing countries in an outdated manner."[4]

The study concluded that firstly, the concept of multi-cultural education, despite national pronouncements to the contrary, is far from accepted and indeed appears to be rejected by many 'all-white' schools.

"The second major conclusion" [the study continues] "which we feel must regrettably be drawn from the findings of this project, is in relation to the widespread existence of racism, whether unintentional and 'latent', or overt and aggressive, in the schools visited. *The extent to which myths and stereotypes of ethnic minority groups are established and reinforced by parental attitudes, by the influence of the media and through institutional practices within the schools, is we believe all too apparent.*[5f]

By the time the white child begins to seriously contemplate a career, he has developed the awareness that to a large extent, there is a social division of labour based on race. The Houses of Parliament were, until the June 1987 general election, entirely 'all-white Clubs'. All political power is concentrated in white hands – both Legislative and Executive. The Judiciary, at least from Crown Court Judges upwards, are all white. Out of a police force of 126,000 only 700 are said to be black and ethnic minorities and there are no senior black officers, to the best of my knowledge.

There are some elected black and brown faces in the Town Halls in England, but they are very few and grossly out of proportion to the size of the black population. Until recently, the white-collar workforce of the Town Halls were literally almost all white; the few black faces were mostly at the typing and clerical grades. In the manual and some craft grades, black people were usually better represented, but found it difficult to make a breakthrough into sections such as Cleansing. In some of those occupations requiring apprenticeships, usually few black people can be found because of the difficulties they encounter at the intake stage.

The top structure of the Civil Service is all-white. At the clerical Executive and Professional levels, there are a few black and brown faces in inverse proportion: the higher the professional/grade level, the lower the black representation.

In education, one comes across the occasional black or brown teacher in the classroom and a few black lecturers in some of the colleges, polytechnics and universities. Throughout Britain, there are said to be only two black headmasters. There are some professors, but these are few and far between, and yet, because of its crucial role in socialisation, if one is to tackle institutional racism, there must be a high black representation among the teacher corps to counter the assumption of inherent black inferiority and the image conveyed to pupils that black people belong more in the kitchen, mopping floors and washing dishes, than being in the classrooms as professional teachers.

In the business world, I have yet to see a black Chairman, Chief Executive, Managing Director or indeed a full-time Director of a large business organisation, either in the private or public sector, except in black-owned businesses. The Stock Exchange is an exclusive white club; if one finds a black face somewhere, it is likely to belong to a potential investor from abroad rather than a broker. The City may not practice 'apartheid' *de jure,* but it is a *de facto* exclusive white structure. Throughout the country, the top and middle management tiers of banks and other financial institutions are all white. The picture in commerce and industry is hardly any different either in the private or public sectors. But you will certainly find black people among the manual workers, cleaners, kitchen staff, clerical and typing staff. Look at the racial composition of the employees of the Employers' Organisations, including the Confederation of British Industries and the Engineering Employers' Federation, as well as their counterparts, the Trades Union Congress and its constituent Trades Unions, and you will appreciate the point being made here.

The picture is hardly any different in the various professions. Take the legal profession, for example. Many black people study for the legal professions but upon completion, opportunities to progress are largely influenced by race (as far as black people are concerned). In a report which appeared in the Wednesday June 13, 1984 publication of *The Guardian* entitled "Bar: sanctuary for white privilege" the Race Relations Committee of the Senate of the Inns of Court and the Bar warned that "discrimination against black barristers raises the danger that black people will regard the law as a white institution, preserving white privileges". The Committee found, *inter alia, "that black barristers are at a disadvantage compared with white barristers of similar ability*" when they try to obtain tenancies in the larger and more established chambers. The result," according to the committee, "is that black barristers end up in predominantly black 'ghetto'. chambers, which often lack senior members and facilities such as Libraries, and are alienated from the rest of the Bar". The Committee found that "80 per cent of 210 black barristers – 4.3 per cent of the total – were in 14 chambers where five or more members are black. Only 34 others of the 320 sets of chambers had a black member". Is it any wonder that there are no black Judges in Britain?[g]

The National Health Service employs more black people than most organisations in Britain. The reason has not been due to a commitment to racial equality by those responsible for recruitment into the service. In the past, the Service has had a chronic shortage of doctors and nurses, with the result that many qualified doctors were attracted from the Indian sub-continent while a recruitment drive was directed at the Caribbean in the 50s and 60s for the supply of student nurses. Once in the Service, however, a definite racial pattern of occupations and promotion prospects emerges.

According to the Camden Committee for Community Relations:

"The Health Service is a major national employer employing about 1 million staff throughout the U.K. Ethnic minority workers are found throughout the service in considerable numbers but are concentrated in particular occupations. For example, in 1976, 35 per cent of all doctors and 85 per cent of registrars in geriatrics were overseas born. A survey of 2,000 doctors by the Policy Studies Institute 'Overseas Doctors in the National Health Service' in 1980 found that 45 per cent of the UK born were consultants compared with 9 per cent of Asians. According to General Nursing Council figures nearly one third of all overseas student nurses are in psychiatric and mental handicap nursing. A London based hospital study *Migrant Workers in the National Health Service* showed that 69 per cent of nurses and 55 per cent of ancillary and maintenance staff were female overseas born, whereas 75 per cent of clerical staff were female British born."[6]

The magazine *Searchlight* commented in 1985:

"... it is undeniable that black doctors are kept in the low-status areas such as geriatrics and mental health; in junior or temporary positions with low pay and overworked conditions. The pattern extends to nurses – black nurses are routinely channeled into SEN courses, with lower status and fewer promotion prospects than the SRN courses favoured for white nurses; and to patients, whose neglect and callous treatment has resulted in, among other things, a far higher pre-natal mortality rate than among whites."[7]

Indeed, as far as black people of African and Afro-Caribbean origin are concerned, the representation is limited largely to the nursing and anciallary services. There are very few black doctors from these groups.

It might be supposed that the under-representation of Asian doctors in the 'consultant grades' in the more desirable fields of medical practice may be attributable to lower qualifications, experience and skills. Such assumptions would be totally false. The Wednesday, April 10, 1985 edition of *The Guardian* reported the award of a record £5,000 to a Sri Lankan doctor, Malila Noone who failed to be appointed as a consultant microbiologist at Ashford Hospital, Middlesex. The London Central Industrial Tribunal said in its report: "The applicant is a 41-year-old, *highly competent, highly experienced,*[h] extremely well-liked and personable woman who has been rejected by the respondents who have preferred and maintained their *preference for the two less experienced, less qualified*[h] – though clearly not less well-liked – persons in a post which was one the applicant was entitled to expect to be appointed to."

The tribunal criticised the seven-strong appointment committee, members of staff at Ashford Hospital and the preferred candidates. "There had been evidence of canvassing for the post from one of the other candidates and a suggestion that *the microbiology laboratory staff did not take kindly to ethnic minority staff.*"[h] The report goes on, "It may well be that the chief medical laboratory scientific officer at Ashford would have preferred a consultant from Roedean or Westminster School rather than from Sri Lanka."

Professor Sidney Selwyn of the department of microbiology at Westminster School, the University's representative on the appointment panel, had given as his first two choices persons not relevant and as his third two women doctors, Drs. K. and T. The Committee had disregarded impartial references as well as "the criticisms of Dr T's inexperience and aggression and the fact that Dr K had qualified for her final MRC (Pathology) at the end of 1983 and had not held any district general hospital positions of any duration nor produced any research."

Available evidence suggests that as the previous shortage of doctors and nurses has been reversed, black people (British-born) are finding it more difficult to get into Medical Schools.

The list could go on and on. Any visitor flying into Britain would observe, particularly at Heathrow, that there is an over-representation of black cleaners and manual staff of all kinds. But what is the position among cockpit and cabin crews on British Airways (the National Carrier) aircrafts, the personnel at the check-in counters, customs and immigration officers, air traffic controllers, managers and administrators to both British Airways and the Civil Aviation Authority? The visitor would find no evidence there of the claim that Britain is a multi-racial society!

This social division of labour in which black people are always confined to the bottom echelon of almost all social institutions and organisations or not represented at all, is one of the most effective weapons of the ideology of racism. The *causes* of this social phenomenon are not readily apparent and will be ignored even when the evidence is overwhelming; but the *effect* is perfectly visible. The conclusion thus drawn is that black people form an under-class in British (and American, etc.) society because they are inherently inferior, they are lazy, they are incompetent, they are unskilled; etc., etc.

The white person, therefore, comes out of school, college or university with an awareness of this reality firmly established in his consciousness. On the labour market, he soon experiences this advantage in competition against black people and, as the ideology of racism would have it, ascribes the reason to his inherent superiority. He might have come across a number of black people at school or college who performed much better than himself academically, but he will soon dismiss such memories: after all, just as one swallow does not make a summer, a few uppity, smart niggers cannot negate the assumption of white superiority, particularly when the socio-economic status of the overwhelming majority of black people makes their alleged inferiority so glaringly obvious.

While in school or college/university, he might have even gone on anti-racist or anti-apartheid demonstrations and carried placards proclaiming his belief in, and commitment to, racial equality. But such 'loony left-wing slogans' are promptly abandoned as he starts his career and in time, as he ascends the organisational ladder and joins the decision-making teams[i], he can be trusted to perpetuate the practice: after all, he would contend, one musn't lower standards in order to get black people into positions of power, authority and responsibility, must one? The exclusion of black people from positions of power, authority and responsibility and their confinement to the most menial, lowest-paying, lowest status and lowest discretion jobs, ensures that they will always be socially, politically and economically dependent. Consequently, to the white members of British society, the black man is inherently inferior, intellectually incapable or low-achieving, morally and socially dependent and demonstrably, by role, non-creative.

This conclusion is constantly reinforced by socio-political evidence which suggests that black people are undesirable in British society. The spectacle of political competition between the Conservative and Labour Parties in the sixties and seventies in which the Parties vied with each other to produce the most effective policy for the control of black immigration served as further public demonstration of the 'undesirability' of black presence in British society. Note that the argument was never about an immigration crisis. Indeed, over the last two decades, there has been a net loss of people, ie migrations have exceeded immigrations. The apprehension of politicians has been caused by the fact that most of the migrants are white while a substantial number of the immigrants are African, Afro-Caribbeans and Asians, thus altering the racial composition of British population. That is why when Mrs. Thatcher made her speech in early 1979 about the fear of Britain 'being swamped' by coloured immigrants, there was a dramatic jump in the 'opinion polls' in favour of the Conservatives.

But then, as always, the ideology of racism ensured that the historical factors were obscured in the equation. The fact that Britain had taken over the countries of the 'immigrants', drafted its people at the point of a musket into the British Empire, ruled and disenfranchised them for over a century and had, prior to colonisation, ruthlessly exploited their economies for centuries, are totally omitted from the social and political debate on immigration. The attaining of independence was deemed to have obliterated centuries of history.

A Conservative MP remarked on television in 1981 that the immigrants, instead of making demands on the community, ought to be grateful for the privilege of being allowed to live in this country. He, of course, did not inform his audience that the immigrants had originally had the status of British subjects imposed on them at the point of a gun. It is this historical dimension which set British black people apart from, for example, Turkish migrant workers in Germany or Southern Italian migrant workers in Switzerland. Many analysts, however, ignore the historical equation, for obvious reasons, and put British black people into the same category as other European migrant workers – an approach which presents a false and distorted view of social and historical reality.

But whatever the merits and demerits of the argument, the debate succeeded in portraying black people as an undesirable group who should be excluded wherever and whenever possible. Lester and Bindman put it aptly when they wrote:

> "It is now conventional wisdom that Britain is too small and overcrowded to absorb fresh newcomers – unless they are white. At the same time, it is also widely accepted that racial discrimination is economically wasteful, socially divisive, harmful to international relations or morally wrong (according to one's particular standpoint). The approach of successive governments has therefore been that Commonwealth citizens should be excluded from this country because they are coloured, but that Commonwealth citizens who are already here should be treated equally, regardless of their colour. Understandably, few pople have grasped the distinction. The more obvious conclusion that has generally been drawn is that if coloured immigration poses a threat to Britain's well-being so does the coloured minority living in Britain."[8]

As for the black man, to be defined inferior is to be treated as inferior; and to be treated as inferior is to be rendered inferior. The overwhelming majority of black children are born into families of multiple disadvantage. The Government's *White Paper on Racial Discrimination,* 1975, acknowledged that while other groups were disadvantaged, "few other groups in society display all the accumulated disadvantages" found among ethnic minorities. The House of Commons Home Affairs Committee took a similar view when they stated: "Racial disadvantage is a particular case of relative disadvantage within society. With the exception of racial discrimination, the disadvantages suffered by Britain's ethnic minorities are shared in varying degrees by the rest of the community... But the ethnic minorities suffer such disadvantages more than the rest of the population, and more than they would if they were white."[9]

The former Community Relations Commission reached the same conclusion in their report *Urban Deprivation, Racial Inequality and Social Policy:*

> "The extent and type of differences between the needs of the urban-deprived and the needs of ethnic minorities is the difference between 'urban deprivation' and what has been called 'racial disadvantage': that is, the disadvantages experienced by racial minorities which spring from racial prejudice, intolerance and less equal treatment in society."[10]

Professor Alan Little and Diana Robbins in a study of 'transmitted deprivation' write:

> "We know that ethnic minorities are disproportionately experiencing the worst that our society can offer.... Evidence is growing not only of a continuation of inequalities over time but possibly of a widening gap between the life chances (especially in employment) of adult and adolescent black people, and between the black and white sections of our society."[11]

Professor Sheila Allen (1979) also writes:

> "At the present time, it is clear that in general terms the colour of one's skin is an important and visible indicator of one's life chances."[12]

Having been born on average into a generally more deprived environment, the black child, like the white child, also experiences most of the socially transmitted racism from early childhood. The major difference apart from greater deprivation is that he may not be exposed to the expression of racist sentiments from parents and siblings. Instead, most will be exposed to the frustration and bitterness of parents who perceive themselves as victims of a racist society. The racism of the media, nursery rhymes, children's stories and films which instil in the white child a feeling of self-confidence, undermines the black child's confidence in himself and makes him aspire to 'whiteness', with some going as far as 'bleaching' themselves with all kinds of chemicals in order to make their skin lighter.

Harold Isaacs in a book *Blackness and Whiteness* in which he reviewed literary and folk images of blacks and whites concluded:

> "It is not hard to imagine the effect on white children who, as they chortle over the good doctor's adventures with the animals, also take in this vignette of the ugly black prince who wanted to be white in order to be loved [this was a reference to the story of Dr Dolittle and Prince Bumpo]. It takes no great art either to imagine how this tale might stab a black child or help give him all unknowingly the same love for whiteness that it nourishes in the white child. The imprint on Negroes of this whole system of ordering 'black' and 'white' has been seen and experienced by many but studied by very few. Every 'black' person obviously has been called upon to reject or somehow deflect from himself the associations of evil and inferiority so powerfully attached to blackness. He has been called upon to do this, moreover, under conditions in which his ego was kept under constant assault from all the conditions of his life. That so many Negroes in every successive generation found the ego strength to meet and resist these identifications is in itself no small miracle. That a greater number accepted the white man's images as the truth about themselves is no wonder at all."[13]

The Association of Directors of Social Services and the CRE in a Working Party Report, came to similar conclusions to the white American author above when they stated:

"It seemed to us that black children were particularly vulnerable because of their need to establish their racial identity and to have positive self-images... David Milner in his study, *Children and Race*, suggests that at a very young age children not only notice differences of skin colour, but actually ascribe a value to colour and a preference for the predominant colour in our society, whiteness. He found that 'black British children are showing a strong preference for the dominant white majority group and a tendency to devalue their own group'. This devaluation of blackness has implications for the health of the individual, for the minority racial communities and for the general public. For the minority communities it leads to a lack of confidence in the potential of the group to contribute to society, and to an acceptance of inferior social and political status. For society as a whole, it represents a perpetuation of racialism and acts as an impediment to the achievement of racial equality. The healthy development of black children in Britain requires an acceptance by them of their colour and a positive encouragement for them to take a pride in their race and culture."[14]

The undermining of the black child's self-confidence and the development of a negative self-image intensifies a great deal throughout the period of his education. History tells him that his people were enslaved for three centuries and that such enslavement and subsequent colonisation was a blessing in disguise, for it gave him the benefit of European civilisation. His ancestors had been primitive savages who had had no history prior to the arrival on the African scene of the white man.

Although now free, and with the benefit of centuries of exposure to European civilisation, he appears to be incapable of making any contribution to the development of human knowledge. All inventions and the creation of the sciences, with the exception of negligible contributions from the Chinese and Indians, were the work of caucasians: from the Greeks to the Romans to the North-Western Europeans. Oh yes, admittedly the Egyptians created a brilliant civilisation, but they are caucasians!

The concept of 'blackness' which characterises his race is also the same one in social discourse that represents all that is vile, treacherous, ugly, unholy, evil, tragedy, ungodly etc. He could not have been made in the image of God, for the Creator is white and so are the angels of heaven. He is a descendant of the 'black' son of Noah who was cursed, with all his progeny, to be a slave to his brothers (the white people), because he had made fun of seeing the nakedness of his drunken father (how Noah and his wife, both white, gave birth to two white sons and one black one, I shall never know!). By the Grace of the white God, he might make it to Heaven, but the Almighty, in His abundant mercy, will 'bleach' him white in the life beyond the grave, before he reaches the heavenly destination.

The attitudes of his teachers send signals of low expectation of his abilities. He is expected to be a low-achiever and a trouble-maker.

Professor Alan Little, analysing the data on academic performance of pupils of Westindian, Asian and white ethnic origins, argued that Asian children as a group function in a very similar way to the indigenous children because they bring to the school a very real alternative culture, an alternative identity, an alternative sense and source of personal well-being and personal strength, to the majority culture. When threatened by the majority community or its institutions the Asian youngster can withdraw both geographically into his own community, and also psychologically, into his own sense of personal worth and well-being. The different language, different religion, different culture and a different set of attitudes, provides the Asian child with a psychological haven in a sea of racial hostility.

But "the West Indian is not in that position. Although there are dangers in pushing this argument too far, the position of the black West Indian is similar to that of the American black. His position represents a variant on the dominant culture, and the dominant culture is rejecting, and therefore there's a danger of community rejection being transferred to self-rejection. There is no religion, no language, no different set of values to fall back on, there is less sense of cultural separateness as a minority.... Perhaps the most difficult fact for the teaching profession to handle is that teachers themselves may reflect some of the attitudes and beliefs found in the wide community. They too may be prejudiced and may actively discriminate. They may have lower expectations for a black youngster."

Referring to a study done by the National Foundation for Educational Research which found that teachers as a group saw Westindian children as being 'stupid' and 'trouble makers', he concludes, "In so far as these stereotypes exist and are communicated to black children, they will be factors in the children's responsiveness to the school, their attitudes to school, and their own views and images of themselves – all the things that teachers professionally know are profoundly important in determining how well or how badly a child does."[15]

The teaching of geography, history, the sciences, art, music and social studies, rather than generating a desire in him to want to know more, confronts him with greater evidence of his supposed inferiority and that of his people. As his awareness of racism deepens, he is faced with at least three options; (a) to accept the label of inferiority and aspire to a status in life which is commensurate with his alleged capability (the thesis); (b) to totally reject the label of inferiority and, with it, the white man's education, institutions and culture, ie total alienation (the antithesis); and (c) to reject the more negative aspects of the curricula and social attitudes, but to accept and learn those aspects of the curricula that he reckons will be of benefit to himself (the synthesis). Note that the process may not necessarily be a conscious and systematic analysis, evaluation and selection of an option.

Those choosing the (c) option, ie, the synthesis, may follow one of three possible courses: (1) while rejecting the assumption that he is inherently inferior, he might accept that his people may be culturally inferior and hence, aim to be as English as the Englishman and thereby hope to earn recognition and acceptance as an equal, on the white man's terms; (2) he might acquire the necessary qualifications and skills and leave the country (this is a course of action which may be pursued not only by those black people born abroad, but also those born and raised in Britain), migrating to a country where the colour of their skin will be no barrier to social acceptability and mobility; and (3) he might totally reject the assumption of inferiority while positively pursuing academic and/or skilled qualifications. Under no illusions as to the obstacles in his way, he pursues a 'realistic' career, determined to succeed without sacrificing entirely his 'blackness' and his black culture and heritage in the process.

The available evidence suggests that only a small proportion of the black population opt for option (c) course (3). This accounts for one of the major causes of the poor academic performance of black children of Westindian origin in British schools.

Before we conclude this chapter, we must take note that there are a few areas of human activities in which black supremacy is reluctantly acknowledged: boxing, football, cricket, athletics, and music. I have already referred to boxing above. The greatest footballer of all time was 'Pele', a black Brazilian. The leading cricket nation in the world is the Westindies. The black domination of several athletic events is well known and needs little affirmation. When Hitler, in the 1936 Berlin Olympic Games, refused to shake the hand of Jesse Owen who had won four gold medals, it was because a black man had shattered his 'myth' of German superiority over all other races. Owen's record stood till 1984 when Carl Lewis, another black American, equalled it in the Los Angeles Olympic Games. The presence of large black contingents in American, Latin American, Canadian and British athletic teams in all international competitions and their gold-winning records is too well known to merit much comment here.

White people, confronted with this aberration to the ideology of racism, counter by arguing that black people are naturally good in these fields – 'they have a natural rhythm'. This becomes not only a defense of the integrity of the basic assumption of the ideology of racism, but is also cleverly used to keep black people from *power* – political, professional, institutional power! It is common knowledge that many teachers encourage black children to devote more time, energy and efforts towards athletics and sports, and as an alternative to academic pursuit.

In the early 1970s, in a debate on black contribution (or noncontribution) to human progress on British Television, a renowned British journalist, parroting earlier 'scientific' racists, claimed that black people had contributed nothing. In music, he claimed, reggae is the only truly black-originated music. Classical music, jazz, etc. were all originated by white people. Such palpable ignorance can be safely ignored, for only the most uninformed or the most incorrigible racist would fail to acknowledge or, at least, accept the contribution of black people to 'Western music' in general, and 'pop' music in particular.

As James R. Flynn observed:

> "When we reflect on what Blacks have added to American culture, their contribution to America's vocabulary, humour, entertainment, cuisine, and sport, the fact that *they have almost single-handedly given America its only claim to artistic originality* (I refer to music and the development of original modes of expression such as jazz, the Negro spiritual, rock and rock opera), the fact that they have produced perhaps the only convincing existentialist literature in America (Richard Wright, Ralph Ellison), we can appreciate the point."[16]

John Wesley had earlier stated: "I cannot but observe that Negroes above all of the human species I ever knew, have the nicest ear for music. They have a kind of ecstatic delight in psalmody".[17] But contrary to European mythology that this was genetic, the black talent for music derives from African social reality in which music and dance play a role in almost every social activity.

Modern 'pop' music owes its origins and most significant developments to black people. Denied every right, human dignity, the use of their African languages and modes of cultural expression, the black slaves of the Americas used their African musical background and their composing ingenuity to create songs that would relieve them of the rigours, severity and monotony of their plantation work. From the 'Negro spirituals' developed the 'Blues', followed by Jazz. As Mark White states:

> "It was somewhere around the year 1900 in New Orleans when a black barber called Buddy Bolden first got hold of a cornet and, to quote, 'blew on it the first stammering notes of Jazz'. Although it is unlikely that the quotation is in fact accurate, Bolden is commonly accepted as being the first musician to start playing what became Jazz as we now know it."[18]

> *"The early Jazzbands were composed exclusively of black musicians* and such men as Freddie Keppard, Mutt Carey and Joe 'King' Oliver among the trumpets were acknowledged 'Kings' of their instruments, along with

clarinettists like Johnny Dodds and Sidney Bechet, trombonist Edward 'Kid' Ory and pianist Ferdinand 'Jelly Roll' Morton.... *The whites had of course learned their Jazz from the black musicians;* and severely criticised they were too by most white Americans for playing what was thought to be 'gutter music', as much because of its origins as because of its sound. Even in the late twenties, Connee Boswell, of the famous Boswell Sisters, was almost cut off with the proverbial shilling by her respectable family when she and her two sisters quit the New Orleans Symphony Orchestra in which they all played in order to launch themselves in a career as a close-harmony singing trio, performing 'that disgusting music'."[19]

Today, Jazz is an integral part of American artistic culture. It was black people like Louis Mitchell, Jelly Roll Morton, Billie Holliday, Gertrude 'Ma' Rainey, Bessie Smith, Ella Fitzgerald, Art Tatum, Johnny and Warren 'Baby' Dodds, Oscar Peterson, Miles Davis, John Coltrane, Archie Shepp, Earl Hines, Art Blakey, Bunk Johnson, Dizzy Gillespie, Duke Ellington, Louis Armstrong and many, many more who were the true originators, innovators and interpreters of 'Jazz' music.

Another branch of 'Blues' (also known at the time as Black Music) developed into 'Rock 'n Roll', a name given by Allan Freed, an American disc jockey to what was 'black music' popularised by performers such as Chuck Berry, Little Richard and others. This brand of music became very popular with the white people who owned most of the clubs and hotels where black artists performed. White people also owned the Recording Studios, Radio Stations (and later) TV Networks. Soon, the search was on for a white singer who could sing like a black person. In Elvis Presley, they found the first of such singers. As Carl Perkins, a songwriter of many of Elvis' songs, put it; "Elvis Presley's Rock 'n Roll was a mixture of the black man's music and white man's lyrics".

From thence, songs by white people, many of them originally written and sung by black people in clubs, were recorded in studios owned by white people, popularised by white disc jockeys, on radio networks owned by white people. All but a few black musicians were ignored by the white establishment in the early days of the development of 'pop' music. Faced with such wanton discrimination, 'Motown Corporation' was formed to give black musicians access to a Recording Studio owned and controlled by black people.

'Fats' Domino, Chubby Checker, Diana Ross and the Supremes, Aretha Franklin, Sam Cooke, The Clovers, Swan Silvertones, Solomon Burke, Otis Redding, The Four Tops, B.B. King, Smokey Robinson and the ·Miracles, Temptations, Ray Charles, Stevie Wonder, Wilson Picket, James Brown, Marvin Gaye, Dionne Warwick, Tina Turner, The Drifters, the Jacksons, The Isley Brothers, and scores of other black musicians were the true originators and innovators; where they led, others followed. Phenomenally successful white groups such as The Beatles and the Rolling Stones were heavily inspired and influenced by black musicians such as Chuck Berry, Little Richard, Jimmy Hendrix and others. Despite the enormous advantage enjoyed by white musicians over black musicians in a largely white controlled industry, the all-time record of sales of any album is held by Michael Jackson's *Thriller* which by the summer of 1984 had sold thirty-five million copies, and was still high up in the album charts. His most recent album, *Bad,* is on its way to setting a new record in 1988.

'Pop' music today is a multi-billion-dollar industry and is a world-wide phenomenon. The greatest beneficiaries are, of course, white people, but the undoubted originators and innovators – from Blues, Jazz, Calypso, Rock 'n Roll, to 'Soul', 'Funky', and Reggae – have all been black people.

It is most important to bear in mind, however, that the world is not ruled by athletes, sportsmen, and musicians. Effective power in society is vested in politicians, judges, business executives, trade union leaders, top civil servants, top professionals in fields such as medicine, education, engineering, the armed forces and the police and these are areas where every effort is made to prevent power-sharing with black people. Hence the black child has few *role models* to aspire to and to emulate.

The 'expectancy theory of motivation' argues that motivational force to perform – or effort – is a multiplicative function of the expectancies, or beliefs, that individuals have concerning future outcomes times the value they place on those outcomes. In other words, the individual must firstly believe that there is a high probability that his effort will result in performance and that performance will result in reward which he values. These conditions must exist if the individual is to be motivated to perform. If the black child does not believe that good academic attainment would provide a route to social status and financial reward similar to what his white peer could realistically expect, what would be the incentive for greater effort? Many black people, consequently, are never able to develop their inherent potential abilities and talents.

Those black people who, in spite of the above problems, acquire skills, academic qualifications or possess special talents, find that they are nevertheless disadvantaged in competition with their white counterparts for jobs; indeed, as W.W. Daniel found in his empirical study reviewed above, the more qualified the black person is, the higher the degree of discrimination he will suffer.

A white child of low socio-economic status may realistically aspire towards upward social mobility through higher education, and transmit the advance thus made to his progeny. For the black child, however, the most significant variable preventing his upward social mobility is not class, but an immutable natural characteristic – skin colour. "We believe that we can show that the mechanisms of transmission of racial disadvantage are not identical with or exclusively those operating for other disadvantaged groups but that an important if not paramount factor for ethnic minorities is racial/ ethnic discrimination."[20]

To the black man, then, the whole process becomes a vicious circle – a downward spiral of disadvantage – in which he is assigned, through a systematic pattern of discrimination, to the bottom of the ladder of socio-economic status; the consequent deprivation is then offered a teleological explanation in which the *effects* of discrimination are cited as the *cause* of disadvantage, for example, the claim that lack of qualifications derives from black low mental capacity. In other words, the assumption of inferiority leads to discriminatory treatment, which results in low social status, which is then cited as further evidence of inferiority, thus justifying future discrimination. It is a vicious circle from which only a minority of black people manage to escape.

From the foregoing, the following can be formulated as working hypotheses. Firstly, to explain the cause of racial discrimination in Britain (and other multi-racial Western countries) in general and in employment in particular, and secondly, to provide an evaluative criteria by which the efficacy of any equal opportunities programme can be assessed:

It is a fundamental assumption of this book that:

(i) The doctrine of inherent black inferiority, originally developed to justify the barbaric behaviour of the slave traders and later, colonial subjugation and exploitation, has been assimilated into British social attitudes and has permeated and become deeply entrenched in all social institutions; and
(ii) decision making in employment is, *ex hypothesi*, informed by the assumption of black inferiority rather than by objective assessment of the black person's actual qualities.

The hypotheses suggest that black people are, in consequence used as a marginal supply of labour; that where two candidates are equally qualified or capable for a post, the white candidate will almost invariably be chosen; and that black people are selected only when there is a shortage of equally qualified, capable and suitable white candidates; or when a black candidate, in competition with white candidates, is demonstrably outstanding. This explains why black people are the last hired and the first fired. In times of recession, black employment prospects will deteriorate perhaps twice as much as white people's because the latter's needs will be addressed first. The fact that both the black and white job seekers may be British citizens – born and bred in Britain – will make no difference to the poorer prospect of the black job seeker.

The higher up the occupational status or the higher up the grade in individual organisations, the higher the probability that this will invariably be the case. The Weberian model of selection based solely on technical competence is largely non-applicable to the black-skinned members of British society. The frame of reference of most personnel managers and line managers are informed by the assumption of the ideolgy of racism and they, in consequence, approach decision making in employment via such negative stereotypes and assumptions of black inferiority.

The hypotheses find strong support in the widespread pattern of discrimination revealed in the empirical researches reviewed above. In a speech to the Equal Opportunity Conference held by the CRE in co-operation with the Confederation of British Industries (CBI), Mr. John Moores, Director of Littlewoods Organization Ltd., distinguished between the various kinds of discrimination ethnic minority applicants might experience, particularly in an inner-city area like Liverpool, despite the fact that black people have been living there for generations. He stated, *inter alia,*

> "The fact remains that for many years there has been discrimination by address. For instance, once you get an application with a postmark Liverpool 8, Toxteth, or the address is Upper Parliament Street, or Princess Avenue, or Granby Street, you know where it goes – straight into the wastepaper basket."[21]

Apart from the effect this would have on unfortunate white people who might happen to be domiciled in those areas, the significance of the practice is that black candidates are 'weeded' out of the initial screening stage with the sole criterion for rejection being racial.

In a replication of the PEP research, op.cit., the Nottingham and District Community Relations Council undertook a study using three candidates – a native white person and two black people of Westindian and Asian origins – to apply for advertised vacancies. Of

the 103 valid tests recorded, the black testers were each discriminated against in 48 per cent of cases, the white tester 6 per cent of
cases and there were 46 per cent of cases of no discrimination.[22] And
this was only at the recruitment stage! The hypotheses predict that
there will be a much higher rate of discrimination at the selection
stage.

Similarly, the CRE, in a research exercise involving 300 London
based firms who were recruiting employees, found 50 per cent
discriminated against black applicants at the point of
recruitment.[23]

The Tavistock Institute of Human Relations undertook an
investigation into the effectiveness of race relations policy, at the
request of the Civil Service Department, in 1976-1977. Examining
records of batches of applications and selection decisions made, they
found considerable differences in the success rates of black and
white groups not explicable in terms of qualifications, experience
and other relevant criteria. Our hypotheses offer causal explication
and would predict the results that the Tavistock Researchers found.

These and many other research findings, as well as the numerous
complaints of direct racial discrimination which are reported to the
CRE annually, the hundreds of racial discrimination cases which
come before the Industrial Tribunal Courts, and the thousands of
cases of discrimination which, according to PEP are not reflected in
the number of reported cases, all attest to the validity of our
hypotheses.

Notes

a. The definition of 'crime' is, of course, problematic. A black person may be
convicted of felony and imprisoned for failing to carry a 'pass' in South
Africa. That, to me, is no crime. The term is used here to denote those wrong
doings defined as such by laws accepted as legitimate by the overwhelming
majority of the populace – ideological hegemony or not.
b. emphasis mine.
c. The original Committee was headed by A. Rampton.
d. emphasis mine.
e. Note that a second generation European immigrant is considered British;
a black person who can trace his ancestral connections to Elizabethan times
is still perceived as an immigrant.
f. emphasis mine
g. There is, however, one Asian judge, Mota Singh Q.C.
h. emphasis mine
i. Of course, not all white people will make it up the social ladder.
j. emphasis mine.

Conclusion

Our analyses began with a review of the empirical research studies which produced incontrovertible evidence of the reality of racial discrimination in Britain. However, we found the causal explication in the literature of this social phenomenon fallacious. Knowing that the extirpation of this social disease is impossible without an adequate diagnosis of the causes, we began a systematic socio-historical analysis of the *causes* of this social phenomenon.

We produced evidence to establish the origin, development, and spread of racial ideology in Britain, some Western European countries and the Americas. We showed how, once formulated to justify the brutality against, and exploitation of, the African slaves and colonial subjects, the European, through his immense power over the African, took steps to systematically render the African socio-economically inferior and to achieve a self-fulfilling prophecy.

We examined, and found to be mythological, the claims of inherent black inferiority and the evidence cited to support the proposition, viz., that black people (of African origin) have never created any civilisation without caucasian influence or direction and that no black individual has ever made any contribution towards the development of science and technology. These propositions were demolished firstly, by the evidence cited from the historians, philosophers and scientists of Antiquity – from Herodotus to Diodorus, from the Greeks to the Romans – that not only was the Ancient Egyptian civilisation (the grandest of all known ancient civilisations) the product of black African initiative, but that what has been arrogantly termed "Western Civilisation", "Greek Philosophy" and many branches of science were originally developed by black Africans of Egypt and passed on to the Greeks who proudly proclaimed that fact in clear unambiguous terms. Secondly, we demonstrated that, despite the fact that the conditions necessary for the development of scientific work have been largely non-existent for black people because of brutal European domination and oppression through slavery and colonisation since the fifteenth century, black people have made significant contributions to the development of science and technology. This contribution, however, is given the silent treatment in the literature and school curricula in the Western world through the institutional racism which pervades every strata of Western social life.

Next, we examined the continuing efforts of contemporary 'scientific' racists to give scientific authority, authenticity and demonstrability to the ideology of racism and the effect their works have had on the life-chances of black people.

Finally, we looked at the transmission of the ideology of racism through the process of socialisation, and its effect on contemporary social attitudes, as well as the effect of the latter on black employment prospects.

As I have stated above, the objective of this book was to undertake a theoretical analysis of the underlying causality of racial discrimination. Prescription for the extirpation of racial discrimination on the basis of the nature of the causes as analysed above has to be the subject of another work.

Appendix A

Extracts from the UNESCO
Third Statement on RACE (1964)

"Certain physical characters have a universal biological value for the survival of the human species, irrespective of the environment. The differences on which racial classifications are based do not affect these characters, and therefore, it is not possible from the biological point of view to speak in any way whatsoever of a general inferiority or superiority of this or that race....

The peoples of the world today appear to possess equal biological potentialities for attaining any civilization level. Differences in the achievements of different peoples must be attributed solely to their cultural history....

Neither in the field of hereditary potentialities concerning the overall intelligence and the capacity for cultural development, nor in that of physical traits, is there any justification for the concept of 'inferior' and 'superior' races.

The biological data given above stand in open contradiction to the tenets of racism. Racist theories can in no way pretend to have any scientific foundation and the anthropologists should endeavour to prevent the results of their researches from being used in such a biased way that they would serve non-scientific ends."

Appendix B

Below is the full statement of UNESCO's
Fourth Statement on Race

Statement on race and racial prejudice

PARIS, September 1967

1. "All men are born free and equal both in dignity and in rights." This universally proclaimed democratic principle stands in jeopardy wherever political, economic, social and cultural inequalities affect human group relations. A particularly striking obstacle to the

recognition of equal dignity for all is racism. Racism continues to haunt the world. As a major social phenomenon it requires the attention of all students of the sciences of man.

2. Racism stultifies the development of those who suffer from it, perverts those who apply it, divides nations within themselves, aggravates international conflict and threatens world peace.

3. Conference of experts meeting in Paris in September 1967, agreed that racist doctrines lack any scientific basis whatsoever. It reaffirmed the propositions adopted by the international meeting held in Moscow in 1964 which was called to re-examine the biological aspects of the statements on race and racial differences issued in 1950 and 1951. In particular, it draws attention to the following points:

(a) All men living today belong to the same species and descend from the same stock.

(b) The division of the human species into "races" is partly conventional and partly arbitrary and does not imply any hierarchy whatsoever. Many anthropologists stress the importance of human variation, but believe that "racial" divisions have limited scientific interest and may even carry the risk of inviting abusive generalization.

(c) Current biological knowledge does not permit us to impute cultural achievements to differences in genetic potential. Differences in the achievements of different peoples should be attributed solely to their cultural history. The peoples of the world today appear to possess equal biological potentialities for attaining any level of civilization.

Racism grossly falsifies the knowledge of human biology.

4. The human problems arising from so-called "race" relations are social in origin rather than biological. A base problem is racism, namely, antisocial beliefs and acts which are based on the fallacy that discriminatory intergroup relations are justifiable on biological grounds.

5. Groups commonly evaluate their characteristics in comparison with others. Racism falsely claims that there is a scientific basis for arranging groups hierarchically in terms of psychological and cultural characteristics that are immutable and innate. In this way it seeks to make existing differences appear inviolable as a means of permanently maintaining current relations between groups.

6. Faced with the exposure of the falsity of its biological doctrines, racism finds ever new stratagems for justifying the inequality of groups. It points to the fact that groups do not intermarry, a fact which follows, in part from the divisions created by racism. It uses this fact to argue the thesis that this absence of intermarriage derives from differences of a biological order. Whenever it fails in its

attempts to prove that the source of group differences lies in the biological field, it falls backs upon justifications in terms of divine purpose, cultural differences, disparity of educational standards or some other doctrine which would serve to mask its continued racist beliefs. Thus, many of the problems which racism presents in the world today do not arise merely from its open manifestations, but from the activities, of those who discriminate on racial grounds but are unwilling to acknowledge it.

7. Racism has historical roots. It has not been a universal phenomenon. Many contemporary societies and cultures show little trace of it. It was not evident for long periods in world history. Many forms of racism have arisen out of the conditions of conquest, out of justification of Negro'slavery and its aftermath of racial inequality in the West, and out of antisemitism, which has played a particular role in history, with Jews being the chosen scapegoat to take the blame for problems and crises met by many societies.

8. The anti-colonial revolution of the twentieth century has opened up new possibilities for eliminating the scourge of racism. In some formerly dependent countries, people classified as inferior have now, for the first time, obtained full political rights. Moreover, the participation of formerly dependent nations in international organizations in terms of equality has done much to undermine racism.

9. There are, however, some instances in certain societies in which groups, victims of racialistic practices, have themselves applied doctrines with racist implications in their struggle for freedom. Such an attitude is a secondary phenomenon, a reaction stemming from men's search for an identity which prior racist theory and racialistic practices denied them. None the less, the new forms of racist ideology, resulting from this prior exploitation, have no justification in biology. They are a product of a political struggle and have no scientific foundation.

10. In order to undermine racism it is not sufficient that biologists should expose its fallacies. It is also necessary that psychologists and sociologists should demonstrate its causes. The social structure is always an important factor. However within the same social structure, there may be great individual variation in racialistic behaviour, associated with the personality of the individuals and their personal circumstances.

11. The committee of experts agreed on the following conclusions about the social causes of race prejudice:

   (a) Social and economic causes of race prejudice are particularly observed in settler societies wherein are found conditions of great disparity of power and property, in certain urban areas where there have emerged ghettoes in which individuals are

deprived of equal access to employment, housing, political
participation, education, and the administration of justice,
and in many societies where social and economic tasks which
are deemed to be contrary to the ethics or beneath the dignity
of its members are assigned to a group of different origins who
are derided, blamed, and punished for taking on these tasks.
(b) Individuals with certain personality troubles may be particularly inclined to adopt and manifest racial prejudices. Small
groups, associations, and social movements of a certain kind
sometimes preserve and transmit racial prejudices. The
foundations of the prejudices lie, however, in the economic and
social system of a society.
(c) Racism tends to be cumulative. Discrimination deprives a
group of equal treatment and presents that group as a
problem. The group then tends to be blamed for its own
condition, leading to further elaboration of racist theory.

12. The major techniques for coping with racism involve changing
those social situations which give rise to prejudice, preventing the
prejudiced from acting in accordance with their beliefs, and
combating the false beliefs themselves.

13. It is recognized that the basically important changes in the
social structure that may lead to the elimination of racial prejudice
may require decisions of a political nature. It is also recognized,
however, that certain agencies of enlightenment, such as education
and other means of social and economic advancement, mass media,
and law can be immediately and effectively mobilized for the
elimination of racial prejudice.

14. The school and other instruments for social and economic
progress can be one of the most effective agents for the achievement
of broadened understanding and the fulfilment of the potentialities
of man. They can equally much be used for the perpetuation of
discrimination and inequality. It is therefore essential that the
resources for education and for social and economic action of all
nations be employed in two ways:
(a) The schools should ensure that their curricula contain
scientific understandings about race and human unity, and
that invidious distinctions about peoples are not made in
texts and classrooms.
(b) (i) Because the skills to be gained in formal and vocational
education become increasingly important with the
processes of technological development, the resources of
the schools and other resources should be fully available
to all parts of the population with neither restriction nor
discrimination;
(b) (ii) Furthermore, in cases where, for historical reasons,

certain groups have a lower average education and
economic standing, it is the responsibility of the society
to take corrective measures. These measures should
ensure, so far as possible, that the limitations of poor
environments are not passed on to the children.
In view of the importance of teachers in any educational programme, special attention should be given to their training. Teachers
should be made conscious of the degree to which they reflect the
prejudices which may be current in their society. They should be
encouraged to avoid these prejudices.

15. Governmental units and other organizations concerned should
give special attention to improving the housing situations and work
opportunities available to victims of racism. This will not only
counteract the effects of racism, but in itself can be a positive way of
modifying racist attitudes and behaviour.

16. The media of mass communication are increasingly important
in promoting knowledge and understanding, but their exact potentiality is not fully known. Continuing research into the social
utilization of the media is needed in order to assess their influence
in relation to formation of attitudes and behavioural patterns in the
field of race prejudice and race discrimination. Because the mass
media reach vast numbers of people at different educational and
social levels, their role in encouraging or combating race prejudice
can be crucial. Those who work in these media should maintain a
positive approach to the promotion of understanding between
groups and populations. Representation of peoples in stereotypes
and holding them up to ridicule should be avoided. Attachment to
news reports of racial designations which are not germane to the
accounts should also be avoided.

17. Law is among the most important means of ensuring equality
between individuals and one of the most effective means of fighting
racism.

The Universal Declaration of Human Rights of 10 December 1948
and the related international agreements and conventions which
have taken effect subsequently can contribute effectively, on both
the national and international level, to the fight against any
injustice of racist origin.

National legislation is a means of effectively outlawing racist
propaganda and acts based upon racial discrimination. Moreover,
the policy expressed in such legislation must bind not only the
courts and judges charged with enforcement, but also all agencies of
government of whatever level or whatever character.

It is not claimed that legislation can immediately eliminate
prejudice. Nevertheless, by being a means of protecting the victims
of acts based upon prejudice, and by setting a moral example backed

by the dignity of the courts, it can, in the long run, even change attitudes.

18. Ethnic groups which represent the object of some form of discrimination are sometimes accepted and tolerated by dominating groups at the cost of their having to abandon completely their cultural identity. It should be stressed that the effort of these ethnic groups to preserve their cultural values should be encouraged. They will thus be better able to contribute to the enrichment of the total culture of humanity.

19. Racial prejudice and discrimination in the world today arise from historical and social phenomena and falsely claim the sanction of science. It is, therefore, the responsibility of all biological and social scientists, philosophers, and others working in related disciplines, to ensure that the results of their research are not misused by those who wish to propagate racial prejudice and encourage discrimination.

This statement was prepared by a committee of experts on race and racial prejudice which met at Unesco House, Paris, from 18 to 26 September 1967. The following experts took part in the committee's work:

Professor Muddathir Abdel Rahim, University of Khartoum (Sudan);

Professor George Balandier, Université de Paris (France);

Professor Celio de Oliveira Borja, University of Guanabara (Brazil);

Professor Lloyd Braithwaite, University of the West Indies (Jamaica);

Professor Leonard Broom, University of Texas (United States);

Professor G. C. Debetz, Institute of Ethnography, Moscow (U.S.S.R.);

Professor J. Djordjevic, University of Belgrade (Yugoslavia);

Dean Clarence Clyde Ferguson, Howard University (United States);

Dr. Dharam P. Ghai, University College (Kenya);

Professor Louis Guttman, Hebrew University (Israel);

Professor Jean Hiernaux, Uniersité Libre de Bruxelles (Belgium);

Professor A. Kloskowska, University of Lodz (Poland);

Judge Kéba M'Baye, President of the Supreme Court (Senegal);

Professor John Rex, University of Durham (United Kingdom);

Professor Mariano R. Solveira, University of Havana (Cuba);

Professor Hisashi Suzuki, University of Tokyo (Japan);

Dr. Romila Thapar, University of Delhi (India);

Professor G. H. Waddington, University of Edinburgh (United Kingdom).

Bibliography

ADAMS, Russell L.,*Great Negroes, Past and Present*, 3rd Edition, (1981), Edited by David Ross Jr., Afro-Am Publishing Co. Inc., Chicago, Illinois.

BOURNE Jr., L.E. and EKSTRAND, B.R., *Psychology Its Principles and Meanings* (1979), Rinehart and Winston.

BROWN, Colin, *Black and White Britain, The Third PSI Survey* (1984), Heinemann, London.

CAMPBELL, H., *Rasta and Resistance* (1986), Hansib Publishing Limited.

CHINWEIZU, *The West and the Rest of Us* (1975), Vintage Books.

DABYDEEN, D., *Hogarth's Blacks, Images of Blacks in Eighteenth Century English Art* (1987), Manchester University Press.

DANIEL, W.W., *Racial Discrimination in England* (1968), Penguin Books.

DAVIDSON, Basil, *Black Mother – Africa and the Atlantic Slave Trade* (1980), Penguin Books.

DAVIDSON, Basil, *The Story of Africa* (1984), Mitchell Beazeley.

DIOP, C.A., *The African Origin of Civilization, Myth or Reality* (1974), Lawrence Hill & Co., Westport.

EYSENCK, H.J., *Race, Intelligence and Education* (1971), Temple Smith, London.

EYSENCK, H.J., *Intelligence: The Battle for the Mind* (1981), Pan Books.

FILE, Nigel and POWER, Chris, *Black Settlers in Britain 1555-1958* (1981), Heinemann Educational Books.

FRYER, Peter, *Staying Power – The History of Black People in Britain* (1984), Pluto Press.

GRATUS, Jack, *The Great White Lie – Slavery, Emancipation, and Changing Racial Attitudes* (1973), Monthly Review Press.

HUGGINS, N.I., *Black Odyssey* (1979), George Allen & Unwin.

JAMES, George G.M., *Stolen Legacy* (1954), Julian Richardson Associates.

KAMIN, L.J., *Heredity, Intelligence, Politics and Psychology* (1973), Invited Address, Eastern Psychological Association.

KAMIN, L.J., *Intelligence: The Battle for the Mind* (1981), Pan Books (Debate between Kamin & Eysenck).

KAMIN, L.J., *Psychology as Social Science: The Jensen Affair, Ten Years After* (1979), Presidential Address, Eastern Psychological Association.

LESTER, A. and BINDMAN, G., *Race and Law* (1972), Penguin Books.

LITTLE, A. and ROBBINS, D., *Loading the Law, A Study of Transmitted Deprivation, Ethnic Minorities and Affirmative Action* (1982), Commission for Racial Equality.

LITTLE, Alan, *Schools and Race, Five Views of Multi-Racial Britain* (1980), Commission for Racial Equality.

McINTOSH, N. and SMITH, D.J., *The Extent of Racial Discrimination* (1974), PEP, Broadsheet 547.

NICOLSON, Colin, *The Iaking of Africa* (1973), Wayland Publishers, London.

SEGAL, R., *The Race War* (1967), Penguin Books.

CERTIMA, Ivan Van, (Editor), *Blacks in Science: Ancient and Modern* (1983), Transaction Books, New Brunswick (USA) and London (UK).

SMITH, D.J., *The Facts of Racial Disadvantage* (1976), PEP Broadsheet 560.

SMITH, D.J., *Racial Disadvantage in Employment* (1974), PEP Broadsheet 544.

SUMNER, Colin, *Reading Ideologies, etc.* (1979), Academic Press.

WALVIN, James, *Black and White – The Negro and English Society 1555-1945* (1973), Allen Lane, the Penguin Press.

WHITE, Mark, *The Observer's Book of Jazz* (1978), Frederick Warne, London.

WILLIAMS, Chancellor, *The Destruction of Black Civilization* (1976), Third World Press.

WILLIAMS, Eric, *Capitalism & Slavery* (1944, 1964), Andre Deutsch Ltd., London.

REFERENCES

CHAPTER ONE

1. Daniel, W.W., *Racial Discrimination in England* (Penguin Books, 1968), pp.79-80.

2. ibid., pp.63, 68, 69, 71, 81, 223.

3. ibid., p.218.

4. Smith, D.J., *Racial Disadvantage in Employment,* (PEP, Broadsheet 544, 1974), p.82.

5. ibid., p.48

6. ibid., pp.51 & 87.

7. McIntosh, N. and Smith, D.J., *The Extent of Racial Discrimination,* (PEP Broadsheet no. 547, 1974), p.26.

8. ibid., pp.35-36.

9. Smith, D.J., *The Facts of Racial Disadvantage,* (PEP, Broadsheet 560, February 1976), p.67.

10. ibid., p.68.

11. ibid., p.69.

12. ibid., p.69.

13. ibid., p.176.

14. ibid., p.184.

15. Brown, Colin, *Black and White Britain, The Third PSI Survey,* (Heinemann, London, 1984), p.293.

16. ibid., p.294.

17. ibid., p.315-6.

18. ibid., p.318.

CHAPTER TWO

1. See W.W. Daniel (1968); D.J. Smith (1976) op.cit.; *Take 7, Race Relations at Work,* Department of Employment, HMSO; Keith Carby & Manab Thakur (1977), Herman Ouseley *et al.* (1981), Peter Braham, Ed Rhodes and Michael Paern (Editors, 1981), *Discrimination and Disadvantage in Employment,* (Harper & Row).

2. Lester, Anthony and Bindman, Geoffrey, *Race and Law* (Penguin Books, 1972), p.27.

3. Walvin, James, *Black and White – The Negro and English Society 1555-1945,* (Allen Lane, The Penguin Press, 1973), p.8.

4. Fifth Report from the Home Affairs Committee, Session 1980-81, Racial Disadvantage (HC424-1 HMSO), p.xlvi and xlviii.

5. Lester and Bindman, op.cit., pp.383-418.

6. Hall, Stuart, *Racism and Reaction, Five Views of Multi-Racial Britain,* (CRE, 1978), p.23.

7. Davidson, Basil, *Black Mother – Africa and the Atlantic Slave Trade* (Penguin Books, 1980), p.53.

8. File, Nigel and Power, Chris, *Black Settlers in Britain 1555-1958* (Heinemann Education Books, 1981), p.5.

9. Segal, Ronald, *The Race War,* (Penguin Books, 1967), p.45.

10. Davidson, Basil, *The Story of Africa,* (Mitchell Beazley, 1984), pp. 105-108.

11. ibid., p. 106.

12. Bosman, William, *A New and Accurate Description of Guinea*, etc., London (1705), cited in Colin Nicolson, *The Making of Africa*, (Wayland Publishers, London, 1973).

13. Davidson, B., *The Story of Africa*, op.cit., p.107.

14. ibid., p.108

15. ibid., p.106

16. ibid., p.107.

17. Cuguano, Ottobah, *Thoughts and Sentiments*, etc. (London, 1787), cited in Colin Nicolson, op.cit., p.42.

18. Davidson, B., op.cit., p.107.

19. Minutes of Evidence taken before a Committee of the House of Commons, 1790, cited in Jack Gratus, *The Great White Lie – Slavery, Emancipation, and Changing Racial Attitudes*, (Monthly Review Press, 1973), p.71.

20. Hope-Hennessey, J., *Sins of the Fathers* (London, 1967), quoted by Colin Nicolson, op.cit., p.36

21. Falconbridge, quoted by Jack Gratus, op.cit., p.56.

22. Davidson, B., op.cit., pp.13-14.

23. ibid., pp. 97-98.

24. ibid., p.113

25. Huggins, N.I., *Black Odyssey*, (George Allen & Unwin, London, 1979), pp.50-51.

26. Falconbridge, quoted in Jack Gratus, op.cit., p.105.

27. Davidson, B., op.cit., p.14

28. Gratus, Jack, *The Great White Lie – Slavery, Emancipation, and Changing Racial Attitudes*, (Monthly Review Press, 1973), p.78.

29. Nash, Manning, *Race and the Ideology of Race*, quoted from *Race and Social Difference*, (Penguin Books, 1972), p.119.

30. Segal, R., op.cit., p44.

31. *The Gentleman's Magazine*, XI (1741), p.147, quoted by Jack Gratus, op.cit., p.144.

32. Williams, Chancellor, *The Destruction of Black Civilization*, (Third World Press, 1976), p.269.

33. Williams, Eric, *Capitalism & Slavery* (London 1944, 1964), pp.42-43.

34. Sumner, Colin, *Reading Ideologies*, etc., (Academic Press, 1979), p.6.

35. Althuser, (1971) p.159, quoted in Colin Sumner, ibid., p.40.

36. Colin Sumner, op.cit., p.209.

37. ibid., p.211.

38. ibid., p.218-219.

39. ibid., p.223.

40. Davidson, B., *The Story of Africa*, op.cit., p.143.

41. Williams, Eric, op.cit., pp.19-20.

42. ibid., p.29.

43. Walvin, James, op.cit., pp.41-42.

44. Williams, Eric, op.cit., p.63.

45. Segal, R., op.cit., pp.45-46.

46. Davidson, B., Black Mother, op.cit., p.83.

47. Williams, Eric, op.cit., p.52.

48. Curtin, Philip D., *The Image of Africa: British Ideas and Actions 1780-1850,* (The University of Wisconsin Press, 1964), cited in *Race & Social Difference,* op.cit., p.135.

49. Hume, David (1898) Vol.3, p.252, quoted from Philip Curtin, ibid., p.136.

50. Long, Edward, *History of Jamaica,*ii, 351-2, quoted by James Walvin, op.cit., p.168.

51. ibid., quoted by James Walvin, op.cit., p.168.

52. ibid., Book III, ch 1, quoted by James Walvin, op.cit., p.169.

53. ibid., ii, p.383, quoted by Jack Gratus, op.cit., p.268.

54. ibid., p.374, quoted by Jack Gratus, op.cit., pp.268-269.

55. Darwin, Charles, *The Descent of Man,* London, John Murray, 1871, 2 vol., 2nd Edition, 1874; edition of 1901, p.276, quoted by Ashley Montagu, *Statement on Race,* (Oxford University Press, 1972), pp.15-16.

56. ibid., p.270, quoted by Ashley Montagu, ibid., p.16.

57. ibid., p.278, quoted by Ashley Montagu, ibid., p.16.

CHAPTER THREE

1. Walvin, James, op.cit., p.160.

2. Quoted in ibid., p.160.

3. Curtin, Philip D., op.cit., p.139.

4. Pinckard, George, *Notes on the West Indies,* (London, 1806, 1816), quoted in Jack Gratus, op.cit., p.271.

5. Carlyle, Thomas, *Discourse on the Nigger Question*, quoted in Jack Gratus, op.cit., p.275.

6. ibid., p.86, cited in James Walvin, op.cit., p.165.

7. Trollope, Anthony, *The West Indies and the Spanish Main,* (London, 1856), p.56, quoted in James Walvin, ibid., p.166.

8. Baker, Sir S., *The Albert N'Yanza* (London, 1898), quoted by Colin Nicolson, op.cit., p.60.

9. Lownes, 1772, p.49, cited in Philip D. Curtin, op.cit., 137.

10. Quoted in James Walvin, op.cit., p.162.

11. Edwards, Bryan, *The History, Civil and Commercial of the British Colonies in the West Indies*, 2 vols. (London, 1793), ii. 82-3, quoted in James Walvin, op.cit., p.163.

12. Know, William, *Three Tracts*, 14; 38, cited in James Walvin, op.cit., p.167.

13. Picard, E., quoted in Colin Nicolson, op.cit., pp.88-90.

14. Long, Edward, op.cit., ii Book III, ch.1, quoted by James Walvin, p.169.

15. *Nouveau Dictionnaire Larousse*, 1905, p.516.

16. *Enclyclopaedia Britannica*, (Edinburgh, 1810), xiv, 750, quoted by James Walvin, op.cit., p.173.

17. *Encyclopedia Britannica*, (1884), xvii, 318, quoted by James Walvin, op.cit., p.173.

18. Houston, James, *Some New and Accurate Observations*, (London, 1725), cited in James Walvin, op.cit., p.168.

19. Cited in James Walvin, op.cit., p.172.

20. *The Times*, 10th April, 1866, quoted in James Walvin, ibid., p.172.

21. Jack Gratus, op.cit., p.178.

22. Quoted by Harold R. Isaacs, *Race & Social Difference*, Paul Baxter and Basil Sansom, Ed., (Penguin Books, 1972), p.149.

23. Quoted in ibid., p.150.

24. Quoted in Joseph Baskin, *Race & Social Difference*, ibid., p.154.

25. Quoted in Jack Gratus, op.cit., p.180.

26. Fryer, Peter, *Staying Power—The History of Black People in Britain*, Pluto Press (1984), p.169.

CHAPTER FOUR

1. See Jack Gratus, op.cit., Chapters 19-20.

2. Hansard, Third Series, xvii, c.1193 on, quoted by ibid., p.229.230.

3. Quoted in ibid., p.230

4. Nicolson, Colin, *The Making of Africa*, (Wayland Publishers London, 1973), p.66.

5. Quoted in ibid., p.66.

6. Quoted in ibid., p.66-68

7. Quoted in ibid., p.68
8. Chinweizu, *The West and the Rest of Us,* (Vintage Books, 1975), p.37.
9. ibid., p.39
10. Lugard, Sir Frederick D., *The Dual Mandate in British Tropical Africa* (Edinburgh and London, William Blackwood & Sons, 1923), p.613, quoted by ibid., p.55.
11. Quoted by Chinweizu, op.cit., p.70
12. Quoted by Colin Nicolson, op.cit., p.91.
13. Quoted in ibid., p.91.
14. Quoted in ibid., pp.91-92.
14a. Peter Fryer, op.cit., 169.
15. Hobson, J.A., *Imperialism* (Ann Arbor, University of Michigan Press, 1965), p.265, quoted by Chinweizu, op.cit., p.56
16. ibid., p.258, quoted by Chinweizu, op.cit., 56.
17. Chinweizu, ibid., p.57.
18. *Policy of the Glenn Grey Act,* South Africa, quoted in ibid., p.58.
19. *Blue–Book on Native Affairs* C.31, p.75, quoted in Chinweizu, op.cit., pp.58-59.
20. Morel, E.D., *The Black Man's Burden* (New York, Monthly Review Press, Modern Reader, 1969), pp.129-135, quoted by Chinweizu, op.cit., pp.59-61.
21. ibid., quoted by Chinweizu, op.cit., p.61.
22. ibid., p.134, quoted by Chinweizu, op.cit., p.61
23. Quoted in Colin Nicolson, op.cit., p.93
24. Chinweizu, op.cit., p.62
25. Quoted in Ludwig Bauer, *Leopold The Unloved* (Boston, Little, Brown & Co., 1935), p.263; cited in Chinweizu, ibid., pp.62-63.
26. ibid., pp. 264-265, quoted by Chinweizu, op.cit., p.63.
27. Morel, op.cit., pp.120-121, quoted by Chinweizu, p.64.
28. Quoted by Colin Nicolson, op.cit., pp. 93-97.
29. Morel, op.cit., pp.121 quoted by Chinweizu, op.cit., p.64.
30. ibid., pp.121-122, quoted by Chinweizu, p.64.
31. Chinweizu, op.cit., pp.64-65.
32. Quoted by Ronald Segal, op.cit., p.32
33. Morel, op.cit., pp.116-119, quoted by Chinweizu, op.cit., pp.65-67.
34. ibid., pp.119-120, quoted by Chinweizu, op.cit., p.68.
35. *British Imperialism in East Africa* (Labour Research Department, London, 1926), quoted by Colin Nicolson, op.cit., pp.99-100.
36. Livingstone, David, *Missionary Travels and Researches in South Africa* (London, 1857) quoted by Colin Nicolson, op.cit., pp.75-78.

CHAPTER FIVE

1. Jenkins, *Pro–Slavery Thought in the Old South* (University of North Carolina, 1935), quoted in Manning Nash, op.cit., p.116.

2. ibid., pp.245-6

3. Putnam (1961), *Race and Reason, A Yankee View,* (Public Affairs Dept., Washington DC), quoted from Manning Nash, op.cit., p.114.

4. ibid., p.117

5. ibid., p.116.

6. Lumpkin, Beatrice, *Blacks in Science,* edited by Ivan Van Sertima, (Transaction Books, 1984), p.68.

7. Williams, Chancellor, op.cit., p.66.

8. ibid., p.71.

9. Davidson, Basil, op.cit., p.26.

10. Lumpkin, Beatrice, op.cit., p.71

11. Pappademos, John, *Blacks in Science,* op.cit., p.177-196.

12. Neigebauer, O., *The Exact Sciences in Antiquity,* (New York, Harper, 1962), p.81, quoted by Pappademos, ibid., p.187.

13. James, George G.M., *Stolen Legacy,* (Julian Richardson Associates, 1954).

14. ibid., Introduction to 1976 reprint.

15. Sarton, George, *A History of Science,* Vol. I, (New York, W.W. Norton, 1952), pp.170, 200, 441, quoted by Pappademos, op.cit., p.182-183.

16. Pappademos, op.cit., p.181.

17. See ibid., p.182 and Basil Davidson, *The Story of Africa,* op.cit., p.19.

18. Newsome, Frederick, *Blacks in Science,* op.cit., p.132.

19. ibid., p.134.

20. ibid., p.136

21. Davidson, Basil, *The Story of Africa,* op.cit., pp.19-22.

22. ibid., p.26.

23. Diop, Cheikh Anta, *The African Origin of Civilization, Myth or Reality,* (Lawrence Hill & Co., Westport, 1974), p.xiv.

24. Volney, C.F., *Voyages on Syrie et en Egypte,* Paris, 1787, I, 74-77, quoted by Cheikh Anta Diop, ibid., pp.27-28.

25. *Amélineau, Prolégoménes a l'etude de la religion egyptienne.* Paris: Ed. Leroux, 1916, p.330, quoted by C.A. Diop, op.cit., p.78.

26. Diop, C.A., op.cit p.45

27. Williams, Chancellor, op.cit., pp.69-70

28. Lumpkin, B., op.cit., p.72

29. ibid., p.73
30. ibid., pp.73-74
31. Davidson, B., *The Story of Africa*, op.cit., p.26
32. *Chérubini, La Nubie. Paris: Collection l'Univers,* 1847, pp.2-3, quoted by C.A. Diop, op.cit., p.56.
33. ibid., quoted by C.A. Diop. op.cit., p.56.
34. ibid., pp.28-29, quoted by Diop, op.cit., pp.56-57.
35. ibid., p.73, quoted by C.A. Diop, op.cit., p.57.
36. Champollion-Figeac, *Egypte ancienne.* Paris: Collection l'Univers, 1839, pp.26-27, quoted by C.A. Diop, op.cit., p.51.
37. *Géographie, classe de 5e.* Collection Cholley, Ed. Ballière et fils, 1950, quoted by C.A. Diop, op.cit., p.133.
38. Diop, C.A., op.cit., p.147.
39. Pirenne, Jacques, *Histoire de la civilisation de L'Egypte ancienne.* (Paris; Albin Michel, 1963), I, p.16, quoted by C.A. Diop, op.cit., pp.291-292.
40. Cited in C.A. Diop, op.cit., pp.205-206.
41. ibid., p.208.
42. ibid., p.209.
43. Williams, Chancellor, op.cit., p.88.
44. ibid., pp.115-116.
45. C.A. Diop, op.cit., p.209.
46. ibid., p.210.
47. ibid.
48. ibid., p.211.
49. Williams, Chancellor, op.cit., p.118.
50. Diop, C.A., op.cit., p.240.
51. ibid., pp.166-167.
52. See C. Williams, op.cit., in particular pp.76, 108 and 118.
53. See C.A. Diop, pp.94-95 and pp.212-213.
54. ibid., p.214.
55. ibid., p.215.
56. ibid., p.219.
57. Williams, C., op.cit., p.121.
58. Diop, C.A., op.cit., p.220.
59. ibid., p.221.

CHAPTER SIX

1. Williams, C., op.cit., p.138.
2. Lumpkin, B., Blacks in Science, op.cit., p.100.
3. Davidson, Basil; The Story of Africa, op.cit., p.36.
4. Williams, C., op.cit., p.136.
5. ibid., p.142.
6. ibid., p.152.
7. Davidson, B., The Story of Africa, op.cit., pp.117-118.
8. Nicholson, Colin, op.cit., p.16.
9. Davidson, B., op.cit., p.121.
10. ibid., p.121.
11. ibid., p.122.
12. Nicholson, Colin, op.cit., p.16.
13. ibid., p.18.
14. ibid., pp.20-21.
15. Davidson, B., op.cit., p.128.
16. ibid., pp.128-129.
17. Williams, C., op.cit., p.291.
18. ibid., p.292.
19. ibid.
20. Shore, Debra, Blacks in Science, op.cit., p.157.
21. ibid., p.160.
22. ibid., p.162
23. ibid.
24. Williams, C., op.cit., p.298.
25. Henry, Paul Marc, Africa Aeterna, trans. Joel Carmichael (Lausanne, Switzerland, Sedo S.A., 1965), pp.83, 84, 89, 94, quoted by Chinweizu, op.cit., pp.199-201.
26. Williams, C., op.cit., p.305.
27. Asante, Molefi and Kariamu, Blacks in Science, op.cit., p.85.
28. ibid., p.89.
29. Duff, H.L., Nyasaland under the Foreign Office (London, 1903), quoted by Colin Nicholson, op.cit., p.102.
30. Nicholson, Colin, op.cit., pp.101-102.
31. Asante and Asante, op.cit., p.87.
32. Sertima, Ivan Van, Blacks in Science, op.cit., p.11. Also see contribution by Hunter Havelin Adams III of the Argonne National Laboratory, Chapter 2 of Blacks in Science.

33. ibid., p.12
34. Quoted by Adams in ibid., p.32.
35. Williams, Chancellor, op.cit., p.211.
36. ibid., p.210.
37. Davidson, B., *The Story of Africa,* op.cit., p.91.
38. Cited in Areoye Oyebola, *Black Man's Burden,* (Academy Press Ltd., Lagos, 1976), pp.35-36.
39. Al-Bakri,*Book of the Roads and Kingdoms,*quoted by Basil Davidson, *The Story of Africa,* op.cit., p.90.
40. Davidson, B., *The Story of Africa,* op.cit., p.91.
41. ibid., p.111.
42. Cited in Cheikh Anta Diop, op.cit., p.161.
43. ibid., p.100
44. Williams, C., op.cit., p.215.
45. ibid., p.210.
46. Diop, C.A., op.cit., p.145.
47. Williams, C., op.cit., p.215.
48. Davidson, B., op.cit., p.99.
49. Cited in Colin Nicholson, op.cit., p.15.
50. Cited in Diop, C.A., op.cit., p.162.
51. Williams, C., op.cit., p.217.
52. ibid., p.219.
53. ibid.
54. ibid., p.220.
55. ibid., p.223.

CHAPTER SEVEN

1. Pappademos, op.cit., p.177.
2. ibid., p.179.
3. Newsome, Frederick, op.cit., p.129.
4. Rogers, J.A., *World's Great Men of Colour,* (Macmillan, N.Y. 1972), p.39, quoted by Newsome, ibid., p.129.
5. Newsome, F., op.cit., p.129.
6. Quoted by Newsome, ibid., p.129.
7. Finch, Charles S., *Blacks in Science,* op.cit., p.140.

8. Newsome, op.cit., p.134.
9. Finch C.S., op.cit., p.140.
10. Newsome, op.cit., p.132.
11. Finch, C.S., op.cit., p.141.
12. ibid., p.142.
13. Ghalioungui, P., quoted by Finch, ibid., p.142.
14. *Gentleman's Magazine*, LVIII (1788), p.112, quoted by Jack Gratus, op.cit., p.254.
15. Hayden, Robert, *Blacks in Science*, op.cit., p.216.
16. ibid.
17. ibid.
18. ibid., p.218.
19. Adams, Russell L., *Great Negroes, Past and Present*, 3rd Edition, edited by David Ross Jr., (Afro-Am Publishing Co. Inc., Chicago, Illinois, 1981), p.61.
20. See Robert Hayden, *Blacks in Science*, op.cit., p.219.
21. Adams, R.L., op.cit., p.65.
22. ibid.
23. ibid.
24. Kaplan, Sidney, *Jan Ernest Matzeliger and the Making of the Shoe*, Journal of Negro History, XL (Jan. 1958) pp.8-33, quoted by Russell Adams in ibid., p.63.
25. Quoted by Russell Adams, op.cit., p.64.
26. Clarke, John Henrik, *Blacks in Science*, op.cit., p.229.
27. ibid., p.234.
28. Meade, George, *A Negro Scientist of Slavery Days*, adapted by Russell Adams, op.cit., p.62.
29. Buckler, Helen, *Dr Dan: Pioneer American Surgeon* (Boston, 1954), cited by Russell Adams, ibid., p.70.
30. Adams, Russell, op.cit., p.73. also see *Negro Yearbook*, (1947), *Who's Who in Coloured America*, (1950), pp.163-164.
30[a]. ibid., p.74.
31. Hayden, Robert, *Blacks in Science*, op.cit., p.225.
32. ibid., pp.226-228.
33. ibid., p.226.
34. Spady, James G., *Blacks in Science*, op.cit., pp.258-262.
35. ibid., p.258.
36. ibid., p.262.
37. See Russell L. Adams, op.cit., p.59.
38. Sertima, Ivan Van, *Blacks in Science*, op.cit., p.269.

39. ibid., p.272.

40. Spady, J.G., op.cit., p.263.

41. ibid.

42. See Gentleman, Kirstie, *Blacks in Science*, op.cit., pp.271-292.

43. Graves, Curtis M. and Sertima, Ivan Van, *Blacks in Science*, op.cit., pp.246-248.

CHAPTER EIGHT

1. Tobias, Phillip V., *Race & Social Difference*, op.cit., p.25.

2. Kamin, Leon, *Intelligence: The Battle for the Mind*, H.J. Eysenck versus Leon Kamin, (Pan Books, 1981), p.91.

3. Quoted by Kamin in ibid.

4. Dobson, et al., *Understanding Psychology*, (Weidenfeld and Nicholson, 1981), p.213.

5. Kamin, Leon, op.cit., p.72.

6. ibid., p.95.

7. ibid., p.94.

8. Dobson et al., op.cit., pp.217-218.

9. Kamin, Leon, op.cit., p.97.

10. ibid., p.101.

11. ibid.

12. ibid., pp.102-103.

13. ibid., p.103.

14. ibid., p.98.

15. Quoted by Bourne and Ekstrand, Psychology, Holt, Rinehart and Winston, 1979, p.231.

16. ibid.

17. Kamin, Leon, op.cit., p.103.

18. ibid., p.104.

19. ibid., pp.104-105.

20. ibid., p.156.

21. Eysenck, H.J., *Race, Intelligence and Education*, (Temple Smith, London, 1971), pp.46-47.

22. Quoted by Eysenck in ibid., pp.28-29.

23. Eysenck, H.J., *Intelligence: The Battle for the Mind*, op.cit., p.76.

24. ibid., p.67.
25. ibid., p.142.
26. ibid., p.143.
27. ibid., p.70.
28. ibid., p.180.
29. ibid., p.181.
30. Eysenck, H.J., *Race, Intelligence and Education,* op.cit., p.84.
31. ibid., p.86.
32. Eysenck, v. Kamin, *Intelligence: The Battle for the Mind,* op.cit., p.76.
33. Eysenck, H.J., *Race, Intelligence and Education,* op.cit., p.60.
34. Eysenck v. Kamin, op.cit., pp.82-83.
35. Bourne Jr., L.E. and Ekstrand, B.R., *Psychology Its Principles and Meanings,* (Holt, Rinehart and Winston, 1979), p.216.
36. ibid., p.213.
37. Eysenck v. Kamin, op.cit., pp.94-95.
38. Bourne and Ekstrand, op.cit., p.212.
39. Quoted in ibid., p.232.
40. Kagan, Jerome, "What is Intelligence?" Alan Gartner et al. (eds.), *The New Assault on Equality:* IQ and Social Stratification, cited in Bernard Phillips, Sociology (McGraw Hill, 1979), p.190.
41. Sowell, Thomas, *New Light on Black IQ,* (The New York Times Magazine, March, March 27, 1977), quoted by Bernard Phillips, op.cit., pp.191-192.
42. *Chronicle of Higher Education,* September 12, 1977, quoted by Bourne and Ekstrand, op.cit., pp.233-234.

CHAPTER NINE

1. See Lasker (1929), *Race Attitudes in Children;* Horowitz (1936); Clark and Clark (1974); Mary Goodman (1952); Steveson and Stewart (1958); Pushkin (1967); Pushkin and Veness (1973).
2. Quoted by Tobias, Race & Social Difference, op.cit., p.28.
3. *Education for All,* The Report of the Committee of Inquiry into the Education of Children from Ethnic Minority Groups, HMSO, Cmnd.9453, p.23.
4. ibid., pp.234 and 235.
5. ibid., p.236.

6. Camden Committee for Community Relations, *Racial Equality and the Health Service* (March, 1983), p.4.

7. Quoted in Asian Times, Friday Dec., 6, 1985.

8. Lester, Anthony, and Bindman, Geoffrey, op.cit., p.13.

9. Home Affairs Committee's Fifth Report, op.cit., p.13.

10. Community Relations Commission: *Urban Deprivation, Racial Inequality and Social Policy* (HMSO, 1977), cited in *Youth in Multi-Racial Society: The Urgent Need for New Policies* (CRE, 1982), p.11.

11. Little, Alan, and Robbins, Diana, 'Loading the Law', A Study of Transmitted Deprivation, Ethnic Minorities and Affirmative Action (CRE, 1982), p.8.

12. Allen, Sheila, 'Pre-School Children: Ethnic Minorities in England', New Community, Summer 1979, quoted from Alan Little and Diana Robbins, ibid., p.5.

13. Isaacs, Harold R., *Race & Social Difference,* op.cit., pp.150-151.

14. *Multi-Racial Britain: The Social Services Response,* A Working Party Report (CRE, 1980), p.19.

15. Little, Alan, *"Schools and Race", Five Views of Multi-Racial Britain* (CRE, 1980), pp.62-65.

16. Flynn, James R., *Race, IQ and Jensen* (1980), pp. 217-218.

17. Wesley, John, *Thoughts on Slavery, 1774,* quoted by James Walvin, op.cit., p.170.

18. White, Mark, *The Observer's Book of JAZZ,* (Frederick Warne, London 1978), p.11.

19. ibid., pp.14-17.

20. Little, Alan and Robbins, Diana, op.cit., p.9.

21. *Equal Opportunity, Positive Action and Young People* (CRE, 1983), p.9.

22. Nottingham and District Community Relations Council, *Half A Chance? – A Report on Job Discrimination Against Young Blacks in Nottingham* (CRE, 1980), p.12.

23. Commission for Racial Equality, 1982, *Annual Report,*